DAVID CARRADINE

The Eye of My Tornado

ISBN: 978-1-926745-28-2

Cover design: François Turgeon
Text design and composition: Nassim Bahloul

Cover photo:
© Michael Lamont

Back and Flap photos:
© Alan Weissman

Transit Publishing Inc.
1996 St-Joseph Boulevard East
Montreal, QC
H2H 1E3

Tel: 514-273-0123
www.transitpublishing.com

Printed and Bound in Canada

Marina Anderson

DAVID CARRADINE
The Eye of My Tornado

CONTENTS

Part I
Begin the Beguine
Before 1995

Part II
Heaven and Hell
1996—May 2001

Part III

Sex, Lies and . . .

1995—2001

Part IV

Dances

May 2001—Present

Part V
The Good, The Bad, and...He Did *What?!*

DEDICATION

This book is dedicated in loving memory to my collie, Lulu–sister to Lassie IX, daughter of Lassie VIII, the love and light of my life, who carried me through the darkest of times. I love you more than the world. More than the universe.

PART I

BEGIN THE BEGUINE

Before 1995

Chapter One

D-DAY

It was a long time ago
And a dream away
When all was exciting
Upon a new day.

—Marina Anderson

June 3, 2009

I was working on the TV show *The Cleaner* again, filming on the CBS Radford Street lot in Studio City. This time as a nurse. Good. I didn't have to worry about bringing wardrobe. It was nice to be back and to see a familiar crew, and it turned out to be an easy and enjoyable day with a decent call-time of 10 a.m.

I felt a shift in my feelings about having to do background work—where you are literally in the background behind the action—and stand-in work—where you stand in for a star while the lighting and camera crew set up for a shot. There was a sort of peace within me about this temporary way of life. I had been doing it only a short time and hopefully it would remain a short time, but it was better than most jobs out there. It allowed me to pay my bills, get health insurance, and accrue another year toward my required retirement minimum with the unions. I also had time to concentrate on other projects for television and film, write children's books as well as expand my jewelry line. I was aimed at a goal and plowing forward, again, leaving my ego at the door. Still, it was a difficult transition, having to do this to make a buck, because I had guest star, supporting, and star credits. Most of my friends were in the same boat. No auditions, no acting work, no money. So in spite of this overall sense of calm and acceptance, there was still an underlying edginess to the day.

Nightmares tormented me the night before, and although I didn't remember what they were, they left me a bit depressed. Maybe it was because my seventeen-year-old cat, Tai, had been sick and I was still extremely concerned and sleep deprived. Getting up at various hours to aid him broke my sleep patterns and I thought that might have contributed to the undercurrent of melancholy I was feeling. That night I stayed up working on projects, cleaning up, catching up. At 2:00 a.m., I fell into bed in an exhausted heap.

June 4, 2009, 7:00 a.m. (five hours later)

My home landline jolted me out of a sound sleep. I *hate* to be wakened that early, especially when I have a day off. Hate it! Who in the hell would dare call me at this hour? I looked at the clock by my bed with glazed eyes, barely able to focus and grappled for the phone. By the time I managed to find it, it stopped ringing. Crap! I was furious. Half asleep I waited to hear if someone was leaving a message on the answering machine and there was . . . nothing. Just as I started to drift off again, my cell phone went off.

Damn! Who in the fucking hell is calling me now? *This better be good,* I thought as I bolted out of bed and stomped over to grab it!

"Hello! Who is this?"

Reception is very blippy in my place, and I had to keep moving around the room to hear the voice on the other end. "Hello! Who is this, and what do you want?"

"Marina, it's Patricia," the garbled voice said.

"Who?"

The voice faltered and broke up, but not because of the reception. "It's Patrrrrrrrrrricia. David's dead!" She started to sob. "He's dead!"

I shook my head, trying to wake up fully, making sure this wasn't a nightmare.

"What?" *No way,* I thought.

"David is dead!" she wailed.

"My David? Our David?" I could feel myself hyperventilating. My mouth started to go numb, and my head got light. To keep myself stable, I grabbed the counter for support. *This can't be. This wasn't supposed to happen yet. He had years left.*

"Yes! Our David!" Patricia started to sob again. She was a producer friend of mine and David's—a constant spiritual light in my life.

My voice went from early morning gravel to high-pitched little girl. "Are you sure?" I kept asking, "Our David?" over and over, hoping the response might somehow be different.

"I got a call. They're three hours earlier. It's on the Internet." She was now on the verge of hysterics.

I tried to get a grip. "No, this can't be. Maybe it's wrong. It's got to be wrong. You know how things can be wrong. Rumors, especially from out of the country, can get distorted. I'm going to check."

"It's correct. It's all over the news!"

"Wh . . . what happened?" The reality of what she was saying started to sink in.

"He was filming in Bangkok on location. They found him dead in his hotel room."

My first thought was that the alcohol finally did his liver in.

Patricia cried throughout a brief description of what had happened. I was in the twilight zone. I couldn't believe what I was hearing, but at the same time the scenario didn't surprise me. My gut instinct was telling me something wasn't right. There was something hinky about it all.

Then I thought, *Oh, my God. Bobby!*

Robert Carradine was David's younger brother, and I had remained close to him and his family. He was usually an early riser, and I wanted to call Bobby before he heard this on the news. It would be awful if he found out that way.

"Patricia, I'm going to call Bobby. I have to call Bobby. I'll call you back. OK?"

"OK."

She was in pieces. I was still in denial, but starting to feel anger mixed with fear. I wasn't going to give in to my emotions until I got confirmation.

My hands shook so much I kept punching up the wrong numbers for Bobby's wife. Finally I heard Edie's Swiss-accented "Hah-low?" on the line.

"Edie, it's Marina," I said in a gaspy, shaky voice.

"Marina, what's wrong?"

"Listen, this may be a wrong report, and I really hope I'm waking you up 'cause it's a mistake, but I just got a call from a mutual friend of mine and David's, and . . . " My voice cracked and I held back my panic. "It's on the news that David, our David, is dead."

A disbelieving "Whaa-aat?" echoed on the other end. "David? Are you sure, Marina?"

"Yes! I didn't want to tell Bobby directly and shock him if it's a mistake, but I'm going to go to the computer and check it out. Please do the same. Maybe they're wrong. I just didn't want you to hear it from the news in case it's true."

I could tell Edie was trying to keep from giving in to panic, too.

"OK, we're going to check it out. Thank you, Marina," she said in a soft, somber tone.

"I'll call you back after I get to the computer," I said.

I dashed upstairs, went online, and turned on the TV. Sure enough, it was there. I stared at the screen, frozen in disbelief. I kept thinking, *No, they can still be wrong.* It felt like it wasn't supposed to happen like this. Like there was a mistake. Something still didn't feel right. I did an Internet search and tried to find a news channel on TV, then the reports came up on screen. I picked up the phone and called Edie back.

"Ya, we found it online. Looks like it's true," she said sadly.

"Is Bobby OK?"

Bobby came to the phone.

"Bobby . . . I'm . . . ," I started to cry, " . . . so sorry. I'm stunned. You know I still loved him. I don't know what to say except . . . I'm . . . just so sorry."

"Thanks, Marina." His voice was weak and sounded stunned. Silence. We were both at a loss for words.

"Ummmm, if you need anything, let me know." I was on the verge of bursting into a torrent of tears.

"Okay. Thanks."

"I'll call you later to check on you, okay?"

"Yeah. Okay," he said slowly.

After hanging up, as I sat there staring into space, my body started to shake uncontrollably. My PTSD (Post Traumatic Stress Disorder), the result of a terrible incident years earlier, had kicked into overdrive and my meltdown of grief began. I called Reverend Rosalyn Bruyere, the minister and healer who had performed our wedding ceremony. She had heard what happened to David from her husband.

"I'm in crisis. Can I see you today?" I pleaded.

"Whenever you want to come over."

Tears were streaming down my face. Reality was setting in. I muttered through my crying spasm, "Heeee'sss gone. Heee'sss gone. He . . . is . . . really gone." I looked around the room, trying to sense if he was there with me, from the other side. Pleading out loud to him, "Johnny, are you here? What happened? Johnny, what the hell happened?"

Usually I get a sense, a premonition or some sort of warning when something is about to happen to someone I know. Most times music—

like a radio on in the distance—is the clue when someone I know is about to cross over. Then I remembered that I did have that experience a couple of weeks before, but I thought it was about my cat Tai being sick. Now I knew it was about David. *Oh, my God.*

I had that same silent, empty feeling I had the first night I spent alone at our house after David moved out. Like the world was put on hold. Half smiling, but with tears dripping into my lap, my mind drifted off to the very first time we met and the day I flew up to Toronto to be with him, to being held tight in his arms for six unforgettable years. It was one long rollercoaster thrill . . . Mr. Toad's wild ride . . . intense passion and emotion.

He was the eye of my tornado.

CHAPTER TWO

HELLO

In 1965, at the Fiore d'Italia restaurant in Sherman Oaks, California, I met Bobby Darin. I was thirteen. He signed his autograph for me with a turquoise-colored pen, "For everything you want in life."

—Marina Anderson

I was in my late teens, around 1971, when I decided to take acting lessons from veteran coach Tony Barr, and Ralph Senensky, who directed many episodes of the *Waltons*. They were fabulous teachers, and I stayed with them for a few years. What made the classes special was that they were held on the Warner Bros. lot in Burbank, California, the same studio where my mother was a contract singer in the '40s.

Most of the kids in class had never set foot on a studio lot before. We'd do our acting scenes either in one of the huge soundstages or, most of the time, inside the houses that line New York Street or a mid-west neighborhood where the famous gazebo that's been in hundreds of movies and television shows is located. The houses are merely facades of what looks like the real deal from the outside, but behind the doors are two-by-four bracings and cables, old furniture and traces of past filming.

Sometimes they hadn't yet struck the set and we had the privilege of rehearsing where magic was just made! I still have a distinct memory of that musty smell, especially if class was held at night, the sound of shoes walking up wooden steps to our "classroom," and the goose bumps that overcame me every time I walked through those gates off Pass Avenue. Little did I know what was in store for me there some twenty years later.

On one of our afternoon class breaks, I wandered over to a soundstage that was totally dark except for the flickering light of hundreds of candles glowing in the abyss. I felt like a fly caught on the tongue of a frog, drawn uncontrollably into the deep, dark stage—mesmerized. Before I knew it, I was standing inside, staring at the mystical set of the Shaolin temple. I felt a presence near me. Yes, there was someone staring at me from behind. When I turned around, I came face to face with a bald-headed man in a monk's robe. It was . . . *him*. David Carradine, smiling gently, with an almost disturbingly amused and intense stare.

There wasn't too much said, at least I don't remember if there was. I was in shock and a bit rattled as I muttered a hello and something about acting class, feeling totally flustered and shy. And then boom! I quickly left, but not before he invited me back, looking at me in that all-knowing way he would later in our relationship, which set off shockwaves in my stomach and throughout my body.

For whatever reason, I never returned to visit. David was a big star then because of his show, *Kung Fu,* and I remembered hearing bits and pieces of a big brouhaha about him in the news. It was his infamous adventure through Laurel Canyon where, under the influence of mushrooms, he wandered nude and broke into a home to play their piano. He had cut himself on the window glass and bled over everything. He was heavily fined and the story hit hard in the press. I knew he had a relationship with Barbara Hershey, who temporarily changed her last name to "Seagull." I was never really a big fan of David's show. I mean, I'd watch it when my father or brother would turn it on and I enjoyed it, but I just didn't pay that much attention to the show or to his career.

But from that first meeting, I always had the feeling of fascination with David—the person, not the star—a sense that I was still *not only* connected to him but *had to see him again.* As the years progressed, that feeling got stronger through more "near-miss" encounters with him and the people near him. Years later, I learned that Gail Jensen was living with David. I remembered her from my alma mater, Los Angeles Valley College. Our boyfriends had been roommates in college, so I became acquainted with Gail via other mutual friends in the theater department, including actor-comedians Ed Begley, Jr. —who is now also known for his ecology efforts—and Michael Richards—who played Kramer on the hit sitcom *Seinfeld*, for which I did a voice-over gig.

There were other odd coincidences. My second husband, actor Michael Anderson, Jr., son of British director Michael Anderson (*Around the World in 80 Days, Logan's Run, Dam Busters, The Shoes of the Fisherman*), starred in the 1966 TV series *The Monroes* with Barbara Hershey. Michael Jr. had worked on a film in South Africa along with his friend Alan, whose close friend was—you guessed it—David. Michael Jr. loved to tell the tale of how they were all arrested on the film and locked up in jail because David was supposedly found with marijuana. Later, Alan was working on a script with Michael, and David was to have them over to discuss the project. There were several invitations to go to David's house, but for whatever reason, I was never able to join them.

With each invite, however, I felt an excitement and kind of gravitational pull activated within me again at the very mention of his name.

CHAPTER THREE

KUNG FU TO YOU TOO

IN early 1992, twenty years after our first and, until then, only encounter, I auditioned for a role in the pilot for David's new show, *Kung Fu: The Legend Continues*. The auditions were held, of all places, on the Warner Bros. lot. I found myself walking through the same gates I had passed through all those years before, but this time as a professional actress with solid credits on my resume. It was a moment I had imagined every time I passed through those gates to acting class. When I heard that David might show up at the audition, I got extremely nervous. I might finally see him again!

Two days earlier, I was in an awful car accident. Someone had run a red light and hit me head-on. My prized 1972 1800ES Volvo that I had beautifully restored was toast, not to mention my head. All those trips to junkyards to find original parts, all the hours in the hands of specialty mechanics and upholsterers were history. I suffered a concussion and had to be taken to the hospital, where I got stitches over my left eye.

Now I was sitting in the reception room at Warner Bros. in a total daze, trying to remember my name, let alone my lines. Being nervous was one thing, but with the head injury, the words just weren't sticking. Suddenly, the door was thrown wide open, and in burst David. He wore jeans and shaggy, sheep-fur-lined moccasins and a coat, and he filled the room with an intoxicating and intense energy. You definitely knew *someone* had arrived. He looked at me with deep, keen interest. It was that same look he gave me when we first met. I could feel his magnetism. Our eyes locked. He smiled. "Hello. Who are you?" His voice was buttery smooth. I think my mouth dropped open. I could feel that magnetism pull me toward him. I rattled off that I was a friend of Michael Sloan, the executive producer of the show, who had directed me in a show in Canada, and I was there to read. Then I blurted out that I knew Gail from college as well. David was amused. He said "I'm going to read with you. I don't read with just anyone," and disappeared into another room.

Oh, God. David read with me? I started to panic. I had never auditioned with the star of a show before, let alone that it would be with *him*. When I was called in to read, David was sitting apart from the suited studio brass, casting director John Frank Levey and Michael Sloan. Just as the casting director was about to begin, David piped up, saying he was going to read with me. I think my brain must have frozen. Whether it was having to read with him or the accident, I don't know, but the audition did not go well. My timing was off and my head hurt. I didn't feel connected to Earth, let alone the material or my body.

I could see the disappointment on my friend Michael's face. But hey! I had a fricking concussion! My head felt like it was about to explode. No one asked about the stitches over my eyebrow, which I thought was odd. Maybe the make-up covered them up better than I thought. I didn't want to make excuses by bringing up the accident. I did tell Michael about it a couple of days later, though, when he called to let me know I didn't get the role, but it was too late. By that time it sounded like a lame excuse.

* * *

Fast forward to the following June. I had moved to Toronto for six months as I had for the previous couple of years for acting work and was called in to audition again for David's show, now being filmed there with a different casting director, Susan Forrest. This time it was for a guest star spot, on the episode called *Rain's Only Friend*, as a demented murderer. Writer-producers Larry Lalonde and Phil Bedard, along with Mario Azzopardi, who was directing the episode, were all people I had worked with before on various shows. They were unaware of my earlier audition disaster in Los Angeles.

I felt I had nothing to lose, so I decided to throw all caution to the wind, take a risk on my approach to the character, and have fun with it, as I had in previous auditions for them.

A few hours later, the phone rang in my basement apartment. It was Larry Lalonde. "Listen," he said, "Uh, we loved what you did."

I was thinking, he's going to give me the "but" bad news now. Here it comes.

"But, since the other role, the new female cop on the show, is so much like you in, well, hair color, eyes, build and all, well . . ."

Just-say-it-for-god's-sake-and-get-me-out-of-my-misery!

" . . . would you mind wearing a wig?"

A wig? I laughed with total relief. Are you kidding? Yeah, I'd wear a wig! What a great idea. It would be fun, fabulous, and good for my reel. Aloud I said, "Is that it? That's the problem?"

"Well, I didn't know if you'd have a problem with it."

"A problem with a wig? No way! I'd *love* to wear a wig! No problem!"

"Okay, then. You got the role!" Larry said happily. "I wanted to be the one to tell you."

I was jumping up and down. Yes, I was ecstatic! And it hit me. I'd be working with David.

The role allowed me to redeem myself with Michael Sloan by proving my acting ability. I had fun at it too, losing myself in the character completely, wigs and all. The funny thing is, had I gotten that initial part in the pilot, that would have been it. Actors are almost never asked back on a show unless they play a recurring character. But because of those wigs, it was different for me. Michael really liked what I did on the first episode, so from then on, he pushed to have me cast again. All in all I guest starred in four episodes on *Kung Fu: The Legend Continues,* playing three different characters. All because of my car accident! It felt destined.

When I arrived on set to begin filming, I found out Gail, now David's wife, was there too. She hung out in David's trailer with a humongous dog named Sasquatch, a Catahoula who wandered around with drool dripping off the sides of its mouth. I'm a dog fanatic, but can't deal with that kind of saliva overload, so I avoided it as I approached Gail, who stared at me in a curious way. I reminded her of all the L.A. Valley alumni connections we had in common, and she lit up like a sparkler.

"Ohmygawwwwwwwd!" she squealed. "You're going to have to come over to the house. Mi casa es su casa." It appeared as though she'd been drinking, and she thought I was someone else, but it didn't matter.

At Valley, Gail was a blue-eyed, tow-headed blonde, a spirited bombshell with a musical talent for composing and singing that few surpassed. She was the girl who male students fantasized about. Every guy wanted Gail. Now here she was, years later, with a sexy but boozy low-register voice, and her beauty straining as it waged a losing battle to keep its throne. Gail started inviting me to their house regularly, even after my episode had been finished. It was the beginning of a somewhat close friendship, not only reuniting me with Gail, but with her and David as a couple.

Between 1992 and 1994, I spent many a day, evening, and overnight at the Carradine house in Mississauga, Ontario, which was about half an hour's freeway ride from midtown Toronto, and ten minutes from the studio. Gail always seemed to be a bit frenetic, often complaining she didn't have enough time for herself, not even for a manicure, although we did manage to occasionally run errands together, grab lunch, and a swim. I was a good excuse for her to escape from the office she and David had in the house. It was a great front-row seat to observe their relationship. I remember thinking, how could anyone not take time for themselves? How could her relationship be that time-consuming?

I came to know a lot about Gail and David's relationship. Not all of it was good. It see-sawed up and down. There were quarrels between them where David started yelling at the top of his lungs and Gail would cower at his rage. And then there were the fun times when I could just sit there and enjoy listening to them play music together. Gail also loved having guests over, so there were frequent parties and a constant merry-go-round of people in and out of the house. Gail got pretty colorful when she was near a bottle and this contributed to an air of good fun. But David was more volatile.

At one point I took up an art project of casting people's lips in bronze. Gail loved the idea and wanted hers and David's done. I planned on giving the casts to Gail and David as gifts. We ventured over to David's trailer on location one day to get his lips cast. Gail and David shared an assistant, Jillian, who told us he was taking a nap. We entered the trailer anyway, and Gail tried gently to wake him up. He arose in a fury.

"Where's the car? Why isn't the car ready?" He growled so loud the trailer literally rattled. "You're waking me up and the car isn't here!"

His rage didn't bother me because I grew up with a father who had similar outbursts. It was all just hot air to me, so I stood there taking it all in.

But Gail's and Jillian's faces turned white and froze in fear. I stood off to the side looking on in disbelief as David continued to rant about why did they wake him up, and didn't they know better? Gail, in a shaken voice, frantically assured him with animated gestures. "Now, now, David, honey, I'm sorry. It's okay. The car is on its way, but I have a surprise for you and wanted to make sure we had time to get this in. Marina's here, and she's going to cast our lips in bronze, honey! Okay?"

He looked at her with disdain for a few moments, then turned his focus on me. Uh-oh. I was holding the molds for the lips and he got curious. He was so distracted he forgot his anger and was more than willing to get his lips cast for posterity. Being the artist that he was, David was fascinated with the concept and very eager to participate. In his drunken clumsiness, however, he was more like a chimpanzee examining a foreign object, which got somewhat tweaked in the process. I had to pull out more of the Styrofoam cups that I was using to fit him for his mold. Luckily, I had brought several.

I was a bit nervous at that point because of the attention he was suddenly giving me. On top of that, he wasn't staying still. His patience factor was sub-zero, so he kept futzing with the materials. I finally got firm with him. "David, if you don't stay still, I can't get this done. I really want to get this right. So can you just sit there for, like, three minutes and not do anything?" This got his attention. He respected my command and calmed down long enough for me to get a couple of impressions that provided beautiful casts, which I still have.

By the time I finished, the car had arrived to pick him up. I tapped Gail on the shoulder to call her attention to the freshly done molds. She winced. Her blouse gave way to reveal a very big, ugly bruise. She immediately, but not convincingly, explained she hit her shoulder on a door. I thought, *Yeah, on top of her shoulder. Uh-huh.* But I said nothing, just took in the whole disturbing situation. Sure enough, Gail confided to me later that David had punched her in the shoulder a few days earlier because she didn't want to make love to him. This supposedly had happened before. She had already gone to bed and was exhausted from a long day working on their ranch. She turned him down, so he socked her in frustration. I remember calling my friend Jennifer in L.A. that night and telling her, "Thank God I'm not married to that man!"

Famous last words.

* * *

One evening at the house, while Gail was off in the kitchen with friends, David and I got into a heavy discussion about the subject of healing. I mentioned having studied with Rosalyn Bruyere in L.A. for several years, so David insisted on demonstrating some chi healing on me. He took off his shirt to show me how he wasn't buffed out with muscles, but he was extremely strong. Then he puffed out his chest like a blowfish, took a stance like a guy on Muscle Beach and said, "See." It was a slightly awkward moment when we locked eyes. A palpable tension could be felt between us. He smiled.

I changed the subject to problematic relationships with parents.

"I resolved mine with my father," he said. Marveling at how wonderful that was, I asked how he achieved it.

"He died."

Silence. Then he chuckled. Was that a joke? No. He shrugged his shoulders and turned his attention to the healing. "I don't do this very often because it takes a lot out of me, but you're special."

He had the gift, too. For the next fifteen minutes, he laid his hands on and over my head and body in various positions and motions, with loud breathing, low groan-like sounds, and tones like Tibetan monks chanting. I felt a definite sensation of power and connection. Whether it was the experience of being touched by him for the first time or something else, I don't know, but I felt totally energized. Then, as soon as he finished, he excused himself to take a sauna in the basement and disappeared.

* * *

On a sleepover at the Mississauga house, I met another longtime female friend of theirs whom Gail had invited from New York. David alleged that they all had engaged in some sort of "dalliance" previously. He didn't go into detail, and I didn't ask. I couldn't tell if it was something he said just to get a reaction out of me or not.

Then, later in the evening, I was in the kitchen with Gail and David, sitting at the table, when the woman walked in wearing a rather transparent nightgown, especially when backlit by the refrigerator door when she opened it to get something. David took it all in with pleasure. The woman got something out of the fridge and said goodnight to us all. Gail was clearly uncomfortable with David's reaction and made light conversation until I excused myself. I looked over at David to say goodnight, and he gave me the same look he had just given the woman. It was a tad unnerving. I really wasn't sure what was going on.

I went to the guest room, closed and locked the door. Minutes later there was a wiggle to the handle and a knock on the door. It was Gail. She didn't want me to lock the door. She said she didn't like any locked doors in her house. Regardless of how I felt, she insisted it was her house, her rules. I didn't sleep well that night.

* * *

Some time later, back in L.A., I got a call from Gail inviting me out with a few of the girls for a night on the town. David was paying for us to have a limo for the evening as a present! Gail relayed he wanted to make sure she invited "the girl with the black hair." That's how he remembered me. I was surprised and flattered.

There were about four of us who gathered at their ranch in Sun Valley where a stretch limo took us on our traveling party. David barely said anything to us. He looked at me and mumbled that he was glad I made it and didn't know why I didn't visit them more often. When it came time for Gail to say goodbye to him, David was lying on the sofa and ignored her. When she reached out to touch his leg, he jerked it away in rejection. I guess it was a "bad hair day" for them.

We went to Dan Tana's restaurant in West Hollywood first. Gail wanted to go bar-hopping. I had no interest in that, so I stayed at the restaurant and hung out with Dabney Coleman and photographer Susan Rothschild, who was part of Gail's party and a longtime friend of mine, until Gail came back with the limo to pick us up about an hour later. David greeted us all back at the house and was pleased we appreciated his luxury splurge. But the atmosphere between him and Gail was uneasy on our return as well. I was glad to get into my car and go home.

CHAPTER FOUR

FLYING FISTS OF FURY

IT wasn't until 1994 that my feelings for David started to take another direction. But I never allowed myself to feel them fully, since Gail was my friend, as he was, and they were married.

Synchronicity never ceases to amaze me. It's that universal timeline, a chain that connects the next link and the next, and if it weren't for the previous link the whole chain would never have held together.

I had snagged an audition for a recurring role on *90210*, the first audition with a new agent Gail helped set me up with. Unfortunately, it was set for the same day I had scheduled to have my breast implants redone. As they did with many women, my implants had ruptured. I had just joined a nationwide class-action lawsuit against the manufacturer. I was worried about my health, especially if I waited any longer, so I decided not to put the surgery off and forfeited the audition. It was an expensive decision: the surgery depleted my savings and I had no work.

I put a call in to Michael Sloan to let him know I was badly in need of a job and to see if there was anything on *Kung Fu: The Legend Continues* for me, but there wasn't. A few weeks after the surgery, he called.

"Got a show for you! *Flying Fists of Fury* episode. It's a parody, and you'd be perfect. The guys had someone else in mind, but I brought up your name. They loved you in the first season. Since you were wigged, you'll look entirely different in this show. You can look like you. So you're hired!"

I screamed with joy and relief. To the rescue in the nick of time. And it was a funny role! Yes! God bless Michael Sloan!

Again, like the car accident that led to my first role on David's show, fate seemed to intervene. If I hadn't been so panicked about my finances, I never would have put in that S.O.S. call to Sloan and never would have been cast in another *Kung Fu* episode.

I flew to Toronto to start filming and found myself running, falling, kicking, and doing a bit of kung fu. I prayed through all of it that I wouldn't hurt my boob job for any reason, since the incisions were still healing. The worry subsided, and everything went just fine. I was feeling healthy again, having the time of my life, and without realizing it, falling for David.

It was August, with high summer humidity, when we went on location in Toronto's Chinatown. The first day I did a fun and funny scene with Chris Potter, who played Peter Caine, the heir to the Caine legacy. I wore a skimpy outfit: leather shorts, tall boots, fishnets, and crop top with metal links. In the scene, Chris gives me this sensational kiss with me bent backwards and then literally drops me flat. Cast and crew cracked up laughing, with me letting out a high-pitched surprised squeal each time we did a take. Of course I had a mattress to land on. He was so concerned about how he was kissing me in our scene, that after the first take he asked if it was "okay."

"Okay? Oh my God! You're a fabulous kisser! Are you kidding?"

He flushed red and looked away. "Really?"

"Oh yeah. Perfect." Which was the truth.

"Good. Thanks," he responded shyly, and we prepped for another take. Ooooooola-la! I enjoyed every one.

David dared me to go out to lunch, with him and Chris, wearing my costume. I took him up on it. He liked that. A lot. We ended up at a bar on Queen Street where my outfit actually didn't look that out of place. David downed a couple of drinks and that was lunch. He told me he was trying to keep it to a minimum. I had the feeling he was testing me on various levels in conversation, but I held my own. Chris was looking out for me a bit, to make sure I didn't get intimidated by David, which was very sweet. Such an adorable guy, but very married with kids.

During another funny scene where Edd "Kookie" Byrnes (of the '60s TV show 77 *Sunset Strip*) slaps me around to get me to stop screaming, we had to wait for something technical and I saw David standing off to the side watching us. He looked thoughtful and a bit sad. We smiled at each other and I walked over, calling out to him as usual in a sing-song voice, "Daaaaa-vid!" As was my ritual with him by this point, I wrapped my arms around his waist and said, "Hi, Daaaaa-vid!" He gave a low sexy growl, which was his typical and welcome response, and then folded himself around me as well. Usually our hugs would break after a few beats, but this one just continued... and continued... and continued. He moved behind me and held me close, totally enveloping me in his arms. We just stood there, not moving, and melted into each other, in full view of everyone. I was having a difficult time in my relationship with actor Dabney Coleman, whom I had met at Dan Tana's restaurant a few years earlier and started dating. So this comfort from David was more than welcome. He told me years later he thought *I* was the one who looked sad and wanted to comfort *me*.

It was a good fifteen minutes before Rob Moses sauntered over and reminded David he had promised to jam with the guys at lunch, as they often did because there were so many musicians on crew. I wanted to scream at this guy to go away. How dare he interfere with our moment! David reluctantly let go, and we parted. It felt like a part of me left with him. I quickly interpreted his tenderness as the genuine expression of a caring friendship, a gesture of affection that I realized I was missing in my life. That hug had been just what I needed, and I missed it already.

My feelings about Dabney, at this time, were conflicted. I loved him, despite our difficulties. But David? David was married. He was just being friendly. When I told my girlfriend Jennifer about it, however, she said she thought David was definitely falling in love with me. I laughed it off. She was insistent and didn't think that was going to be the last of it either. The next day we filmed my scenes on a rooftop where David was standing nearby, watching. I strolled up to him after giving the day before considerable thought, and said, "You're the only man, outside of my father, that had ever hugged me like that with no ulterior motives, no double intentions, or innuendos. It was truly a beautiful gift you gave me, David. I just wanted you to know and to thank you."

He had a sparkle in his eye and gave me a wry half-smile. "What makes you think I had no ulterior motive in mind?" he asked, and walked away. Butterflies flew through my stomach. It was that same feeling I had when we first met over twenty years before, except that it was more profound, more intimate. A blushing "Oh!" ran across my ego.

* * *

August 10, 2003

I just came in from walking Lulu on this summer evening. Warm and balmy, much like the night I had dinner with David at the end of the shoot on *Flying Fists*. My God, was that nine years ago? Tears started to flood my eyes as Lulu tugged at the leash, wanting to play with another dog she caught sight of. The teardrops splattered across my face and onto my blouse as she jerked me forward. Almost nine years to the week. I looked at the moon. Almost full. Just like it was then.

* * *

Filming had finished on *Flying Fists,* and I was scheduled to leave for L.A. in a few days, after my Canadian citizenship ceremony on August 31. I had waited four years for this moment. Ex in-laws Michael and Adrianne Anderson sponsored me and Michael Jr. so we could live in Canada and write for their production company. I instantly fell in love with Toronto. My gratitude to the Andersons was the reason I kept the last name. I've remained in touch with them over the years as well. They opened up a new world and life for me in Canada.

David invited me out to dinner at the "IC," as we called the InterContinental Hotel on Bloor Street, along with Chris Potter and Kim Chan. Kim was quite an endearing character. He played the Old Ancient on the show and, after spouting oriental wisdom on set all day, would invite people to his dressing room after filming for martinis. The IC had a fabulous gourmet restaurant, and we dined in luxury. For the wine, David ordered Château Margaux. I kept the cork for years after our divorce. Sitting across from each other, he showed me how to savor the wine, how to tell if it's a good vintage. A true connoisseur, David relished teaching me all about it.

I was a bit nervous because all through dinner, he was paying keen attention to me. We'd continually lock eyes. It was difficult to break his gaze. There was definite chemistry, but I put a wall up to protect myself and tried not to let any fantasy creep over it. We were friends, and he was very married. After dinner, we all piled into his newly purchased, but used, burgundy Maserati. He kept the car parked as we listened to tracks of music he had recorded with Gail. He boasted about her talent and their writing together. I thought, *How wonderful!* Two talented people in love working together like that. That's what I wanted for myself one day.

I did write scripts together with my hubby number two, Michael, but that's all that seemed to work in our marriage, although we did manage to stay friends. Looking back on the marriage, I guess that's what my angels had in mind for me. If it wasn't for Michael Sr. and Adrianne sponsoring us for landed immigrancy, I would never have been able to live and work in Toronto with Michael Sloan, Larry Lalonde, Phil Bedard, and Mario Azzopardi, all of whom hired me for David's series. Synchronicity again.

* * *

I was in constant touch with Gail, who had been living at their ranch in

L.A. for chunks at a time, and told her of the dinner. I could sense in the stilted and awkward beats in our conversation that she was concerned about something. The way she asked questions indicated something was not right between her and David. She seemed suspicious and even joked about creating some publicity stunt for him. She suggested taking pictures of David and me and selling them to the tabloids, saying that we were having an affair. She laughed at the possibility of us making money off the stunt. At first it sounded fun to pull off a joke like that, but it also felt weird to me, so I nixed the idea. She brought up that David asked every so often about "the black-haired friend" of hers, meaning me, and why I didn't come to the ranch to visit?

"He said that?"

I reassured her that he appeared to be very much in love, *with her*. This seemed to have a temporary calming effect on her.

* * *

Winter, 1994

Back in L.A. one pleasant evening in December, I got a phone call from David. "Heeeeyyyy there!" he said in the same cheery tone he always used with me.

"Daaaaa-vid!" I smiled back into the phone, excited, yet wondering why he was calling me.

He was phoning from the IC, where he was staying and celebrating his birthday, *sans* Gail. He called me on his birthday! He said Calista, his daughter, was there with an exotic dancer friend of theirs and that he was having a really good time, maybe too good of a time from the way he described his female friend.

He said it was a relief to get away from Gail, and this saddened me. I had heard her unhappy side of their difficulties, too. They were definitely having problems as he told me of the ins and outs of trying to stay sober.

Our conversation went on for at least an hour, at which point he said he had to get back to his birthday party and would talk to me again soon.

I thought of all the people he chose to call on his birthday, he called me. Wow!

CHAPTER FIVE

SPRING FORWARD

Spring, 1995

I hadn't heard from David in a while, but I did talk to Gail. Things sounded dicey. They took a vacation and it seemed to help. Now they were back in L.A., waiting word if *Kung Fu: The Legend Continues* was going to be picked up for a fourth season. The conversation changed suddenly to her unhappiness. She laughed that David joked with her about how he only keeps wives around for twelve years. Then she told me she had everything prepared if the bottom dropped out of the marriage and already had planned what to do with the horses. She also didn't want to go back to Toronto.

I could relate. I was having a hell of a time letting go of my tumultuous relationship with Dabney, or the Dabster as I now fondly refer to him. We had just returned that March from a trip to New York where we saw Jerry Lewis in *Damn Yankees*. It had always been one of my lifetime wishes to meet this funny man, and Dabney was able to take me backstage so I could have Lewis autograph pictures for me and my brother. I was a major fan and so jazzed at finally meeting him.

I thought my year-and-a-half affair with rocker Don Henley was steamy, but my four years with Dabney were far more intensely hot, heavy, and. . . long distance. It took a toll on me emotionally and I was at a turning point. I felt stuck. So, as I often do when I need new insight into my life, I went to see a psychic.

He was nothing like I envisioned he would be. Christian Dion was different. Flamboyant, glitzy, and rather short, he had huge, sad blue eyes; long, blond, professionally coiffed hair; and a voice that sounded like ET, but with a thick British accent. I didn't give him any information except that I wanted a reading. He had me shuffle a deck of cards that were very different from the traditional Tarot and, as soon as he laid them out, began a dissertation that lasted without interruption for a solid half hour.

"It's bollox!"

That was how he described my situation. He was to the point about my problem and circumstances. He told me that it was a type of addiction and that I had a choice to make. He suggested ways to help me deal with the relationship and warned of temptations, and emotional traps.

Christian went on to say that, after three months, I would feel a release. I would then take a trip, within six months, possibly for work, which would take me to an involvement with someone, leading to a long-term relationship. But it wouldn't happen unless I got serious about getting over this other person. I took his advice and was glad I did, because I ran into all the traps he predicted. But thanks to his warnings I was prepared for everything that happened!

In the meantime, Christian's parents, Tom and Christine Fishwick, both gifted psychics as well, came to L.A. for a visit. His father, who had an accent as thick as oatmeal you could stand up a spoon in, told me I'd be moving east. I had briefly fantasized about trying out New York for a while, but it was a fleeting thought.

"Could be, huh, maybe not, but I see ye in the east. Overlookin' a river, I'm tellin' ye." He said I'd be living in a new place, standing by a window and, when I looked out, would see a river. That would be the sign that I was in "the" long-term relationship, "the one," and that I could marry this person. Ooooooh, how exciting!

CHAPTER SIX

SPECIAL FORCES

August 1995

T RUE to the title, it was a special episode, with many forces behind it.

This time it was David himself who requested me to guest star in an episode called *Special Forces*. In a phone conversation, after I was cast, he told me he wanted this role to be recurring and that I'd probably do another episode later in the season. I was thrilled. He was also very keen on my getting together with his daughter Calista, whom I had met briefly before. He thought we'd have a lot in common and become good friends. It seemed important to him. She would be on the same plane coming up to Toronto, along with her ex-fiancé Patrick Culliton, who was also going to appear in the episode, and David's stepbrother Michael Bowen. One of David's brothers, Robert Carradine, would be in Toronto as well. David was looking forward to getting us all together.

Indeed, on the shoot Calista and I bonded quickly. She was down to earth, a say-it-like-it-is, take-it-or-leave-it gal. We soon developed a strong, sister-like friendship. Filming the show and life behind the scenes were both a blast. Calista and I would venture off with the stunt crew, riding in the Hummers, climbing hillsides for shoot preps, inventing our own cool adventures and laughing a lot. She filled me in on the drama between her dad and Gail—that they were living apart—and said that David *really* liked me. A lot. She thought we'd have a shot at a relationship and hoped it would happen.

During a fun field trip to see a show with Calista and David in Stratford, about two hours down the road from Toronto, we all bonded further.

We were looking for a place to stay overnight and a woman who served us lunch, homemade strudel, invited us to stay at her place. The "strudel lady," as we called her, clearly had a crush on David, and he was leaning toward staying there. This rubbed me the wrong way. I couldn't understand why I felt so territorial about him, but I did. Calista and I voted for "the dorm" instead, a room in a house where the daughter had left for college. Calista and I stayed up all night, gabbing in whispers, eating snacks and laughing like two college girls ourselves, while David slept in the bed on the other side of the room. Or so we thought. "I wish you two would talk louder so I can hear what you're saying," he joked. "I think I'm missing out on some good information!" We all laughed.

The next day, we headed for the theater. It was a beautiful day and we had a chance to mill around the grounds before we went inside. During the show, David sat in the middle holding hands with both of us, Calista on one side and me on the other. I didn't want to let go of his hand even to clap. Calista leaned back and smiled at me like she was saying, *See? He really likes you!* It was a wonderful weekend escape.

After we got back to Mississauga, David threw a big get-together. It was a full house that night for stay-overs. A very sexy guy and I got along great during the shoot. A short time after we all went off to bed, however, I heard a knock at my door. I opened it to find the guy standing there in the buff. "I'm heeeeeere. Izzzzz gooooood!" he said in a funny European accent he had often kidded me with over the weeks. I was stunned. He came in, closed the door, said, "Let's talk," then pulled me over onto the bed.

"Uh, not a good idea." But for the next several minutes we played cat and mouse around the room as he tried to convince me it was. As tempting as the situation was, it didn't feel right. Probably because I was trying to sort out my feelings about David. I thought if I went to bed with anyone close to him, it would ruin any chance of being with David. I didn't want to muddy the water. I finally grabbed a camera from my bag and said, "If you don't leave, I'll take a picture of you and show it to everyone." He didn't, so I did. He still wouldn't leave, so I went into the living room and fell asleep on the sofa. When I woke up early in the morning I looked down to find David asleep beside me on the floor. Odd, I thought. When he got up, he told me I looked uncomfortable and in need of protection. Years later he confessed it was just to be near me.

A week later, just before I was due to move back to L.A., David threw yet another party, a huge birthday bash for Chris Potter, who played his son on the show. There must have been a hundred people in and outside of the house, with the later hours whittling the throng down to a core group of family and friends. I was sitting in the den talking to Chris when David loomed in the doorway. He climbed over the sofa edge and pushed me back so he was on top and leaning over me, staring down into my eyes. His long hair obscured my view so I had to hold it back. It was so soft to touch. I held his face. We stared into each other's eyes for a long moment, and he kissed me. His lips were soft and sensual. The moment felt so right. I couldn't believe he was kissing me. The question in my mind was finally answered. I realized I was, for the first time in my life, falling in love with a man with brown eyes. My heart was pounding. I kissed back.

"David, what are you doing? Are you nuts?" Chris asked him.

To which David lifted his head and responded, "Hey man, I know what I'm doing. I'm not letting her get away."

I sat up and excused myself from the room. I could faintly hear bits of their conversation and caught the words *Gail, married,* and *separation.*

David came out of the den, took me by the hand, and we made out in practically any room where we could find privacy. "I want you to stay," he told me. I said I had to go back to my apartment, to pack, because I was moving back to L.A. He winced, as if someone punched him in the stomach. He was crushed. "You can't go back. I want you here with me. Live here with me."

I knew instantly that's what I wanted, especially since others had already informed me he and Gail were separated, but I still had reservations. So to play it safe, I thought maybe I should keep my apartment in Toronto as a safety net.

I called my psychic friend, Michael Bodine. "I don't know what to do."

"Well, hun, it's like this. There's a possibility of marrying this guy, but you might be better off just doing business with him. But, uh . . . " There was a pause as he concentrated on the information he was getting. "Nope, don't think you're going to do that. Yep. I think you're going to live with him. The apartment is a good idea too."

I immediately called my landlord and got my apartment back, on a month-to-month basis. The next day, I called my longtime dear friend and clairvoyant, Marilyn Mazzotta, and told her what happened. She responded, "He really does care for you, luvvy. You'll be a busy gal."

Regardless of what Michael and Marilyn said, and even though sparks flew between David and me, it wasn't what Tom Fishwick had predicted. It couldn't be *the* relationship, since I didn't see a river anywhere, let alone from a window. Nowhere. Bummer.

CHAPTER SEVEN

I GET ALL *THAT?*

For the next two weeks, after I flew back to L.A. from the *Special Forces* shoot, David and I courted on the phone for hours at a time. One conversation lasted six hours! Count 'em—six! The subsequent calls each day were not as long, but still extremely lengthy and spontaneous, whenever and from wherever we could squeeze them in.

We talked about anything and everything. We took particular delight in recalling how I succumbed to David's seduction in the Mississauga house. We planned our future, talked about having a baby together, discussed our mutual love of art, music, and philosophy.

During one of the phone marathons, we had made a pact: no lies, total honesty, no secrets, have a baby, get matching tattoos and do sculpting together. It was all part of our secret plan to share life. I carried the "contract" in my wallet throughout the relationship.

It was difficult to hang up each time, but knowing we'd soon be together again in Toronto helped to make things easier. We were on a countdown for my return to Toronto.

The night before my flight, I stuffed my suitcases to the brim with my designer clothes, along with a wide assortment of sexy lingerie. While we never talked about what David might like to see me wear, I tried to out-guess him by packing what I thought would please him the most.

September 8, 1995

On the evening flight to Toronto, I was a bundle of nerves and full of excited anticipation. During a five-hour flight that seemed like an eternity, I thought about David and our marathon conversations. I was also looking forward to catching up with my dear friend Marilyn, who was coming to meet me at the airport.

She was always the first to volunteer to help me with my treks to Toronto, and one of the first in which I always confided. I couldn't think of a more ideal person to deliver me to David. Marilyn did warn me that the relationship would be a difficult rollercoaster ride, full of extreme ups and downs, but said that David was definitely in love with me, adding, "Luvvy, he's falling for you hard."

Well, that was good to hear, because I was falling faster than a comet hurtling to earth.

The plane was on time and so was Marilyn. In a flash, we arrived at David's house on Prince John in the Sherwood Forest Estates. Maid Marian was coming home to her Robin Hood. I was so nervous. David wasn't sure when he'd be finished filming, but said he'd leave the house unlocked and I could let myself in.

We no sooner got the luggage out of the car than the headlights from another vehicle startled us as it pulled up into the circular drive. It was David. My Robin Hood. I thought, what perfect timing. Nope. David later admitted he had been waiting in his car just so he could watch me arrive. Awww . . . how romantic!

He wore a heavy sheep-lined suede coat with brown jeans and a hat from his character on his show. We looked at each other, smiled, and like two magnets, locked together in an all-consuming kiss and embrace. His arms seemed to wrap around me twice. We swayed side to side as we hugged. He smelled like cigarettes and alcohol mixed with the damp, brisk evening air. God, he felt good! I never felt so wanted. So safe. So secure. I was finally home.

After a long and awkward silence, Marilyn did her signature clearing of her throat and said, "Well, luvvy, I better get moving and leave you two be. Give me a call when you settle in later in the week." And with that, she drove off as we hauled my luggage into the hallway, but not before David picked me up and carried me across the threshold!

Inside, David looked me over and smiled as he pointed, "Go to your room!" in his low, distinctive, resonating voice. My body pulsed with anticipation. I instinctively knew what he meant and headed off to the bedroom to wait for him, but not for long.

When I entered the room my heart was pounding. I turned the overhead lights off and just left the bedside lamps on to illuminate the room. I debated on what lingerie to wear, but ultimately decided not to wear anything at all. I turned down the bedspread and stretched out on the huge king-sized bed, trying to find a comfortable, yet provocative pose with which to welcome him. I wanted this first vision of me lying naked on his bed to be an indelible image in his mind. I lay on my side with one arm stretched overhead and my left leg bent at the knee and crossed over my front, so he'd only see a hint of everything. My left arm rested on top of my left side, over and down my hip. This was one of many poses I had tested out in the mirror at home. In between trying to settle into a Kodak moment for him, I could hear various noises in the kitchen.

I no sooner got in my final position than David entered the room. He beamed, a broad smile filling his face, and in that booming voice roared, "I get all *that*?" I couldn't help but laugh.

David began tearing his clothes off as he dove onto the bed, revealing his body as a canvas for the most beautiful tattoo artwork I had ever seen. Not dark black lines, but a full rainbow of beautiful muted colors. A tiger against a backdrop of mountains. Chinese carp. The images wrapped around his body, inked by some of the foremost tattoo artists around the world. My hands traced over his physique, admiring their beauty . . . feeling his body. David, the artist, was a walking canvas himself. I lay there taking in every detail of this live portrait.

When he removed his Speedos, I was pleasantly surprised to see his genitalia displaying an assortment of gold chains in various lengths, linking to several "family jewel" body piercings. I thought to myself, "Wow! Now *that's* different!"

"I wanted to dress up for the occasion," he stated proudly, showing off his dazzling gold regalia. He was very pleased that I liked it.

It was totally rock'n roll, avant-garde, and made him appear even sexier, if that were possible. He said he had a couple of the piercings done professionally, and a couple he did himself. Himself? In particular his Prince Albert piercing. To pierce one's own penis and testicles I thought would be unfathomable. And without anesthetic? I cringed at the thought. Was he kidding me? No. Capital O-U-C-H! It certainly was intriguing though . . . I had to take a closer look.

David's sexual advances were exotic, sweet, and such a turn-on. It was as if centuries of past lives melted away and we were finally united again. An overwhelming feeling of completion and peace came over me. I found him *again*. It was as if I had waited all my life for him and this was the way it was supposed to be. Everyone else had been just marking time for me until I could be with *him*, again. He was my love and no one was going to take him away from me. Not ever. He was from that moment, on that night, inseparably, my Johnny, and I was his Blackie.

We made love for hours. It was fun love, new love, exploring, hot, and heavy. We laughed, talked. We were hungry for each other, taking delight in finding new little secrets and hidden pleasures. David was gentle and took great pleasure in caressing me admiringly. The artist in him emerged. He kept running his hands over my body, my face, feeling my bone structure, particularly my hip and collar bones. "You've got a fabulous clavicle," he told me. As he explored my throat, where he indulged in kissing, he took his hands and smoothly ran them over and around my neck in a caressing motion, so they were positioned on either side, and gently used his thumbs to trace down the middle to my collarbone. No matter where or how he touched me, my body shivered with delight. "You're one entire erogenous zone," he chuckled.

Then he asked me to open my mouth slightly, but instead of kissing me, we locked lips and he inhaled so that the air from my lungs was sucked into his. As quickly as he did this, he exhaled back into me. This totally unexpected maneuver startled me. He smiled and asked me how I liked it. "Uh . . . different. Never did that before." He just kept smiling and chuckled, "There's more."

Suddenly, he got up and disappeared from the room, only to reappear with a dinner feast. He strode nude back into the bedroom and placed a huge silver platter before me. There, centered among the colorful array of grapes, kiwi and other fruits and vegetables, was a fish cooked in its entirety, head to tail, stuffed with even more edibles. It was the first time I ever ate a fish with its head attached, let alone served to me in bed by a nude lover! It was the oddest, yet the most delicious fish I've ever tasted to this day. We devoured every morsel, feeding each other with our hands, and then fell asleep in each other's arms, exhausted and satisfied. Oh, was I satisfied!

The morning started with a knocking at the bedroom door. It was Johnny Mac, as we all called him, short for John McIntyre, David's personal driver. It was time for David to go to set. Knock, knock, again, louder this time, and David finally started to stir. "Give me another ten minutes!" "Okay," and we could hear footsteps on the carpet retreat back down the hallway. He rolled over and we started to greet each other a passionate good morning, as each subsequent morning would start. We couldn't get enough of each other.

After David left the house, I unpacked and tried to organize myself. Even though I had all my belongings there, I had retained rental on my basement apartment from Rick Rode, the same sweet landlord from the previous year. It was my "just in case" safety net, which came in handy later.

As I darted around the house, it felt like I had truly arrived home, yet at the same time, seeing that Gail's belongings were still there, I felt very odd. David and others around him assured me that they had separated. Every time I thought I should call Gail, I stuffed the idea away. I didn't want confrontation or anything to spoil my joy. But nowhere did I see the river that British psychic Tom Fishwick talked about in his reading. He said that I'd move to the East and I'd know it was "the" relationship when I saw a river from a window in the house where I'd live. Sigh. Oh, well.

* * *

The first weekend of our romance, I got coveted invitations to the traditional Toronto Film Festival barbecue hosted by Norman Jewison at the Canadian Film Centre. We declared it our "coming out party" and took command of the event. Even though we only had two tickets, we insisted Calista join us. "What are they going to do? Turn David Carradine away? They wouldn't dare," he laughed.

We walked around the grounds with David in the middle holding our hands. I "worked the lawn" as David would always brag about me, introducing him to producers, directors and other stars. News crews gathered around us to grab photos and film footage ops as we were escorted to the celebrity area on the patio where even more photographers were crammed. It was the most fun I ever had at the annual event.

David spotted a very large, unusual dog at the end of the lawn area. All three of us being major pet lovers, we headed in its direction. David, as usual, didn't take the expected route, politely snaking around the throng of people that were milling about. The crowd stared as he made a beeline for the dog, hurdling over a high hedge in true "grasshopper" style. Calista and I looked at each other and laughed as we followed over and through the greenery. Coming upon the owners of the canine, we were introduced to our first Bernese Mountain Dog. "That's my next dog," David declared.

The next day, I set about making calls to the States to find a Berner Sennenhund breeder. The owners of the dog we met told us that Robert Redford was responsible for introducing the breed into the United States, so I called his office. What the hey, go to the source! His assistant gave me several referrals and by the end of the day, our dog Rocky was on order with Bobbie Hefner of Swiss Star Farms. I was told it could take a year to get one, and I knew David would be extremely disappointed. He wanted one of those dogs now! So I explained to Hefner that David used to breed dogs and how fabulous he was with them, hoping to get the wait time reduced. After she interviewed us for two hours on the phone, we were put on a short list and got Rocky within a few months. We had a chance to thank Redford in person a few years later at Sundance, where he met David's second Bernese, Thunder.

CHAPTER EIGHT

TARANTINO TARANTELLA

September, 1995

LATER that week, like two school kids, we crashed parties and galas at the Toronto Film Festival and declared them all celebratory parties for our romance. We roamed the upstairs at Bistro 990, sort of my Toronto "home away from home" version of Dan Tana's restaurant in L.A., and sneaked into yet another industry party because we heard Drew Barrymore was there. David's family and the Barrymores go way back. The bouncer at the event hesitated to admit us at first, but acquiesced because he was a *Kung Fu* fan.

We found Drew, and they were both delighted to see each other again. When she was a kid, I used to socialize with her and her mom at various parties Don Johnson's sister, Jamie Skylar, would throw. We reminisced a bit about friends in common. David pulled out a photograph of his granddaughter, Sienna, who looks quite a bit like Drew.

She stared at the picture and said, "We're related, aren't we? She looks like me."

David smiled and said, "I think so."

Then, on the opposite side of the room, I noticed that Quentin Tarantino had just arrived. I thought, "Now there is a director who would be great for David to work with. Two rebel personalities who color outside the box." I remembered all the buzz about Tarantino being the one who helped rejuvenate John Travolta's career in *Pulp Fiction*, and I just couldn't let this opportunity pass by.

David refused to make the first move and approach Tarantino, due to a combination of ego and extreme shyness. I couldn't believe he would risk passing up this chance, so I said, "Okay. If you won't, I will," and headed straight for Tarantino. I mingled with people alongside him and got something to drink, waiting for an opportune moment, when I overheard him saying to someone, "Carradine . . . Yeah, man."

That was a cue if I ever heard one. I tapped him on the shoulder and said, "Hi, Quentin, I'm Marina Anderson, and my boyfriend would love to meet you. He's quite a fan of yours."

He looked me up and down skeptically and said, "Oh? And who is your boyfriend?"

"David Carradine. He's over there," I responded as I pointed across the room.

His eyes popped, and he blurted out, "Oh my God! *David Carradine* is your boyfriend? You're *kidding!*" He seemed to shudder with excitement and started to talk even faster. He admitted to me that he was a major fan and that he had spotted David entering the party but was too intimidated to go up to him.

I said, "Well, let me introduce you. C'mon."

So I took him by the arm and guided him over to David, where they talked for quite some time. Tarantino told David that he had a copy of *Americana*, a 1983 film David had directed and starred in, and even relayed parts of his favorite scenes of other films David had done. Tarantino mentioned that he'd love to work with David someday—of course the feeling was mutual—but was very blunt in admitting he had reservations. He had heard about David's wild reputation and his drinking and had concerns. We both refuted the stories, of course, but it was hard to get around David being known in Toronto as GLASShopper, for the highly publicized incident where he shattered the glass on a backstage door after trying to shove it open at a Rolling Stones concert.

I assured him that the stories were overblown and that the alcohol never got in the way of his filming or resulted in production problems, but Tarantino didn't appear convinced. I knew I had to do something else to secure his confidence. The conversation was coming to a close, since other people wanted Tarantino's attention, but I didn't want it to end on that note. I couldn't allow it! I had an idea: lunch! I suggested we meet the following day at the Sutton Place Hotel, knowing the hotel had a piano that David could play to entertain and impress Tarantino. They could talk in more depth in a quiet atmosphere. Tarantino was delighted at the invitation.

Sure enough, mid-afternoon the next day, we met in Alexander's Bar at the Sutton. To my pleasant surprise, Tarantino brought along fellow director, Toronto-based Atom Egoyan, who was quickly gaining international recognition. We talked through lunch, trading stories, and David kept the drinking to a minimum. At the piano, David sang away for a good portion of our two-hour lunch with the best of his own compositions as well as cover songs. As he played, I did my best to schmooze both directors, to convince Tarantino that David was back on the road to being a bankable star once more. Tarantino seemed very pleased and expressed that he really wanted to work with David one day.

We left the meeting feeling elated . . . like something clicked into place. When we got home, I faxed a note about the meeting to Army Archerd, the celeb columnist at *Variety*, and called my longtime psychic friend Michael Bodine. He assured me that David and Quentin would indeed work together one day on a film that would benefit David. He couldn't pinpoint a time, but said that "they would." My dear friend Marilyn also confirmed the prediction. It all sounded so promising.

Now all *I* had to do, and did for the next several years, was to try and make sure that Tarantino knew David went sober and stayed sober. I left messages, sent notices, kept up with different personnel changes, any-thing we could think of to keep in touch and keep him updated on David. We invited Tarantino to numerous functions, like our engagement party, wedding, screenings and music venues with David's band. I also submitted David for a few roles that Tarantino's company, A Band Apart, produced, thus furthering the contact. We would always mention David's recent projects, awards, and publicity, and that he was *still sober*, but David was never called in and Tarantino never attended.

A couple of years later, David's stepbrother, actor Michael Bowen, invited us to the wrap party for Tarantino's film *Jackie Brown*, which he had a nice role in. David was miffed that he wasn't cast in Robert Forster's role in the film. He thought Tarantino was never going to cast him in anything. So to avoid confrontation—he *so* did not like confrontation—he balked at attending. Trying to get David to go to an event when he was in that mood was almost impossible without getting into a major argument. By the time I would convince him and get out the door, I was so exhausted I didn't want to go anywhere! David said he'd rather not go to the party than have to hide his angst toward Tarantino. I could have clobbered him! I explained again this was a prime opportunity for Tarantino to see him in person for the first time since Toronto, and this time sober! That turned David around.

We arrived at the party fashionably late and I immediately zeroed in on Tarantino. David shifted into one of his quiet, but intimidating moods. We greeted Tarantino, but David barely said anything. He kept Tarantino in his strong gaze, and stayed aloof by turning his body away, addressing Tarantino with little eye contact while he scanned the room here and there. It was a rather dismissive tactic that he often used, which resulted in people feeling uneasy and not important. David knew this disturbed people, so he did it on purpose. His own "Art of War" method. This made Tarantino babble even more than usual, held together by awkward, quiet moments from David.

When David walked away to get me something to drink, Tarantino turned to me and asked if David was angry with him. I said that he was miffed that he hadn't been considered for the Forster role. I said, "Look, Quentin, David would kill to work with you. He likes you. He really does. He's understandably disappointed he wasn't cast in that role. We thought this would be the movie for you two to work together. Besides, he's doing that to intimidate you. Don't let it get to you. That's just David wanting to punish you." We laughed, but Tarantino was still bugged by it.

When David returned, Tarantino promised that he would definitely find something for them to do together, and urged him not to be upset. David grinned, a great big one, and said, "find something soon." Tarantino reassured him that they would "work together in something that would be great." He didn't want it to be just anything, "but the right thing." David's defining moment had been set into motion.

Even after David and I separated in May 2001, he called me about being at a crossroads on whether to go to Austin, Texas, because Tarantino was going to be there. He was concerned about the cost and whether it would be beneficial. I tried to be encouraging, reminding David that it was some time since they saw each other at the *Jackie Brown* party, and pointing out that this would be another key opportunity to reconnect in person. He was depressed and wasn't going to make the trip, but I said just put it on the credit card and go. He did connect with Tarantino, which further solidified their friendship. It all obviously paid off for David because finally, in 2002, just a few months after our divorce was final—on December 12, 2001, Lady Guadalupe Day—Tarantino came through with his promise and cast David in *Kill Bill*.

Someone sent me a copy of what was supposed to be the script when Warren Beatty was originally cast. I thought how perfect it was for David. In the version I read Bill was more like Warren—typically handsome, debonair, almost "Bond-ish," not a "Kung Fu-ish" character. That's what David dreamed of—an A-list movie to star in where he could get away from the Kung Fu branding.

It was a great disappointment that David never acknowledged what I did, and I never got to share in the end result of my efforts. It was like having a baby and being forced to give it up for adoption, having other people enjoy the experience and being left behind in the dust.

Hayley, girlfriend of David's brother, Keith—now his wife—called me to tell me the news about David being cast in the movie. David took his girlfriend and Hayley and Keith out to dinner at Le Sanglier, *our* favorite French romantic hideaway restaurant in Encino, to make the big announcement. At first the news really stung me. I felt it was a betrayal to celebrate with this new person in his life at *our* favorite place. David supposedly had a slightly melancholy reaction to a comment made about the offer just coming to him, like it just fell into his lap with no back story involving my efforts.

David knew better, but I was not brought up in conversation. After recovering from the initial shock, I actually liked the fact he chose our restaurant. That's the place we would have chosen to celebrate together as we did for anniversaries, for intimate times, or just to get away from it all. In a way, it was like David wanting to be with me but that was as close as he could get.

Intellectualizing only lasted so long. After I hung up the phone, I screamed into my pillow, then had a good cry.

CHAPTER NINE

NO SECRETS, NO LIES

I did everything to turn the energy away from myself and into David, not in a calculated or planned way, but as a kind of natural priority. I made him more important than me, and it stayed that way, in spite of my internal conflicting feelings. My grandmother and mother had put family first, and I thought I learned from their patterns. Yet here I was doing what I thought I never would—repeating what they did. A laugh and a half.

There were battles. Not only with his alcoholism, but also with the other demons that lay in wait, ready to devour the next innocent victim—me. It wasn't until David knew I was hooked into the relationship that the demons slowly crept further into my life and our marriage. I didn't know then that there would be no healing. They had damaged others. They were held in tight security in the darkest corner of the perpetrator's psyche, and only the edges showed. The rest was hidden under the illusion of mystery and allure with captivating charisma.

There was a familiar energy in David, something I couldn't pinpoint, sexy and intoxicating, yet unsettling. I was a butterfly caught in a Venus flytrap, with no way out. I was addicted to him. He had me and he knew it.

We agreed to teach each other how to be like each other, regarding the qualities we liked best. I just never knew he had such a stunning secret, begging to be brought to light.

One evening it all made sense . . .

It was in the fall of 1995. We purred along in David's Maserati Quattro Porte after playing billiards, which we loved to do together. David was plastered from his favorite rum and coke, and my hair smelled of all the English Oval cigarettes he had chain-smoked in the small neighborhood billiard hall. His cigarettes were suffocating in the tight-quartered environment. The air outside was brisk and fresh, with a slight hint of burning pine. I could breathe again! As we rode along, David began talking about X, and his role in X's life, helping X.

"X is the love of my life."

I thought it was odd, to refer to this person as that. Shouldn't that phrase be reserved for a lover? Then I thought since he was drunk and I was tired, maybe I mistook what or whom he was talking about or . . . My pulse quickened. No, he was talking about X. My little gut feeling told me something was off about *the way* he made that comment, the tone of his voice. I froze with anticipation.

We kept motoring along slowly. Glancing at me in his drunken haze, he crushed out his cigarette and began, "Blackie, about our pact . . . no secrets, no lies . . . I don't want to hold anything back from you. Nothing."

I held my breath. Then, as he pulled the car to a stop, the blow came. "I slept with *X*." My face froze. I'm sure my mouth dropped to the floor mats. My gut was in my throat, my heart was pounding, and my thoughts were spinning. I tried to stop my mind before it crashed into the reality of his statement. This had to be a joke. He's testing me. Yes, that's it. This was only a test, right? To see if I could handle him saying such a thing? He liked to psych people out.

My nose was red from the cold, but I suddenly felt a flush of panicked heat. Our eyes locked for what seemed an hour, me waiting for him to flash a smile and say "psych-out!" Instead, he proceeded to relate that it had only happened a few times. Actually, semi relief washed over me as I thought in a warped way, "Oh, it was *only a few times*. It's just his . . . Wait a minute. His . . . how many times? *What?* Doooiii-yoi-yoiiinnng! Ohmigod! Ohmigod! Ohmigod!" My body started to shake.

I instantly started to justify what he was declaring, but still questioned myself. They were adults, right? *Consenting* adults. Then it was okay? Right? It's not illegal, is it? That's with a *child*. This was *an adult*. But they *are* related. Morally that's . . . ? Geeeeez . . . but, but, but . . . My mind was looped in a repetitive inner dialogue. It felt like a scenario in *Chinatown:* Adult, *smack*, related, *smack*, adult, *smack*, related, *smack!*

He wasn't a child molester. It wasn't like he was a pedophile. Or was he? Why now, as adults? Maybe something did happen before? *What the hell was this?* If I had had clear healthy boundaries, I would have gotten out of the car, grabbed a cab, packed and flown back to L.A. But I didn't.

It was too much for my brain to handle. I didn't find out until later that he had approached X when X was barely a teenager. And even though I was told no physical action was taken at that time, David supposedly made it verbally clear what he wanted.

A flash of other justifications popped into my head. Take it to a "higher level." A spiritual outlook. Maybe this was life's plan for me, a way to finally forgive my uncle for molesting me when I was a child. Hey! This really was a test after all. That was it! This was *my* test. Only a test!

After all, David was the first man I ever fell in love with who had brown eyes. My uncle had brown eyes! This was my test of forgiveness! Right? I could forgive him. It was part of my healing. That had to be it! Forgive and heal.

I reminded myself that David was also drunk at the time of the act, but how could they justify it happening more than once? *How could X justify this?* I was so dumbfounded, I don't remember saying anything.

Then he offered, "It's over. I just wanted you to know everything."

Oh, okay. It's over. It's done, as in the past, which is where it will stay. Finished. Good! I could push it back into the closet. I could put this behind us. A wave of relief washed over me. Breathe! It seemed to cleanse my feelings and a new slate was drawn.

Suddenly, I felt closer than ever to him. Wow! He had confessed his darkest secret to me. He trusted me *that* much. All the "dirtiness" of the deed didn't seem to matter anymore. It was over, and he wanted me to know everything. It was all okay now.

Or was it? When we subsequently met up with X, without hesitation, David blurted out that he had told me their secret. X's eyes bugged out, horrified.

I said, "It's okay. I understand." But I didn't. I was still in shock.

It was obvious X was greatly relieved about my reaction. I felt empathy with them and wanted to discuss it further, the three of us, but David insisted everything was fine and walked away. X and I would have private talks about it later.

CHAPTER TEN

THE GRAND PLAN

I had a game plan. To restore David's reputation as an actor who could be depended upon. That meant he had to get sober. We also had to embark upon our damage control campaign. The publicity tour for his autobiography *Endless Highway* was the perfect avenue to begin. People would see what a "sober," funny and great guy he really was.

At the same time, I was concerned I was losing the credibility and respect I had built in Canada as an actress because, as someone pointed out, I was now hooked up with this "rebel." Therefore, people might start to think I was "out there" as well. Guilt by association. It also didn't benefit me that he had been married a few times and people didn't always know which wife I was. Over the years, I was consistently confused with one of the others, which caused me problems. After I separated from David, a producer friend told me "Honey, we wanted you to be happy, but at the same time we wanted to scream 'are you fucking nuts?!'"

I didn't get called in to audition for a role that I thought I was perfect for, and that coincidentally had the same writer-producer friends as the *Kung Fu* show. I was told the director didn't want David on set. Upsetting to say the least. Because I was not called in for other auditions, not the way I used to be, I started seriously thinking about this problem. I had no concept how dim was the light in which David was looked upon by people.

I rationalized that the reason I didn't get that particular audition was because the director of that episode had previously worked on David's show. Once, I was in the trailer and they couldn't find David for a scene. The director bolted through the trailer door upset because I didn't know where David was. He appeared to blame *me* for not knowing where David could be found, since I was "in charge of Sparky." That was his code name.

There was also the infamous incident in Canada where David was taken into custody at a Rolling Stones concert. He supposedly kicked a backstage door, which caused the glass to shatter. A newspaper article dubbed him "Glasshopper." David told me he had to deal with court, more embarrassment, and pay out thousands of dollars in damages and attorney fees. He was very hurt and upset by this because it was purely an accident that the glass broke. He didn't feel he got a fair deal, or a chance to have his say in court.

That was just the beginning of more problems to overcome, including the difficulty in getting David work in LA. I knew the damage control I had to exert would benefit not only David, but also me. Because of my background in publicity and writing, I had the tools to use for our PR campaign. I declared this not only a challenge but also a terrible injustice to this man, and me for that matter, that had to be set right. We embarked on our warpath to turn his reputation around. My chant: I can do this. We will overcome!!

I started with cold calling one of the producers of *Inside Edition*. "How would you like to do coverage on David Carradine turning his life around?"

They came out to Mississauga within two weeks and filmed us with Calista and her daughters to show an affectionate, warm and "together" family man going sober. Even though he was still drinking, he did taper off for the shoot.

The segment came off great and was a definite incentive for David to do more. I pursued other media in Toronto and worked that in with the press for his book promotion. The plan was working!

It spurred me on to think of other ways to show David in a more positive light, which included introducing him to my circle of influential friends. Well-known columnist Rita Zekas, who was Toronto's version of *Variety's* Army Archerd, helped get the ball rolling in the *Toronto Star* newspaper.

My birthday rolled around, October 5, the same day as Gail's birthday. What are the odds of that? David wanted me to go shopping with him to get *Gail* a gift. I thought it was a very sweet thought on his part. Then he wanted to buy furniture for the office. I thought it was for me. At least that's what he said at first. Later he retracted the intent and said it was for Gail. Well, if they were separated, then why would he buy furniture for the office that she wouldn't use? The answers kept flipping back and forth. Friends said to ignore it. He was drunk and didn't know what he was saying. I didn't find out until a year later he was still hoping to get her back, and there we were living together trying to have a baby!

Nevertheless, on that first birthday he gave me a beautiful silver bracelet with a large chunky heart that dangled from it. "His heart," with a note that said, "For you, my love. This is not enough."

And all else was forgotten and forgiven.

* * *

It was November, two months into my hectic life with David, and winter was setting in with an occasional snow flurry. I was in the bedroom one morning gazing out the window at the woods, as I had many times before. The panorama of trees was beautiful. I saw that the leaves had dropped from the branches. I looked up at the treetops that held a bit of snow and scanned the winter scape. My eyes focused on the site below, then back up at the trees again, then . . . Gasp! Wait a minute! What was that? Boi-oi-oi-ng! Rack focus! There, before my eyes, beyond the thick of the trees, was . . . *the river!* I stood in awe, stunned at the revelation. "The river! Ohmigod, it's the river!" Just as Tom Fishwick described. The adrenaline rush and goose bumps that overcame me at that moment, I can feel to this day.

The fruition—the reality of Tom's and Christian's predictions crystallized before my eyes, confirming this was *the* relationship I was supposed to be in. I felt as if my life was actually just beginning, that I had been asleep all this time, waiting for this man, and *this was it*. *He* was *it*. They told me it would happen! *This* was the start of my dreams coming true! I was convinced all the problems would work themselves out. It was going to be okay.

* * *

The Friar & Firkin bar in Mississauga is where David had his meltdown. He was trying to cut back more on his drinking, with no success. He was conflicted about his relationship with Gail. I found a letter recently that he wrote to me saying their sex life had dwindled a great deal during their time together. Even though he had a double incentive to move forward with me, fourteen years with her was still a lot to let go.

So there we were in the bar after a day's shooting, with David surrounded by several of his buddies from the crew including Rob Moses, Johnny Mac, Calista and myself, watching as he sobbed into his drink. "I can't do this again. I can't go through another divorce. I just can't do this."

I stood there feeling like chopped liver as the group consoled him. Many felt David had a destructive relationship with Gail, but he had me in his life now. He agreed, but was still tormented with the decision. He knew if he didn't make drastic changes, he'd probably never get sober and move his career forward—if he lived that long. They were rooting for our romance to work.

More than once, Johnny Mac talked me out of leaving David in those five months in Toronto. The last time was after I found a love poem David had secretly faxed to Gail from his trailer. I was in tears as I ran to my car. I could hardly wait to get back to the house, pack up and grab the first plane back to Los Angeles. Mac happened to be passing by the trailer and bumped into me, literally stopping me in my tracks. It was fate. Thirty seconds later he would have missed me and I probably wouldn't be writing this book now.

David loved me and the poem, evidently, was just the last gesture in what he had with Gail. Had. Past tense. That's what I was reassured with anyway: he would be crushed if I left. I wanted to believe it. I wanted to be loved . . . so I stayed.

Calista also helped further my belief and ease my angst. I suspected she had another agenda, since she and Gail were at odds, but it was more than nice to have her support for me to take over as the woman in her dad's life. Not that there weren't other fabulous women her father came into contact with. There were three on the show who could be candidates. But when I came along, Calista acted like cupid and brought me and David together. Because of that, I asked her to be my matron of honor for our wedding.

The next step was for David to file for legal separation. He finally made up his mind and through a series of phone calls we were referred to an attorney in Los Angeles. We met with Lisa Brandon at the Polo Lounge in the Beverly Hills Hotel. David was sweating bullets about the meeting. I thought maybe he'd back out. He downed a few drinks before and held my hand tightly as we sat with Brandon.

She was warm, reassuring, matter-of-fact. David felt comfortable with having her represent him, so she was signed up. With that, he set in motion his commitment for legal separation from Gail—a life changing decision.

CHAPTER ELEVEN

WORKIN' ON THE CAINE GANG

August, 2003

Summer is still underway, but there's already a hint of fall. Whether it's the certain slight coolness to the late afternoon air, or just the way the leaves sound as they rustle along walkways . . . it's changed. I can always tell. The sun's light hits the trees differently, enveloping all in its clear golden cast. My memory flashes back to Toronto, 1995.

* * *

Fall. It's the time of year I looked forward to most in Toronto. The smell of wood-burning fireplaces beginning their winter initiations, the wisps of smoke from above. There was an incredible view right outside the backyard of our house. It extended into a thick forest with red-tailed foxes scampering through, dense tall trees filled with leaves turning stunning colors of fire red, orange, yellow and russet and drifting to the ground. I loved the sound of boots crunching through them, and the smell of damp, mossy woods. There were a few field mice that would pay us a visit, crawling up the drapes as our cat sat and watched and ran away from them! My face was cool from the brisk air, then warmed as I walked into the house to a man I was so madly in love with.

Planning a rendezvous with David, after his day of filming, downstairs in the basement Jacuzzi was always a treat. Downstairs was like a house unto itself, complete with kitchen, fireplace, his editing equipment, sauna and Jacuzzi built in a private room, storage areas where he would work on his sculptures. I'd preset the tub with a new fragrance, candles and other sensual surprises for us to enjoy together. Kitchen aromas wafted down, a stuffed chicken maybe or an apple pie. No warmth or sensory experience ever filled me like that fall in Mississauga did. And I was in love. Those few months in Toronto were the best. Sigh.

When I moved in with David, I thought I finally had a place in the world . . . a purpose. I thought my life had really just begun. Not that I didn't think I had one with my career, I did. It was *always* my acting career. I just thought this was more important *for the moment*. It was my significant relationship. It had a bigger mission attached. Here was a man who needed my help. He was drowning, had touched bottom and reached out for someone to rescue him. He wanted to work with me creatively on projects, and appeared to absolutely adore me. Again, as I had done in the past, I placed the priority and importance on someone else, and it became my mission to fix his problems.

I saw him as an underdog and wanted to help him get sober. I also had this grandiose idea that helping him would help the world, by giving it back his talent. He was multi-gifted. But there was something about him. Maybe it was the wounded little boy in him and the wounded little girl in me that we identified with and clung to in each other.

Had I been as emotionally healthy, with half the belief and self-esteem then that I have now, I would have realized what a mistake it would be to neglect myself and undertake such a task. It would have been run, not walk, and leave him to his drink.

However, I remember what I was told by clairvoyant Mae Bodine, Michael's mother, years later when I asked during one of my meltdowns, "Why on earth was I with David? What was that all about?" I was told I was the angel sent to show him the difference in two paths. The higher one—with me—getting him sober and back on track, or the lower, dark road he was on that would lead to more alcohol abuse, degradation and ruin.

As Michael Bodine reminded me, David had a choice and a chance to be a better person before he died, which is what David told me he wanted. He chose that higher path for a while, for the six years we were together. Little did I know then about the power of addiction and the true core of his being. A diehard, I wasn't about to give up. No, not me. I-can-fix-that, I'm-going-to-rescue-him, I-can-help person that I was. Ultimately, he drifted back into the dark. I couldn't save him anymore. No one could.

The situation with David's personal life was chaotic. He had personal assistants, but whoever was taking care of the banking and daily routine office work wasn't great at spelling or balancing a checkbook. The office was an unorganized mess. The housekeeper would rearrange things in the house, which drove David crazy when he couldn't find where she'd put them. It was actually pretty funny because she would put things where common sense would tell you to find them, but not where *David* would put them. Outdoor boots went into the hall closet, but David always put them in the den, never thinking to look in the hall closet. He'd start screaming, sending us into a frenzy looking for the absconded boots, or cigarette lighters, which were another consistently "lost" item, or whatever, only to find them in their "proper" places.

Friends and neighbors would walk into the house unannounced day and night—the door was kept unlocked—to say hi or hang out. David also suspected that Gail hired people or had neighbors spy on him and report back to her, especially after we started living together.

I had the locks changed and made new policies regarding visits to protect our privacy as well as David's energy. He didn't like confrontation and didn't have the heart to kick anyone out if they overstayed their welcome. He would just disappear into another room, leaving them with me to entertain them or send them on their way. That was okay for a while, but it had to stop. And it did. He liked my way of taking over and bringing a new organization to his way of life. The "riff raff" got sorted out and were not allowed back once he placed me in charge.

Because he was also one of the producers of *Kung Fu: The Legend Continues*, he kept things as professional as possible. However, David could make production difficult. The drinking, the drama and disappearing from the set with crewmembers constantly trying to find him—it was like "finding Waldo" except it was "find Sparky," the code name for David— amongst the pubs close to location and the studio. Production gave him a walkie-talkie so they could be in constant contact with him. Well, that is, if he kept it on.

The ADs and PAs on crew were constantly sent on a treasure hunt. In the walkies we'd hear, "We're ready for Sparky on set."

PA: "Copy. Traveling. Retrieving Sparky." Five minutes later, "Has anyone seen Sparky? Copy."

Second PA: "Negative."

Second AD: "Does *anyone* know where Sparky is? Copy."

First AD: "Check the closest bar!"

A director in the background, screaming, "Where the fuck is he?!"

* * *

Gail was living at their Sun Valley ranch in L.A. where, according to sources, she stayed when "they separated." David supposedly went to Toronto on his own when filming started. It never occurred to me to question if they were indeed truly separated or why a good portion of her belongings were still in Toronto. I just accepted what David and the others told me—they weren't together anymore. And technically, they weren't.

I didn't know at the time that it wasn't a mutual personal "agreement," but more of a Mexican standoff. Evidently, David took her staying in L.A. for months and not with him as "separation."

It turned out it wasn't the kind of separation I had been led to believe. A game of semantics? Had I known what the real truth was, I wouldn't have moved forward at least until an official legal motion was filed. What's the saying? What do you become when you assume? Take the first three letters of the word. Did I learn from it? Yes. Bottom line, she wasn't there and from David's explanation, she not only had no desire to return, but he was clear about wanting to keep our relationship. So that was it. I believed what I wanted.

I started helping David out by making sure he was functional, which meant getting him to the set on time so that production didn't fall behind. He was notorious for being hours late on set. There was always a just reason in his mind for why he delayed going to set. David complained that they'd give him a call time, but wouldn't use him for at least a couple of hours after he got there. That was time wasted he could be putting into being home and working on his music, editing his *Mata Hari* film, or artwork.

The situation got better once production knew I was on board and helping. Between his schedule being changed and showing up closer to call time, the tug of war eased up. I certainly didn't want them to think I was the cause of making him late. Rumor had it that Gail was trying to put the blame on Calista, while others blamed Gail for David's tardiness. It was actually David who was responsible for his own consistent delinquency, and no one else. Everyone seemed to be passing the buck to everyone else, but unless you were living with him, how would you know for sure?

* * *

I was becoming a bit overwhelmed between putting in a sixty-plus-hour week helping out at the house with a variety of personal and administrative duties and gradually easing into being David's liaison with his *Kung Fu*, TLC producers. In addition, I was overseeing all of his personal business and being placed in the hot seat of overseeing communications between David and Gail. The producers on the show were worried about how all of this personal upheaval was going to affect their star.

Upon our return to Toronto from the meeting with Brandon in L.A., David had a grueling film schedule. He was very irritable and drinking even more. The decision to file for separation took its toll.

In the make-up room at the studio, one of the young actors on the show was having fun and horsing around with David. David "joked" back, but instead of giving the kid a slight nudge with his leg, kung fu style, he accidentally pushed him into the wall. I was told the kid wasn't hurt physically, but was stunned with hurt feelings. He supposedly looked up to David and couldn't understand why he kicked him. The young actor thought David wasn't his friend anymore.

David told me later that the kid ticked him off and he wasn't in the mood to joke around or "play." David intended just to push him away so he would leave him alone. He obviously didn't know how hard he pushed.

Production claimed the upset parents were going to file complaints with the unions, and we thought we were on the verge of a lawsuit. Publicity would be really bad if this got out. I told the producers I thought I could explain to the parents the hell David was going through and maybe turn things around, so they allowed me to intervene.

I appealed to the parents' empathy, said that it was purely accidental. David was trying to go sober, the separation, it was just too much for him to handle at once. It had nothing to do with David not liking their son. David often played that way with his kung fu antics, I assured them. They evidently took sympathy because a lawsuit never materialized. The producers were gratefully relieved.

David knew I still had my apartment in town and was afraid I was going to bail since I was getting too frazzled, so he had production put me on salary to help compensate for my time for running the ship.

"Running the ship" meant getting David to the set on time—well, I tried my best; making sure he wasn't drinking too much—that didn't work, since David would order me drinks, which I wouldn't consume, so he would drink them for me; making sure he ate—I called it the disappearing act, he'd say he wasn't hungry, yet I'd make myself a sandwich, go to the ladies' room, and while I was gone, he'd eat it; and helping out with the David-Gail problems—like setting him up with an attorney, taking care of his office work, dealing with publicity, and so on. Not that I didn't want to do this anyway, but being on payroll did pull me deeper into the situation and into David's world with more obligation.

Things started to run more smoothly, but there was still way too much to keep up with. We ended up hiring an assistant for me. Julie Harding joined as my comrade. The two of us worked full-time just to keep up with all that had to be done. Highly recommended by my friend Marilyn, Julie was my British shoulder on which to cry, my confidante and *the* savior of *my* sanity during that very difficult time. And, best of all, she was someone David and I could trust with anything.

David was about to start promotion for his autobiography *Endless Highway,* which would take us in and out of town. Production was afraid he would do something on tour resulting in bad press for the show, and the publishers were also afraid to commit to any extensive publicity tour because David was considered unpredictable. After the publishers found out I was on board, they were not only relieved, they expanded their promotion and in-person appearances because they had my personal promise and assurance I would make sure David would not only be okay, but he would exceed their expectations.

I had great faith in David. I gave my word I would be there every moment and would see that he represented the book in the best possible light. I also helped booked several promo interviews for him in Canada.

As I often did over the next several years, I put my professional make-up artist background to work—since he was so pale, a light bronzer worked great—and helped with his wardrobe, to make sure that he looked his best at all times. David held to his promise to monitor the alcohol consumption during that time. He'd bring the mini bottles of choice from the hotel in his pocket or his personal flask and take just enough before going on-air with Howard Stern or Charlie Rose or Dick Cavett or to a book signing. Then in private time, he'd indulge up the yinyang.

Thing is, David didn't usually get sloppy with his talking or physical movements. Sometimes, it was very difficult to tell if he had been drinking. It all depended on how much. If he drank more, his reaction time was slower, physical expression, phrasing in speech, and gestures were wider and vocally more intense. He could also get "testy" and tended to be unpredictable, which kept everyone on their toes.

There were times when he was in a bad mood or wanted more to drink I'd hold my breath and walk on eggshells for fear of him bolting and missing one of the promo venues. But he had a double incentive going— wanting the book to be a success and wanting to please me, so he'd turn on the charm and all the angst melted away.

At the first bookstore signing in New York, David was excited but equally anxious. He was concerned that there wouldn't be a lot of people and it would be embarrassing. "No way, Johnny. You'll be inundated." Sure enough, there was over an hour wait in line for him to sign books. He was greatly relieved and a very happy camper.

Every city we went to, it was the same turnout. Throngs of fans wanting to meet him, take pictures and have him sign their books. It was fabulous hearing their comments, seeing tears in their eyes, listening to them credit David with turning their lives around with martial arts and just loving his show.

Sometimes, if the person captured his interest, David would draw doodles with his autograph or include a quote from the show to make it extra special. On television talk shows the producers would sometimes take me aside just to give them reassurance he was "okay," but they could soon see for themselves he was. David always came through shining. He was entertaining, funny, and held it together. As soon as we were in the limo though, out came the flask or mini bottle, with instructions for the driver to head for the nearest restaurant or bar.

The publishers were very happy with the press tour and the book was doing well in sales. David did indeed exceed their expectations as well as his own. He had a great time doing it and felt good about himself, which was probably the best part.

CHAPTER TWELVE

HIT 'EM UP, MOVE 'EM OUT

DAVID got a request from producer Bob DeBrino to meet regarding some project. We thought it would be a good excuse to take a trip to New York and get out of town after his filing for separation, so arrangements were made with production to fly to the Big Apple for a couple of days between his film dates.

As soon as we got to the airport, David wanted to grab a quick drink so we headed for the first bar. I remember not wanting to do this because I didn't want to spend the next half hour in a bar and it was cramming time before the flight. He could get his complimentary drinks on the plane. But he insisted, so in we walked. To our stunned surprises, there sat Gail. She had obviously flown in unannounced and had planned to go to the house to pack up her things. The encounter was extremely uncomfortable for all, especially after she kissed him. I was very upset with the whole situation – seeing the two of them together, and feeling like a third wheel, since I didn't feel that David was paying attention to me as his girlfriend.

I suddenly realized if she was going to be at the house, my belongings might be at risk. I had my designer clothes, audition wardrobe and other valuables there. I had visions of her grabbing my clothes and shredding them with a pair of scissors. Not that she would, but my trust factor in general was zero.

David and I argued about giving her the key. He told me when I moved in that the house was "our home." Now he was saying in front of Gail that it was still "their house," and "She's still my wife!" That stung badly. So what the hell was I? I had a real bad feeling about this as I handed over the key.

I immediately called Calista and asked her to gather all my belongings as fast as she could, find the kitten, David's adorable all-white Himalayan cat that he named Blackie, and take her too. The kitten was originally purchased for Gail, but because they were "separated," she became mine. I was extremely attached to her. There was no way Calista was not going to come to my rescue! She was totally on my side. An SOS call went out to our assistant Julie as well, to keep an eye on things and report back. She immediately headed out to the house and was there when Gail arrived.

I was on pins and needles for a few hours waiting to get word. I remember Calista telling me she was in the middle of packing my clothes in suitcases when Gail arrived and asked what was going on. I understood Calista told her they were her own clothes and Gail let her be. Clever, fast thinker. Thank goodness she was able to collect everything, except Blackie. My heart sank.

Thinking we had a handle on the situation, David and I enjoyed our meeting and schmoozing the NY scene with DeBrino until we got the call the next day. One of David and Gail's mutual friends and neighbors spotted a huge moving van pulling up to the house. Gail supposedly told them she was moving the house out. The *house*? Not what David had in mind.

DeBrino, an ex-cop, contacted the Mississauga police department and explained the situation. They sent a team out to the house, where Julie met them. There wasn't much the police could do except make sure our pets were okay and leave. It was a civil matter and it appeared they didn't consider her taking communal property as theft.

That's when David called the teamsters who worked on his show to intervene. They were able to block the driveway with trucks and hold position until we got back into town. We took the first flight back to find a flurry of activity.

I immediately looked for Blackie but couldn't find her anywhere. Neither could anyone else. I was sick to my stomach. There was only a new collar and tag on the kitchen sink, evidently purchased to replace the one she already had. If she got outside, the wild foxes would kill her or someone could steal her. Then again if she was found, Gail would take her back to L.A. I couldn't bare any of the scenarios.

With us back, and Gail and a friend of hers there to help her pack, what were the sleeping arrangements going to be? They had no plans to leave for at least another day or two and weren't about to pay for a hotel room. It was almost like a sit-com.

David was not about to let me go back to my apartment either. Nope. We slept on the sofa bed in the den, while Gail took the master bedroom and her friend took the guest room. I got the distinct feeling that by us sleeping together in full view, he was in a way getting revenge, showing her he could get someone to replace her. I felt horrid about it all. I wanted to go back to my apartment, but at the same time, I was afraid if I left, Gail might seduce him back. I wasn't about to let that happen.

They worked it out between themselves what was to stay and what items were to be moved out, but the constant tension in the house was unbearable. David was at the studio filming, which left me and Julie to monitor things and deal with the daily chaos. I didn't want to be there, but my loyalty was to David and to protecting his interests. Gail and I barely spoke. I let Julie deal with most of it. At one point Gail had had enough, packed up the last of it and headed for the airport. It was as if an over inflated balloon had been released, flinging about, making sputtering sounds, with people dodging its path, then finally lying on the floor in silence. All was quiet again, but not for long.

Soon after the Mississauga invasion, Gail filed for divorce. I would have done the same thing.

The whole experience left me drained. It took a while for the house to get back to normal. Rocky was fine, but still no sign of Blackie. I spent hours after Gail left for the airport looking top to bottom in the house.

Every nook, under and over, around the neighborhood, asking people, tracking paw prints in the snow. I stayed out in the cold until it got dark. Teary eyed I walked into the kitchen and there on the counter top was . . . Blackie! She looked at me and gave me a single meow, like "hi." I cried out with joy and scooped her up. Where was she all that time?! She purred in my arms for the next couple of hours until David got home. He laughed. "Well I guess she knew who she wanted to live with too."

Chapter Thirteen

BLUE CHRISTMAS

THE stress of the first few months finally got to me. Each day I felt more ill, but I ignored it because there was too much to take care of. Finally, three days later, I accepted the fact I must have a fever and should do something about it. There was no thermometer in the house, so I just carried on with deskwork. Didn't have the energy to walk outside the house, let alone go to the store. David was tunnel visioned and blitzed out, so he never offered to even warm up so much as a cup of soup for me. Besides, he was off to the studio every day. I made up excuses for the situation so his lack of attention wouldn't upset me.

Julie made dinner as she often did for us, and went to the drugstore to get a thermometer. I was like a wet noodle, couldn't even take my temp. The next day, even though I was feeling better, I checked it out. When I pulled the stick out of my mouth, I couldn't believe what I saw. It had to be wrong. 104? Recheck. 104! And I was feeling better? If that was better, then what was my temperature before?

Julie was at the studio with David so I poured myself into the SUV and drove to the doctor's office. All I wanted to do was lie down in the car, but I knew I had to get to the doctor's office. I was a blob clinging to the steering wheel and staggered into the reception room. Dr. Babb couldn't believe I wasn't in the hospital. He shook his head and scolded me for not getting in earlier. A prescription was handed to me and back home I went, to plop myself into bed. When David got home, knowing how sick I was, he still didn't offer to get me even a cup of tea. If I could drive myself to the doctor, I guess he thought I could get myself to the kitchen. He left me alone while he went off to tend to his buddies at the local pub. That did not go over well with me. At all.

Years later, when David had the flu, I waited on him hand and foot. It's what I do for people I care about when they're ill. He was so appreciative. "Haven't you had anyone take care of you when you got sick?" I asked.

He rarely got a cold, let alone the flu, but he wasn't used to anyone looking after him when he did. He couldn't understand why I would do that for him. It was a "What-are-you-kidding? Why-wouldn't-I?" factor for me. I was nonplussed. Maybe that's why he left me on my own in Toronto. He didn't have an example set for him? Nah.

When I had surgery after blowing my knee out on Roger Corman's *Stray Bullet II (Dangerous Curves)* in 1998, which we filmed in Ireland with David's brother Robert, David waited on me hand and foot, bringing gifts, accompanying me through a storm to the Steadman-Hawkins clinic in Vail for the surgery. David even made sure he oversaw my procedure himself. The surgical staff allowed him to watch it on screen with one of the nurses. I guess he was trying to make up for the time I was so ill in Toronto. I too, rarely got sick, but that was the most attentive David had ever been with me without being asked, including all the fertility procedures we endured.

* * *

The holidays were upon us in Mississauga and I was excited about spending our first Christmas together, as well as it being a white one. The closer the holiday got, the more morose David's attitude became. It was clear he did not enjoy this time of year. Or was it just *this* Christmas? David wasn't up for discussing why. He just wanted to go away until the holidays were over and ignore Christmas. Well, that was just great. This was my favorite time of the year and I love to get into the whole holiday scene—baking, decorating, making crafty gifts for friends. To know he didn't want to participate in anything—with me, shopping, trimming the tree let alone selecting one, was a big let down. It wasn't the joyous, sharing experience I had anticipated. My balloon burst.

There was no getting through to him. He was in his own world, wallowing in drink and melancholic misery. I knew the separation from Gail was difficult, but he was supposed to be in love with me, wasn't he? I was at a loss what to do and broke down into a major crying jag. "It's our first Christmas together, Johnny!" It's like he didn't care about anything or anyone. Finally, I told him I was going to go back to my apartment. I just had to get away from the negative environment.

He left the house for a few hours and came back with a beautiful white angel made of sugar to top the tree. We used it every Christmas after that. Looking at me with a timid smile, he said "Well I guess this means we have to get a tree to go with the angel, huh?"

We took hours to pick out a huge gorgeous pine that had to be cut back to fit the door and ceiling. He got a kick out of seeing it in the room and his spirit seemed to lift.

That Christmas, he gave me an entire outfit from hat to shoes, literally right off the mannequin in a store window display. I bought a silver ring that had three bands intertwined with a word in Latin on each band, for courage, love, strength. He hesitated and said, "You know by wearing a ring such as this, it means I'd be committing myself to the relationship." It fit his ring finger perfectly.

Yes, all was better, but still not right. David remained in a funk. So we made an effort to change it up as much as possible. Each holiday in the years after that had a similar, but lesser, effect on him as things improved in our lives, although he still preferred to spend at least part of it somewhere else.

Birthday or other celebrations, he was all in for the party, but when it came to gathering at homes of families for the holidays, that was different. He was uncomfortable. You wouldn't know it once people were there, but earlier, he seemed to dread the anticipation of it. Maybe because he didn't have much in the way of happy Christmases growing up and it brought back sad memories.

David loved opening surprises, as much as he loved buying them for people. Even when we didn't have the money, he'd just charge it. He spent large and tipped well. Even in hotels he always made sure the maids were left a cash tip on the coffee table. After all it reflected who he was—David Carradine—and he was not going to have people think he was a stingy star. He certainly didn't want people to know he didn't have money, even if he meant going into hock!

When we did have a bit of money, he'd go hog wild. When he saw an outfit displayed in the store window, he'd buy it exactly as it was on the mannequin, accessories and all. David really got into wrapping the presents as well. If it was a wallet or purse it had to have money inside, or some other "gifty," as we called small presents. Nothing could be presented "empty." He was ingenious about not using tape or ribbon to hold the wrapping together either, creating special bows and writing personal notes. Every present, no matter how small, came with a special loving message for me. Some would be store bought with romantic themes, some personal doodles on hand cut paper, some were ingenious artwork he did on his computer. All expressed his affection.

Our first New Year's together we decided to head for the beautiful Millcroft Inn. It was a winter wonderland, where David had stayed on one of his attempts to get sober. He said it had good memories for him, so we thought that would be a quiet, romantic place to toast in our first New Year's. And it was. We took walks in the snow, drank a lot of herbal tea instead of alcohol, and loved each other up. It felt like the start of a beautiful New Year.

Chapter Fourteen

WESTWARD BOUND

The time came to pack up the house for the big move back to Los Angeles. The series was cancelled and the last show wrapped. The cast party was celebrated, people moved on with their lives and jobs, and depression set in with us both.

It was tough for David to say goodbye to everyone who had become his extended family on the show for four years, and he was insecure about his future. The thought that he had to give up the editing table he had in the basement was painful. This is where he'd spend countless hours working on his pet film project *Mata Hari*, starring his daughter Calista who had been in her mid-teens at the time of filming. David took great pride in screening footage for guests. He longed to get the funding to finish the film, but that never happened.

There were no projects on the horizon, just financial and emotional stress with his pending divorce and the unknown to deal with.

David wanted to sever ties with most anything that had to do with the past and start fresh, so there was no turning back. We thought he had a new agent in the wings to help set things in motion, but didn't hear a word for weeks. Upon calling, we found they closed their theatrical division. No one notified David! Here we were less than two weeks from leaving and he didn't have representation. David was a sixty-year-old actor considered dead in the water after a cancelled series. His alcohol consumption was widely known and considered the key factor of his career demise. He had no agent, no home, no manager, no income and a few thousand dollars in his pocket. He had not only reached bottom, he was staring up from inside a hole that it didn't seem he could get out of.

In order to get David going again, I set aside my plans to go back to teaching acting, make-up work and freelance writing, and made the decision to take the next step to put all my efforts into managing his career myself.

Things were set in motion for us to move back to Los Angeles. There was a baby grand piano worth several thousand dollars that David absolutely loved and spent many an hour during the four years at the house hammering out old and new songs on the keyboard. He had great affection for Chris Potter and wanted to give him some parting gift. So what could be better for his surrogate son, than to give him the piano? David inscribed his autograph under its lid. Chris was blown away. That's how generous David was with his possessions and people he liked.

Years later he presented personal manager Jay Bernstein with the western gun set from the Lone Ranger, holster and all. This too was worth several thousand dollars and he gave it as a birthday present to Jay. We were at the Bistro Gardens restaurant where David stood up with the guns and whipped them around to demonstrate for us. We didn't know George Clooney was taking in the action as well from a nearby table. It made a great excuse for table talk with Clooney as we left the restaurant. I met him years later and he remembered the event. Yes, it's difficult to get rid of an image of David flipping around a gun in a restaurant.

Julie and I organized the entire monumental move, which was complicated by the fact that it was across the country and from Canada. Customs requirements were a pain in the butt. We wanted to get estimates, but David would say, "Do whatever." He often seemed very nonchalant about financial issues. When we did get a few estimates and showed him that we saved about three thousand dollars by not going with the first company, he was *very* pleased. Still, the cost was about $10,000 to move the contents of the home. It was $10,000 more than David had at the time, but he didn't stress about it.

To add to the chaos, Rocky got a hold of David's hairpiece used on the show and mangled it considerably. It was extremely upsetting to David, since he was counting on having it for possible future filmings. Having one made would cost a few thousand dollars. "Don't you have insurance for something like that, Johnny?"

By the time we left, he had the payment from the insurance company, which came in handy for the first few months in L.A. David's Canadian bank accounts were closed and his money was now tied up in his divorce. He also got slapped by the IRS for approximately $750,000 worth of owed taxes, and later another $150,000 from the State. This sent him into a further spin with alcohol. A friend referred him to a tax expert who, for the next several years, battled the ongoing problem for David.

So we looked back at the Mississauga house, its apple and pine trees, the forest, the river, the circular driveway and the porch on which we kissed hello. With Rocky panting out the car window, Blackie in her carry case, and the baggage crammed in, we headed to the airport for our new life together on another coast.

PART II

HEAVEN AND HELL

1996 – May 2001

CHAPTER FIFTEEN

TOMORRAH IS ANOTHAH DAY!

THE six years with David were heaven and hell. At times it was the happiest I had ever been in my life, at other times the worst. With the exception of my beloved collie Lulu passing away, I've never felt those peaks of joy or extreme misery before or after. And it was definitely the most passionate six years ever.

Marry one of Hollywood's rebel bad-boys? Me? Nah. Become his manager and the one responsible for rebuilding his long-suffering career *and* getting him to total sobriety? Huh, yeah, right.

I didn't know that all my life experiences and production background would be put to use in this one relationship, and with such intensity. I took on the ultimate challenge: to accomplish what David feared was nearly impossible. I'm proud of reaching the goal we set—to get him back on top and back into the theatrical film A-list. I just never thought it would happen without my being a part of the celebration or basking in the experience and rewards with him. No one knew what was going on behind closed doors at home or in the limo minutes before a public appearance. My smiles for the camera were sometimes a total facade to cover the havoc or pain that we would leave behind for a few hours. A good portion of the time, I was relieved to get away from the desk and the turbulence. Of course I beamed for the cameras. Other times, it was pure bliss to be having nothing but fun with David for a change. But to get him out the door sometimes took hours of prodding and argument. I had two people to get ready for any meeting or occasion. David and myself. By the time we got to the event, I was exhausted, not looking or feeling my best, while he sparkled and was just getting rolling for the evening.

His resurgence didn't happen overnight with the success of his key role in Quentin Tarantino's *Kill Bill*. It took approximately twenty-five years for David to get back on the A feature film list. His last few A-listings included *The Long Riders* and *Bound For Glory* which resulted in a Golden Globe nomination. David admitted to a sort of "love-dislike" between the industry and him. He knew it was due in part to his behavior. It took the six years we were together to finally get him back on top again.

He told me he walked away from the original *Kung Fu* series after four years, when it was one of the top four rated shows at the time. (He wrote a different version of this in his autobiography.) He said he got bored with it and was high on LSD and/or peyote during most of that time—he'd mix it in with his drink and take sips all day. His bizarre adventure through Laurel Canyon and the tangle with the law was an example of being under that influence.

After the original series was over, David filled his resume with a grab bag mix of B-list movies, straight-to-video flicks and cult classics like *Death Race 2000* and *Lone Wolf McQuade*. A few of them—*The Long Riders*, *Boxcar Bertha*, *North and South* (a mini series), and *Bound For Glory*, the last two of which got David Golden Globe nominations—were highly popular and acclaimed films.

His pride and joy, *Americana*, which David starred in, wrote, produced, edited and wrote the original music for, received considerable recognition. At the Cannes film festival's Director's Fortnight, the film garnered the People's Choice Award. Then came along the highly rated *Kung Fu: The Legend Continues*, his last series. It kept his spiritual persona in the hearts and minds of the public and the industry. But again, the demons took over and the alcohol made each season more difficult.

After *Kung Fu: TLC*, the following six years consisted of orchestrating a new career to restore his tarnished reputation to a shining, untarnished star, with A-list productions again.

Under my "regime," David did at least twenty-two films, five prime time highly rated movies for TV—*Last Stand At Saber River* was one which hit top all-time ratings for Turner Network Television—a mini-series, ten voice-overs and cartoons, eleven prime time episodics, a long list of fundraisers supporting various charities, and talk shows. And sobriety brought David to that prime casting decision by Quentin Tarantino. It was a hard road with butt-busting work because David was basically starting from scratch again, not like "easy capitalization" on a hit film to spin off mega bucks and just take phone calls.

My career was blooming in Toronto, but I soon neglected it when David's life became mine. I had begun to establish myself in the Canadian entertainment industry with supporting and guest star roles on numerous shows and principal actor spots in several national commercials. Like the *Chorus Line* song "What I Did For Love", right? Besides, it was to build a life for *us*. Well, I thought it was anyway. The plan was to help out until he got on his feet after a few months, but that didn't happen.

Six months turned into six years. David's lack of self-esteem caused him to self-destruct and made my journey to get back on track arduous. I didn't know what I had gotten myself into until it was too late.

David didn't acknowledge my efforts to others, and led people to think the opportunities came to him directly and effortlessly. His ego wouldn't allow him to do otherwise. If he expressed anything to other people, he certainly did not let me know about it. It felt as if there was no gratitude or appreciation for what I did, probably because in all those years, he thanked me for my efforts only a few times. And that was after I prompted him. It's as if it was expected of me, as if I had nothing else to do with my life, but to cater to him. The greater the lack of acknowledgement, the more I pushed to prove my love and belief in him. His attitude in this respect intensified after we got married. It seemed as if he knew he "had" me and put even more responsibility and pressure on me.

My true reward was seeing us progress with our goals, but if he wasn't going to show me his appreciation in a simple verbal acknowledgement, then it all felt so empty. It seemed I could never do enough to fill his void. But whenever I reached the depths of thinking he didn't care, David would do something to counter it. Like our first Valentine's Day together, he gave me a sterling silver dragon pin he designed and made himself. It has ruby eyes—red for love—and the body was shaped the way I signed my nickname, using the B in the shape of a heart. I was born in the year of the dragon, which he knew made it extra personal. So that's where he disappeared to when he'd go off to the pub for a drink in Missisauga. It was for a drink and a design! He got as much delight out of making it for me as I had in receiving it.

When the series ended and we moved back to L.A. in March 1996, David didn't have a manager, an agent or money. He had a few thousand dollars in cash and that was it. His belongings in Canada, including his Maserati Quattro Porte, were on their way out to L.A. via the moving company, to be delivered and stored. We started out by living at my condo in Valencia while we tried to find a house to rent where we could plot strategy. David didn't like living in a place that wasn't his and it was far too small for two people, a large dog and four cats, even though all the animals got along.

Yes, I had three felines waiting for me in L.A. and we brought Blackie with us. When David still claimed ownership of her and wanted to give her to Calista, I put my foot down and declared her my cat, and there was no way he was going to give her away to anyone. That was the end of that. How could he even think that, after I helped raise her for the past five months? David never said otherwise all that time. He knew how attached I was to Blackie. He eventually got his daughter a relative of my kitty, but that cat was unfortunately killed when someone ran over it with their car.

We also needed a house with hard wood floors and a room large enough for his concert grand piano, which he wanted to get out of storage. His cigarette smoking—dropping ashes everywhere and burning holes in my carpet—was testing my patience and understanding. Neither of us had the money to replace the carpet so I literally sat on the floor doing a cut and paste with carpet fragments to camouflage the damage.

I was always on pins and needles because he was careless about keeping his hands clean, dropping food . . . overall, to be blunt, he was a housekeeping nightmare. I had all designer matching upholstery and drapes and pristine carpet. Every room was the ultimate in interior design as I had purchased the model unit of the complex. The faux finish and color washed walls I painted myself.

It's not that he didn't respect my property. He was under the influence of the booze and got careless. At least that's what I thought at first. It did cause some friction and he always felt bad about ruining something, but that didn't make me feel any better. I didn't have to push hard for us to find another space and fast.

Years prior, I ran into actor Mark Harmon, star of the current hit TV series *NCIS*, who put me back in touch with his cousin and my childhood friend, Lisa Knox. Lisa and I kept in touch over the years and the timing was now perfect for my call. So happens, she was going to rent out the house she grew up in, a house I remember having many sleepovers in, with us watching *Man From U.N.C.L.E.* on a *color* television set and eating the French toast her mom would fix for us in the mornings. It was just down the street from my childhood home and elementary school. It not only had a room for David's grand piano, but hard wood floors and a huge backyard for Rocky. Best of all, she gave us a great rental price! Never in my wildest imagination would I have pictured my future living there, let alone spending my honeymoon night with David in Lisa's mom's bedroom.

We had just signed the lease when David's youngest daughter, Kansas, popped into town for a visit. We wanted to show her our new digs, so we all took a drive out to the Valley Vista house. David and I were excited about having plenty of room and private time together. No maid, no neighbors knocking at all hours . . . just quality time. Just the *two* of us. No sooner were we inside the door than Kansas says, "So which room is mine?"

David and I looked at each other. Uh-oh! I adored Kansas, but neither of us thought about her living with us. We thought she was going to live elsewhere with friends in an apartment or go to college. I certainly wasn't going to say no, she was "daddy's little girl." Besides, even though it wasn't planned, I thought it would be wonderful to have her there. They could make up for lost time over the years, and I would have a chance to know her better. There were only two bedrooms, so we pointed to the guest room. She seemed delighted. David shrugged his shoulders as if to say, "Oh well." That was that until she left for an out-of-state college.

David was always pushing the envelope with safety. He hated to lock the doors let alone set the alarm. We had been followed on occasion— David suspected by Gail's friends—and we were to take extra caution: our new address was to be kept for selected people, and we would get a security system. I had to plead with David to get one installed. The day after we moved into the Valley Vista house, we had to leave town for a few days. At the airport, I got an emergency page from the security company. Evidently someone tried to get in through the sliding doors and the alarm went off. In plain view was a row of David's most prized guitars, including three Mossmans, not to mention all of our other valuables. The alarm scared them off before they grabbed anything. So the $2,000 investment saved David at least $20,000. No one knew we were going out of town except the movers. Turns out David bragged about our schedule, when and where we were going. Smart.

Did he take precautions after that? He tried, but only to please me. It just wasn't in his nature to keep it up. I never felt protected enough. Eventually, I ended up hiding my things in weird places, just in case, but our pets were my first priority over materialistic things, so I was always worrying and thinking maybe it will get better.

* * *

Every relationship has its common denominators: whether the two people involved are public figures or not. We were no exception. The bickering, the differences, a lack of communication at times, money squabbles . . . it comes with the territory of being in a relationship.

Living at the Valley Vista house and being central in location to the studios, grocery stores, favorite restaurants helped ease daily life. Restaurants, by the way, could not be in a franchise or chain, with only a few exceptions. David never explained why. Just didn't like them. One of his quirks.

We crammed in the furniture David brought back from Toronto, creating organized clutter. Our coffee table was actually the two coffee tables that he had in his television series dressing room, sitting back to back. Beautifully colored paintings of Asian women on black lacquer background—they showed their wear and tear, but sufficed. The peach colored leather sofa ran along one wall and the green suede couch paralleled the sliding doors to the yard. In the corner was the Schimmel grand piano and hanging from the beamed ceiling was an array of carved colorful Balinese flying goddesses, which inspired my company name and jewelry line, and frogs and dragons.

The cubby hole leading to the hall for the guest bedroom was David's office. It overlooked the front of the house so he could keep an eye on who was coming and going at the house. It was also great because his cigarette smoke went mostly out the window instead of into the house.

We got into a flow in spite of the continuous chaos. The months flew by and before we knew it, in a whirlwind of events, travel and personal crises, another year had gone by.

Looking back at letters between the two of us over the years, I saw a constant push-pull and meshing of our wants, our needs and how we wanted to live our life with each other. It worked most of the time. I was in constant struggle with myself about how to deal with everything thrown my way. David seemed to flow over it all.

Showing affection wasn't a problem for David. Verbalizing it was the glitch. He loved the fact that I was very demonstrative, verbally and physically. Well, I'm part Sicilian! Speaking affectionate words were awkward for him. He showed me as best he could. It was easy for him to write it in love notes and artwork and he kept assuring me in unspoken ways. But speaking the words, "I love you," was difficult. He said I should be patient. He didn't want to say the words without fully meaning them. And if he did say them, it meant he had given his heart to that person. That was fine with me. I had lots of that, so it wasn't a problem.

Then, one ordinary day about eight months into the relationship, as we were doing ordinary daily chores, David approached me for no particular reason. He looked at me very shyly and said softly, "I love you, Blackie."

"I love you more than you know, Johnny." I smiled. He looked slightly flushed and gave a short Gary Cooperish chuckle. The moment was so tender and innocent. From then on, he had no problem verbalizing his affection for me to me, or how he felt about me to others.

In 1997, David asked my mother for my hand in marriage—my father had passed on—promising her he'd take care of her and me both. It was an old-fashioned courtesy and a gesture that won my mother over. She felt included, wanted, and approved.

October 4, the night before my birthday, he asked me the big question in bed after we made love with the "stage" set to soft burning candles. The question was stated very simply, "Blackie, will you marry me?" The answer I had ready for two years. When I gave him my "yes," he got teary eyed and we started to laugh because I started to cry. He apologized for not having a ring for me yet, but he did have something to hold me over in the meantime. In a black velvet box was a delicate, beautiful gold Tiffany watch, with a band of hearts that intertwined into each other. I instantly put it on. He was very relieved I liked it and wasn't upset he didn't have the ring. He could have presented me with a cigar band and I would have been ecstatic.

So we decided to celebrate my birthday and our engagement at my favorite restaurant, Dan Tana's. Sitting at the corner table in the main room, David suddenly pops up from the table and shouts in his booming voice, "Excuse me everyone! I'd like your attention! I'm David Carradine and I have an important announcement to make!"

I didn't know whether to slide down in the seat, or laugh, or what, it took me by such surprise. He pointed to me. "I'm going to marry this woman! We just got engaged. Her name is Marina and she's going to become my bride, Mrs. David Carradine!" The room went nuts with applause and cheers and in true Dan Tana tradition, the bartender, Michael, threw a stack of napkins up in the air that floated down upon the patrons. David sat down and gave me the biggest smile. I did too. "Let's eat!"

* * *

The week before our engagement party, we went to dinner at my cousin Sebastian's restaurant nearby. As I sat down, on the plate was a little gold box. Inside was a smaller red heart-shaped box and inside that was my engagement ring. He chose the setting and the stones, to create it especially for me. Blue sapphire with two diamonds on either side. He knew I wasn't a fan of white diamonds because they're rather cold looking, so he chose stones that had yellow warmth to them. Even the color of the sapphire was the lighter color I loved. When he placed the ring on my finger, we kissed and I cried.

The engagement party was set for the end of October at Chasin's new location on Canon Drive in Beverly Hills. The restaurant personnel were supposed to be there to help, but no one showed up. That left me and my friend Wendy, whom I had known since fourth grade, to decorate the entire room and do table settings within an hour and a half. We had already spent half the day at the flower mart selecting vases, Chinese lanterns for the centerpieces and autumn leaves for table garnishes. I had only one hour to dash home and get ready for the party.

It was a wonderful celebration with live music to sing and dance to. David took over the microphone and sang a couple songs, one of which was "our" song, *Come Rain or Come Shine*. My mother even sang along with the pianist we hired. I wore the dress he bought for me at a celebrity auction. David looked very debonair in his white jacket, black bow tie and brocade vest. We celebrated into the early morning hours with Frank Stallone, Stacy Keach, Dabney Coleman, actor-artist Aron Kincaid, Stefanie Powers, and close family members.

It was also a year to celebrate David booking better-paying films to showcase his talent—such as *American Reel, Last Stand at Saber River, Lost Treasure of Dos Santos*—and receiving his gold star on the Hollywood Walk of Fame. Things were moving forward, small step by small step.

Nineteen ninety-eight was supposed to be a heavenly year for our wedding, but it turned into a year from hell. As soon as we got married something in him seemed to change. He made less and less of an effort to make me happy. It was definitely a traumatic time and with each year it got worse. But whenever I questioned myself, if I really wanted to marry this man, he'd do something so sweet or look at me in such a loving way, any doubt was erased.

Thunder was David's dog (the Bernese he got after Rocky), and I grew very attached to him. I trained him and was his caretaker—his "mommy." But something was missing. It had been many years since my valiant Golden Retriever, Dalton, passed away and I figured if I'm taking care of David's dog, then two isn't much more. Besides, Thunder would have a playmate, and I should have a dog of my own.

When I decided to get a large dog to buddy up to Thunder, I thought "you don't see collies around much anymore." But where to get one that wasn't over-bred was the question. David suggested I track down Bob Weatherwax, owner of Lassie, and see what breeders he might suggest. Brilliant idea! After a couple of days, I got a number for him through people in the industry and called his home in Canyon Country.

A gruff sounding voice answered the phone. It was Weatherwax himself. After I explained who I was and what I wanted, he said, "Well we've got three litters. Most are spoken for, but you're welcome to come on down and pick out one." I nearly dropped the phone I was so excited. We zoomed out within the hour and I found myself at his sister's house, sitting on the floor playing with the puppies.

There was one I was holding that was a live wire and I thought maybe that would be the one, but I wasn't sure. David said, "Check this one out." He pointed to a sable-colored ball of fluff lying quietly beside her bowl of food, taking in all the chaos around her. She calmly ate her food like she was having dinner and watching TV. After she finished, I picked her up and we looked into each other's eyes. There was an electric connection. Like I was looking at my soul in her eyes. Her name was already picked out months prior—Lulu. I held her close and we cuddled. That was it. She was mine.

Coincidentally, her birthday was December 7, 1998. December 7 is Pearl Harbor day. Honolulu means safe harbor. It was fate. Since it was a week before Valentine's Day, I declared her my present and thanked David. He hadn't planned on spending the $1,500 for her. I was supposed to pay for it. I could see him clench his jaw, but he footed the bill for her anyway. She was a bargain. She became the love and light of my life for nine years. The best thing that came from my marriage with David. The most perfect dog and companion I could ever have dreamed of or wished for. She was priceless.

* * *

The years of struggling within the relationship with the core issues wore away my energy to a point where when he'd go out of town for a few days, I would choose not to accompany him. Until then David and I had been inseparable. It was the only time I could take a breath and recharge. I'd be free of cigarette smoke, noise, picking up after him. I could go out and not worry about what might happen when I was gone. It used to be that days before his departure, in anticipation of him leaving, we'd say "I miss you already." And a line I got from my grandmother, "I love you more than you know."

It was summer, balmy. I had short "vacations" at home by myself, looking at the sunset and the dark silhouette of the palm trees that lined the street, and feeling at peace . . . calm serenity. I'd go to Color Me Mine and paint a surprise gift for his return. It was the only free time I had to do any artwork . . . I could play my favorite music of Gypsy Kings, Juan Luis Guerra, Ottmar Liebert . . . I could feel my *self* again.

As soon as he walked in the door, as glad as I was to be back in his arms, I dreaded the tornado that would start to whirl all over again.

There was more traveling, the lawsuit with a publishing company, my knee injury and rehab, continuous IRS problems, ongoing drama with David's daughter and her girls, and on and on and on. It was David's world, not mine. I barely had any time to keep up with my longtime friends or with my family. When we made out the guest list and chose the bridal party, they were mostly his "clan." It hit me that I had to make room for the people important to me and mine again, and not be passed over because there wasn't any room left after him and his.

One Fourth of July, David and I attended a party on the beach front in Malibu. We cuddled up with each other on a chaise lounge to keep warm as we watched the sun set, and I noticed a woman who had come with a date, but stood off on the side gazing out at the ocean. She had a misty eyed, wistful look of longing on her face. I thought how sad that she was with someone, but it was obviously not the right person. As I buried myself in David's embrace, I thought how lucky we were to have found each other. I felt bad for that woman. Later she came up to us and commented how sweet and lovely it was to see two people so much in love. How could I ever think at that moment that one day some years later, I would be that woman, standing off on the side and wistfully looking out over the ocean?

* * *

The house got to be too busy with meetings, and people and personal assistants coming and going. I felt we had no privacy. It reminded me of David's lifestyle in Mississauga, so we decided to rent office space a block away. It was a very comfortable, large, impressive space, and we filled it with whitewashed wicker furniture I had in my condo. It lasted only a year. Even though it was just down the street, it still wasn't as convenient as working out of the house and there was a considerable rental expense. We had to let the assistants and the office go because of low funds again, and we downsized our operations. Lisa, my friend and our landlord, decided she wanted to sell the house and wondered if we would be interested. As much as we loved our cozy abode, per our "experts," it was a feng shui nightmare. There also were too many architectural things we'd have to change. With our lifestyle and schedule, there wasn't any time to take on such tasks. So a-hunting we did go for a change.

We must have looked at seventy houses in a few months' time. The real estate agent brought David to look at one house, since I was too burned out to go, and he came back with the news that he had found "a great house." He wanted my candid reaction first. Well there were a lot of "great houses" we looked at, and we passed on all of them, so I wasn't getting my hopes up. This one was just listed, but hadn't been officially on the market yet. We got the preview. The minute I walked in the door and looked at the backyard through the sliding glass doors to the waterfall and lagoon pool, I said, "This is it!"

The real estate woman told me that's what David thought I'd say. So we struck a deal with the sellers, though not at the price I wanted to bargain for. David didn't like haggling over a mere $30,000 or the fact it needed a new roof. He said he was going to make more than enough money, so it wouldn't matter. What he lost sight of was that my mother was taking out the loan for the house and I was putting in the money for the down payment. But, that was it. He blew up at me for possibly screwing up the deal and losing the house, so I acquiesced. I found out later that they were willing to drop the price $20,000. Who knows. If we waited and haggled, another buyer might have paid full price and we might have lost the deal.

By the time we planned on moving, his movie *By Dawn's Early Light* was rescheduled to film in Vancouver at the same time. Grrrrreat. That meant I'd have to stay in L.A. and do the move by myself. He'd be up there filming. David did travel back for a couple of days to help, but fizzled out on me and didn't do much, except pack his personal office space. I enlisted the help of one of his friends and between the two of us, we packed and self moved most of it except the heavy furniture. I looked at it like it was my exercise get-in-shape boot camp.

A couple nights before David was to come home to our new place, I was carrying a box and hurrying down the hall toward the kitchen. Just as I looked up, I saw what I thought was a tall person wearing what I perceived to be American Indian clothing. "It" had a blanket over one shoulder. And I walked right through it. Whoa! Okaaay. I froze, analyzing the experience. I didn't feel any cold draft, in fact as I passed through, it felt warm. Very odd.

Once we were in our new home—The Rosita House, spring 2000—it was wonderful to feel we finally had enough room. Two thousand two hundred square feet of it, two fireplaces, maid's quarters that became his office, three other bedrooms, one of which was my office, walk-in closets, and that incredible yard.

I had my numerology chart done and the guy said the house number was very bad for our marriage. We had to see about getting the house number changed because it meant divorce. Good numbers for David, but not for me. I jumped all over that, as well as city hoops to get it done, but it obviously didn't help. Can't say I didn't try everything to save the marriage!

Another evening I was in my office and I heard clopping footsteps coming down the hall. They hesitated, then started up again. I shouted out, "I'm in the office, Johnny." And the footsteps sounded like they veered off into the bedroom. I looked in the bedroom, no Johnny. Down the hall I could see Thunder asleep. If David had come out of his office, Thunder would have been up and about. So down the hall I went into David's office, where he was working at his computer. Now chills ran up my spine. I told him what happened, but he didn't give much reaction. It was interesting and that was it. I had several other experiences at the house, seeing and hearing things. I found out later that the house as well as the entire neighborhood was built on Indian ceremonial grounds. Needless to say, I was on the phone with my clairvoyant friends about the house.

When it later came to selling it, based on the fact that the first owners lost the house in a foreclosure, and we were separating, it didn't have the happiest vibe. The people we bought it from had children and they seemed happy. The family who purchased the house on a short sale from my mother, also have children and they are happy there. The house went on the market in June of 2001 and got not one offer in over ten months. Nine-eleven didn't help the real estate market either. I changed real estate agents three times, saged, did feng shui, consulted astrologers, clairvoyants. I re-saged, did other affirmation ceremonies, called in a psychic to chase away any negative entities, all to try and attract a buyer. I redecorated, recarpeted . . . anything I could think of, and still not one offer.

So I had a little heart-to-heart talk with the spirits of the house. "Look, I'm not the right person to live here and David's not coming back. You need a *family* to live here, right? Let me go and help me find the right buyers so you'll be happy too. You won't be alone."

Within a couple of months, I happened to mention my problem to a new acquaintance who said she thought she had a buyer for my house: the Carmody family from out of state, with three kids. And guess what?

They bought the house. It was just as three psychics told me would happen. The family and I are not only friends to this day, but at one point I was their son's agent.

Oh happy house!

Chapter Sixteen

THE DAILY GRIND

Managing David wasn't 24/7, it was a 48/8 job. It wasn't just managing his career, but his entire life. From making his phone calls, setting his alarm clock, and helping to choose his wardrobe to getting him to appointments on time, which was a nightmare because he was notoriously late, and making sure he remembered birthday presents and important dates of his family. He refused to take charge or be responsible for any element and phase of his personal life for the most part. He'd consistently put things off he didn't want to deal with, which forced people to do the task for him. Uh, passive-aggressive, do you think? Hmmmmmm, let me contemplate on that a moment.

The basic routine may sound simple and easy, but it wasn't. The workdays were anywhere from 14–16 hours, not counting any social functions, which I considered work a lot of the time. I felt I couldn't let one thing go by without taking advantage of it, for fear of losing an opportunity that might lead to an interview, job or publicity for David. I was continually working it. It could be taxing for David as well because he felt he had to be "on" and not always the "self" he wanted to be, but rather what he thought they'd be looking for. Sometimes he put a considerable damper on his natural way of shocking people with either what he said or did, especially around a "suited" corporate crowd or at an elite venue, like attending the Oscars. In other words he'd behave more "normal" or low-keyed versus "eccentric." After he started getting work, and he was more comfortable with his career, he loosened up. Around friends and people he was familiar with, he did whatever he wanted. He was just himself. In short, he made adjustments depending on what was required.

If David wanted to call friends of *his*, I would literally punch up a phone number and hand him the phone. That lasted about six months. I finally threatened if *he* didn't dial, then the call wouldn't go through. He started to make his own calls again.

In the meantime, I contacted Stephen Viens, who worked for the tabloid *The Star* and told him of my battle plan for damage control and a new sober image for David. Viens wrote a two-page article, with pictures, about David going sober and me as the positive influence and love in his life.

Along with *Inside Edition*, which had recently aired when we were in Toronto, the ball started rolling on getting attention in a positive light. The new image of David was now being projected around the world.

David's habit of being late continued when we lived together, and from what I heard after that, didn't change. I was listening to the early morning Adam Carolla show on the radio a few years ago when they announced David was supposed to be a guest. They kept making explanations to the listeners because it was well into the hour and David hadn't yet shown up for his on-air interview. I called the station because I was laughing at the whole situation—how typical it was and how he obviously hadn't changed. They were going to interview me instead, but Carolla's segment was ending and David finally arrived in time to be interviewed on *the next show!*

* * *

Typical day, I'd set the alarm for David to get up for an appointment and . . . he wouldn't get up. He slept through alarms. I'd go into the room to rouse him, and he'd ask for ten more minutes. Ten minutes would go by and he'd want ten more. I'd always be on a tight schedule and the last thing I needed was to play nursemaid and alarm clock for him, but this is what I did for years. Then after half an hour, I'd run out of patience, get irritated and start giving him ultimatums: "Go ahead be late! I don't care anymore!" This in turn would tick David off, so when he finally did get up, he would complain that I ruined his morning.

No matter how nice or patient I'd be, I would ultimately be the excuse he needed to blame his bad mood on me and display his "bass fish" face. That's how I described his sour expression when he was sullen. His mouth would turn down and he'd look like . . . a bass fish.

It took a few years before I got a handle on the tough love theory and started putting attention on my own career again and not catering to him all the time. That meant that sometimes I'd wake him up, but he had better make sure to follow through on his own or else he'd miss his meetings, as it sometimes happened. He learned. It gave me a tad more freedom, but the more I pulled back energy for myself, the more he appeared to resent it.

At the beginning of the New Year 2010, I was watching my friends Ed Begley, Jr. and his wife Rachel in a segment of the Dr. Phil show. Dr. Phil was talking about couples' conflicts and compatibilities and said he'd wake up every morning and ask himself what could he do that day to make his wife's life better? When I heard that, I started to cry. How fabulous to have a mate like that. Not once did I feel that from David.

* * *

One day, I had an acting job on a film and David had an important interview for a project. The alarm was set in plenty of time for him to get ready. He was to sleep on the couch so he'd be close to the door to hear the knock when his transportation arrived for his pick up. A night owl, he would usually go to bed around 6 or 7 *a.m.* and sleep the day away if he didn't have anything going on. I'd get up around 8 a.m. to work in the office. I thought how nice not to have to worry about him that day of all days. I could concentrate just on *my* work . . . *my* career.

On location, I got an emergency page from the driver that David was not coming to the door. They were now half an hour late. The driver was frantic. I'm being called to set while trying to instruct the driver how to get through the gate to find the bedroom window to pound on it, since he didn't see David on the couch. He didn't pick up the house line or his cell phone. Nothing. I asked the driver to keep me informed if he were able to find and or wake David up. No matter what I did to pave the way and secure the situation, David would do something that caused me or others to scamper about and spin our wheels, draining away time and energy we needed for ourselves. Yes, it was the tornado again!

In between scenes, I was still calling the house and the driver to see what the update was. Did David call to tell me he finally made it to the appointment? Nada. The *driver* called to let me know.

Music was part of David's soul and mine, and we were anxious to get a band together for him again. It had been years since he was able to do that. I remembered that my friend, Harry Dean Stanton, played at The Mint. Another friend, guitarist Jamie James was part of Harry's backup band. We went to see Harry's show, which was always such a gas. He had the audience in the palm of his hand, banging out Mustang Sally or crooning a Mexican ballad. David wanted to perform his music so badly we could both taste it, so we talked with the booking manager and without hesitation the Mint booked David into his first venue. After getting his feet wet with that, we looked at other clubs and venues in towns where he was scheduled as well and he played to packed houses.

Managing David's career, I handled the announcements, mailers, everything to do with promotion. I "directed" his photo shoots, got a website going and even did his make-up for various shoots as well as public appearances and quite a few of his film and TV shoots. As I said, it was a 48/8 job. Up at seven or eight a.m. and in bed usually by two a.m. David couldn't understand why I was too tired to have sex with him whenever he wanted or why I got upset over a phone bill that wasn't corrected after the tenth phone call. Hormones from the many IVF attempts didn't help. I was often out of kilter. It didn't seem like he took any of this into consideration before he'd criticize me.

"You're always so angry."

Until one week I put those tasks in his lap and he got a taste of what it was like. He was then the one yelling at the billing department and stomping out of the room. Made my day!

It was like Mr. Toad's wild ride when David was at the wheel. I'd white-knuckle it while clenching the side arm in the car. He loved to speed along Mulholland Drive, thinking it was a short cut when traffic was heavy on the freeway or Ventura Boulevard. At traffic lights he'd light up a cigarette and even after the light had turned green, we'd still be sitting there as he futzed with this or that or he fidgeted with the cigarette lighter or performed his routine of taking a dust brush from the glove compartment, which was more like a paintbrush, and whisking away ashes from the gearshift.

In the meantime, people would honk their horns in anger and zoom around him. I'd keep looking back, turning white, at oncoming cars as they got closer and closer, afraid we'd get rear-ended. Often. I thought we had had it. "They're not stopping! Johnny, move the car, dammit! They're not slowing down!!!" He'd then berate me for getting upset over "nothing."

David would often make illegal U-turns or back up half way down the block for a parking space. Once, when he wasn't paying attention and I had briefly turned away, he drove us into the wrong lane of on coming traffic. We were going the opposite direction on a one-way street. Yeah, that was a screamer. Times like those, I would cover my eyes and brace myself as if I were on an airplane prepping for a crash landing. Thing is, we never got into a crash. However, he did cream the entire side of my Miata when he parked his Maserati in our driveway one day. We made different parking arrangements after that.

If he did get pulled over by the police, they would always let him go with a warning . . . because he was David Carradine and they were fans. It didn't work for me though. We were coming from Calista's place one day, cruising along with David encouraging me to pick up the pace. We joined the pack of other speeding cars when some cop picked me out of the crowd. We asked why he would ticket us versus others who were going faster? Because . . . he saw David in the passenger seat. "Kung Fu, huh? Didn't watch it." He was not a fan. I have to admit David did his charming best to get out of it, but that only made the cop more determined. He wasn't going to be swayed by "an actor." Yeah he'd show that celebrity a thing or two! Celebrities weren't special to him and he showed us alright! I had David pay for the ticket, but still had to go to traffic school. That was a kick in the rump.

* * *

David wasn't the most organized person in the world. I couldn't keep track of everything so when it came to things like his car registration, that was his department. Problem was, he'd often lose or misplace things in this stack of files or on that shelf of papers. It was constant and I'd end up spending considerable time trying to find miscellaneous items for him. On occasion, he'd spend an entire day reorganizing everything, only to spend even more time trying to find something in its new location. His car registration wasn't the only thing he lost in his office shuffle.

He tended to have a sort of tunnel vision of concentration. When he was focused on a mission, that was it. He wasn't great at multitasking. We were in a frenzy to get a life-size stand-up poster print of the sexy photo Alan Weissman took of David for one of his gigs. David offered to pick it up at the printer and as usual, he took Thunder with him to keep him company. OK! One less thing for me to do. He came home to show me the poster, which turned out fabulous, and headed for his office. I looked around. Something was missing. "Uh, Johnny, where's Thunder?"

After silence from the other room, "Oh, I must have left him in the car."

I ran out to get the dog and . . . no Thunder. Could he have jumped out the car window? *"Johnny!"*

He comes running out and looks at me blankly. "He was with me in the store."

"Was he in the car with you?"

David looked at me blankly.

"Johnny, do you remember him getting back into the car?"

He looked around, panicked . . . checked the car . . . turned white. "I must have left him at the copy store."

"You're kidding me, right?" Sure enough he did. Running into the house I shouted back at David, "I'll call the store." As I heard him peel out the driveway, the guy at the store on the other end of the phone says, "Yeah, there's this great-looking dog sitting outside the store."

"Don't let that dog go anywhere! His owner is on the way".

"You mean he forgot his dog?"

"Yep".

The guy laughed. "You got your hands full, don't ya lady?"

* * *

Socially, we never stopped schmoozing, and I was notorious for "working a room," as David would brag, introducing him to important people, setting up the conversation—like a talk show host would do—to allow David to segue into telling his funny stories, or gear it to whatever we thought that director or producer might be looking for in a role. It became an art to do this without it being too obvious it was a pitch.

This wasn't a gift that came naturally. I had to overcome a lot of insecurities over the years to grow the cahoonas. He also called me "the most organized person in the world." David referred to me as his "floppy disc." He relied on me to remember everything and everyone including birthdays of friends and relatives. My ego liked the boost, but it was just another responsibility on my plate and the pressure built to a point I felt I was short-circuiting.

There were many times David would also forget who people were, even if he had known them for years as personal friends. It was embarrassing sometimes, but David was good at faking recognition and I was usually able to gracefully play detective and give David the information before anyone realized.

If someone were approaching, I'd whisper in his ear who it was or what they did in the industry to give him a heads up. Or if he did remember them, but not their name, he'd be "busy" taking a drink of soda (his favorite was root beer) or bite of food and I'd extend my hand first and say, "Hello, I'm Marina, you are . . . ?" And I'd get the name of the person. By that time, he could clear his throat of the drink or food and say, "Hey man! Good to see ya again." We had it down!

Once in a rare while he'd get busted. "You don't remember me, do you?"

David would smile and say almost like he was singing, "Nnnnnnnnah, I donnnnn't." There'd be apprehension mixed with a laugh, like "am I in trouble?" The combination with his facial expression was hysterical. Afterward, I'd do an impression of him and we'd have a belly laugh over it. He could be alarmingly honest and so charming no one took offense.

The problem was, with most of the emphasis placed on David, I'd forget how to relate to people for myself. I got used to people not paying attention to me, not caring what I had to say. If I got two words in edgewise during a monologue David was giving, it was a miracle. David not only took the spotlight, but if I did say anything, he'd cut in like he didn't hear me and take over the conversation or invalidate me by saying, "No that's not it, it's . . . " and he'd paraphrase or turn around what I just said, as if it was his own idea. People would listen to him and I'd stand there feeling like I had egg on my face, because I was made to look like I was wrong or inept at telling a story or entertaining people. This happened many times and occasionally I'd literally back out from the circle which would close around David and no one would notice I had disappeared until the end of the party. Then he'd start to wonder where I was because that conversation circle would bore him and he'd look to me for the next intro.

It got to a point after a couple of years , I got so self-conscious that when anyone did pay attention and really focused on me, whether David was present or not, I'd get anxious and self-conscious, thinking "Hey, they are really listening to me!" It would throw me off to the extent that my words would come out too fast or get mixed up or fumbled and like an idiot I would say things like gumble bum instead of bubble gum, or stutter. Then I'd walk off feeling like a jerk, incompetent, inarticulate, and retreat into my shell.

David wasn't one to ask many questions in conversation because that meant the attention shifted to the other person giving the answer. He liked the attention on him, so he was one to make statements and tell stories. Getting to know someone by asking them questions? Seldom.

David had the intelligence of a Rhodes scholar that kept me and others on our toes and constantly learning. There wasn't anything he couldn't talk about or that he didn't know enough about. He was witty, and one of the most naturally funny men I've ever met. Sometimes my face and stomach would ache from laughter, and he could spin a story or joke like no one else. He could be oh so incredibly sweet, vulnerable, captivating, charismatic. There was never a dull moment with the man.

Even though he rebelled against convention, there was a part of him that wanted to belong. Almost as though he was saying f— you before "they" could. He seemed to be constantly torn between being his rebel self and compromising in a world of rules he didn't agree with.

We had a fun ongoing "gotya" that helped lighten the day or situation. One of us would pretend there was something on our clothes, to cause the other to look down, at which time, one would take a finger and flick it quickly under the other's nose. It was sometimes hard to get him. He was so quick he'd grab my hand before I could flick him. I guess snatching all those pebbles was good training!

One look of his could freeze a person or warm them with comfort, like basking in the sun. For the longest time, it made up for what was lacking, which was just enough incentive to get through the daily grind and charge on!

CHAPTER SEVENTEEN

"S" for SOBRIETY

Think beyond the door
Think beyond the wall
Open the window . . .

—Marina Anderson

W HEN David was filming his series, he was all too aware of how concerned the "brass" was about his drinking. Once, he pulled off a very clever maneuver. David was trying to get as many of his buddies as possible to work on the show, which was difficult because of the Canadian content factor—they had to use mostly Canadians. He told me he arranged for a friend whom he called his sponsor to fly up to Toronto not only at the expense of production, but also so he could be cast in one of the episodes. This way, he was able to get another friend a gig on his show under the ruse they were there also to help try and get him sober.

It was a great idea, but I was really expecting this sponsor to actually get him to stop drinking. What did I know? When I saw that nothing was actively being done to help David, I confronted the person. After all, he was there to look after David—to help. Isn't that what a sponsor was for—to help someone get sober? Why was he not helping? He did, however, give David a book on AA with the 12 Steps, which David did read and kept on hand over the years. The friend explained there wasn't anything he could do to force David to stop drinking.

"We carry the message and not the alcoholic."

That was my first lesson about sobriety and dealing with an alcoholic. I still felt there had to be some other proactive things to help. There just had to be! What do you mean there isn't *anything* anyone can do?! It was explained that David would have to take the first step, and evidently he wasn't quite ready. I was very angry with the sponsor and held a grudge until I really understood what he was talking about. With time I gained first hand understanding what he meant, and the sponsor and I eventually became friends. I sputter at the thought of people asking me for advice on the subject. I can only relate my experience and how we dealt with it.

When David drank, he kept his energy closer to himself and was focused. That is, until something triggered him to explode in a rage. Drinking or not, he knew his lines and hit his marks. He did get more physical after a few drinks, though. He liked to use his arms to emphasize whatever he was saying, but sometimes he went too far. He would tap people a little too hard, for emphasis, and once hit a kid actor on his show, which got David into considerable trouble. In 1995, he unintentionally chipped my front tooth when, waving his arms about while saying something, he accidentally slammed his ringed hand into my mouth. He was very upset and had his dentist file it down, but a fracture line remains. At the time I thought it was endearing, how much emotional agony he was in about accidentally hurting me.

* * *

It felt great to accomplish goals. People credit me with his sobriety and say I was his savior. That's a really nice compliment, but I wasn't the one who got him sober. He got himself sober. David hit bottom and knew he had to climb back up or he'd disappear into oblivion and poverty. I provided part of the support, incentive and motivation. The other incentive was that getting sober was the only way to get his life and career back. However, he knew if he lost me, he'd lose that opportunity too.

I came along just in time—the catalyst for it all to come together and work—but David had to want to stop drinking to begin with. If I hadn't come along, he probably would have died years ago. I, and others, say I remained his *main incentive* for staying sober the years we were together. As the old saying goes, you can lead a horse to water, but you can't make it drink. I also had "approval" and support from his brothers, Keith and Robert, who thanked me for giving them their brother back—the David they felt they had lost for so many years to the booze.

Looking back now I realize I was addicted to saving him. I thought David was brilliant and underrated for his abilities and accomplishments. I came to understand how he sabotaged himself and I tried to intervene, but I got caught in the line of fire.

I saw everything going down the drain with the alcohol and felt it was a tragedy for that to happen. When I told David he was depriving fans by keeping his true talent from shining through, he looked at me curiously and smiled. He never thought of it that way.

David and I admired the various strengths we saw in each other. We wanted to be more like each other. This was something that was in our original "pact." We agreed we'd each teach the other how to nurture the qualities we liked best. One quality of David's I admired was that he questioned authority and was a non-conformist. He was not easily intimidated. I, on the other hand, was always a "goody two-shoes" and I admired his defiance. He loved the fact I was pretty much a teetotaler, so giving up drinking entirely to help David was certainly not a problem for me. I have had barely anything to do with drugs my entire life. For me, taking an Advil was a big deal. This was a strength David wanted to tap into, to help him maintain his sobriety.

We shared mutual curiosity about and experience in spirituality and metaphysics. He didn't pooh-pooh healers, psychics or my work as a healer. I studied for many years, both independently and through the Healing Light Center Church; just call me "Rev." Anderson. It was frustrating for both of us when sometimes our deep-seated natures conflicted with changes necessary to become more like what we admired in each other.

* * *

"David, I want to talk to you about death ... "

David was very open about his doctor—Dr. Babb—giving him a serious talk. His liver had become very enlarged and the numbers in his liver test were so abnormally high the doctor said he had about six months left to live if he continued on this path.

Before we started our relationship, there were several attempts, lasting a few weeks or maybe a couple of months, to stay sober, but he eventually slid back into his old pattern. He was unable to achieve total sobriety with Gail drinking and the house full of liquor. David explained he was never into alcohol to a large extent until he began his relationship with her. He indulged more and more as time went on. So it wasn't like he started the habit in his early years. It was a late onset problem. As with a lot of things in life, it's easier to get into a habit when you have a mate who likes to indulge in the same thing. I'm told with an addictive personality, it's also easy to substitute one habit or addiction, thus sliding into another.

David also had the disadvantage of alcohol use in his family—his father was one to indulge heavily so David supposedly had a genetic predisposition from the get-go. I felt he deserved extra understanding and consideration. It was, I believed, tougher for him than for most. Maybe.

To try to counter the effects alcohol had on him, he took large amounts of Chinese herbs, including a brew called ditijou. It consisted of over thirty herbs and snake and lizard and goodness knows what else. He got it in Chinatown in downtown Toronto, cured in vodka and/or gin in a jar. The jar was buried underground for a period of at least six months. A section of the backyard looked a bit like a mine field had exploded when he dug up one of the jars the size of a huge keg of beer.

David shared this potion with guests at the house, including me—

snake, lizard and all. My mouth contorts at the memory. Problem with that theory is the brew was alcoholic! He said he also took a slew of other exotic herbs, and we both believed that they extended his life. He continued taking many concoctions of herbal remedies, sans alcohol, throughout our relationship, not only for his liver regeneration, but also for his arthritis. His father had it bad and David was starting to see and feel the beginnings of it in his hands.

As much as David told people he wanted to get sober, however, he just couldn't. The house in Mississauga was full of alcoholic beverages. The only way he could quit, he said, was if there was absolutely no alcohol around. So we ceremoniously dumped every bottle of alcohol we could find down the drain. It took a couple of hours to find and gather his collection scattered about the 3000 square foot house. With every bottle glugging down the drain, he had a mixed look of fear and determination, especially when he came across a rather tasty favorite. It pained him to see it all go without tasting, but he did it. The more expensive wines and liquors he gave away to very appreciative recipients.

The now depleted home stash forced him to go out to drink, but at least it was a step in the right direction. He'd head for the pub when it opened at 11 a.m. The downside was unless he was filming, in which case Johnny Mac would do the driving, *David* had to drive the car if he wanted to get to the pub! I would drive him on occasion, but it was too time-consuming to make the trips and sit at the bar while he tanked up.

The first few months together, he cut back somewhat. His book tour dictated it, but David was averaging about a quart and a half a day, mostly vodka. At one point, he suggested I hide the car keys so he couldn't drive to the bar. He instructed me that no matter how he screamed or pleaded, I was not to give him the keys. That's what the man wanted, so I did exactly that, but it didn't last long. He got so desperate one evening and so frantic to find something alcoholic, that when the screaming and intimidation didn't work on me, he grabbed me by the shoulders and shook me, demanding that I give him the keys. When I refused, he made a search of the room and found them. We fought over the keys and he grabbed my hands so hard I cried out and let the keys go.

"Here. Take them. Go get drunk!" I thought he'd break my wrist if I resisted any more. I was scared and angry. It was a flash of the angry David I had seen with Gail. Mostly, I was upset that I allowed myself to be put in that position in the first place. I had no idea he'd get violent. He immediately looked painfully apologetic and embarrassed, but it was only for a split second as he hurried out the house to the nearby pub, Friar & Firkin, to get there before they closed. Sometimes they would stay open past closing for him because of the amount of money he'd spend.

When he got back an hour later, he said with a tentative chuckle, "Well, I guess that wasn't a good idea. I don't think we should try that again." I couldn't have agreed more. David didn't ask if I was okay or verbalize an apology, but I could tell he was worried that I might change my mind about staying with him because he offered to fix me some tea and a bubble bath. That was his way.

* * *

One night coming back from playing pool at our favorite spot, I suggested that I drive, but no, David insisted he would. He was an extremely careful driver at that time because he was overly cautious not to get pulled over. Nevertheless, he was under the influence, and sure enough that evening in the rear view mirror we saw red flashing lights. David was cited with a DUI *warning*. They took his license, and the police made sure I drove home, a few blocks away. How I hated driving that tank of a Maserati! You could hear the motor from blocks away and it was difficult to handle. Definitely a man's car although it was a good arm workout. At least it was a solid car. I felt safe driving it in the snow and in L.A.

David had to go back to the police station the next day to pick up his license. He didn't have to pay a fine since they all were fans of his. He chatted away with the officers for quite a while making sure all was "good" in case he was ever pulled over again. He showed them some card from some organization in the States confirming his support of the LAPD. They loved that. Regardless, from then on, I drove most of the time, which was more than fine with me because I lost a childhood friend to a drunk driver and I am to this day adamantly against people driving under the influence. David rented a SUV from Johnny Mac that I declared my car of choice.

* * *

When David and I met with divorce attorney Lisa Brandon at the Beverly Hills hotel in 1995 to initiate his legal separation from Gail, I also arranged to have psychic Christian Dion give David a jump-start healing for sobriety. We were both believers and practitioners in the transfer of energy from one person to another. We both studied this for years, and Christian was able to meet with us on our tight schedule. He spent about half an hour working on David, who said after the session that he felt more energetic, was more focused and drank less in the next few weeks. A clairvoyant, Christian assured me David would eventually get sober and it would stick as long as he was in his relationship with me. Years later a couple of other psychics including Christian's father Tom, also affirmed the same thing.

* * *

After we moved back to L.A., David wanted to hit just about any bar he could find and to revisit old haunts as well. It got to be a tedious routine and I considered it a waste of time for me to accompany him and sit there for hours at a time, having a fruit juice while he got . . . juiced, and was surrounded by other drunks, which I hated. The worst was being in a dark, stank bar at 11 a.m. watching the "hard cores" come through the door shaking, desperate for their first drink of the day. It was very disturbing and sad to be around.

Some weeks later, I arranged for a meeting to book David and his band at Smokin' Johnnie's, a rib joint in the Valley. The owner was dubious because he could tell David was under the influence, but with David's name, he felt they could pull in a crowd. I thought it would be a shoe-in to have David on their billing. He did a few songs for the booker and afterward I talked privately to the owner. The guy loved the idea, but wasn't going to risk putting David on stage if he was *that* drunk. On the way back to the condo, I relayed to David exactly what the man said about him.

We were zipping along on the 405, heading back to Valencia in my little Miata. Traffic was easy for a change. It was silent for the longest time. Then I added gently, "You know Johnny, if you want to resurrect your career, you're going to have to make a serious change. You said this is what you want to do. This is your chance. Now."

More silence. He stared out the car in deep thought, his cigarette burning away quickly in the open window. Then breaking the drone of the motor, he announced that he was going to choose a date to go sober. Cold turkey. Butterflies of excitement fluttered through my stomach at his news. He had my total support. We reflected on a meeting we had some months prior with an intervention specialist who helped many celebrities, but this doctor wanted to put David in the hospital for several weeks, and at major expense, with intravenous medications and tests in order to get him sober. There would be no visitors and it would be a very strict environment. Not even phone calls were to be allowed. I remember a brief look of astonishment on David's face, which probably reflected mine. No communication with each other or anyone for weeeeeks? No, no, no, no, no. Spooky. IV medications? Severe. It was soon replaced with a look of defiance when the man told David he didn't stand a chance of getting sober without doing it that way. Not a chance, huh? We looked at each other, thanked the man and walked out.

"Bullshit," David grumbled. He had "I'll show him" written all over his face.

I agreed. Nothing made David more set on doing something than when someone said he couldn't do it. No one was going to separate Johnny from his Blackie. It wasn't going to go down that way. Nope, not for David it wasn't!

When March 10th rolled around, he said he forgot about the commitment date and wasn't ready. He wanted to delay it until the following week. I didn't buy his bluff tactic. I said that wasn't what he promised and *this* was the day. He didn't give me any flack either. "OK. If you say so."

David was very apprehensive about "S"—sobriety—day. We stocked up on numerous herb teas, Chinese herbs, videos of favorite films and healthy foods. I prepared myself for the worst. I had seen movies and heard stories about people with the shakes, hallucinations, straightjacket-like fits. I had images of Ray Milland in *The Lost Weekend* in my head. I thought that's what it might be like for him. I was in total anxiety. It took me a couple of years to stop worrying. I was fearful of setting him off because he might start drinking again, until a friend reminded me if he started to drink, it wouldn't be because of me. He was responsible for his own actions.

I looked around my condo and removed my favorite breakables just in case. I was ready. Kind of. The first few days he was edgy and cranky. I tried to have things as normal as possible, but at the same time to cater to him more, so it would ease the tension.

After the first week, we both were pleasantly surprised at how well he was adapting. I kept encouraging his progress, saying how proud I was of him. And I was very proud. I made sure others knew as well to lend their support.

He'd get on the phone and announce, "Hey man, how ya doin'? It's been two weeks now . . . " As the months and years went on he'd make his proud progress reports.

David didn't have the shakes, cold sweats or any other obvious symptoms. It didn't seem like he was having nightmares either. Not that

I could see by observing him sleep or by his reports. He actually fell into very, *very* deep sleep, and it was difficult to get him into a waking state. This trait never did change. Most times, we'd set three alarm clocks. He could sleep through yelling, phones ringing, alarms . . . Sometimes he was so deep in, he didn't wake up to relieve his bladder. Walking Rocky helped occupy his attention and he busied himself with writing, drawing or talking on the phone. Anything to keep his mind off drinking, except he did not get into any exercise program or practice Tai Chi on a daily or even monthly basis as people thought. Not while we were together anyway. The only time he "tuned up" was before he did a taping for one of his Tai Chi videos. After a time he even stopped walking the dog. Probably because we had a huge backyard when we moved into the Valley Vista house a few months later. As time moved on, I was surprised to see that David didn't appear to be having any further problems. He never expressed much about his symptoms even when I asked.

"Naw. I'm fine. I'm grrrrrrreat!" he'd say, like Tony the Tiger, the cartoon character.

His energy was picking up and even the way he was moving and talking quickened. He was more alert.

We had a three-foot high rolling four-shelf bin full to the brim with vitamins and herbs in the kitchen. He'd sit there for a good fifteen minutes, gulping them by the handful, with his juice or coffee. I often had to remind him to eat something with them or else they could be hard to digest. No, no, he was a macho man, until he'd feel sick and then I'd fix him something to eat.

The six years David was sober were the first years since childhood, he said, that he was totally substance free. It scared the crap out of him, yet he was excited. Everything was new, uncharted territory again. The exhilaration seemed to spur him on. He loved adventure. One fear that most concerned him, though, was that maybe the lack of being buzzed would cause him to lose his edge in his acting abilities. For most of his successful acting career, he was taking one substance or another. It was difficult for him to tell if he was doing a good job or not and would constantly ask for my opinion and suggestions.

I did what I could to assure him that sobriety would not interfere with his ability, that his acting would be even better—and it was—because he was more open. Vulnerable and present. That hadn't occurred to him. He liked the affirmation. The proof was his being cast and receiving accolades in project after project.

David was actually like a little boy, being born again, with a new outlook on everything. He said even food tasted different, better than ever. All his senses were being rejuvenated. His extended liver was gradually subsiding and tests showed it was regenerating. Mentally, he wasn't in a fog anymore. This clarity helped David let the last of everything go in his feelings toward Gail. He could see and feel things in a new reality. The last of their divorce settlement set him free in that area as well.

On the downside, he was moodier, edgier, and more difficult to get along with in general. Under the influence, he was more of a pussycat. Everything seemed to go down easy. Of course it would, he wasn't all there. Only a couple of times during our six years did he tell me about a nightmare he'd have about taking a sip of alcohol, which bothered him a lot. So much so, he was jittery through the next day, but we would just keep busy with projects, he'd work at the computer or go out for a coffee. David didn't like to let people in on his innermost fears. It was like giving the enemy an advantage. Something he learned as a kid. His armor of defense.

Sometimes, he'd call his sponsor buddy or we'd visit, but even that was only on occasion. Within a month, he started to lose weight and the extended stomach and bloated look in his face began to disappear. The new David began to emerge inside and out. He started drinking espresso in increasing amounts. First double, then triple and quadruple shots, and Coca Cola in excess—unless he could order root beer. These beverages remained his habit over the next several years—caffeine and sugar.

It was suggested that David take a full spectrum of vitamin B in high dosages each day because alcohol depletes it from the body, but David hadn't adhered to this advice while he was drinking. He did of course keep up and even increased his nicotine intake: his two and a half to three packs a day habit of English Ovals. Had to be English Ovals unless he was smoking a Cohiba. He'd often leave them lit and ashes would cover tabletops and floors. Burn marks would be his signature in wood and carpets . . . or people if they stood too close. My hair got singed a couple of times. Other objects would sometimes catch fire if the cigarette got knocked over onto a piece of paper. Sniff, sniff . . . what's that smell . . . ? Gasp! And then we'd see a spark of flame burst from the table. Would be funny in a sitcom, but not in real life. Okay, sometimes it was funny!

The cigarettes were tough for me, a non-smoker, to be around. I finally had to send him outdoors to smoke because my condo was small and I could barely breathe. Cigars, which he loved and smoked often as well, he definitely had to take outside. When we moved, he'd smoke in a room by a window or in his office on the other side of the house, which he kept shut. It would be so thick with smoke, you'd open the door and couldn't see across the room! Of course the air-conditioning unit would allow the smoke to infiltrate the rest of the house. It was a real problem but at least he wasn't drinking anymore.

He said having a smoke and drinking something went hand in hand, so he'd spend considerable time at cafes doing both, sitting there doing crossword puzzles to wile away the time. He spent about as much time in cafes as he had in bars with the alcohol. Inevitably someone would recognize him or he'd run into someone he knew and it turned into a social outing for him, which he liked.

David went to a handful of AA meetings at the most, to please his sponsor and to celebrate his year anniversaries where they present a cake at the meeting. David's main beef was that people would approach him to pitch a project, ask for autographs or ask him to read their scripts. It never happened. People were very respectful, but nevertheless, he never wanted to go and offered one excuse after another. David said he didn't *need* to go.

Besides, David didn't even think of himself as an alcoholic.

At one AA meeting in Malibu, David told the high content of celebrity and powerhouse attendees that packed the room that he didn't go to meetings and was there for his "birthday cake" that night. A large wave of hisses and boos showed David the audience disapproved of his being glib and arrogant. His sponsor and I were on stage with David, and we looked at each other, wondering if we should make a quick getaway out the back before the mob overtook us! It wasn't quite the thing to say to avid AA goers, especially in a gathering with so many industry people. David's speech did not win him points, let's put it that way. But then, David rarely wanted to do anything in a conventional way and there was that naive honest quality that came through. He quite often spoke before considering the consequences. I remember wondering how was I going to do damage control on this debacle. We had a laugh later at the hypothetical scenario of explaining he didn't know what he was saying—he was drunk!

* * *

Our home in Valley Vista was our new sanctuary. I did my best to keep it that way. David liked the fact that I kept the "riff raff" away, the "hangers-on," acquaintances he didn't want to say no to because he didn't like confrontations. He told me he didn't like all the people hanging around their ranch house night and day doing whatever, including recreational drugs. Valley Vista was truly a clean, fresh start and it felt good to him. It certainly was very different from his past. The fact that David felt he was compromising by not being able to drink sometimes made him irritable. He wanted to feel he could down one or two when he wanted, and then stop. He didn't want to feel the fear of not being *able* to stop. David did not like to compromise. He was self centered—centered around one's self. Always.

He would often get frustrated because his career wasn't progressing as fast as he wanted and lament, "What's the point of staying sober?"

He was on the good and narrow, unfamiliar territory, and needed constant encouragement, which I happily supplied. When he'd have a low day, he thought all the work, the jobs were for nothing. He was tired of waiting for the big break the clairvoyants said would happen. He couldn't see the forest for the trees. I reminded him we were taking one step at a time and it was building up slowly but definitely building. And it was. He was getting recognition and respect from the networks, directors, executives, who were putting him back on their "lists" again for prime projects. But he was blind to this. *The big break* hadn't come yet and he was losing faith. Our love, he told me, was what kept him sticking with it.

"Nothing else seemed to matter," he said.

But I still sometimes found myself walking on tiptoes, afraid something might set him off into a rage or to drinking again. I attended a few Alanon meetings, but not until after we were married and were having more problems. It strengthened my resolve that I didn't want to spend the rest of my life catering to and dancing around someone who was putting less and less effort into the relationship or his career. Something had to change. I tried changing my attitude, but David continued to drop everything into my lap. I couldn't bear to hear more people get up and tell the gathering that they spent the last sixteen years of their life making sure their partners did this or that, or how they gave up something important because their drinking partners went off the wagon or . . . or . . . or . . . I went home screaming in the car. I felt so stuck.

Shortly after moving into the Valley Vista house, David got a computer and found a new passion in computer art, which occupied a considerable amount of positive creative time. I kept all of his artwork he gave me, even our wedding program, doodles, cards and notes—romantic, erotic, poignant—most are signed, personally noted and titled. His gestures and expressions of love through his art melted my heart, even to this day. They are what he couldn't verbally express. He was constantly encouraging me, "Blackie, find time for your art. You should start selling your work again." I still feel him around me when I sit at my design desk to work on a sculpture, jewelry or painting.

But some of his habits and attitudes were still difficult to deal with. His sponsor and other AAers said it was "dry drunk" syndrome. It happened to people who have gone sober but have not made any internal or emotional changes, or have returned to chaotic and unrealistic thinking. Boy, did that sound familiar. I waited for David to get sober, hoping certain things would change, but they didn't. Then I waited for the dry drunk syndrome to pass, but no one could tell me when it might, or *if* it would at all.

I kept hoping beyond belief and faith that if he got sober and got through the dry drunk syndrome that he would get help with the "secret," and we could overcome the damage and move forward in a constructive and healthier way. But he didn't. Day to day I was left with the constant reminder and the question of how long I could deal with this? With someone who refused to step up to the plate and be responsible. Someone who wouldn't help the other person and change the matrix of the damage. If he had been anyone else, I wouldn't have had anything to do with him. I didn't with my uncle, so why was I allowing this now? It was a constant inner battle I dealt with. I was hoping David would—could—change. Ultimately, I found that a nature is a nature and certain things just do not change.

One of the positive things David did do was read the AA twelve-step book and he did refer to it occasionally. David had always held to the philosophy of keep your friends close, but your enemies closer. Now it was time to make amends. At a time when he needed all the friends in the business he could get, David was reaching out. His original motivations aside, he felt really good about letting go a lot of harbored feelings and repairing damaged friendships.

One person David tried to make amends with was writer-producer Larry Cohen, whom he knew since his army days and had worked with on the movie Q. Cohen, who also attended our wedding, related to me that years after our divorce, he saw David drinking at a bar in the Sportsman Lodge. At that time David was nice and friendly, but the last time Cohen saw him, in 2008 at a screening of *Defiance* at Paramount Studios with brother Bobby, David was like Jekyll and Hyde—mean, rude, just the opposite of when they last encountered each other. When Cohen asked David about the attitude change, David responded with something like, "Times have changed" and walked off. From the way Cohen sounded, it must have been very disappointing. I felt badly for him and at the same time I could identify with that disappointment. My last conversation with David that same year, 2008, was similar.

* * *

We were invited to a fundraiser in Tucson, Arizona to benefit Ronald McDonald House, which we jumped at because we were active in anything to do with children and animals. As usual, David brought his guitar to keep himself entertained if he got bored. There were various celebrity activities going on, like a tennis match, which David did not want to do. On occasion, he did a golf benefit, but golf was not his forte and he didn't want to look inept. So we did some schmoozing at the lunch and realized that none of the celebrities were going to the hospital to visit the children and none of the children were at the event. I asked one of the reps to take us over to the facility. David packed up his guitar and I grabbed a bag of whoopee whistles for the kids and off we went.

There were a dozen or so children and nurses gathered in a recreation room. David entertained everyone for about half an hour and I handed out the whistles. It was magic seeing how these kids lit up hearing David play. Afterward, we were taken to the rooms of some who were too ill to attend the gathering. David and I talked to the kids, told jokes and sang a bit. The staff said it made their week. After we left each room, you could hear the whoopee whistles going off like they were talking to each other. One nurse told me it was perfect for one patient who they had a hard time motivating to do lung exercises but by getting involved with blowing on the whistle, they were getting the job done. The nurse jokingly rolled her eyes and said, "Now if it could just have a mute button on the whistle. We're going to hear it all day long!"

On our way back to the hotel, we were both caught up in thoughts about meeting the children. It was quite an emotional experience, especially since we were trying to get pregnant. We remained quiet for the ride.

Back at the venue, Rick Springfield was the new host for the fundraiser and the big entertainment bash was set for that evening. I said to David, "Wouldn't it be super if you played with him?"

He looked at me like I was half nuts. Well, he had his guitar!

"What, with no rehearsal?"

I first convinced him that he had his act down, since they were all his songs, and he could jam with anyone. David had this look of yearning, but he was very hesitant. "I can't ask. What if they say 'no'?"

"I just know they won't".

Off I went to talk to the entertainment co-coordinator and when he found that David could sing, had his own music *and could play with Springfield,* they were sold. Now they just needed approval from the guy himself—Springfield. We got the green light, but David started to panic. It would be the largest crowd he had played to since being sober, let alone playing with no rehearsal.

"Johnny, just do what you always do. Have fun!"

That night, he was a bundle of nerves, but as soon as he hit that stage, the nerves disappeared. He did a few songs and they wanted more. So he performed one I insisted on, *Cosmic Joke,* and had the entire audience sore from laughter. In the song he does this knee slapping laugh and it's so contagious, you just can't help but laugh and laugh some more. It was a showstopper. Then he had a hoot of a time jamming with Springfield, and the audience ate it up.

Afterward, David was glowing. He was on a natural high from it for weeks. It bolstered his confidence that he could do it—sober!

* * *

A couple of months after we separated, I was to get together with David for coffee, so we met at his storage space in Studio City. When I arrived, he was still inside and the gates were closed. And locked. He didn't get out in time and was locked inside. I had a throw-away camera in the car and took a snap of him "behind bars." I thought it was a hoot. He was tired and seemed a bit disoriented—could he be drinking?—but there was minor humor in the situation. "Yeah, okay, ha ha." I figured we should take advantage of the situation and make lemonade out of the lemon, so we agreed to try and sell the picture to the tabloids because we could use a few bucks. The picture got published and paid a whopping $150. In the meantime, it took two hours for him to figure a way to get over the fence. Good thing he didn't have Thunder with him or they'd have had to spend the night there.

* * *

About five months after we separated, I started to get many reports of "David sightings" from friends and strangers. David's return to alcohol might have been a self-imposed punishment because he did not want the divorce. There were other first-hand reports and conversations from various sources regarding his state of being and health. There was always controversy and conflicting information surrounding David.

Even though I could tell David was back to his old patterns, he'd make a point of mentioning in various interviews he was sober. Why talk about it unless there were suspicions or he was trying to do damage control? His appearance on the Sharon Osborne show was a typical example. There he sat appearing to almost nod out at one point, but talking about his sobriety. I got a half dozen calls from friends, some of who were AAers, who watched the show. They thought he couldn't possibly be sober.

I asked Tom Fishwick, that all-knowing and seeing clairvoyant from my past, why David went back to drinking after all we accomplished. And why so soon after we separated? He told me it was because David was lost and didn't know how to "reach me" anymore—he couldn't reconnect, get back together with me. His security was gone. He was in pain. Fishwick had told me years prior never to leave David. I asked him about that later. It was because Fishwick saw that if we separated, David would return to the drinking. And he reminded me that I didn't leave, David did.

Who knows? Alcohol is used widely to numb feelings and from David's emails and our phone conversations, I believe that's what he was doing, along with other methods of "indulgement." I think he lost himself in the process, couldn't find his way back to *himself* and sold out . . . compromised. He told me he didn't want or plan to get stuck in another relationship. He didn't like confrontation, so I guess he just gave up. Holiday time in 2001, he expressed to me that he didn't know how to get out. I thought maybe the brothers would help with an escape plan, but that never came about. David couldn't have been happy. If he was, I think he wouldn't have started drinking again and doing goodness knows what else, including battling me in court. But then again, I felt he had other people telling him lies, and instead of believing the one person who proved over and over that he could trust— me—he chose to trust people who had other agendas. People who were not looking out for him, but for their own interests, and attempting to make David lose his love for me.

Some reports said David looked and acted sober, yet others said although he didn't appear drunk, "something" was "off" about his behavior. Looking back now, he was probably using pills or some other "feel good" substance. Word gets around the industry quickly and he was openly seen drinking after a while. I knew too well how he could pace himself for an important meeting and appear "fine," but half an hour later be three sheets to the wind.

In 2002, I attended a screening for the movie *Monte Walsh*, produced by friend Michael Brandman, starring Tom Selleck along with David's brothers Keith and Robert. David was there, and thinner. His cheeks were sunken and he looked frail and old. Not only did he appear to be looped, as he was standing in front of the bar, but his speech didn't sound right either. When he gave me an ultra friendly hello, he brushed his hand against my breast, copping an ever so subtle feel. He had been living with his girlfriend for some time and here he was making a pass at me. When I hugged him back, he swayed to the side so much I thought he was going to fall over if I didn't hold him in my embrace. He felt as light as a feather. Like if I puffed on him, he'd blow away. I could definitely smell alcohol on his breath as I moved close to his face to hear him over the din of the room. This verified the reports I was hearing that he indeed had started drinking again.

As soon as I called over my date, Randall, David's smile turned to a sullen frown and his attitude immediately dampened. I could see him clench his jaw too. Randall England, a ruggedly handsome Oklahomian actor-producer, was someone we had met before, when we were married, and I knew David felt insecure about him. David excused himself and moved further into the party although I caught glimpses of him keeping an eye on me.

* * *

A mutual friend recounted how later in the year 2000, at a dinner party, the hostess walked into the kitchen as David, apparently, seemed like he was just about to take a sniff off a wine bottle. It wasn't clear exactly what he was doing, but he put the bottle down and appeared embarrassed. Being a considerable wine connoisseur, I'm sure he was sussing out what he was missing. He'd done that before. Kind of challenging himself. Daring himself to take a deep inhalation of the fumes, but not drink the drink. It sounded this time he was on the edge of temptation, but didn't give in, as there wasn't a hint of any alcohol on his breath that night.

After *Kill Bill*, his list of work was long but for the most part straight-to-video types of projects. On one actress's website, I viewed a scene of her and David from a film they did together. She looked young enough to be his granddaughter. My friend who sent me the link and I myself found it to be revolting and sad, because I could tell he was under the influence. I felt after such a success as *Kill Bill* was, certain choices were not good career moves and he must have taken the project for the money. I couldn't believe he did a commercial for a phone directory either. They must have offered a pretty penny for him to want to do it.

David considered himself manic-depressive. I wasn't too sure about that, but he did have consistent mood swings. He went from happy to morose within an hour, but he was never suicidal, and never talked about the subject in regards to himself. Could an occasional pill pop affect someone like that?

Some family members and a close family friend related to me that there were a couple of occasions when David hid out at a center in Hollywood to supposedly get sober. Perhaps not because he wanted to, but because it was more or less demanded of him. The attempts evidently didn't last long. An ex-boyfriend of mine saw him at Birds restaurant bar, which is across the street from the center, ordering a few shots of hefty alcoholic beverages.

I ran into another longtime friend of David's, Roger, who attended AFM (American Film Market) with him. He related that David was actually in the next room at the bar putting away a few vodkas. Roger actually grabbed one of the drinks and had it in his hand to show me. Yes, I took a sniff. Vodka. I was tempted, but didn't go running in to see David. I sat there shaking inside. The wounds still felt fresh, even though it had been many years. After Roger left the table, I eventually did check out the bar, but David had left.

* * *

In the car one day on my way to an appointment, I turned on the radio to hear David in an interview. He sounded like he had been drinking and when asked how long he was married to his current wife, he said six years. They weren't even together four years, let alone six, at that point. We were together for six! Ooooops!

In a 2006 edition of the *Toronto Star*, published when David was filming the feature *Camille*, the columnist detailed David's drinking Absinthe in an article titled *Cowboy Bob*.

Theory is: secrets are toxic. Booze and drugs—they are an easy road to deter a person from dealing with the truth . . . away from the pain or fear of reality. Jane Velez-Mitchell in a television interview said something profound: that honesty is a process, not an event. I highly agree.

To be truly honest with yourself, sobriety is needed in order to see things clearly. David got close. He was on the verge of his personal breakthrough, but chose the "easy" road again. He didn't want to come clean with the "secret" and stayed toxic, and that carried over into other areas of our relationship. When you take a hard look at it . . . was it really the easier road? Some people prefer to stay happy in their misery.

Deep down, I believed he felt unworthy and attracted that kind of situation and people to himself, which I tried to fend off for six years. I was burned out from it all, but still fought to maintain our marriage. It was a very sad thing to watch him succumb to negative influences all over again.

Our time together was, I believe, the first time in his life he really gave it his all, in the capacity that he had, but it was too much for him. The part of David I fell in love with—Johnny—was the potential I saw in David. Tears well up in my eyes when I think of how much he must have loved me to try to continue to be the Johnny I fell in love with—the side of him that was moral, ethical and loving. But the "David" in him thought that was taking away his edge, interfering in his acting progress. The resentments of his childhood, of feeling abandoned, the non-trust, took over and wouldn't allow the Johnny in him to continue. Once we got married, he stopped trying for the most part. He knew I was "in" and then started to turn more and more toward the "David" direction. He sank back into his old beliefs, patterns, allowed the riffraff back in . . . the sycophants, the leeches who kow-towed and weren't honest with him, along with the alcohol and other "comfort" habits.

Other rumors and stories about David drinking continued to circulate, even up until his death. One in particular had him visiting local "cat-houses" while filming a television show in South America. Some stories stay rumors because people in the industry are afraid to talk "bad" about anyone. Maybe if more people let the cat out of the bag, so to speak, it would be more difficult for others to enable the person with the problem, and that person would be forced to get help.

And so the stories continued.

Chapter Eighteen

WHISTLE WHILE HE WORKED

Each project David did, whether it was a television show, movie, voice-over, on location or in town, carried its own unique adventure and story. I vicariously enjoyed David's happiness in working and was as thrilled as he was, even though he didn't show it often, each time he booked.

David's life seemed to parallel his previous series—seeking happiness. Unless he was working, he wasn't truly fulfilled. When he was working, unless something went wrong with the production, David was on cloud nine. It was hard to shake him off that cloud. It wasn't work for him, it was life, his oxygen, his being—to be in front of an audience or a camera. It's what he lived for.

I asked David once what he did to prep for a role, any role, since in all the time together I never once saw him do anything. Not even run lines. He said he didn't do any prep. For *Bound for Glory*—maybe he listened to the music or watched footage, but even in that role, he didn't try to "act" like Woodie Guthrie, he just absorbed the essence of the character or person.

He always kept a small stack of the book *Acting: The First Six Lessons* by Richard Boleslavsky, handy in his office. He'd give them out if he felt a particular person was worth bestowing one of his "secrets of the trade" on. He gave me one of his personal copies—the 27th printing with water stains, tattered cover and all. Originally issued in 1933, it's a very small, but powerful book. That was his mini "bible."

* * *

David didn't bother to study his lines the night before. He'd take a look at the schedule of scenes that were to be shot and scan the "sides." That was it until the next day, when he'd take another look at it in his trailer or make-up room. He had a type of photographic memory. It wasn't much different when he was drinking either. Only occasionally did he need a few "cue cards" when filming *King Fu: The Legend Continues* if there was heavy dialogue. As amazing as this ability was, after seeing so much of his work and knowing what went on behind the scenes, I could tell by his phrasing and eyeline—where an actor looks—or other body language if he was trying to remember the lines in front of the lens. There was a speech pattern he'd get into or he would make a facial expression. By the time they came in for his close-up, however, he pretty much got a grab on the lines, but most of the time I could tell when he was grasping.

* * *

I wanted to get back into an acting class and throughout the years since the '70s, Milton Katselas' name was one that kept popping up as one of the key coaches to take classes from. David not only thought it was a great idea, but knew Milton.

I called the Beverly Hills Playhouse to get an appointment for an interview. Yes, you had to interview in order to get into his class. The instant I walked through the office door and had to fill out paperwork, I had the gut feeling that the woman who scrutinized my resume was going to be my road block. After about an hour of conversation, she told me there was a waiting list of at least a year to get into Milton's Saturday Master Class and, regardless, I'd have to start off with one of the other teachers and classes.

When I told David what happened, he thought it was "bullshit." The next day, he put in a call to Milton and by that evening, after their half hour conversation, he put me on the phone with the man. He had gone over my resume from the office and didn't see any reason why I shouldn't be in his class. I was in.

The next Saturday, I was there at 9:30 a.m. for the four hours, and every Saturday for the next year and a half.

The Master Class was full of casting directors, directors, producers, name actors and actresses. I got a kick how, when Milton arrived each Saturday, the entire room would stand and applaud his entrance. Now that's admiration. Oh yes, David joined too. He thought Milton held the key to unlocking his talent and moving forward with his career. Again, David's lack of confidence in his talent was getting in the way. Milton didn't have the key to unlocking it for David. David held the key the whole time himself.

* * *

During our six years and his sobriety, he was alert and had a new snappy energy in himself and in his approach to his work. It showed in his performances. We made special effort to choose roles that were as far from Kwai Chang Caine as we could get. He wanted to set all of that aside and distance himself from the character. He was extremely shy, insecure about not only his talent, but physical attractiveness. Being sober, his "point of reference" he'd judge himself with was new, and made him feel apprehensive. David constantly asked my opinion and re-assurance about his performances.

Other problems in our relationship also contributed to turning my energy back around to what I needed to do for myself, like my acting career. I began to push for small roles in various indies as well as in ones David had been cast in. Production cast me by either audition or viewing my demo. My producer, director, and casting friends who had worked with me before cast me in other projects.

David liked to brag about me after I got a role, because he thought I did a good job, but with the exception of a few films where his brothers Robert and Mike Bowen pushed for me, David didn't *voluntarily* do much to help with my acting career. And even then, I still proved myself. Occasionally he'd help me with taped auditions for Canada by reading off camera or even directing a couple, but it got to a point where he was taking too much control and we'd bicker, so I stopped asking him to participate. As proud as he was of my work, David didn't like the fact that he wasn't getting 200% of my time anymore. His resentments began to grow and overlap into other areas of our life.

* * *

Whether it was David being generous, naïve or self-sabotaging, he'd sometimes push for other actors on a movie instead of himself. Maybe because he was so anxious to make people think he was a good-guy, I don't know. All I know is it nixed several chances for work when we desperately needed the money.

There was one big-budget fiction film, for which David was in a meeting with a room full of producers and the director. I waited out in the hall with my ear to the door and heard David pitching William Shatner for it! He went on about how he worked together with Bill, directing one of the *Kung Fu* episodes and barely talked about himself.

After the meeting was over, he walked out into the hall and said, "Well, I don't think I got that one."

No sh—t, Sherlock!

I didn't plan nor did I want to stay his assistant, manager, secretary, PR rep, gofer, agent or publicity person. I just wanted to be his love and continue with my own creative pursuits in art, writing and acting. I had the background to handle it all for David, years of production and administrative work to fill in between the acting. I've done a bit of just about everything in the business from teaching, writing, PR, publicity, make-up, wardrobe to producing. I was one of the youngest producers to join the TV Academy—in 1976. I knew what had to be done and how to get it done for David. It was part instinct, how to guide people. David knew and trusted that.

We tried to get other agents or managers, but it was very difficult. In the beginning, we couldn't find anyone that would take him on until he started booking by way of our own efforts first. The larger agencies kept saying "no." His damaged reputation preceded him. Others lasted a short time.

For the first two months we were back in L.A. from Toronto, in 1996, we'd go over the breakdown service, an online service where agents and managers see what's being cast and where to submit their various clients for roles. Each day we'd go over page after page, checking to see who each of us knew, to try and get interviews and auditions. Finally, it started to pay off. Sidney Furie was directing a film called *The Rage.* David lit up. "I know Sidney."

I immediately called casting as David's manager and arranged a meeting. In the room with Furie, David insisted on auditioning. He held to this approach and attitude throughout our years together. David would chuckle "Hey, since this may be the only chance I get to play the role, I want to give it a shot!" It took the sting and any embarrassment out of anyone asking that he read for them. People respected him for that.

He also wanted to prove to Furie he was "okay." We were ecstatic when David landed the role. It took him out of town on location and there wasn't any budget for me, so I had to stay behind. It was agony for both of us. The gig also didn't pay what David was accustomed to, but it's not like he was in a position to bargain. The film was food, rent and moving money, as well as the start of the career snowball. He also had a good time working with Furie. It brought hope back to David.

It wasn't until after I started booking David on a few projects that agencies gave him a try, but that eventually fell by the wayside. It was one problem or another. We were shocked at how little some people knew, not only about the business and negotiating, but about how to rep an actor properly.

I called my own agent in New York, Marv Josephson, asking if he'd be interested in repping David for East Coast territory. After a long talk about David going sober, he agreed to take him on. He was, after all, a fan. When we made a trip to NY for them to meet, Marv pushed hard and got us many meetings, including one with heavy-duty casting director Georgianne Walken.

A couple of other agents in L.A. almost lost David jobs we actually brought to the table, specifically one that Keith pulled David in on, *Last Stand at Saber River*—which coincidentally reunited me with its executive producer, Michael Brandman, whom I knew from when we both worked at Lorimar.

The deal was already set between David and production, yet the agent tried to override it in order to jack up the price. We had to do damage control to make sure David wouldn't lose the role. That was one agent he did not want to pay commission to. And he didn't.

* * *

To further restore David's reputation as an actor who could be depended upon, and get the word out that he was sober, we used letters from producers he recently worked with as recommendations. It helped to a degree. David had ideal "pipes" for voice-overs, and he was eager to get that going. Even before we moved back to L.A., I connected him with a voice-over agent friend, and with the professional recording studio David had in the living room, we recorded some auditions, and David created his own Taco Bell song to include in the audition. He didn't get the Taco Bell, but it did put him in the running for other commercials, which he booked within weeks.

The sexy leading man image was next on the to do list. We got Alan Weisman to take some great shots of David. I did his hair, make-up, wardrobe styling and was emphatic about him posing with the jacket unbuttoned, showing off his now toned physique —that is, when I reminded him to stand up straight and tighten his abs.

"Like this?" as he took a stance and started to chuckle, being self-conscious.

"Yeah! That's it! God, Johnny, you should see how sexy you look."

He got that big ear-to-ear grin on his face and Weisman clicked away capturing it all. We got the shots! It was probably one of the sexiest pictures David ever had taken. He said he never thought of himself as sexy or good-looking for that matter, so he gained new confidence in himself by seeing the results of the picture. It created new perspective for casting and got David consideration for other types of roles.

"Wow, he looks great!"

The change in his career continued upward.

The more work I got him, the more requests we started to get, the more there was to handle and the more I was letting my career go to the back burner. The less I had of my own to feel better about, the more I shifted to do for him. The more he didn't acknowledge the work I did get for him, the harder I'd push to get his approval, love and appreciation.

It was a vicious cycle. Did he plan it that way? Is that what happened to Gail? She was an actress, talented composer and singer. That's when I made a conscious effort to look for acting work for me, as well as David. No matter how small a role, as long as I kept working, I was happy—well, at least happier.

The one thing his resume needed more of was comedy, so I focused on the prime sitcoms and other projects. It was more of a long shot, waiting for a role to come out in the breakdowns and then submitting to casting. That was a whole other barrier to get through, so I decided to target directors, producers and writers of the shows directly.

One day I was scrutinizing the list of popular TV comedy shows in the trades and came upon a list of producers. As I scanned each name, one in particular stood out. Hmm. My instinct compelled me to call that one as my finger stopped at a name. I zeroed in and cold-called Kevin Slattery. He actually answered his extension instead of a secretary. I was shocked. Usually people get detoured by an authoritative assistant and never get a chance to talk to *the key* person. But there he was on the phone.

I pitched David for the show saying he was a major fan (he maybe watched one episode) and knew George Segal. I explained we were moving away from the Kung Fu image and were looking for something more leading man for David.

Turns out Slattery was a fan of David's, liked the idea and said he'd find a spot for him. Jackpot! I kept in touch with Slattery for a number of weeks, nudging ever so lightly, "just saying 'hi,' " and he finally came through with a role—an episode with Jenny McCarthy guesting! David was the "special guest."

I could tell David was delighted by the way he called his friends and told them about how *he* booked the sitcom, as if it came to him with no effort from anyone, but he never expressed appreciation directly to me. No thanks. No "good job." No hug. No . . . nothing.

"You need constant validation?" he'd bark.

It was a typical response. What's wrong with *some* validation? I still kept hoping that would change. It was like waiting for Godot.

* * *

One show, *Family Law*, had an ensemble cast that included stars Tony Danza and Christopher McDonald. I saw in the breakdowns what would be just the ticket for David. A wonderful role as Andrew Weller, the mentally challenged brother of McDonald's character, Season 2, episodes 5, 6, and 7.

David's agent wasn't able to get David in via casting and gave up trying. I wasn't about to let this one slide. Getting this role would be a big break for David. Researching the production, I discovered that one of the producers was my friend Mark Harris. We had just worked with Harris on his film, *Kiss of a Stranger*. I put in a call to Mark, who agreed David would be good for the role and said he'd put a call in to the other producers. In the meantime, I sent over the "arsenal"—finding and making video copies of recent footage, updates on recent projects, new pictures and so on to pitch David, which took hours to put together. The report back was they liked the idea but Fred Gerber wanted to meet with David face to face, which we immediately arranged.

David was nervous about the meeting, which took place at the production office on the MGM lot, now Sony Studios. We sat across from Gerber at his desk while the two of them made small talk. I could see Gerber honing in on David, sussing him out. Without much ado, Gerber said, "I'm going to be frank with you, David." He was upfront in telling us the reason for the meeting was to make sure, to physically see for himself, that David was sober. I thanked him for his honesty and we were glad he took the time to meet with David.

Right then and there he said, "Okay, David, you got the role."

That was it. David got it! We all shook hands and walked out of the office. This was a turning point. It was a break we were hoping for—special guest star billing in a three-parter! It was something major to capitalize on with publicity and more work.

Strolling down the lot between the famed soundstages, David was stone-faced. I stopped our stride and faced him. "Aren't you even the slightest happy about this?"

"Of course."

"Why aren't you smiling?" I said sweetly, making a funny face. "It would be so nice to see you smile. And you know what would make my week? Hearing you say 'thank youuuuuu Blackie.' I puckered my mouth and made another funny face. He started to smile and blush. "C'mon Johnny."

He started chuckling, imitating me. "Thank youuuuuu, Blackie."

I beamed back, "You're welcome. Johnny."

We continued our walk to the next building where friend and producer

Bob Christianson, who cast him in *Lost Treasure of Dos Santos,* had an office. For the next half hour, David bragged how he just snared his prime role on the show with no mention of my unrelenting efforts.

* * *

David asked me to put in a call to Stacy Keach because it had been a long time since they had communicated. Their friendship went back before they filmed *The Long Riders* together with their other brothers: James, Keith and Bobby. In David's phone book, there were listings for both Stacy and his brother James, but I accidentally punched up the wrong number and found I had called James instead. I couldn't say "Oh, thought I was calling Stacy, so 'bye.' " By that time, David had picked up the other line and engaged in an unintended conversation. By the end of the call, David and I considered it fate. Regardless of James suggesting David work with him and his wife on their TV series, David was genuinely glad to reconnect with him, show or no show.

James and his wife, actress Jane Seymour, were in production with her television drama *Dr. Quinn, Medicine Woman* so they brought David in to guest star on one of the episodes. Their friendship deepened again for David and led to bringing him in for one of the leads to film *The New Swiss Family Robinson* in Puerto Rico, starring the couple. Aside from Jane getting seriously ill from swallowing swamp water, the shoot went well for David. We were all very concerned about her. Production arranged a special visit with the orangutans they used on the film as well as a chance to tour the city. Jane couldn't have been nicer to me. Very open, supportive and, unlike a lot of women, especially in the entertainment industry, she was not "catty." We all went into town to visit the home and studio of a local artist who did amazing work. Jane purchased a painting. We wished we had the room for one.

* * *

Director Jean-Marie Pallardy contacted David to do a film—*Le Doneur, The Doner*—on location in Turkey. The handsome male lead, Pierre DuLat, was to play opposite David. The director was also still looking for a female to play DuLat's wife. When we met with Pallardy for the film, he thought I'd be right for the part and after viewing my demo, he cast me in the co-leading role.

The flight to Turkey was a long one with a stop in Istanbul. People were suddenly being escorted outside from the terminal. A security guard who looked more bored than worried told us it was yet another bomb scare and we were ushered outside with no particular rush. After about a half-hour delay, everyone was let back inside and we were able to board our plane.

It was incredibly hot at the resort where they filmed the production. Sweltering was more like it. By eleven o'clock in the morning it was already 120 degrees. So we had to film from about six in the morning until eleven, and then again after four in the afternoon into the evening. It was a beautiful location and one of the producer's sons took me into town to a bazaar where I bought some beautiful plates and other trinkets. We jet skied and got a chance to see a bit of the area, which was quite a contrast to the ritzy resort. Desolate looking shacks for homes, barren land, and yet ten minutes away, beautiful beaches and scenery.

They created their own buzz in their newspapers by publishing the rumor that David was having an affair with the producer's girlfriend, who had a role in the film. It was funny to see a picture of all of us, like in the tabloids here, except the article was in Turkish. Every day there was something new in their newspapers on David.

Working in that type of heat was difficult on everyone, but experiencing the authentic food and drink, including Turkish tea and coffee, was what David and I really got into. Nevertheless, the production dragged on and even though we both loved working with Pallardy and DuLat, because of the heat we were both getting very impatient about the delays. The hotel wasn't supposed to charge us for phone calls, but did and we had a huge tab to pay. There were other complications and aggravations and we could hardly wait to come back home.

We were so anxious to get out of Turkey we changed our flight to an earlier one. On the way back, it was even more frightening. In the shuffle at the airport, security decided to inspect not only our luggage, but us. David and I were escorted over to the side, away from all the other people, and not only had to turn over our passports, but were separated from each other while we were questioned and frisked.

As they led David away, we looked at each other like maybe it would be the last time. My palms were clammy and my heart was beating hard the whole time. I was so scared that someone might have planted something on me or David. Worse than that, what if David took it upon himself to do something stupid and had something in his baggage?!

It occurred to both of us that this could end up being one of those horror stories of how people disappear and end up in a "midnight express" experience, never to see the U.S. or each other again!

After they were satisfied we didn't have a bomb or drugs, we were reunited and given our documents back. We couldn't wait to get our hands on each other again. We clung to each other like little kids who just woke up from a nightmare. Even as the plane taxied out, we were still clinging on to each other, afraid something still might happen. Not until we landed on American soil did we breathe a sigh of relief. That was probably the only time I can say David was actually paranoid.

They decided to shoot another scene for the movie with Karen Black playing my mother, but it was slated at the time I lost a pregnancy. I was incredibly depressed and beyond anything I could deal with at that point so they filmed without me. Actually I didn't even take the call. I asked David to deal with it for me. I couldn't talk to anyone for a couple of weeks. David didn't understand how I could turn down the money. He also didn't know how to verbally console me either, so he made a beautiful card showing a landscape of mountains against a multi-blue sky, and the sun with birds in flight, with encouraging words telling me to hold on—

that our love would conquer all. I thought so too.

It turned out to be a decent film, it just didn't get the distribution everyone had hoped for. We fondly referred to it as the tasty turkey we filmed in Turkey.

* * *

I saw a project in the breakdowns that sounded like the perfect showcase for David's musical talents. *American Reel* was a low-budget flick that also starred Mariel Hemingway—whom we worked with on *Kiss of A Stranger*, and British actor Michael Maloney. What it lacked in money, it made up for in the role. David's character was a struggling singer-songwriter who faces the prospect of overnight success after languishing in the music industry for twenty years and finally hits it big. David got to do his cowboy character and sing a variety of his own songs and show his comedic chops again.

Well after contracts were signed, the producer told me there were a few small roles left and asked if I'd like to play one of them. I didn't like the two female roles, but the one written for a man, the commercial director, I thought would be fun. I insisted they look at my demo first to make sure they thought it would work. He and the director did just that. They thought it was a novel idea and gave me the part. David and I had a great time working together again. Location was in Indiana with a small, but mighty crew. We were together, both acting and David was doing his music and getting paid for it all and the producers were wonderful. Life was good.

The one particular scene where David is making a credit card commercial, he drives the commercial director—me—crazy with not getting his lines right and his cell phone going off. What was especially funny and frustrating for the real director was that my character yells "action" and "cut" to the "acting crew" and the *real* crew kept thinking it was their real cue when it wasn't. It took a few takes, but all was accomplished and made a very funny scene, not to mention off camera laughs from cast and crew.

In a recent conversation with Mark Archer, the director and co-producer, he revealed that they could hardly wait until I arrived because I could stabilize David and neutralize the situation, for example, when he locked himself in the dressing room during the live concert sequence. Evidently, someone promised him they would be making a music video out of this live concert, but Archer had no knowledge of that promise. All he knew was they had an extremely tight budget and only so much film left. There certainly wasn't enough to shoot a music video and David was understandably pissed.

I was just as upset, but there was nothing we could do, so I got in there and turned David's attitude around. He wanted to do the video so badly he told me he'd pay for the extra footage until he calculated how much it would be. Besides, there was no time to run out and get the film. We'd have to deal with the producers later. The standoff would only sabotage everyone's efforts and it had nothing to do with the director. He agreed. Once he walked onstage with the lights on him, in front of the large live audience, hearing the hoots and applause, he forgot all the angst. For the moment.

I left to come back to L.A., but David still had filming to do. There was another problem and again he locked himself in his dressing room. This time, they thought David was just being a difficult ass.

What was eye-watering for me to hear, was that David told Archer I was the best thing that ever happened to him. What makes it so difficult for some people to say these things directly to the other person, where it really counts? Why is it so much easier to tell others? David had a funny way of showing it sometimes. The most treasured things in his life . . . me, Rocky, Thunder . . . he sometimes didn't cherish or treat with respect. His expression for what he loved was countered and contradicted constantly. He took the loves in his life for granted, therefore destroying them in the process. Almost like he couldn't help himself.

* * *

I was called in by producer Mark Harris to audition for *Kiss of a Stranger*, which had a long list of star names attached including Mariel Hemingway, Corbin Bernsen, Dyan Cannon. It was an excellent role, the ex-girlfriend to a drugged out musician, and I landed it. The musician hadn't been cast yet and even though David was contracted for *Family Robinson*, I suggested David for the role. Mark loved the idea. David, however, for some reason wasn't too keen on it. He wanted more money, one, and two, he would be in Puerto Rico, so logistics didn't look good. David wasn't above sliding around filming schedules in order to do two projects at once either. This was a perfect case in point.

I was bent on David doing this tour de force role, and determined to make it work. David read the script and agreed it would be worth doing, but the nightmare of getting production schedules to work was another matter. Ordinarily, one production doesn't want to let an actor out to do another role, especially if they are in a far-off location, as he would be, because of insurance purposes and possible snags like missing planes and messed up production schedules. I worked with the *Kiss* production staff back and forth for days to get it lined up.

David didn't want to tell the *Family Robinson* people what he was doing for fear they would not allow him to go, so he kept it all secret. We had to find what days they wouldn't be using David on *Family Robinson* and coordinate it with *Kiss*. Those days changed a couple of times, which put me through the roof because it meant changing airline schedules as well. I screamed at myself many times for ever thinking of this.

It was extremely stressful because the flights and plane changes were so close getting into L.A. and back out again. Everything had to go perfectly with both productions in order to make it all work. We held our breath before, during and after, until he was back in Puerto Rico. We're talking down to the hour timing. Coming back to L.A., David was up for almost twenty-four hours, yet performed flawlessly. He was running on adrenaline and the sheer happiness he felt in pulling off such a "caper."

All went well with the filming and as soon as "cut" was called on David's last scene, he was off on a flight back to Puerto Rico. Whew! That was a close one!

CHAPTER NINETEEN

$$$

Even when David had an agent, I still kept watch to protect him. If we had hired people to do what David had me doing, the price tag would have been a minimum of $15,000 a month. Publicity would have cost about $3,000 up just for very basic services; a PR specialist, $5,000 to $10,000; a personal assistant, $4,000 per month. You get the idea. The stress was monumental and we thought it the key reason why I wasn't able to get pregnant. But there was no help in sight. David kept telling me to let things go, take a break for a week or two, knowing full well it wouldn't happen. It couldn't. If I did take a break, nothing would get done—he certainly wouldn't deal with the daily routine—and therefore no work would come in, which meant no money to pay the bills. Yes, much easier said than done.

David offered me commission for my work, at a whopping fee of 5% to start, and only on work I procured for him, nothing from any residuals or other work. After the first year I gave myself a raise to 10%, because he never offered to bump it up, and finally after we were married to 15%. Again, he didn't offer it, I had to declare it. In addition, I paid my own bills, and covered personal supplies and needs from my percentage as well. I also often paid for half the groceries and other costs.

I eventually reached my limit of sacrificing myself and not having enough for my own essentials, in order for David to have enough money to deal with his enormous debt and family obligations. When he did have money, he'd squander it. The IRS wanted almost $750,000 and the State another $150,000 from the days he was with Gail. The government placed liens on David's income from his residuals and we were usually strapped for money. His accountant constantly worked to negotiate and dance around the situation, to get David out of the crisis. That bill was a hefty chunk each month as well, and we were behind in paying a lot of the time. The debt problem was ongoing, even after we separated.

I asked myself why I was scrimping so he could have more money to spend on $500 cigarette lighters—which were frequently lost or stolen because he'd leave them out in the open with his back turned—or lend friends money to pay their phone bills or their rent when we didn't have enough money to pay our own. He knew they had no intention of paying him back. They never did in the past when he "loaned" them money.

It was laughable when David would say, "Half of what's mine is yours." The money would go through his accountant and out to whatever debts there were, and there was barely anything left. It would disappear so quickly there wasn't any half to get. If I didn't demand my percentage, there wouldn't be anything left over for me. When money did flow in, and we had spending money, he would splurge on expensive gifts. David had a disproportionate budget sense and would commit to large expenses before any money came in to fund such endeavors.

He took out a loan from me in order to spend $15,000 to buy his youngest daughter an SUV when he could have spent half that on a different car. Instead of her going to public college near home, $30,000 went to sending her to a private school for one year out of state. Why? He didn't say it was because he loved his daughter and wanted the best for her, but "Because she's a Carradine. A Carradine can't be driving just any car!" Ego trip? Yes. But deep down that was also his way of saying he loved her.

Yet he didn't invest in education for his oldest daughter or grandchildren, or help his son out in any way that I was aware of. And I know he loved them too. It was irrational. As was the time he held on to

Calista's residual check from the series for over a month. Even though I had to keep at him to get it to her, he brought it to a friend to give to her instead. She left urgent messages that there was an apartment she needed the money for, but he never responded. Control issue? Keeping people on the string gave him more attention.

He liked to live large and was very generous and considerate, including tipping big at restaurants. He'd even leave large tips for maid service in hotels we stayed at. If it was a foreign country, he'd leave behind any leftover currency, which sometimes added up to about $30 or more. That was grocery money for us, but he'd insist. David was impulsive and would avoid paying off his debts whenever possible. I was brought up in a very frugal family and wasn't used to that logic, or living in that type of financial insecurity.

There was a certain pattern to his business method. The strategy was basically when he built up a bill, people were afraid to tick him off or do a bad job because then he wouldn't want to pay them. So he consistently kept behind on payments and gave dribs and drabs to string people along. They would consistently work even harder because the debt to them was more and more and they had more at stake, more to lose if they quit or got him upset. He'd usually keep the relationship very sweet so people would feel guilty even thinking about suing him. This way he kept total control over everyone and in some cases caused one person to be pitted against the other in competition for his money. He handed out a bone here and there.

If we debated where money was to be spent, and I was adamant in not approving something, David would go behind my back and devise creative ways of getting his way.

Typical example is when his youngest daughter chipped a front tooth. Instead of getting that one tooth capped or veneered, David took her to a dentist to have several front veneers done. We didn't have the money to cover such a thing so it wasn't to be done. Or so he told me. I needed cosmetic dental work too, but didn't have enough from my own earnings or that kind of money in our joint budget to spend on me, so it created a type of competition between his daughter and myself.

After we separated, I needed a crown redone and was told by my dentist there was no more money available in my dental insurance policy. *Huh?* Other than getting my teeth cleaned, I hadn't gone to the dentist for anything else. When the insurance company was called, we found out what had happened. David evidently made an arrangement with a dentist to do his daughter's veneers and bill the insurance for various gum procedures supposedly done to me in order to cover payment for her teeth.

* * *

For over a year, David boarded one of his favorite horses, one he'd fought for in his divorce from Gail at a ranch. He stopped making the payments and ended up giving the horse to the rancher as trade for the debt. A beloved horse he never went to visit. I could see he agonized about it, but somehow he was able, as he could with people and relationships, to flip a switch and turn off the emotion. I couldn't imagine loving an animal as much as he said he did and not going to visit. Was he being cold? Or was it that it hurt him too deeply? Could it have been that he wouldn't be able to stand the pain of leaving it behind again, and start drinking? Did he have to buy that $400 Dunhill cigarette lighter when he could have put the money toward his horse in order to keep it? Why did I feel bad for the horse and not for David?

* * *

When our budget loosened enough, I started to assert myself more and insisted that a few of my bills be paid directly by David via his accountant, to which he agreed. Several weeks later I started getting late fee notices because no payments were being made. It was so upsetting to find that outside of payments for essential bills, other people got paid before me.

Even if I was the one who booked the job, the agent was getting paid before me. The bills he promised to take responsibility for were not getting priority either. I felt I should have come first.

The accountant gave me what I considered excuses and said they could only go by orders from David, since that's who hired them. Really? The person was already given "orders" by David. This carried on after we were married. I didn't know who was really the culprit—David or the accountant. I blamed David. Bottom line, he called the shots. The delay in paying me my commission and my few bills was putting my credit at risk. That was it! David and I had a huge blow out and I had to threaten a "deal breaker" —I get my money first! He seemed to have "respect" for everyone but me. Did he adhere to his promise? No. I was forced to start paying my own bills again since I wasn't going to allow anyone to ruin what I worked so hard for.

David could also benefit by taking me as a tax deduction, since agent and manager commission fees were deductible. That's a sweet deal. I often joked to friends that looking back on all the hours I put in managing his career versus the money I made, I worked for minimum wage!

It was a common occurrence that David would leave certain decisions to me but then complain about how he had to conform to those decisions. He would say I was controlling when he left the "control" up to me. He didn't want to deal with most things so he would usually pass them off on me, or others. This was another pattern that built resentment between us.

He had a habit of not reading contracts or other legal paperwork before signing them. Not with everything, but with a considerable number of contracts. Too trustful, too lazy, or stupidity? A few times he led me to think he hadn't read something, testing me to see if I'd catch certain items that needed to be amended. He'd rather let others take the reins and inform him or instruct him, like in his divorce from Gail. That always took me aback.

* * *

We were constantly trying to think of ways to get extra money. One way would be to create some project for David to star in. Back in Mississauga, he came up with a basic television show idea for him to play a priest. I reminded him about Robert Blake's show and suggested he play a judge instead. Cop shows are always "in." He loved the idea and we set about working on a series for him to star in again. An initial treatment was done but when we moved back to L.A., it took a while before we picked it up again and wrote the script.

There was a role in there for me, of course, as well as for some friends. A fabulous ensemble cast. We finalized the script after living at the Valley Vista house, but it was just one of those things where it never got to the right person. And it was still too close to his past reputation for anyone to consider him as a series lead so it got shelved. I came upon my revamp of the script and my initial treatment again this year while looking for pictures for this book. It's a fabulous vehicle for an actor of David's age. Would have launched him again in another series.

* * *

We were invited to a celebrity driven live fashion show auction at the Century Plaza Hotel and were looking forward to having a fun, inexpensive night on the town. It was a lovely gathering where all the clothes were donated and modeled by celebrities. David ran into a multitude of people he knew and he was looking fabulous. The fashion show started and David said he wanted to bid on the foxtail sweater that the model was strutting down the catwalk in. I'm an anti-fur, PETA and mega animal supporter and was appalled at his gesture. He knew how I was about animals. In spite of my "definitely not" protests, he kept bidding and won the sweater.

"It's only $450." At least it was a previously owned garment and not new, but just the same, it revolted me. What was he doing?

"Well, we can't just sit here and not bid."

Oh yes we could. We went to many such auctions and I could tell it bothered him to be one of the few name celebrities that didn't bid even once. His ego wouldn't allow it this time. Besides, he just got paid for a film and in his mind there was cash to burn. Reality was we got just enough to be flush for a change and not worry about the next month's rent.

Next down the runway walks Tippi Hedren in the most eye-catching black tulle, beaded peek-a-boo ball gown. Our engagement party was around the corner and I hadn't shopped for my dress yet, because we didn't have the money.

"Wow!" David said.   "That would look great on you, Blackie." David popped his hand up with the numbered paddle to start the bidding war. He wasn't about to let anyone get that dress. Before we knew it, "Sold!" was shouted out and the dress was declared ours for $750. A Paul-Louis Orrier for Giorgio of Beverly Hills Couture, made in Paris. Now that was a bargain. It put a smile back on my face and wore the dress for our big engagement party. The foxtail sweater? I donated it back to charity.

* * *

During the fight with Gail over their divorce settlement, the IRS put a lien on David's residuals from the *Kung Fu* series. She was to get a percentage of that money. A large check for about $26,000 slipped through from the studio and didn't get snagged by the government. David did not notify her of the "mistake." After all, he was being truthful that the IRS had a lien. Why should he tell her about this little "goof" and pay her?

That really bothered me so I called her attorney anonymously and told him about it. I actually don't remember if she ever got her money or tried to sue him, but I do know David always wondered how she found out.

* * *

In another creative maneuver to "distract" funds, David ran money through a type of trust fund or money market account in his daughter's name, who I believe was unaware of this. This kept other funds, particularly cash income, off the divorce radar because it wasn't in David's name. I found this out by accident when I overheard a conversation. It had been set up for quite some time and David never told me about it. Why not? He said he thought he did. I didn't buy that at all. I was concerned about any legal "fall out," to which he explained that if it was questioned, he'd just say it was money set aside for his daughter and not to worry since he had it all under control. In other words, it had nothing to do with me.

I thought, "Would he do that to me? Naw. I'm the one who's resurrecting his career, who's really helping him. He loves me." Laugh. Wasn't I the one who said, "Thank God I'm not married to that man!"

* * *

When it came time for to David to get paid for work, he used his past experience plus additional advice on how to, shall we say, get the best for his buck. It was easy to make arrangements with independent companies to contract on paper at a certain price, but have a side deal where he'd get cash "under the table." David initially hated doing autograph conventions because he felt like he was a has-been and more of a loser. He soon discovered the plus side to the venue since he'd rake in a few to several thousands of dollars each time, pretty much all cash. (Autograph conventions now have a higher status level than they did when David first did them. A-listers now participate.)

Sometimes he'd take a large sum of cash and stash it either on himself or in his carry-on to take back so it wouldn't go on the books. He wouldn't deposit it in the bank either, just hide it in discrete places in the house. These "creative" tactics made me very nervous because I didn't like having large amounts of money in the house and, according to David, he was always in Dutch with the IRS. There was always a risk he could tick someone off who knew about the arrangement and that person could turn on him. So after we got married, I insisted things change.

After our divorce, I had to sell my condo and moved in with my mother for a while during my recuperation time from a surgery that depleted my funds. I laughed with glee when, upon moving into my apartment, I opened a box to find a vase we had kept stashed in a back kitchen cupboard, with $2,000 in it! Now that's flower power!

* * *

During our divorce proceedings, a paper presented to my attorney stated David hadn't attended any autograph conventions during that last year in which I was to be paid commissions. Funny, I went online and found evidence to the contrary. That's when I learned the word disingenuous. Why would he do that to someone he loved? Why would he do that to a friend who helped turn his life around? It was beyond my comprehension.

* * *

When David, Bobby, and I filmed *Stray Bullet II* (aka *Dangerous Curves*) in Ireland, I blew my knee out toward the end of the shoot in an action sequence. Bobby's wife, Edie, doubled me for the last couple of scenes, in one of which I had to run into the shot. Good thing I was wearing a wig because she was blonde. It worked seamlessly and no one could tell. Problem was my knee was extremely painful and I had to be driven to the hospital. They couldn't do an MRI because they didn't have the equipment and we couldn't drive two hours into Dublin, so we had to wait and have it done when we returned to the States. Turns out I had a bucket handle meniscus tear and needed surgery. The operation was performed by one of the best knee specialists in Vail, Colorado at the Steadman-Hawkins

Clinic by Steadman himself. He couldn't repair the meniscus because too much time had elapsed and had to remove half of it.

I spent months doing rehab on the knee and it took about a year before I got enough confidence back to even think about running at full speed. David was very supportive during my surgery and healing process and I was amazed at all the attention he gave me. At the same time, I thought how sad it was I had to be injured to get that kind of attention.

When a settlement was paid out for my injury, however, David wanted half of my money. I couldn't understand or accept that. I didn't think it was right and something within me turned completely off. He did the same when I was awarded a settlement from the national breast implant class action suit. That action went on for years before I even met him and was only settled after we were together. David's true colors about money were starting to show.

* * *

We eventually took Jay Bernstein on board as personal manager for about a year. Jay was known for being *the* star maker in Hollywood, and he was looking for another celebrity to manage. I thought he could take over so I could get back to my career. However, I found myself doing everything I had been doing, and Jay was collecting his full 15% on *all projects*, not just jobs he booked for David, as my arrangement had been. That really burned my popcorn! David didn't want to negotiate, as he bonded quickly with Jay, who considered him his "co-maverick."

As eccentric as Bernstein was, he was also very supportive of me and the work I was doing. He said I reminded him of a female version of himself—thank you, I think—regarding my creativity in getting David's career going. Yes, that was a big compliment, but there were glitches in the working relationship with Jay. Aside from him getting top percent from all project income, he didn't subscribe to the typical industry breakdowns—a subscription service where agents and managers find out what's being cast in order to submit their clients. That was and is like the casting bible for submissions. David didn't care. He had me to cover that base and, besides, he said, "Jay was working his magic."

Magic? Going out to restaurants and clubs and mingling was evidently Jay's magic, still leaving me to do the grunt work for nothing, literally for no money since I got a percentage only on work I got David. I was in a way Jay's secretary. The schmoozing at the top restaurants in town was great, but c'mon guys! Magic. Yeah here's magic for ya . . . see the money from the project? See fifteen percent disappear before your very eyes and the magician doesn't move! Poof! All gone! Jay was however, a very thoughtful, loyal and sensitive person. There wasn't a lunch or dinner he didn't bring some trinket or "party favor" for everyone. I liked the man a lot, but the business side of the relationship had to be changed.

Somewhere deep inside I felt the pings that signaled falling out of love with him. It scared me. I confronted David and told him that, like Jay, I deserved my 15% from all projects. Jay booked David only one film and even that was questionable, because David was already being pushed for the role in *Swiss Family Robinson* by other top sources on the production. David took a look at all the money being paid out to Jay and decided to get out of their contract.

Did I get a raise? No. Not until after we were married. And even then I had to claim it with a contract. Why didn't I just take the money I felt I was due? Funds went to the accountant and David approved the expenditures.

* * *

Curiously, our monetary struggles drew us closer together at the same time they pushed us further apart.

David was on a conference call I set up with one of his business advisors. I was waiting to ask one more question. Before I could speak, I heard "re-think your wedding date," so I decided to listen in. The person on the other end of the phone, who spoke in an irritating voice, suggested we get married earlier in the year because it would be more beneficial for David's tax deductions. If we waited until September, the year would be almost over and he couldn't write-off as much. Businesswise, I guess it was good advice, but I didn't feel this was being sensitive to the romance of his client's relationship. Well, that's what David hired them for—business. It still bothered me though. I could picture their squinty eyes and thin smile. Even more disturbing, when the conversation ended David suggested bumping up our wedding plans. He told me in a rush of enthusiasm he didn't want to wait until Sept 8th—the anniversary of our romance—to get married and call me his bride. Why put it off? I let him know what I heard, that I knew it wasn't because he "couldn't wait," not in the way he wanted me to think.

He put me on the defensive. Well, didn't I want to help him save money for *us*?

Before we set a date, I consulted with Weiss Kelly, who had been doing my chart updates for the past twenty-five years. I remember she wasn't enthusiastic about any of the dates for the early part of that year, but February 20th was the best date out of that time frame. The downside was it meant the responsibility would fall on my shoulders. Well, wasn't I dealing with everything anyway? So to David's joy, and relief, the date was changed. I had mixed feelings. I was disappointed because the date had no special significance, but I was happy because I was that much closer to being Mrs. David Carradine, his bride.

* * *

A publication not only printed a detrimental caption about me that wasn't true, but the picture of us was printed along with other major stars, which meant it would get extreme attention to that particular section. I wanted to get on the phone with an attorney immediately, but David initially couldn't have cared less. He was lying on the living room sofa with his nose in the newspaper and didn't even look up. "So?"

So? I immediately started making calls to find a lawyer. After he realized how it was going to affect *us,* he changed his mind. When he saw the potential of what he could gain from the lawsuit, what was good for him, not me, then I had his full support. We retained Neville Johnson to represent us. An attorney with a lot of passion. One of the best in the field.

To have this printed the same year of our marriage threw me into PTSD (Post Traumatic Stress Disorder). I had the most horrific violent nightmares for years. I'd wake up yelling or crying. In the morning I'd get up totally spent. It took its toll on me—affected my energy and daily life—and us.

David realized later that it did impact our lives, but his initial reaction and lack of support flipped yet another switch inside me to "off."

* * *

There were many other instances where I felt David could have acted differently in business, including paying agent commissions, but these were ultimately his decisions. And with those decisions, being his manager, I got mixed up in the negativity as well.

David didn't like to sign contracts either, so if we booked him on a project on our own, the agent often didn't get commission unless the agent contributed to the negotiation. And of course the agent didn't like that. David pulled this off with several agents. I spoke with yet another casualty of this tactic while researching for this book. Someone who repped David after we separated. He supposedly assured the agent they would get commissions off a big project, but when residuals came in, reneged on that portion, saying he never promised such a thing.

So David shifted from one agency to another trying to find the right fit, with the list growing longer and longer. He was looking for a business relationship with a personal interest, the kind that existed with the agent he had for years when he booked the original *Kung Fu* series, who was more like a personal manager to David. Switching agencies nixed the possibility of my trying to get any number of them to represent me in my career. It burned bridges for me professionally that I believe have stayed burned to this day. Guilt by association. It singed me.

Winter of 2001, after our divorce, within weeks of David withholding commission on a cartoon voice over, I was dropped by the voice-over agent we shared. The agent related to me a phone conversation he had with a woman who was calling on David's behalf, inviting him to one of David's music events. The agent responded with something to the effect that he would not attend because of being stiffed for commissions, to which the woman supposedly pointed out, well, I was David's manager. As if I was responsible for the lack of commission to the agency? That was very upsetting to say the least and I set out to prove I had nothing to do with it, that it was David. Even though the agent said the situation didn't have anything to do with my being booted, and he acknowledged my efforts in tracking the money to try and get the commission paid, he decided to drop me from the roster anyway. Coincidence?

At the time of writing this section, out of curiosity, I tried to reach the agent for further comments, and to see if the issue was ever resolved with payment. After half a dozen messages over two weeks, he never returned my call. Do I smell something burning?

* * *

Because of the huge IRS problem, I was told David could not invest in any property—namely a house for us. Evidently his credit wasn't good enough because of past and current problems. We badly wanted to buy a house of our own.

This was the primary reason we had to figure out an alternative way to buy the Rosita house in Tarzana. In 2000, I invested my life savings of $32,000 as the down payment and my eighty-year-old mother took out the $650,000 loan in her name, she wanted us to live in a beautiful home and consider the house as ours. David promised not to default on his obligations and to make the mortgage payments. There was no other way for us to get the house at that time.

A retired singer and housewife, living on fixed income, cautious and thrifty her entire life, my mother trusted David implicitly. We hoped that eventually when the IRS lien could be lifted or paid, we could change the property over into our name, but that didn't happen during the time we were together.

In early 2001, one of David's financial advisors gave him another creative idea in order to take bigger tax deductions. David wanted me to talk my mother into signing him onto an unrecorded deed to the house. It would look as if David was part owner of the house for tax benefits, but the document wouldn't be fully recorded, and therefore not totally legal. The purpose was to write off interest from the mortgage payments on the loan as a full tax deduction.

If the IRS investigated, and my mother was caught, it would have not only landed her in deep legal trouble, like possible jail time—she was eighty-two years old at that time—but also lumbered her with fines and goodness knows what else. It would put David in legal jeopardy as well. And since I was his wife, I'd be sucked into the mess too.

He couldn't be on title, which is why my mother took out the loan to begin with, because of the lien the IRS had. There was the risk one arm of the government would catch up with the other and the house could also be taken from us, along with my life savings that was used as the down payment.

I was brow beaten by David when I refused even to talk to my mother about doing such a thing. Because of questionable business advice David was listening to from others and allowing, I first threatened, then filed for legal separation and got my own accountant, the one I had prior to David, to do my taxes separately. Since David and his advisor weren't taking "no" for a final answer, we conference-called my accountant, Kathy Roat, to discuss the matter further. Thank goodness I had Kathy supporting me for the final "No."

This incident along with the other personal problems David and I were having in the marriage sent me over the edge. I previously threatened to file for separation thinking that would scare him into making changes, but it had only a temporary effect. I knew he didn't want a divorce and thought the threat of one would shake him up. But now, I knew I had to protect myself legally from what I considered his shady dealings, and I was told by filing for separation, it would protect me. I had no intention to divorce him. I was desperate to find a solution to help save the marriage and to help me. When this situation with the house came up, I felt my entire future security was at risk. I didn't want to have anything to do with something like that. I heard the "innocent wife statute" doesn't always work when the government wants their money. According to my advisors, the only way to keep out of the fray, should something happen, would be to file for legal separation.

Coincidentally, a short time after this happened, David moved out. He said he never cared about money, but his actions told me a different story.

CHAPTER TWENTY

GOTTA HAVE A GIMMICK!

As it says in the song from *Gypsy*, in order to get applause, you have to have some kind of gimmick. In this business you really do have to have a gimmick—to get ahead as well. Especially nowadays. When David and I were working at promoting various venues for him, we didn't have the Internet. It took a lot more grunt work to get publicity and attention.

If we attended a premiere or made an appearance with the press, I made sure we did something fun, funny or romantic to catch the eye of the photographers, which gave us more of a chance of getting print or film coverage. David liked the fact that now he had a playmate who thought like him in that department. It was fun to come up with ideas and bounce them off one another for reaction.

He loved to smooch for the camera. With his new sobriety and me on his arm, we started the social rounds at press promotions, parties and fund-raisers. One of the first was the promo for *Last Stand At Saber River*. The press had all the stars for the film in attendance, but when David and I locked lips for the cameras, that's the shot they printed. From then on, we kissed in practically every photo event and the pictures usually got into the media. In Cannes and all over Europe where we traveled, the public and press ate him up with attention and adulation. Our swooping kiss on the grand steps of the Palace in Cannes made a big publicity splash a couple of years in a row. Europe loves love.

David's choice of wardrobe was important. A conversation piece in the form of a pair of Icon shoes—a brand that has the work of famous artists printed on the shoes, like Starry Night by Van Gogh or Warhol's Campbell Soup can—was a conversation piece. The Botticelli Venus De Milo necktie he wore to receive his star on the Hollywood Walk of Fame created interest for the press. His wardrobe was always a consideration before we stepped out the door. It worked.

David didn't have the usual color sense. Some men are color blind and see shades of gray. David could see colors, but differently. He described colors as being more saturated. He would see a green more in shades of red and that made for some interesting color combinations in his wardrobe. He'd usually run his choices by me to make sure he wasn't going to walk out of the house looking like a clown. He may have behaved like Bozo at times, but I certainly wasn't going to let him look like one.

* * *

Sometimes it was a giggle to see the results. Like the time we bought a "cheapo" replica of the sapphire necklace shown in the movie *Titanic*, and I wore it to a movie premiere. The caption under the ensuing picture read like I had an *expensive* duplicate!

It was still more difficult to get press on him here in the States versus Canada or Europe because, for the most part, the attitude here is more jaded and there's more competition. There weren't too many projects David was doing that the press considered prime. At least not enough to give us the attention we wanted. Especially in a heavily star-studded event, the competition for press attention is fierce. I'd often get *we're just not interested in David Carradine, the Kung Fu guy*. That just made me push and network harder.

There's only so much space available in the press and it usually went to the stars in demand unless there was an unusual gimmick or hook, or they were clients of a high-powered publicity company. I was constantly trying to create something to gain press interest and get more coverage for David. That meant capitalizing on various projects he was doing. And even then, there was only so much time in the day to delegate to such a task.

The big publicity companies had an edge on getting clients into premieres, award celebrations and other events. For a few years we just winged it on our own, as we had done in Toronto, and started crashing various venues. It worked to a great extent, but then David put on the brakes. Unless we were invited, he didn't want to go "begging." That was fine by me. It was nerve wracking worrying that we might be embarrassed by being turned away, as we were one year from the Vanity Fair Academy Awards party. That was the turning point for David. He was not going to be turned down again!

But I must say, we had a great time at the ones we did get into, like Sir Elton John's yearly Academy Award party! We merely showed up on the red carpet and walked along as if we belonged. Jay Leno was in the middle of doing an on-camera interview when David—who had been on his talk show and in various skits, and even one we did together—tapped him on the shoulder to say hello. Not missing a beat, Leno included David on the spot. David responded to one question with "No, man, we're not invited, we're crashing this party!" I couldn't believe he said that! Then again, people probably thought he was just being funny. Leno did!

We turned to walk through the door with a security guard blocking the entry, and he didn't even check the list, just let us go on in. Guess he thought since we were on camera and welcomed by Leno, we had an invite. No sooner had we stepped inside, than there stood Sir Elton John himself, who welcomed us to the celebration. Were we relieved! He couldn't have been more gracious and friendly. "Thank you for dropping by, David." Other celebrities like Sharon Stone schmoozed with us during the evening. It was glittering, dazzling, the epitome of an elite Hollywood A-list party, but David yearned to be on the actual A invite list. Even though we were inside the party, we still felt on the outside.

* * *

In the past, David had participated in many charities. Now, I made sure we got involved in new organizations and fund-raisers as well as part of the positive image campaign. However, if I didn't make the effort to set it all up, David didn't make the effort to get involved. He waited until called upon. Not that he didn't care, he was just . . . lazy, and focused on other things.

Whenever it involved donating himself, as a performer or as an artist, David thoroughly enjoyed getting into the art of it all. He came up with some fabulous designs that helped several charity auctions. Sometimes he asked me to participate, which was a joy. When it came to animals, children, battling abuse, or ecology, we put those first on our list to contribute.

Before the career revamp took hold, David was asked to contribute one of his drawings for a foundation that grants wishes for kids and adults, which he did gladly. But the drawing wasn't getting bids at the live auction, so the foundation put it on its online website auction. When it still wasn't getting bids, David felt very embarrassed, and I felt badly for him, so we had a friend start the bidding. There were only a few bites, but it did eventually sell. It put him in a funk for quite a while. However, a couple of years later he contributed again, and this time his work got snatched up quickly—no, not by one of our friends—and raised a good amount of money for the charity. This reenforced the fact that we were progressing with our goal of repairing his image.

* * *

Years prior to my relationship with David, he was rejected for membership into the Motion Picture Academy. He felt like an outsider in his own industry. A couple of years after we got together, and after a few more films were released into distribution, it was time to try again. We re-applied and he was granted membership in the Academy. David finally felt accepted and a part of his peer group. His attitude changed. He felt more confident about himself, especially when he socialized.

Still, in the usual debate of whether or not to attend a function, he'd say, "I have nothing to tell these people. There's no project I'm doing. What am I going to talk to them about?" A part of him always felt inferior and lost perspective. Once in the mix of people, he had no problem telling jokes or stories. He just needed a kick start to get through the shyness and know he was accepted.

He'd forget that most people in the biz are between jobs. "So you talk about projects you want to get done. Now you can tell them you just joined the Academy."

"Good idea."

Thing is, people automatically assumed he was always a member.

* * *

It took the Hollywood Chamber of Commerce to get David a star on the Hollywood Star Walk of Fame and considerable money. I provided the Chamber with publicity on how David was sober and was now a "good guy" and on his past major accomplishments. He wasn't known just for television, but film as well. I thought he should get two categories, but television was the media in which he became a worldwide icon.

After months of waiting, they finally gave us the nod! Yes!

Then there was the problem of how to pay for it. I co-coordinated with his fan club presidents Caroline Toye and Maria Porak, who reached out to David's fans and raised the $7,000 needed to pay for the star. The price is much higher now. We worked feverishly for months with the various fan clubs around the world. Caroline and Maria spearheaded the tasks of taking ads out in the trades and their publications, getting donations from their members, newsletters . . . they really covered the territory. Once the money was in place, we got word that David was to get his star on April

1st—yes, April Fool's Day. We got the money just in the nick of time. David's star truly came from his fans.

The placement of it was another matter. It couldn't be just anywhere. Not if we had a say in it. It wasn't like you could just request the location either. We were given a few choices where they had open spaces, but none of them seemed right. We wanted him along the main street of Hollywood Boulevard, not on some side street. David wanted to be next to a star he liked. Part of the Boulevard was undergoing reconstruction because of a sinkhole and that limited some selections. I thought the front of the Hollywood Entertainment Museum would be a prime location because of the other stars placed there, and it's a main tourist attraction, but we were told we'd have to get permission from the storeowners. There was a space right next to Stan Laurel that David drooled over. He loved Stan Laurel and did the funniest facial impression of him. This was a once in a lifetime event and I was going to make sure he got the right spot!

Because the star would be right outside selected stores, it could attract a lot of business from tourists. I took on the mission of showing the owners what changes David had made in his career and image, and convincing them that it would be a major boost to the stores' revenue to have it there. Some gave their approval right away, only a couple were hesitant. I couldn't believe it. Well, talking to them on the phone wasn't working, so I dropped by in person. David went with me to make the in-person schmooze with the Hollywood Entertainment Museum, where David had donated numerous memorabilia and we had attended many events.

It took several weeks of communication to get all the stores on board, but we got them for David's prime placement at 7021 Hollywood Blvd., next to Stan Laurel, in front of the museum, and across the street from the Hollywood Roosevelt Hotel!

The ceremony for David's star was very exciting and I had a special surprise for him that day. Tom Selleck, whom David had recently worked with on *Last Stand At Saber River*, made a speech, as did the executive producer of *Kung Fu: The Legend Continues*, Michael Sloan. About a thousand people lined up along the red carpet with the press and television cameras. People were shouting for autographs. Johnny Grant, mayor of Hollywood, declared April 1, 1997, officially David Carradine Day.

Since it was on April Fool's Day, how could I not take advantage of the publicity factor? David chose the date, which expressed his own ironic "ha ha" sense of humor, but I took it a step further. On various errands, I'd cram in secret trips to the souvenir shops along Hollywood Boulevard to find a Walk of Fame Star I could copy and turn into a life-size mock-up. I took pictures of actual "stars" along the walkway to get more authentic details for color, size, the font for the lettering, the coloring of the granite . . . While David was out of town for a few days, I scrambled to make the "Star plate" to go over the real star he was getting, so when they unveiled it, it would reveal: *Robert* Carradine!

David was disappointed when I said I wasn't feeling well and couldn't go with him on a short gig out of town. He never suspected what my plan was. It took three solid days of intense work on this art project and quite a bit of "secret service" co-ordination to make it and get it to the Chamber of Commerce in time to set up before he got back, but it was done.

When they peeled off the cover to reveal David's star, the April Fool's star for Robert Carradine showed up in all its realistic glory! April Fool's indeed. I looked closely for David's initial reaction. He was stunned. His autopilot protection system took over and I could see him clench his jaw. After the on-lookers gasped and you could hear a kerfuffle, Johnny Grant quickly unveiled the real star with David's name. I thought they'd let the fake star get a little more "air time," but I think they were afraid of what David might do since he looked to be on the verge of getting angry! This would have been a great prank for Ashton Kutcher's show *Punk'd*. When David saw *his name* revealed, he gave a big smile and laughed. Got him! The press ate it up.

Someone, somehow, walked off with the fake star, which we wanted to keep. It was very disturbing to have it stolen. All those hours put into it and we didn't have it to keep as our souvenir. Whoever grabbed it, I hope will one day return it to me!

The excitement wasn't over yet. On our way to the limo, I caught a glimpse of Gail in the crowd and a photographer next to her. David and I made a beeline for the car with a bodyguard and just as we scrambled in, an arm reached over to try and serve him with court papers. I blocked the arm and the photographer with my body so David was not on camera or legally served, and we sped off. He chose not to argue it though, and went through with the court procedure.

At the after-party at Drai's restaurant on La Cienega Boulevard, word was out as to what had happened. We believed it was part of a set up to try and sell to the tabloids. His divorce proceedings were still ongoing at that point, but to choose a key happy moment in his life to serve him papers, when there were other methods and times to do so, well . . . it did not go over well with friends, family and people in the business. David and I did not allow it to spoil his day. It added to our victory that we foiled the "enemies" efforts. There were no scandalous pictures for the tabloids on this special day. David was elated about getting his well-deserved star. He was truly happy.

* * *

The star on the Walk of Fame gave me the needed "hook" to promote him further and keep up the buzz. The campaign snowball slowly started to roll. Unless you had the budget to hire a publicity company, and even then unless you have one of the more high-powered ones behind you, it was very difficult to get any sort of article about any celebrity into magazines or the media.

We found the Hollywood Entertainment Museum had a special program going for at-risk kids on probation. Their school attendance was practically nil. The museum actually held regular conventional school classes there, and invited name people in the entertainment industry—

producers, directors and other production personnel—to come in and teach. Because of the economy, they were forced to change locations and the museum auctioned off the artifacts, including those that David donated from his series, in order to raise more funds to keep the school going. David was called upon many times to lend his support to raise more money, which he did every time they called him.

Just this year I caught up with the museum president, Phyllis Caskey, who heads up its newly named school, The Education Center For The Entertainment Arts. She told me they achieved an eighty percent success rate with the kids graduating from high school, with at least half going on to college and a good number placed in actual jobs in the industry. David's efforts helped them keep the school going. He could identify strongly with these at-risk kids because he had it rough in school and was a rebel himself. He joked that if it wasn't for his interest in the arts he might have ended up behind bars. "Hell, I did anyway!" And he'd laugh.

* * *

It was imperative to make sure he looked his best. A lot of make-up "professionals" didn't have a clue how to do his make-up right, especially on the majority of indie projects he did. They'd fill in his eyebrows too dark or use eyeliner. David had me make adjustments or simply had me do it to make sure he had the look we thought he should be projecting. This also applied to his in-person appearances.

If he was looking too pale, a bit of bronzer worked well. Even with hair implants, David still wanted more coverage so he'd use Couvre to cover the increasing balding. Instead of getting more implants done, he opted to spend money on one of his passions, cars, and bought a Crossley Hotshot. Since his teeth were permanent titanium implants he didn't have to worry about bleaching them and always had that big, bright smile.

A few other beauty tricks I used was to tint his lashes to make his eyes stand out and color weave his hair a dark ash blonde, keeping the temples his natural grey. The ash color, even when it started to fade, didn't give off that orange-red shoe polish tint that men get when they color their hair.

When we both had liposuction done, David also got his face laser resurfaced, which improved the texture of his skin greatly, but as usual, he didn't follow-up with sunscreen or other after care and the effects didn't last long. He wasn't as happy with the lipo results as I was. He wanted more of his love-handles removed, but I was very pleased with Dr. Abergel's work in getting rid of the under eye puffies with a laser and my hip side-pockets, which also improved the look of my rear. All that sitting at the desk can get you "secretary spread!"

It all added up to giving David more confidence and helping him feel as sexy inside as he looked outside.

* * *

When I heard the Bata shoe museum in Toronto was having its next major exhibit, I called and asked if they would like to have a pair of shoes David wore on the series. They were very keen on this acquisition for their prestigious museum, so we made a trip up to Toronto for the launch, where David's Capezzio dance shoes—which he wore in *Kung Fu: The Legend Continues,* were the center of attention in the news. Hard Rock Cafe, Planet Hollywood and The Hollywood Entertainment Museum were similar publicity venues that helped promote David as well for his contributions for good causes to help various charities. Shoes, jackets, flutes, pebbles—he'd always carry around a pebble in his pocket—were some of the items David liked to donate. It was a win-win for everyone.

* * *

Wherever we went, if there was a piano or a guitar, David had his hands on it. He couldn't resist seeing what make it was or how a piano sounded when he tinkled the keys. Then as if compelled by a force stronger then himself, he had to play it, and before you knew it, he had his hands on the keyboard wailing away and drawing a crowd. Not just because of who he was, but because he was darned good! Only a few times was he ever shut down, to which he'd say under his breath, "Fuck'em if they can't take a joke."

Most of the time, David would give a mini concert for the appreciative crowd and it served as an excellent attention grabber since, on location, it got David into the local papers many times. I so miss David's entertaining with his music.

* * *

One of David's brainstorms was to pitch *Playboy* on the idea of a celebrity, him, taking nude photos of their playmate, me. The idea intrigued them, but we were told they wanted us to come up with another couple as well as us. David thought of Mickey Rourke, who at the time was with Carrie Otis. I played Rourke's nurse in *Johnny Handsome,* which was directed by our mutual friend Walter Hill. I contacted their PR person, who initially took our call, but delayed for the longest time in getting back to us. Long story short, after contacting *Playboy* again, we were told that just Mickey and Carrie were going to do the photo shoot and not us. David was furious. Too bad. It was a great gimmick.

CHAPTER TWENTY-ONE

ME, MYSELF AND I

I once had a nightmare of standing in front of a large crowd with nametags and seated in metal folding chairs. On many of the tags a name was crossed out and replaced by a stickie with another name. Then the second name was crossed out and replaced with another stickie, and with another one . . . and yet another. There was a podium in front of me with a microphone that was wonky and squealed as I attempted to start my speech:

"Hi . . . uh . . . my name is (slight pause) Maa . . . uh . . . Coco . . . Coco d' . . . no, em Carradine . . . uh . . . Anderson . . . and I'm (I get a little choked up, then boldly) a nameaholic!" Proud to expel the word *Name-a-holic!!*

There's a response from the audience. "Hi Coco!" Then an awful feeling came over me and I said . . . "Wait! I'm not Coco, I'm . . . Marina! No, I Am Cindy! No! Blackie? No . . . wait Coco . . . No . . . No . . . Noooooo!" Then I bolted awake in a cold sweat.

So what's in a name, right? Shakespeare wrote: A rose by any other name would smell as sweet. Well, not really. I should have had my numerology chart done *before* changing my name, instead of after.

Since Gail had supposedly acted as David's previous manager, we felt it would be better that people didn't know he had yet another wife taking over the same job. A wife wouldn't have the same credibility as an "independent" professional would. Yet we couldn't find anyone else to take on the task. We couldn't afford to have any more doors closed to us either, and saying, "Hello, I'm David Carradine's wife and we were hoping the producers would take a meeting . . . " This wasn't going to cut it. So the character of Cindy was created, and she ran our management company. David thought I was great with my character acting work, so he knew I could pull this one off. He was all over it. Whatever it took.

To give you some picture of the set-up, at my desk I had two phones to my left. The office had two lines for incoming calls and another separate phone for outgoing. To my right was the computer, in between were mounds of papers, files, four full Rolodex files and desk paraphernalia. Behind me on a filing cabinet was the fax that also had a phone I'd use.

Sometimes, I'd be on three phones at once—on hold on one, dialing out on another and talking on the third. It was a bit dicey and schizoid at times, but I was trying to pack in as much as possible and "Cindy" added credibility to David and then some. People liked her.

Oftentimes, I'd talk to people we knew in production, but as David's manager, Cindy, and they wouldn't realize it was *me* bantering on and making the deals. To lead people to think we had a staff, I'd shout into the other room for our assistant to do something, like catch the Fed Ex guy, then answer back in yet another voice. Or put someone on hold while Cindy checked to see if David or I was available. David would sometimes add background noises and disguise his voice as an assistant.

Finally we hired someone to help, but that didn't last long. Their one assignment while we were out of town for the week was to organize our Rolodex. They didn't get beyond the letter *E*. We found evidence they were too busy copying our entire address file! At one point a friend helped out, but she fell months behind in fulfilling the number of hours of work required in lieu of paying money for renting my condo. It dragged on and I was forced to not only fire, but also evict her. We never did get anyone who could really take the reins.

We'd see people at parties and they'd comment on how helpful Cindy was or how much they liked doing business with her. On occasion, it could get pretty sticky although they never suspected. David and I would share a little secret smile and say, "Yep, she's the best" or "Yeah, don't know what

I'd do without her . . . She's like one of the family." At the same time, I'd feel a bit guilty about deceiving people, but this was survival for us. David had no guilt at all. It was all a theatrical production and he was certainly the star. We felt there was no way we could get in the door otherwise and we had to project and maintain a successful image.

Every day, I played the role of Cindy, who had an entire background. Well, she had to if people asked, and we had to stick to our script. That's what I'd create for any role I'd play. She was a fortyish blonde, green-eyed, single Brit, from Uxbridge, England. Her voice was a cross between Maggie Smith and our assistant Julie. If Cindy got excited, a bit of Hayley Mills got thrown in. For the most part, I kept her voice low and a bit on the rough side. She had a great sense of humor, was authoritative, competent and pushed the envelope for her client.

As Cindy, I could put people in their place as only the British can do so eloquently. Cindy never took meetings in person because of an overloaded schedule, but she could be seen at a distance. On a few occasions, I dressed in disguise in a short blonde wig, colored contacts, glasses, changed my make-up and wardrobe—the tailored look was best—so if I drove David somewhere, they'd see "Cindy" dropping him off. David even bought me some "Cindy clothes" for my costume changes. Our favorite was a red plaid jacket.

David was careful who he told about all this at first, and it didn't appear that his family even knew for quite some time. I guess he didn't want to spoil the illusion. Gradually, others close to us found out, but David wanted it to appear as if offers were just coming in to him on their own. Years down the line and with selected projects, I started to let Cindy slide to the side a bit and I, as me, handled the management end of things. It depended on whom, what and where.

Because I was handling just about every job, I melted into a jack-of-all-trades blob—I'm David's, pick a hat, any hat. Someone asked me what made me happy and my answer was "when David's happy." They then asked, "No, what are you doing for *yourself* that makes you happy?"

My answer was still doing something for David instead of commenting on something I did just for *myself*. A light was switched on in my head. Where did *Marina* go? I was losing my identity and not liking who I was. Where were *my* projects? I couldn't speak a sentence without having David entwined in it. It was all David. Oh, I'm picking that up for David, or, I'm surprising David with this . . . this event would be good to go to because David this and David that. And it was wonderful to a point because he was my world. But at the peak, I looked around and there wasn't anything that was . . . just for me . . . for Marina.

When we married and I took the name of Marina Carradine, my life became more difficult. There was a myriad of problems. I'd wake up in the morning in fear thinking, "What next? What are we going to have to battle today?" Instead of getting up energized and excited. Various lawsuits, all the disappointments at not getting pregnant, drama with his daughters, and being consistently mistaken for David's ex-wives did not serve me well. I felt some of these mistakes hurt me professionally, personally and financially. Somehow, I got mixed up in a tax problem David had with Gail, and my accounts were to have liens placed on them. We have different social security numbers. How could that happen? But it did. They eventually cleared things up after several months, but what a nightmare! It was always something. I kept turning to alternative counseling to get a grip, and some understanding of why. Astrology, numerology and consulting with clairvoyants helped in that quest. I found conventional psychologists were more of a band-aid and it was difficult to find one I felt comfortable with. The others involved in metaphysics offered me more of what I needed to move forward, especially in a spiritual way.

After years of mix-ups, I had had it. Changing my name to Coco d'Este in 2000, the year before our separation, would, I thought, help get *me* back. "Hey, I'll just become an entirely different person!" I stuck with the name Coco for seven years. Taking my cousin's nickname, Coco Brown, with the name of my mother's ancestor, Cardinal D'Este of Villa D'Este, put a smile back on my face. I found out later this was one of the things sexually abused people do in order to start over—give themselves a new identity. My hopes were that maybe this change might also help the marriage. If I was happier, then the marriage would get better. I was desperate, trying anything and everything possible.

David didn't like the change at all. It bothered him I was no longer using the Carradine name and he felt hurt. He wanted me to stay a Carradine, but he gradually got used to introducing me as Coco. Mostly he stuck to "this is my bride" and in our private life he still called me Blackie. The shift was good initially, but I never really adjusted to it. It always felt I was looking in on myself as a second entity.

Finally, I decided it was time to get back to the real me, a *me* I was okay with, comfortable at being in my own skin. Back it went to Marina Anderson-Carradine for a year, and then after a moving spiritual experience Christmas day 2008, where I had a vision of Lulu, I felt compelled to drop Carradine from my name in March 2009—yes, the year David passed away. It felt like a weight was lifted to get back to Marina Anderson, but I think I drove all my friends nuts in the process.

CHAPTER TWENTY-TWO

THE FANS

Aʜʜʜʜ, the fans! The fan mail kept coming, but I had less and less time, and I was the only one to take care of it. David would only occasionally read a letter if it was brought to his attention, but for the most part he had no interest in them. He did care about information getting into the fan club newsletters and the "fun" stuff and he enjoyed writing directly to the club presidents, but even that petered out and he wanted me to fill them in more and more. I barely had time to take a pee, let alone handle one more part-time job for him. Besides, he was supposed to be helping lighten my load since stress was not helping us get pregnant.

I'd also get flack when a stack of pictures was organized for him to sign. He'd put it off, saying he was too tired or not in the mood. This was one more thing I had to keep track of. When he had time, he couldn't find the pictures or they'd end up with coffee spills or cigarette burns. The fans probably wouldn't mind since they were his!

For the fan club newsletters, he'd get on the phone with the club presidents and give reports or stories, but most times, he wanted me to relay or write things for their newsletters. The feeling of being unappreciated by David further increased the resentment. I felt like a slave at times.

One day on overload I said, "If you don't deal with your fan mail, then hire someone who will. I quit." And I did.

The boxes built up and a pile of unopened mail sat in his office for months. If he saw there might be a picture he didn't have, he'd pull it and keep it for himself. A good deal of the time, people didn't send envelopes or return postage. Occasionally, a book was sent for signature, which he kept, or other materials arrived that they wanted autographed. We certainly didn't have a budget for that kind of mail response. Eventually, he got a friend who had a side business to handle it for a while. Maybe they saw it as an opportunity to get a database of fans for future sales. But at least it was being taken care of.

I felt bad since those fans helped David get that star on the Walk of Fame, but it was either I had a meltdown or turned it over to David.

Later on, he got his website going, after much prodding and pleading. "Johnny, this will help promote you. You can put pictures, announcements for your band . . . ." That piqued his interest and he decided to put more and more time into the endeavor. He went from "I don't want or need a website," to "This is really cool to have!" He quickly got into contributing stories and interviews, posting pictures and communicating with the fans. He liked that he could put out the same effort he would have with an individual fan letter, but with the new website and its maximum impact and visibility, he could reach thousands. It remained one of his pet projects. He just hated opening envelopes.

* * *

For the most part, David liked it when a fan approached him. Of course it could get annoying if we were in the middle of dinner and they wanted to carry on a lengthy conversation, but most of them had good intentions. If some overstayed their welcome, or were an annoying "show me some moves" type, David would literally end the conversation abruptly, turn away and pretend they didn't exist. Other times, David might say, "You wanna take it outside?" Or "You wanna go a few rounds?" To which the guy would meekly back down.

He often got complimentary drinks sent over, which were exchanged for coffee or a non-alcoholic drink, or the other guests at our table could enjoy the gesture.

There were some strange individuals who were referred to as "troll people." They meant well, but lived in a bit of a fantasy world where they couldn't separate David from his characters in films or TV. We had a file of "profiles" on people who sent letters obsessively or who we thought might be a security problem. It was spooky, especially when we were followed a few times. But they were no match for either of us when it came to losing them in traffic.

Sometimes a timid person approached him, wanting to make sure he was really David Carradine. "Excuse me, you're David Carradine, right?"

If David was in a mood, he would stare them down with his poker face and deep intimidating delivery, "Yeah. You got a problem with that?"

That response usually took the person totally off guard. That alone made a few back off. Others hung in there with a compliment, at which point David warmed up. He liked it when people stood up to him.

If we were in a larger building like an airport, for example, David would simply walk away, and I might say he's hard of hearing, but I'll relay your compliment to him. That scenario occurred often when David first started doing autograph conventions. He resented having to do them in the first place. These venues didn't have the status then that they do now, and he felt they were below him. Second, he was there only to make money. If there was a long line, and there usually was, he just wanted to get it over with. He'd do a cordial hello, sign a picture or pose for one—he didn't smile much with the fan, then he wanted it done. If the person wanted to chat, he'd turn his attention to the next in line.

For some it was a big let down. You could see him fall off their pedestal. That's when I couldn't help but make an excuse like, he wasn't feeling well, or use the hard of hearing line or anything else so they wouldn't walk away feeling bad. It didn't happen that often, but more than it should have.

When he realized how much money he was making in cash, however, his attitude lightened and started to enjoy the opportunity.

We were sitting outside a restaurant with my mother once when David was approached by an attractive woman who knelt down on one knee in front of him. She looked up at him, said, "I just love you," and reached for his hand to kiss it. David ate it up, of course. When she wouldn't go away, David looked at me, like "uh-oh, get me out of this." My mother, thinking the whole thing was absurd, stood up and said our table was ready and she needed David to help her inside. He hopped up and escorted her in. The woman hung around for a while waiting to see if he would come back outside.

At one venue we attended, David and I were holding hands when a woman abruptly busted in between us and shoved me out of the way in order to talk to him. Well excuuuuuuse me, lady! Ever the gentleman when it came to adoring females, even if they were rude to his mate, he took in the attention. I had to wait a good ten minutes until she was done babbling about his Tai Chi video. David looked up and could see the steam blowing from my Sicilian ears and knew her time was up, so he excused himself to "get back to my bride." He knew that would soften my mood.

Better yet, we were at Sundance with a group of people who were packaging a project with David as the star and enjoying the party when I noticed one of the married female producers from the film paying a little too much attention to David. Ladies, you know when you get that vibe off another female, right? Back in the car he blurted out the woman Frenched him when he said goodbye. Rrrrrrreally? Bobby was in the front seat and looked back. The color dropped from his face, because he was either cold or because he never saw me give "that look" before, I don't know. "Now Blackie . . . " trying to diffuse the situation. He knew where I was going with this before David did.

"Did you have to kiss her back?"

David laughed, "Well, I couldn't insult her and make a scene." He knew how to push my buttons. Sometimes it felt like he did it just to play with me, to get attention and reassurance. This time he got a kick out of my being "territorial."

Let's just say it wasn't just snow and sleet that was making it freezing inside the car.

* * *

March 2001, *The Academy Awards*

It was hard to believe that David had never attended the Academy Awards before. Neither had I. A very special virgin voyage for both of us. The tickets were very expensive, but we knew it was an opportunity we couldn't pass up. I called the Academy office to see about an invite to the Governor's Ball, which is a very tight invite list. When I explained it was not only a first for both of us, but how long David was sober, the woman went out of her way to call us back a week later when a cancellation came in. She put us on the top priority list so we could attend. It was a major score since the crème de la crème could see for themselves, up close and personal, that David looked great and was sober!

We were so excited and nervous. The limo let us out at the beginning of the red carpet, where they had everyone go through a security check in a tent, and then we were "on the runway" with all the press and the fans in the bleachers that lined the sides of the Shrine auditorium. It was a familiar scene since I covered the event as a roving reporter for WCCO Radio, but I had been on the outside of the perimeter in street clothes. This time, I was part of the event. David looked so handsome in his cream tux he wore for our wedding and I wore the incredible silver Bob Mackie gown he bought for me.

The second David stepped out from the tent, you could hear people shout his name and yell out to him. He lit up in a big smile and waved to the fans, who screamed louder. It made him chuckle. The reporters were yelling for pictures and for us to pose, and as was our tradition, we smooched for them too. Among the many mini interviewers along the carpet was Joan Rivers, who was charming and funny and spent considerable time talking to David.

Inside they served food and drinks and escorted us to our seats up front close to the stage. Fifth row! We were surprised and delighted they sat us by Sting and his wife, in front of Mary Hart. I could see David taking it all in. I knew he badly wanted to be a contender and gain recognition from the industry again. The longing was written all over his face and in his demeanor. I could see also how proud he was of himself. He knew he looked great and he felt confident. I couldn't have been more proud of him. One celebrity after another came up to him to say hello.

After the awards, the Governor's Ball was around the corner. The decorations were beautiful and everyone looked so elegant. Not to mention Wolfgang Puck's food was incredible! David went out for a smoke, but didn't return in the ten minutes he promised. When I went outside, I found him chatting away with one of his fans about the industry and his movies. Half an hour went by and people were leaving the dinner. I kept nudging him that if we didn't get back inside, we'd miss meeting this director or that producer, but he ignored me. Finally, I reminded him that the people who could hire him are inside and we should get moving. The more people that saw him and spoke to him, the better the word would circulate about how he looked fabulous and he wasn't drinking. He knew this, yet he stayed put. I went back inside to pre-schmooze, set up conversations and at least make some contacts myself. By the time David came back in, a good portion of the party had left. I couldn't understand why he did such a thing. He was sabotaging another major opportunity. Getting an invitation to a venue like this doesn't come along often and he needed to keep up the momentum to make more connections. But there he was, shooting the breeze with one single fan who was a novice in the industry. We did manage to mingle with a few who stayed longer, like Jeff Bridges, who was very receptive to David and chatted up a storm.

I watched news interview snippits on TV and the reporter was commenting on David and his tux, but referred to me as "the woman with David." I called the producer of the segment and told him that was no "woman," that was his wife! Me! He offered his apology by booking us on E! Fashion Emergency for the E! Entertainment Network, which we had a lot of fun doing and played in syndication for the longest time.

It was an evening of pure elation and frustration.

CHAPTER TWENTY-THREE

DOGGIE BAG

WE left David's beloved Rocky with "Jane," a close friend, while we went to Cannes, my first time in France and the festival. I never had a good feeling about her buying property up the street from where David and Gail had their ranch. It was one of my gut-wrenching, dark and negative feelings. But no one listened to me when I advised her to invest somewhere else. David stuck to the decision and that was that. This also marked the first of his years of criticizing me for being "too protective" and "worrying too much," in spite of the fact that Jane told us she felt someone was intruding on the property and keeping tabs on her. David ignored the warnings.

So instead of leaving Rocky, his first Bernese mountain dog, in a kennel, David wanted to save money and left him with Jane. Again, I never felt good about it. My guts were twisting inside, but Rocky, who was also a bit of a wanderer, was *his* dog. At the Mississauga house, he got out and wandered a few times. Once, a posse of us scoured the neighborhood and couldn't find him for hours. When he was finally spotted trotting along the road, David leaped out of the car and descended on the puppy, screaming as he flailed his fists and, to our horror, pummeled the poor thing. You could see David's relief turn into pure anger—how dare the puppy scare and abandon him like that! At least that's what I thought he might have felt. We actually had to intervene and pull David away so the dog didn't get hurt. I was appalled, and again, people made excuses for him, and blamed it all on the alcohol. It was a silent car ride back to the house.

We spent one glorious week in Milan and Cannes only to come back to the usual chaos. When we arrived back in L.A., David put in a call to pick up Rocky. There was awkward silence on the other end of the phone, then Jane said hesitantly that Rocky had disappeared. She had assured both of us that she would not let Rocky out of her sight. The event related to us was that it had been very early in the morning and Rocky was let out to pee. He should have been kept on a leash, but he wasn't. She opened the door to let him out, thinking he'd come right back, then unintentionally fell asleep again. When she woke up, she realized there was no dog!

It happened within days of our leaving for Cannes. Anyone who has had to rescue animals knows how crucial time is in claiming an animal at the pound. In some shelters, animals are put to sleep, sometimes in less than a week. David pushed down his anger and fear, but I could see his classic jaw clench. I, on the other hand, was extremely upset that David hadn't listened to me. We had to check the shelters fast. There was no Rocky.

The idea hit me to go to the press to help us find our dog. I turned to Stephen Viens at the *Star* tabloid again and asked to print something to help. And boy, did they come to the rescue. There was a huge full-page spread of us with our dog posters and a story on the missing puppy. We got many phone calls and leads, including about twenty psychics and clairvoyants offering their services. I called every one of them. They gave descriptions of people Rocky was with, his surroundings and lots of details. One psychic saw impressions from the dog's perspective and gave an uncanny description of David's ranch on La Tuna. Who knows if they were getting images or vibes from David and not the dog.

Out of the twenty clairvoyants and psychics, only one related a very different scenario. She didn't think we'd see Rocky again unless we got to him in time. She saw him trapped in an area he couldn't get out of. Like he fell through the flooring of a deserted, burned out building or house.

David said the area she described fit the area surrounding the ranch, but it would take a search on horseback to look. He didn't want to do it because that meant he'd have to deal with Gail again to get a horse and get to the area the psychic described. He tried to justify his decision by dismissing the psychic as probably wrong.

We even hired Sherlock Bones, a known animal detective out of San Francisco, who distributed posters and mailings for at least two months. It was non-stop scouring the streets and following up on tips. Our lives became nothing but looking for Rocky and that was not good for our relationship. David started to back off the search. He was giving up when I was still pushing, and I wanted so badly to check out that deserted house the woman had described.

Another psychic described a beach area with a boardwalk, and said to look for a Harlequin Great Dane. This dog was supposedly in contact with Rocky. Find the Great Dane and we would find Rocky. This time, David decided to pursue the lead. For a couple of weeks, we searched and posted notices in the Santa Monica and Venice area.

One weekend, we were walking along the Venice walkway and spotted a Harlequin Great Dane, but the owner of the dog denied seeing or playing with any dog like Rocky. We were deflated, but hopeful at the same time, since this was the exact description the psychic gave us. We decided to inundate the area with posters, we handed them out, posted them everywhere, talked to people . . . we exhausted ourselves.

One night about 2 a.m., we re-checked an area where we'd posted and found that they had been taken down. It was disheartening because we just put them up a couple of days before. Just as we were staple gunning a poster to a pole, we hear this booming voice in a thick Boston accent yelling at us, "Hey! Stop posting that crap!"

We looked up to find a woman with a baseball cap and flashlight, riding a bike. "You can't do that. You'll get fined."

David and I explained our plight and we got her immediate sympathy and attention.

"OK. But I gotta tell ya, you're doing this at your own risk."

Her name was Boston Dawna. That's what the neighborhood knew her as. She told us her mission was to keep her home turf safe and that she busts the perps in her territory. Dawna traveled around on her bike with nothing more than a pair of handcuffs, flashlight and phone. That's it. Of course, one could say her voice was certainly a weapon, since it shook us up a bit. It was reassuring to know she also worked with the police department extensively.

Dawna escorted us around as we posted a few more flyers, telling us her story. We ended up talking at her apartment until four in the morning. I told her that her life would make a great script, which she said she was working on. Fast-forward years later, I kept in touch with Boston Dawna and we have been working on getting her story produced.

A couple of days later, we get a call from none other than BD, saying she thinks she found Rocky! We hauled out to Venice where Dawna took us to the yard of a house in her neighborhood. We got to the gate of the yard and saw a Bernese mountain dog!! The dog turned around and . . . ugh, agony. Not David's dog. Upon checking his tags, this dog's name was also Rocky! Just not our Rocky. Is that weird or what? Well, the psychic was right. We did find *a* Rocky, just not our Rocky. It was heartbreaking we never found David's dog. I got a last call from that one particular psychic who described the deserted house. She was in tears saying she had a vision of the dog fading out, that there was no more time left and he had left this earth. I truly believed in her gift and that what she felt was right.

Everyone else believed pretty much the same scenario, that Rocky got out and wandered down the street and found himself in the hands of another family who kept him. Even though they knew who he belonged to, they didn't want to give him up. We will probably never know for sure what really happened and it haunts me to this day.

That was 1996 and Rocky was almost a year old. This breed doesn't have the longest life span expectancy, that's why they call it the "heartbreak" breed. Usually ten years is the average. I called the same breeder, Bobbie

Hefner at Swiss Star Farms, and inquired about getting another dog. I told her everything and she was so understanding about it. She put us at the top of the list and within a few months, we got a cousin to Rocky, Thunder. They shared the same grandfather. Thunder wasn't a wanderer, just a big bundle of happy love. He made David laugh. We took him everywhere we possibly could and didn't let him out of our site unless it was absolutely necessary. However, David never liked to keep his dogs on a leash.

Something clicked for David when he finally gave up the notion of looking for Rocky. His attitude toward Gail changed. Some time after we were married, I overheard a conversation he had on the phone, which stunned and deeply hurt me. He told this friend that he never lost hope of getting back together with Gail, until the Rocky disappearance. He felt she had the dog at some point and that was the turning point for him in letting go and focusing on other things. It made perfect sense to me. David did suddenly change his attitude toward me. He was more loving, more attentive, more everything after that event.

Maybe that's what Rocky was placed here on earth for. Maybe that was his angelic mission—to help David see the light, to let go of the dark road and turn to the light. I had no idea he harbored any feelings like that for those nine months we were together. I kept buying the excuse people gave me that it was the drinking that made him somewhat detached, not giving me the kind of affection I wanted. Then the excuse was "the dry drunk" syndrome. Maybe it played a part. But there was always some excuse.

There I was busting my buns trying to get him on track with his career, neglecting mine. He was talking about having a baby with me, sharing the new life and career, and privately, secretly, he was hoping things would change with Gail! I felt so deceived. Something inside me tweaked. What else did I not know?

From that point on I looked at everything within the relationship differently. Suddenly, it felt like the blinders had been pried off my eyes.

* * *

I helped raise the adorable bow-wow, Thunder, from puppydom. Went through obedience training with him—the Matthew Margolis team came to the house—early mornings while David slept in, cleaned up after him, fed and groomed him, even saved his life. I loved that dog. David did too. Outside of me, Thunder was the one thing David supposedly loved the most. But his actions could be contradictory. He never used a leash unless he was forced to and, well . . . some people have a funny way of taking care of what they are supposed to value the most.

Returning from a trip, leaving Thunder in David's care, I walked in to find one of his friends, Roger, sitting on the couch, with David in his office smoking away. There was something awkward in the feelings coming from Roger's "hello." David, who was preoccupied and seemed in a weird fog—which I thought was because he had a friend over and he couldn't multi-task—greeted me back and went about his visit with Roger, who eventually brought up the subject.

Evidently the day before, David had Thunder outside and he wandered to the edge of the driveway—no, he was not on a leash—where an elderly man was walking his pit-bull. Even though the pit-bull was leashed, the man couldn't control his dog, and it lunged at Thunder, and bit him. The pit wouldn't let go and David had to literally kick the dog in the head in order to get Thunder out of its jaws. David usually went barefoot. This time luckily he had on cowboy boots and the pit was not seriously hurt.

I was aghast and went to find Thunder, who did not get up to greet me as usual. He was lying down and whining softly. Roger pulled me aside and told me I had better get Thunder to the vet.

"You better do it quick. It's not good."

I gave Thunder a hug and gently felt under his belly. It was shocking to find a two-inch gaping hole in his stomach area. David said I was being paranoid and it would heal itself. Roger and I looked at each other as if

David was out of his mind, and I raced Thunder to emergency where they immediately operated. About $1,500 later, Thunder was going to be fine. He must have been in such pain. Thank goodness the vital organs were missed and they stitched him up. An infection had started to set in because David didn't even disinfect the wound, so Thunder was put on heavy antibiotics. Had I not come home that day, we could have said goodbye to Thunder. I got there just in time.

Summer 2001 was busy for Thunder. First, he wandered off while David was having his computer worked on, out of some guy's garage. I was on my way to meet up with David when I passed by a dog that looked exactly like Thunder. Eh . . . it was Thunder! Needless to say I picked him up, but waited until David   found him missing and got worried before I screamed at him, pointing out that I found the dog before he noticed his canine was missing!

Another memorable time for the pooch was when David was sitting in an outdoor cafe in Hollywood near his apartment having his coffee and we were actually having a pleasant conversation on the phone. After about ten minutes of conversation, I asked how Thunder was doing.

"Oh, he's great. He's out with me here. We're . . . " Beat. "Thunder?" "THUNDER?!" Panic set in his voice. "I don't see Thunder!" I could hear him calling out in the background and asking someone if they'd seen his dog, then muffled conversation, then his voice booming in the background, "THUNNNNNNNDERRRRRR!" He came back to the cell phone. "He's gone! Thunder's gone! I gotta go find him. Gotta go." David's voice cracked and got high pitched. I never heard him so upset. He was like a scared little boy. My heart went out to him and I was panicked myself since I adored the dog. I told David I'd call the press immediately and get them out to cover the story and get word out on TV. He thought that was great and we hung up. I immediately called all the news stations.

Two hours later, with my heart in my mouth and in a state of shock, after twenty phone calls and faxes . . . I set up news crews to meet David at the spot of the dog-napping. I called David to make sure he'd meet the crew, but he didn't answer his cell. "Got three news crews coming out to meet you. They're on their way! Call me!"

After another half hour, David calmly answers his phone. I hear him saying good bye to some chum on the other phone and a chuckle and he comes back to my line. "Oh, uh I got him back".

"You got him back? WHEN?"

"About a half hour ago".

"WHY DIDN'T YOU CALL ME?!"

"What are you so upset for? I got him back! Some group called the Green something saw him and thought he was lost."

It didn't make sense because if Thunder was by his side as he told me, how could the dog be mistaken for lost?

"I set up news crews. You knew I was going to get press for you to find him and you don't call me to say you found him? You talk to a chum on the phone instead of calling me right away?!"

"The phone rang, I answered it and got to talking."

"I have to call them back now, you ass, and stop them before they come out. And you don't even thank me!"

"You didn't give me a chance to."

"You could have called half hour ago you !#!*#!*#!"

I spent the next hour retracing the calls to cancel the crews.

* * *

April 19, 2003

Easter is tomorrow. I used to love to decorate eggs and package Easter baskets for presents. But reality kicks in. I remember Thunder was a party poop. He'd play for about five minutes and then want to sit the day out while Lulu was just getting warmed up for an hour race. Lulu and Thunder were parallels to David and me. He'd be crashed out on the couch and I'd want to do something social.

Then there's Thunder wanting to pee on everything. Most of the time, he couldn't help it with a chronic infection from not being neutered and his stinky gland getting clogged. Even though it would have helped Thunder's health, David refused to get it done.

I thought today would be the day to get the court accounting done and just relax for Easter tomorrow. Had already sent a birthday email to Kansas—today's the day—and she emailed back saying there were a lot of changes and transitions leading up to today. I sent off an encouraging self-esteem "pump," reminding her she is beautiful, smart and talented, and one day she will find a man who will value her. I was so much like her at her age.

Anyway, got up around 8:30 to Lulu's nudges to go for a walk and proceeded to put myself together for the day, slapping on some sunscreen when the phone rang.

"Hello, this is the West Valley Animal Shelter . . . "

My heart raced and not having my senses fully together for the day, I looked around quickly for Lulu, thinking for a split second how could it be her? Did a cat get out? How could they be in West Valley?!

"Are you the owner of a dog named Thunder?"

My eyes popped open. It had been a couple of years since I had seen Thunder, but I didn't want to let the shelter worker know that. I told her she had the right number, but how did she get it?

"We checked for the microchip. Someone brought him in this morning. Would you be able to pick him up?"

I asked if anyone else had been contacted and was told they called another number on a tag. I recognized it as David's cell. They said they left a message over an hour ago. The girl then asked if Thunder had been vaccinated and did I have his records. I said I didn't remember and I didn't have the records handy. She told me that unless I ok'd the vet to give him his vaccination, he'd be kept for a week, since they do not let dogs out without verification or the shot. I said to go ahead thinking it would be horrible for Thunder to be there for a week *if* David was out of town.

Even though it's a good shelter, I didn't want to take a chance on anything happening to Thunder there, not to mention he would be distressed.

I quickly slicked on some gloss, grabbed Lulu and hurried out the door. On the way I decided to call Bobby and Edie to see if David was out of town, but couldn't get them on the phone until later, after I got Thunder. I told Edie it would be interesting to see how long it took him to realize Thunder was gone and to call. We both had a chuckle.

I got a spare leash out of the car to use for Lulu and Lulu's for Thunder, since it was stronger, and marched into the animal shelter building. I was so nervous and excited about seeing Thunder again.

The woman inside at the window told me to get the card from the cage and bring it back to her. When I approached, I called out his name and you could literally see recognition flash across his tri-colored furry face. It went from I'm miserably scared and why am I here to . . . ohmygod, it's mommy! He whined and wagged his tail. I grabbed the card and ran back to the counter where she told me they like to neuter animals before they leave.

I said his dad would not like that at all and he stays untouched. She sent me across the way to the other counter to pay and get our dog . . . My heart was beating so fast. I was afraid they wouldn't let me take him and he'd be stuck there, but it all went fine. When they brought him out, he pulled hard on the rope toward me, almost dragging the worker off balance. It was difficult to get a hold of him because he was jumping around so happily . . . wagging his tail, moaning, talking.

Finally, with leash attached, we headed out for my car with Lulu barking her head off. I put her leash on and they bolted for each other, dancing around in reunion . . . heading for the grass area to mark their territory and play and smell. Happy dogs. Happy me. We headed into the Valley to run an errand and then home. Excited pants from behind, slurping water from the bowl I set out, and heads out the window to feel the wind against their faces.

My mind journeyed back to earlier romps, and when we first brought

Lulu home, and the two of them playing . . . this was definitely going to be a Kodak moment. I wanted to make sure I had something to record this visit, since I was feeling I might never see Thunder again. He weighed so much more than the last time I saw him, over 1 1/2 years ago. He went from too thin to overweight and had a skin tag on his eye that should have been removed. I just sighed and hugged him.

We arrived at my condo where they bolted up the stairs and were greeted by the cats, who Thunder gently sniffed hello. It was like no time had passed. Smittie meowed and licked his nose to greet him.

Lulu and Thunder spent a couple of hours on the cool patio, barking, playing and snoozing. At about 3 p.m. the phone rang. It was David's cell phone. He sounded very upset and out of breath.

"It's David. You have Thunder?"

It felt as strange to hear him say David instead of Johnny, as it did for me to call him that myself. "Yes, I have Thunder. It's like the tenth time this has happened, David. You insist on keeping him off-leash. How'd he get out this time?"

"None of your fucking business!"

"You'll never learn, will you? You're lucky he didn't get hit by a car."

"He's only been missing a couple of hours."

"You mean it's only been a couple of hours since *you noticed him missing*. He's been missing since early this morning. That's hours ago. I picked him up at 11a.m. and it's now 3 o'clock and you are just *now* calling!"

I couldn't help but think what an irresponsible twit he was. Maybe I was making a mistake by turning this dog back over to him, putting this precious pooch in jeopardy of getting loose again . . . and someone keeping him or . . . but . . . he was David's dog.

"When can I pick him up?"

"Whenever. I'm here."

"How long will you be there? I . . . I'm in the middle of Kansas' birthday party and I've already missed an hour of it by going to the shelter. Where are you?"

"Where I live, David, in Valencia."

He had this incredulous tone to his voice, as if he was so put out at the thought he'd have to make a 20-minute drive to retrieve his dog.

"You mean I have to come all the way out there?!"

I calmly replied, "Yes, this is where Thunder is. With me."

I heard his girlfriend's voice in the background, yapping something, and him snapping back at her, "she's not going to want to do that . . . "

"Uh . . . I'm going to have to call you back," he said. "How long will you be there? I'm in the middle here?"

"You tell me when you want to pick up Thunder and I will make sure I'm here to meet you."

He calmed down a bit when I offered to be extremely accommodating. I'm sure he was thinking I might pull a "number" by trying to keep or hide the dog for spite or revenge. After all, we were in a bitter court battle. "Remember the twenty-seven dollars it took to bail him out, though . . . and I want it in cash."

"Big fucking deal!" He snapped. I remained calm.

I thought it would be just like him to "forget" to reimburse me. "Fine. Just remember I won't hand him over unless I get the money in cash. I won't accept a check."

"I'm going to call you back later when I can figure this out."

"Fine." About twenty minutes later the phone rang again.

"Yes, David . . . "

He was ever so sweet. "Hi! Uh . . . listen, what's your address?" He chuckled.

"You mean to tell me you don't remember where I live?"

"Well, I don't have the street address."

I could tell something was up. "You mean you're telling me you don't remember how to get out here? You've been here how many times? Lived here, cruised the property looking for me at one point . . . "

"I'm having someone else pick up Thunder."

"I see. Well I don't want to give my address out to anyone. Who's supposed to pick him up?"

"A limo."

"A limo? You're sending a limo to pick up your dog?"

"I can't leave the party. I'm in the middle of Kansas' party."

That wasn't the real reason, I thought. And why was he sugar sweet to me now? I let it go and said I'd meet the driver at the supermarket.

"What time?"

"You tell me."

"Ok . . . I'll call you back after I talk with them."

"Fine."

A short time later, the phone rang again. "Hello, Johnny."

A brief hesitation, hearing his pet name. "Hi. Okay . . . is it alright if I give them your number to coordinate the meeting?"

"Yeah, sure."

"Great. I really appreciate your being so concerned about Thunder." I couldn't believe he was being this nice and appreciative. "Well, Thunder is . . . " I almost choked, " . . . one of my kids."

Another brief hesitation, then he asked, "So how was the reaction to Lulu and all?"

So now he wants to make conversation too? Hmmmmm. I told him how Thunder greeted me, instantly recognizing me.

He replied, "Yeah, they told me at the shelter they only released him to you because he looked like he belonged to you . . . how happy he was . . . that he went right to you."

I thought, yes, he was happy to see me, but no, the reason they released him to me is because I matched the I.D. and I was in the microchip registration. But I didn't want him to know that. I then told him that Lulu was elated and they played together. We talked like old friends, not enemies. It made me feel sad. Here was this conversation, like parents talking about their kids, and there were the court papers on my table with all the accounting I had to do to try and get the money I felt he was trying to screw me out of.

I reminded him the driver better have the cash. He assured me he would and he signed off with a soft and affectionate "Thanks, honey." Honey, huh? Whoa. The girlfriend definitely wasn't in the room!

I took more pictures of us, running back and forth with the self-timer, and my neighbor snapped a few on our way to the car. Thunder said goodbye to the cats. Smittie licked his nose goodbye and we bounded out the door. Pulling into the shopping center, I immediately spotted the black town car and waved to the driver.

Lulu and Thunder had a last goodbye nuzzle and lick . . . and I said to Lulu, "You may not see him again, Lulu . . . Thunder has to go back now." She looked up at me with her ears bent back, whined, looked at Thunder and nuzzled him again. He nuzzled back and I escorted him to the other car where he bounced inside. We had a last moment and, before I could start crying, I closed the door and turned to the driver.

Laslo handed me the money. At that point I looked at the twenty-dollar bill on top and wondered for a moment why he was offering me money, forgetting completely it was the money David owed me. My emotions were definitely taking over. Laslo said he remembered meeting me with David before, and he wanted to know what I was up to. I wasn't about to say anything, knowing full well it could get reported back to David. He was very friendly. And maybe a little too interested.

"So did you remarry?"

I looked up in surprise "Please, I'm not done dealing with this mess yet. I'm still having to take David to court . . . it's . . . " and I left it hanging there with gestures that said I've had it.

I switched the subject back to Thunder, getting more pictures taken, and called it a day, shaking hands as we departed. I suddenly remembered "I just want to show you the receipt, just in case."

He added "Just in case the 'accountant' wants to know?"

I pulled the receipt out and showed him.

"Oh, I believe you."

"I want you to see so you can tell David."

He smiled and said he understood. We waved goodbye. I didn't want to drive yet. I sat in the car, lost in thought, and pulled out my cell, pretending I was on the phone, just in case he was still watching. I sat there for several minutes on the verge of a crying spell. A few tears spilled onto my denim jacket. Since the photo store was right there, I popped in to get the film developed. Then I debated whether to call, and finally decided I'd tell David the rendezvous was successful.

"Just wanted you to know Thunder should be arriving momentarily." He sounded a bit tense again.

"Yeah, the driver called."

"Good. Just wanted to make sure you knew. That's it."

"Yeah, thanks again for your concern. I appreciate it."

Ohmygod, he thanked me! He actually said the words. I was astounded, but acted nonchalant.

"Okay, bye."

He was very cheery-sweet with me now.

"Okay, bye baby."

Baby. Now I'm baby. No, she definitely wasn't in the room. He delivered the line the same way he had when we were together. Like no time had gone by, like we were still together. Which was an eerie thought. I felt the overwhelming yearning to have what I used to have with David—our menagerie family, me, David, Thunder, Lulu and the cats. I remembered our "in-joke" of baboons on the road. A line from his film *Safari 2000* where Christopher Lee's foil, Hamilton Camp, sings, "I'd rather see a rain of toads, than the sight of baboons on zah road!" We'd always crack each other up with that line.

I missed that. I missed the "in" jokes, comments, looks, thoughts that we shared as a couple. We had delighted in the fact that only we knew and appreciated what they meant from prior moments and the history we shared. Oh God, I ached for it so much. I called a few friends and Edie to give the updated report on the event of the day. Lulu sat on the porch looking around. We had fun. Got my "Thunder fix" and some pictures to fill more frames with my beloved Thunder-dog and our adventure!

* * *

Lulu and I never did see Thunder again. I was told that he passed away only a couple of months before David. I can only hope they are united again. There's one thing you can be sure of, he won't have him on a leash!

CHAPTER TWENTY-FOUR

BABY TALK

Before I tell my tale of woe about trying to get pregnant, I'm going to start at the end, because I can't wait to get this information out to people. I hope it will save couples tears of anguish and anxiety, unnecessary blaming—your mate or yourself—and thousands of dollars. If you have been trying to get pregnant and it hasn't happened, get a cross-match (also known as an "antibody") detection test. I suggest not even waiting until you're trying to get pregnant. Get the test *before* you try. This test costs about $150 in the U.S. and it's a simple blood test.

Here's the technical explanation: This test determines the level of recognition by the female immune system of the differences in the transplantation antigens between the female and the male partner. In pregnancy it is essential that the female immune system recognize that there is embryonic tissue present. It is necessary that there be big enough differences in transplantation antigens between the woman and the sperm provider, that the embryonic tissue—the fetus—will perceive the differences, which will trigger the female immune system into recognizing pregnancy.

Having recognized the presence of embryonic tissue, the female immune system produces anti-idiotypic antibodies, which then specifically protect the foreign embryonic tissue from being attacked by the female's own immune system.

In my case, my test showed a low level of recognition of the differences, therefore I had a treatment with David's white blood cells, in order to pre-sensitize my immune system to the differences. This process is called leukocyte immunization treatment (LIT). The goal is to increase the cross-match to a point where the immune system is able to afford a sufficiently high level of protection for the pregnancy to take place.

That's the technical explanation. In simple English, we had the test done and found our "bands" were too much alike. Which was the reason I wasn't getting pregnant. When there isn't enough difference in the antibody levels, a pregnancy won't happen or it won't hold. In my series of treatments (leukocyte injections), they injected David's white blood cells (they took a blood sample and separated out the cells) under my skin in hopes that my anti-body levels would increase (making more differences) at least enough so that the next pregnancy attempt would hold. It was not a pleasant procedure, but it was tolerable. It was nothing compared to what I went through before.

Although my antibody levels did get higher, they didn't reach the desired numbers. We tried another in vitro fertilization anyway, which was futile. Blood type, by the way, has nothing to do with this problem. I thought it might because David and I were also the same blood type, but it doesn't. It's the "bands." If they are too much alike, this is what happens. The closer the match, the bigger the problem. Yes, David and I were too much alike.

To nutshell it, because the bands are too alike, it causes a rejection factor when a woman conceives. The pregnancy either doesn't happen, or the pregnancy is lost early. The leukocyte immunization program— the treatment that I went through—is not done in the U.S. anymore. Dr. Bronte Stone, who performed the white blood cell immunization/ treatment on me, related that the FDA pulled the plug on the treatment program here. Why?

Because the FDA wanted the white blood cell preparation used for the immunization, even if it was from your sexual partner, to be registered as *a drug!* The person producing the cells would also have to be screened as if they were a blood donor, and the results of the testing would also have to be known before the immunization was done. David would have loved that—to have the FDA officially label him as a drug!

What this boils down to is, even if a couple got diagnosed here in the U.S., they'd have to go to Mexico or Canada for treatment. I will still shout as loud as I can to every couple who has a problem getting pregnant, to *get the test*.

* * *

Back to the beginning. Since day one, David and I talked about having a baby together. We didn't use contraception and eagerly enjoyed trying to reach that goal, but I wasn't getting pregnant and we couldn't understand why. I saw a doctor in Toronto who did a post-coital test and it showed David was shooting blanks. Under the circumstances, given David's alcohol use, the doctor thought it might be part of the problem, but unless he got sober, it would be difficult to tell. David took the news in stride. Actually he didn't even comment on it. It was more of a grunt. Just one more incentive for him to get sober.

His daughter Calista didn't want to see me get hurt, so she gave me a heads up warning on David. Supposedly people felt he left Barbara Hershey when his son was two years old because too much attention was going to the baby. David wanted all the attention, so he strayed to another woman. Calista didn't want that happening to me. His own recounting in his autobiography has different details, but this "inside info" isn't something I think he'd admit to. Maybe there was something to that. I felt even though David was all for having another baby, it also scared him. Was he afraid that he might stray again because he knew the attention would go to the baby and not all to him? Or that he was so much older, and didn't know if he had the energy for it?

After he got sober and it still wasn't happening, a path of research, experiments, further tests for us both, and treatments opened up before us. Since we didn't have money in the beginning of our relationship for the expensive procedures, we tried holistic approaches. I busied myself with sussing out doctors in order to find out why we weren't "getting lucky." After the test results for David in Toronto, he went to an urologist and had to be treated there. Then we got the low-down on his "swimmers"—sperm. After he got sober, they were still there, but not the greatest. Good news was, in artificial insemination, they spin all that down and only the very best are used for the procedure, giving the maximum possible chance of pregnancy. Along with fertility drugs for me, we thought it was a done deal.

Far from it.

What was most disconcerting to me was that I was continually looked upon by the doctors as the one with the problem, or the cause of the infertility. I hated being called infertile. Why is the woman labeled? Like it's always the woman's fault? In my case, they initially accused me of having old eggs. My family history was very fertile on both sides and it didn't make sense that I was the problem. After about $40,000, five specialists, so many physically invasive and painful procedures and tests I can't remember them all, fertility drugs, pills, shots . . . getting the timing of cycles right, monitoring everything . . . the hopes, the let downs . . . I was leading a second life. All David had to do was enjoy donating to the cause, as it were. He expressed disappointment, but not depression or grief over not getting pregnant. He had his kids, but I didn't.

Each time it didn't happen, I was devastated. And with each subsequent disappointment, I was less and less consolable. The hormonal ups and downs weren't as bad as we anticipated, but it still affected me considerably and back-lashed on David as well. I felt the stress was hurting my chances of getting pregnant and David wasn't helping in that area. The dream shattered. To this day, I have to turn away sometimes and head for a bathroom or corner to cry in after seeing a mother and her baby. It remains extremely painful for me.

A female celebrity friend referred us to Dr. Richard Paulson, a doctor who had helped her conceive her twins. After a few IVF attempts, followed by the "I'm sorry" phone call from the doctor again, I melted down and crawled into bed sobbing for hours until I was dehydrated. David did his best to console me, but I didn't even want him touching me. That same time, I was supposed to stay home calmly in bed, but Thunder got out, and I had to race over the neighborhood to find him. I blamed David. He was supposed to have fixed the fencing so Thunder wouldn't get out, but he didn't. I blamed God . . . I blamed me. Why was I being deprived of having my own baby? So many people have them by accident and here I desperately wanted one of my own and couldn't have it.

I couldn't understand it. Each time we harvested my eggs, we got from ten to fifteen embryos. Those were the results typical of a healthy, much younger woman. Each IVF, we placed four to six embryos. Sometimes in the thawing out from storage, we lost a few, but . . . So why were they not taking? Was someone "upstairs" telling me something? I had at least half a dozen psychics tell me there was a little boy around me. They saw a pregnancy. I guessed the child-to-be knew better not to become our kid.

Mostly, at that moment, I blamed David. Managing his career caused me so much stress. It was a monumental task that I didn't want to do for him anymore. I just wanted to get pregnant and enjoy married life as a wife and mom.

It was with Dr. Paulson that we got the luckiest with one of the IVF attempts. We had pictures of our embryos to be implanted—which I taped above my desk to talk to each day—and I was sure it would work this time. I was disappointed when David had to leave town for a film. I didn't want to be alone, so I called upon Reverend Rosalyn Bruyere, a hands-on healer who was the minister for our wedding, to be by my side and do a healing on me and the embryos.

Her presence calmed me down and I felt protected. She ran energy over the embryos in their container before Dr. Paulson did the implantation and ran energy on me as she held my hand during the procedure. This time, the absence of David's strife, the positive atmosphere and Rosalyn's energy boost helped me, I believe, to get "technically" pregnant—the numbers go up to a certain level when they declare it's a pregnancy. But two weeks after getting the good news, I was on the freeway coming back home through Westwood, turning onto the 405 on-ramp after another argument with David on the phone, and felt a very sharp pain in my abdomen. And another. I knew right then, I lost the pregnancy. "*Noooooo!*" It was difficult to drive while crying hysterically.

We went in to Paulson for yet another procedure. Unbeknownst to me, David took his cell phone in with him, but didn't turn it off. While Paulson was in the middle of the implantation—at the most spiritual moment, when he's about to implant the embryos—David's phone goes off, to a Mozart tune! He didn't take the call, but didn't turn it off either. In a movie it might have been funny, but not in person.

Dr. Paulson looked at me, then David. The nurse's eyes widened and then squinted disapproval. I was... stunned. Instead of getting upset, I tried to make a joke, "and now for our musical interlude..." It brought a small chuckle, but underneath we all were upset, except for David.

With the embryos in place, I was supposed to lie still for an hour, during which time David was to be by my side, holding my hand, making it a beautiful and loving, instead of clinical, moment. We were to talk about our future and do more visualization on the implantation taking hold. Instead, his cell phone rings again. He not only takes the call, but leaves the room! Our special time together he treated like an everyday office visit and left me alone, ignoring what we planned. I thought maybe it was an urgent call and he'd be gone a couple of minutes. After all, he knew how important this was. But time went by... tick, tick, tick, tick...

Fifteen minutes later the nurse came in to check on me, thinking David had returned. Nada. She left to try and find him. More time passed. She came back and ... nada. She was appalled that he just disappeared. I broke down sobbing. The nurse stayed with me the remaining time, comforting me. David returned *after the hour was up*. He couldn't fathom why I was upset. I couldn't talk to him I was so distraught. He stayed outside to smoke, and I got into the limo and vented to our trusted driver, Carlos, whom we called upon frequently. He was a sympathetic ear and was upset for me. When David got into the car, I let loose on him. He said that I was ruining *his* experience of the event!

Was the phone call urgent? No. He was "just catching up" with one of his buddies—I found out later it was his friend Alan—telling him about the procedure. Needless to say, that IVF didn't take either. And another attempt failed after he threw an apple, hitting and bruising me in the abdomen during an argument.

We even made a trip to St. Louis, Missouri for a GIFT procedure with Dr. Sherman Silber. In this procedure, instead of implanting the embryos via the vagina into the fallopian tubes, they cut into the abdomen to implant. We stayed at a hotel just ten minutes from the hospital with Thunder and Lulu for over two weeks. Our small room was made into a mini home away from home. We took walks, watched a lot of television, made a few short side runs to see the sights, including the Gateway Arch, and played with Thunder and Lulu. It was April and the tulips were in full, glorious bloom. There were large patches of them in every color outside our door along the walkway. Whenever I look at a tulip, I think of Missouri and a melancholy feeling overcomes me.

By chance I heard of yet another celebrity my age getting pregnant. I knew her from Tony Barr's acting class, tracked her down, and she gave me the number of Dr. Jirair Konialian. In our first visit, Dr. K sat there looking over my intense medical records and said, "I don't see any antibody test." Any what? He explained what it was and before he was to do any procedures, we were to get tested, which we did that day. The test results came back showing we had a cross match problem. A what? Evidently that was the main reason I wasn't getting pregnant. The daily high stress level wasn't helping. There was nothing wrong with me or my eggs, with the embryos or with David. It was us.

We were referred to Dr. Bronte Stone who performed a series of leukocyte immunization treatments. Along with that, we tried a few more

IVF procedures, but they all failed.

At which point we were told that if we wanted to use my eggs, the only way for me to conceive was to use donor sperm. That way the antibody problem would be resolved. David looked to his side of the family, but the males were not options for various reasons. Keith, as much as he wanted to help us out, was in his relationship with Hayley. The four of us sat in our living room discussing the matter, with Keith in tears because he didn't want to let his brother down. It was very emotional for all of us. David told me Bobby wasn't an option either since he had three of his own already. I understood. It was awkward at best. But when David wanted to ask his son, I nipped that in the bud. Now that was a little too liberal for me and I said "no." That's when David lost interest. Adoption wasn't an option he would go for. Neither was the idea of sperm from an anonymous donor or from a friend. Why? The child wouldn't have his genes. If he couldn't get the Carradine genes to get me pregnant, then he wasn't interested in having another baby.

It was another considerable factor, in the last year we were together, in the demise of our marriage. He had his kids, and yet he didn't want me to have a last shot at having my own. I was forty-two years old. At the end he said, "You don't need me for anything anymore. You can have a baby on your own, so what do you need me for?" I looked at him dumbfounded.

"Because you are a part of me. And I love you beyond words." His eyes got moist. But there was no further talk about babies. I chalked it up to fate, that it wasn't meant to happen for me. I wasn't going to divorce him over it.

After we separated I went so far as to try artificial insemination via a cryo bank. Searching on the internet for a donor was a surreal experience let alone being inseminated with a stranger's sperm. It creeped me out. It was too intimate and yet so impersonal. It didn't feel right. Determined in spite of the experience to try again, I ventured to Canada to score fertility drugs at half the cost, but decided that I didn't want to raise a child alone, especially under the financial circumstances I was facing. Adoption?

Couldn't afford that either.

There was still hope, I thought. Maybe I'll find another love and I could still get pregnant. But the right man didn't come along and the door to that path slowly closed.

CHAPTER TWENTY-FIVE

THE WILD, WILD WEDDING

WE've got a sighting!!! We've got a sighting!!!

Sure enough, just past the corner, around the hedges, there it was. Dark, looming, staring back at us, and another lurking in the shadows just across the street, poised, in position ready to spring forward, waiting to feed on its prey! We were hidden behind drawn curtains, but we knew we were being watched! The paparazzi were there!

Between the two of us, there were seven marriages, in various locations. My first wedding was in the Fern Grotto on Kaui and my second was actually on the Mark Twain ride in Disneyland—on the marriage certificate it actually says married in Disneyland. Michael (Anderson, Jr.) and I couldn't get official sanction from Disney head Michael Eisner, but we decided to do it anyway—hey, we figured they couldn't stop the ride. Michael's brother, David, a movie production manager and mail-order minister, did the honors. I thought I'd never top that if I ever got married again. Who knew?

We bounced around ideas for weeks. Where could this internationally known kick-ass icon tie the knot with his Valley Girl? We wanted to make a big splash, but had such limited funds it wouldn't even make a faucet drip. There *had* to be a way of getting it paid for. I mean, this is Hollywood!

Then it hit us. David and I thought it was the perfect romantic tribute to how and where it all really began for us—the back lot of Warner Bros. Studios in Burbank, on the western Laramie Street (it has since been torn down). This was the street on which he filmed his original *Kung Fu* series. It was the nearby soundstage that I wandered onto and met him for the first time in the early '70s. We thought it would make for a good publicity story.

David, being the ultimate romantic, actually asked my mother's permission for my hand in marriage.

Speaking about permission, we needed to get it from the studio, and got not only the blessing, but help from executive Barry Meyer and staff for the wedding plans. Meyer substantially discounted prices for us and allowed us to use the *entire* Laramie Street, including the Saloon for our reception. The street and interior of the Saloon was professionally decorated by the pros at the studio. Talk about having the best and doing it right! It was literally right out of a television show!

We hired Cesare Bonazza as our official photographer, who captured many "Kodak" moments on film of celebrities such as Pierce Brosnan and Jane Seymour. He made the deal for our print exclusive with international magazine *Hello!*, which brought in just enough money—actually almost to the dollar—to pay for the entire wedding. Cesare was a gem to work with and took the most beautiful photos. You knew he was there with the camera, somewhere, but he didn't distract from the most intimate moments.

News of our wedding was carried internationally by hundreds of publications. *Access Hollywood* had exclusive television coverage. We had no staff per se, no wedding planner, no florist to work with. It was David, a couple friends and myself. I was a totally frazzled bride working the wedding to the last second, with all the preparations and anxiety. David took charge of the invitations, which were perfect. He even wrote what was inside.

For the canopy under which we were to stand, I went downtown and bought silk flowers and ivy at the mart to cover it, and my close friends Wendy Miller and Steven Berg decorated it at the studio.

The added stress of planning security not just at the house, but also at the studio, was intense. It wasn't easy because it wasn't on a soundstage that could be locked off. It took place on the famous Laramie Street, which was out in the open, and we had to scout for places where paparazzi could hide out, in the rafters or even on the hill using zoom telescopic lenses. There were passwords, codes and lists upon lists.

Because of the budget problem, David used his martial arts connections to hire our security guards. Ahhh-soooo-very-clevvah! They were honored to protect one of their idols. Kam Yuen, martial arts expert and teacher, who knew David from the old *Kung Fu* series, became the foreman, and our entire security staff consisted of volunteer students and teachers from Kam's school. We had about fifteen martial arts students on guard at every entry, and in the storefronts lining the western street, observing with keen eyes and binoculars to make sure no one had cameras except our own approved videographer, and *Access Hollywood.*

I got the idea of being kidnapped and whisked away by a couple of western bad-guys—we hired actors in full western costume—which David wanted to nix. "I don't want my bride kidnapped!" Instead of horseback, we would use two white limos.

It took some convincing that the press would love it before he finally gave in. *Access Hollywood* did indeed love the idea and wanted exclusive coverage. They did a fabulous job. There was one camera to follow me on a side trip on the way to the studio and another to follow David, and of course the wedding.

I designed my bridal bouquet in the shape of a heart with sweet peas, gardenias and other fragrant flowers, taking great pains to research what flowers were in bloom at the time so the florist would have them in stock. I specified that I did *not* want a bouquet of roses, as the insistent florist suggested, just a few tiny rose buds.

Well, the camera crew was there at the house filming, when my bridal bouquet from the florist in Sherman Oaks to the *très* elite social scene arrived late. And what was inside the elegantly packed box? An *all rose* bouquet. I went into a quiet panic, but was seething inside. I did not want to have *that* bouquet as part of my wedding, but how was I going to get a replacement? I didn't want to throw a conniption fit in front of the cameras and there was no one who could deal with it but me. We were running late with our schedule, I was supposed to be dressed and didn't have the time to arrange my hair the way I intended either. I wanted to scream.

I ran into the other room to call the florist. They didn't want to put me through to the owner so that's when I put it to them.

"This is a major celebrity wedding. You all know that. It's not only the opposite of what I ordered, but I will not have this as my bouquet. Send me the one I designed to the house—*now!*"

The owner got on the phone and started to give me a song and dance about the issue and that's when I pulled out "the guns."

"This is being highly publicized. I have *Access Hollywood* in the other room, so I guess you won't get the free positive publicity. Everyone will know who screwed up because I will make sure I mention it on camera. This is *my wedding* bouquet!" I was trying not to go to tears, but my hormones were in overdrive from our recent IVF procedure, for which we were supposed to get the results that day. I decided to wait, however, until after we returned from our honeymoon.

"I will not use this bouquet! You will be publicized nationwide for spoiling my day!" I was about to explode. The owner finally saw the light and my bouquet arrived, not only just in time but also to the specifications of what I originally designed! Now why in the hell couldn't they have done that to begin with? I've never ordered flowers from them since.

We could see a couple of unfamiliar vehicles parked across the street. One of the *Access Hollywood* crew said he could see guys with cameras through the tinted windows. Ahhhh, the paparazzi! We found out a couple weeks later via an inside source at the tabloids, that supposedly someone who used to be close with David sold our address to them for money.

We were totally prepared with A, B and C plans to hide behind coats and umbrellas and lose the paparazzi. Even though they got a few pictures, which ended up in the tabloids, we were so obscured, you couldn't even really tell it was us in the pictures, let alone what we were wearing! Had we lost the exclusive, there wouldn't have been any money to pay for the wedding, which would have put us in major debt to the studio. One of the paparazzi tried to rush through security with their car, but friends of ours following right behind alerted the guards and they were halted in their tire tracks! Yaay, for security at Gate 7! Ha!

David was enjoying the drama and espionage. He looked so handsome and was on cloud nine with happiness. We both were.

I went in one limo and made a sentimental journey to my grandmother's house nearby to get orange blossoms to add to my bouquet. She once told me she had them as part of her wedding bouquet and this way, even though she had long passed on, I felt she was with me. The new owners of the house were delighted to be a part of the event and on camera, since *Access Hollywood* was with us every step of the way interviewing us inside the limo on our journey to the studio.

The ceremony was a mix of Bon Po, Irish and American Indian. We and our guests sang an ancient love chant. The vows were given by Rev. Rosalyn Bruyere. There David stood in his cream-colored Brioni tuxedo, with me in my white French lace dress from Celeste, full of multi-colored cascading silk and satin flowers. It was as if I had walked though a magical garden and the blooms clung to the dress and train. The wedding was perfect except we all froze our asses off, it was so cold! At least it didn't rain as it had all week. In most of our pictures you can see my nose was as red as Rudolph's! It went without a hitch, except of course that we got hitched.

David's brother Robert flew in from location and had barely any sleep in order to be there as our best man for the ceremony. Calista was my matron of honor. Over a hundred and fifty guests included family, friends, VIPs and celebrities. James Keach attended, Jane Seymour couldn't because of filming for the *Dr. Quinn* show. Eloise and John Paul DeJoria, mogul of John Paul Mitchell hair care, 24 director/producer and KFTLC director Jon Cassar, John Blythe Barrymore, Drew's brother, and Robert's daughter, actress Ever Carradine, along with my Academy Award winning lyricist cousin Ray Evans, Roger Corman, and Stacy Keach. We invited Quentin Tarantino, but his assistant said he was out of town. So was David's other brother, Keith, who had to attend his son's sports event. That was a huge disappointment to both of us. I had always loved the song *Come Rain or Come Shine*. My mother had sung it and over the years we declared it our song. Instead of the typical wedding march, the harpist and musical trio played that song as my brother walked me down the aisle. Through all our trials and tribulations, it had seemed to speak our dedication to each other. David loved to sing it, like at our engagement party. And then there were the two songs he wrote for me. One was called *And Then She Smiles*, which was an anniversary present for the day we started our romance.

I made my entrance from the back of one of the street storefronts. My brother and I stood there waiting for our cue, looking at the same bracings and 2x4s I had seen on the lot when I first met David in the '70s. My white 'walk way' was placed over the bumpy dirt street, which was difficult to walk over in high heels. I was half weepy, half giggly, clinging to my brother for balance. Then I looked up at David and we locked eyes. I never saw him happier or looking more proud and loving. After the vows, we were greeted by guests blowing bubbles, as we walked down the aisle as husband and wife.

For our first dance as newlyweds, they played one of the songs David wrote for me, *When Blackie Lets Her Hair Down*, accompanied by the harpist. It was like out of a movie—beautiful, romantic, theatrical, magical and emotional. He held me in his arms like he did when we first hugged during the filming of *Flying Fists* on his television show . . . the wind blew gently . . . my hair softly floated as if in slow motion . . . I forgot how cold it was. Looking into his eyes I felt the warmth of summer. We were in our own movie. There's one picture that Cesare captured that personified it all for us.

In the Saloon many toasts and speeches entertained us all. David gallantly tossed his glass of champagne onto the floor to mega applause and cheers. It was replaced by non-alcoholic bubbly. We couldn't afford to pay for lighting the street—an extra $20,000—so the celebration had to end when the sun went down.

The two actor-kidnappers who bride-napped me had a hoot of a time trying to pick me up and pile me into the first car, with David the hero in hot pursuit, chasing me in the second limo. That was how we ended the wedding party. We rode or rather drove off in our modern day version of two white horses . . . two white stretch limos as planned. We met up at the end of the studio entry, where we got into one vehicle and sped off home into the sunset. Literally. Strangely and sadly the route we took to get to Gate 7, down Forrest Lawn Drive from Barham Boulevard, is the same one that the funeral-goers had to take to attend David's funeral at Forrest Lawn about a half mile further down the road.

We didn't have the budget to pay for any wedding dinner and we didn't want to risk losing the exclusive, so instead, we hid in the house and had our wedding feast delivered from my cousin Sebastian's restaurant. Over dinner, I presented David with his wedding gift—a small erotic nude bronze of me. It's now somewhere with who knows whom, but I have the original model and pulled some molds from it to duplicate. It's titled "Ahhhhhhhhh." I'm working on others as well and I have David to thank for pushing me more into that arena. Part of our pact was to do a sculpture together, but it never happened. Best of intentions.

Our wedding certainly made history at the studio. There was a huge billboard at the entry of Laramie Street, where they would take the tour trams. It listed all the historic westerns filmed there. Aside from the fact they listed the year wrong, it read: *"DAVID CARRADINE'S WEDDING – Not a movie, his actual wedding!"* They had 1988 instead of the correct year 1998, which I had to laugh about, because this was so typically symbolic. Just about everything that had to do with David got mixed up, had to be saved, corrected, or sidetracked, caused problems, or chaos ensued. Nothing was easy or just flowed. It seemed to me that everything he was involved in or touched got tweaked some way or another.

You just have to smile at the irony. It still pangs. Blackie and Johnny ... come rain or come shine. I never felt as married or as close to any man in my life as I did with Johnny.

February 27, 2010. As I was sorting through boxes of pictures for this book, I came across two video tapes of footage from our wedding taken by two of David's friends. It was footage I asked for time and time again. Evidently, David forgot to tell me he received the videos and placed them in the book case with the *Access Hollywood* tapes. I never knew until I viewed them some twelve years later, that it was the "lost footage" of our wedding. It was a two-hour sobfest.

CHAPTER TWENTY-SIX

DAVID, THE HERO

DAVID loved to be the good guy, especially if it challenged authority. Larry Beckerman, a longtime friend of mine, was stricken with lung cancer and was in his final weeks in the hospital. He talked about the pain and process and how he wished he could get hold of a joint—pot. When I told David about Larry and that I wanted to fly to Seattle, he immediately grabbed his phone and said, "We're going to grant his wish. I know where we can get some." He had that little devilish smile on his face. An escapade was afoot!

Five minutes later he tells me he's going out to a friend's house in Laurel Canyon and to wait until after he comes back with the stash. He was going to go with me and I should make travel reservations to leave ASAP. He came back home with a bag full of marijuana, which he relished in preparing for my friend. Okay, he kept some for himself too. I hated the smell and we were very careful never to have anything like that in the house just in case something happened, like an impromptu raid. That's all we needed, to have him in the headlines again associated with something that could hurt all the effort made to rebuild his image. David laughed at the thought of getting caught. "I escaped South Africa!"

As we packed, it suddenly occurred to me: how in the hell were we going to get this past security?! Even though this was well before 9-11, it was still very risky. David sported his biggest grin, and caressed my face with his gentle hands, "Not for you to worry. I'll take care of this. If anyone takes the fall, it will be me. Besides, they wouldn't dare." And he gave a big laugh. Uh-oh. Wouldn't they?

He didn't want to chance the airline losing his luggage, so he expertly hid the joints inside his carry-on. But what if they had drug-sniffing dogs? "At LAX?" He laughed and reassured me again. "If anyone's going down, it's going to be me. I don't want you going to jail. You'd look good behind anything, my bride, but not that." Geeee, thanks, hun!

It was an intense, nerve-wracking time for me at the airport. Going through security, he was recognized by the security guards who were too star-struck, engaging in conversation with their hero, to check him or our carry-on. I pretended to be preoccupied with the usual—putting on lipstick, and being "bored" with all the airport shuffle. David was as cool as a cucumber and didn't behave any differently than he had in other numerous trips we made when he was in a good mood. As we cleared the area and strutted down the hallway away from security earshot, we looked at each other and took a deep breath. David gave me a wink and a theatrical cowboy-like, "Whoooo! Glad that's over!" then uttered a big "Ha! Let's get something to eat. I could use an espresso!" He was nervous after all.

At the hotel, David repacked the joints into a small, pretty wooden box to conceal them for Larry. He took extra care, as if he knew my friend, even though they never met or talked.

We spent a few hours at the hospital and David was very supportive of me, Larry and his wife. Larry was grateful for our efforts and our presence bolstered his day. It was a tough visit, but David cracked jokes and told stories until it was time to leave.

A few weeks later, we were in Ireland filming when I got word Larry passed away. He never got a chance to indulge in the gift because the one short trip out of the hospital was cancelled. Because of the equipment and strict rules, he couldn't light up in the room. The news hit me hard and I needed David's shoulder to cry on, but he wasn't there for me. He turned a cold shoulder and said something like life sucks and left the room. I just needed to be held. His actions compounded the pain I felt on losing my friend. I didn't understand David's change of emotion and lack of support. I turned to Bobby and Edie, who were there with us for consolation.

Years later when one of David's dearest longtime friends, Stan Unger, died, David didn't go to the funeral. I couldn't understand that either, especially since he didn't hesitate to attend a memorial at the Troubadour for its owner Doug Weston. Maybe it was too close to home and he couldn't deal with any of it.

CHAPTER TWENTY-SEVEN

WHAT A TRIP

WHEN I was little—and even now—I'd look up in the sky and watch the planes and jets crossing overhead in the distance, and wonder. At night, the wing lights blinking in silence, on board, the low drone of the engines lulling the passengers . . . some reading by the overhead lights, some sleeping with blankets pulled up tight . . . up into the skies until the small bright dot disappeared into the distance. Where were they going? Why were they traveling? Were their destinations far away places or nearby jaunts? Were they traveling alone, with their lovers or families? Were they arriving in L.A. for the first time? Who would be there to greet them?

Other than Hawaii or London, I never really longed to travel much. Probably, mostly, because I loved my animals so much—they're like my children—and I hated to leave them behind. Clairvoyants always told me I'd travel extensively in my life, but that information was just set aside. Okay, yeah, sure.

When I started making a list of the places David and I ventured to, all of a sudden I realized how extensive our travels were. There were so many wonderful places we journeyed to for location shoots, personal appearances, his book tour, festivals, fund-raisers, it was mind-boggling and seemed non-stop.

A good deal of the time we'd travel coach, because the project budgets were so low and sometimes they didn't allow for me to travel with David. So he'd trade in his first class ticket for two coach seats. Other times, the airline would bump us up as a courtesy if there was room. When David started booking better gigs, we made it standard in his contract to include an extra ticket. No matter where we sat on the plane, we were always treated special—extra nuts, caviar or whatever they could to make the trip more enjoyable. Ah, the small perks of traveling with a celebrity.

Something *almost* comical happened each trip. David would often fall asleep with his mouth wide open and I'd lean over to nudge him, so he'd wake up briefly and reposition himself, but in the process he'd knock over a drink spilling it either on himself, or me, or someone next to him, causing ruffled feathers. Once, he nodded off while working on a crossword puzzle, with me asleep on his shoulder. When I woke up, he was in exactly the same position, but there was no pen. Someone literally lifted the sterling silver pen out of his hand. We had all of first class looking for the pen. No pen. To snatch it right out of his hand—baaad karma!

Other times, David would forget things in the airport, or on the plane. Many times, I'd call the airline or a restaurant to do a search for one of his lighters or cigarette cases, glasses, books, only to find it in his inside pocket or briefcase where he'd overlook it. David never allowed enough time to get to the airport or plane. Our drivers would always be in a frenzy. I started to fib about the departure time, telling him it was half an hour earlier. That only lasted for a few trips and he caught on.

It was usually a last minute jog to the gate because he wanted to get a cup of coffee, magazine or have a last-second smoke. Always a panic, but never missed a flight. One time, they actually closed the plane doors and re-opened them because it was David Carradine! It got to the point, because we ran to catch the plane so often, I bought a special pair of Bally wedgy shoes to look classy with the black velvet travel sweats I always wore, so I could sprint in them with the best of the plane-runners. They were worth the investment. I wear them to travel in to this day.

As soon as we got home, there were other trips in the works. China, Cannes, Milan, Spain, Puerto Rico, Puerto Vallarta, Turkey, Alaska, Austin and Dallas, Texas, Indiana, NY, Vail and Telluride in Colorado, Park City and Moab in Utah, Vancouver and Toronto and Montreal in Canada, Hawaii—swimming with Hoby the Dolphin—Paris. Not to mention "local" locations—San Diego, Palm Springs, Santa Barbara. Each has very special memories and stories. There wasn't a place we traveled to that David wasn't recognized as "Kung Fu," from the neighborhood corner of our house to the most remote streets of China, Mexico and Turkey. You name it, people asked for an autograph.

No matter where we went, we always sought out small side trips, to art galleries or to our other favorite pharmacy drug stores. Odd, I know, but we both loved it. We'd troll down the aisles and find tchotchke items like reading glasses, cigarette lighters, hand cream or souvenir pins with the city's name on it for my pin jacket collection—a jean jacket full of souvenir pins from my travels—or a gift to bring back home for my mother. Unlike the commercial, it wasn't a credit card David never left home without. It was pebbles. We would buy special selected stones for him to bring on our travels, to Ireland and China, for example, to hand out to fans or co-workers. On the surface of some, he'd etch out an Asian symbol or his initials with an awl or roto tool I had.

Travel meant alone time, just the two of us. Concentrated, necessary bonding times that were romantic, exciting, fun adventures together. There are so many memories and stories to tell. A few stand out.

* * *

In 2000, David got a call to narrate a documentary on China, where they were to film at the Shaolin Temple outside of Zhengzhou. *The* Shaolin Temple. I suggested to the producer that instead of having David doing just a voice-over, how about having him on the trip as the tour guide and host?

Next thing we know, we're getting our pre-travel shots at the doctor's —a whole series, including hepatitis and malaria. The trek was a long one, but flying first class, who cared? Armed with an interpreter and the producer, we stopped in Beijing and took white-knuckled cab rides to various locations. You think driving is crazy here? There, there's no such thing as driving on one side of the road. It's a free-for-all. One of our flights was delayed two hours and the airline gave all the passengers courtesy key chains as an apology. Now that's good PR!

Seeing such extreme poverty in contrast to the wealthy clientele at our posh hotel was a culture shock. It's one thing to see it on TV, but to be amidst it, the smells, sounds and sights up close and personal, is gut wrenching.

The Abbot himself invited us inside his private chambers at the Shaolin Temple. It was surreal looking at the real thing, as if we were on the soundstage for David's show. Any minute we expected to hear over a walkie, "Scouting for Sparky." We were transported in time, space travelers landing in this strange village of temples and fragrant burning incense.

Only David was invited to eat with monks, as a gesture of honor. The food was basically soup and bread. Extremely simple diet and lifestyle. The martial artists performed for the cameras and we were introduced to the youngest "prodigy" being trained in the monastery. He was about seven years old and already a legend in China. They gave us T-shirts with a caricature of the kid on them. Children from the most remote regions of China, we were told, are sent by their families to study there at the school.

The Abbot looked like the stereotype happy Buddha, only he seldom smiled. We did manage to see a glimpse of his not so pearly teeth when David showed him a clip from the Kung Fu TLC show. He thought it was funny seeing David as a bald monk in a flashback scene. Before we left, the Abbot gave me two books he wrote and cracked a parting smile for me. One of these days, I'll have to get them translated since they're written in Chinese.

The producer treated us and the crew to a feast at one of the local restaurants outside the village where we were staying. That's where I got an intestinal bug of some kind and got sick. There was no hot water and goodness knows if they used soap to wash the dishes. The director got sick too. My gut felt as if it was being pulled in ten different directions and any minute "Alien" was going to pop through. David had more filming to do so I had to stay in the room, alone. No phone, no one who spoke English. He was very hesitant to leave me—not half as much as I was—but he did, with the assurance they'd be gone only a couple of hours. They were gone longer and I was totally anxiety ridden. Some of the symptoms started to subside into a kind of dull gnawing in my stomach, so I tried to curb my paranoia and focus on a book we brought. Ohmygod, it was so good to see him walk through the door! David was just as relieved to see me.

We left the next day to go back to Beijing where a doctor was called in to my aid. It was no big deal to him. He gave me a few bags that contained little round brown pills and instructions. Overnight, the pain went away, and after a few days, so did the weakness. Magic herbs. I think. He spoke little English so we didn't know what was in those pills, but they saved the day. Never did find out what the diagnosis was either.

The two weeks went by so fast. We toured all around Hong Kong, bought silk jackets and cashmere sweaters for peanuts compared to U.S. prices, filmed at the famous harbor, and toured Tiananmen Square when we were in Beijing. We also filmed atop a mountain, where we had to take a long tram ride up to the top. I was trying not to look down and clung to the tram, while David took it all in and made fun of my being silly. "Oh, come on. What's the worst that could happen? Fall a few thousand feet?" He laughed. We had the most incredible bird's eye view of China. Part of the documentary took us to a film studio where David interviewed Jackie Chan. That was a special moment for all of us. We spent the afternoon with Jackie, who gave us a personal tour. I made sure we stayed in contact after returning to the States and Jackie later invited us to the premiere of *Rush Hour*. Very humble, gentle and funny man.

* * *

David was asked to be a presenter at the International Televison Awards—

Telegato Awards—in Milan, which is a huge event, equivalent to the American Oscars. Everyone who's anyone turns out for the event. We got a call from a talent booker for the show who offered not only a nice price for David to be a presenter, but first class service start to finish, from limo pick-up at the house to helping us make arrangements to attend the Cannes Film Festival in France. Most of the time, we had to pay for our own transportation to LAX.

It was a special thrill for me to go to Italy for the first time because my ancestors were from Sicily and cousins to Cardinal D'Este, who lived in Villa D'Este. David, being the avid and experienced traveler and anxious to share "his city's" favorite haunts, had already lined up places to see. He did this whenever we traveled to places that he had previously trekked.

We stayed at the five-star hotel Principe Di Savoia with its 19th century interior designed rooms that overlooked the Piazza della Repubblica and were given one of the coveted Imperial Suites only because the Presidential Suite was booked. Every inch of the hotel had magnificent architecture and decor. It was like a palace and we felt like royalty.

A car soon whisked us off to the award ceremony where the traffic soon backed up bumper-to-bumper on the way to the venue, very much like Los Angeles for any award show. As we pulled up to the red carpet area, we could see hoards of fans.

When David rolled down the dark tinted window to smoke his cigarette, we were taken by surprise by the crowd screaming his name. Like a cloud of locusts, about five hundred fans descended on the limo. Even David was taken aback.

"Now I know how the Beatles or the Stones must have felt."

As he quickly tried to roll the window back up a hand tried to reach inside. It was funny to see it kind of groping around, trying to touch him. He signed a napkin and put it in the hand, which immediately retracted back outside.

The security guards couldn't hold all of them back and the ones that got past, about a hundred, were screaming out his name and started pounding on the car and waving. Some put their faces to the window trying to look inside. We waved just in case they could see us. The driver said they too wanted his autograph.

David grabbed more napkins from the car's bar, signed them and handed them out to the grasping hands. Thank goodness the car started moving again—we ran out of napkins.

Finally inside the building, a flurry of people on crew scurried about and led David backstage for his entrance. I stayed off to the side of the audience seating area, near the cameras, to watch. When David walked on stage, the applause was thunderous. They whistled and "whooped" their support. Italiano—very demonstrative!

We had a couple of days of sightseeing, which was our well-deserved playtime together. Those moments were part of what I waited and worked so hard for, just the two of us enjoying and focusing on each other for a change. David bought me a Borsalino hat and we walked hand in hand around town to the La Scala opera house, where they gave us a VIP tour, to the cathedral, which was equally jaw dropping, and to the Ducati motorcycle factory. I set David up with an Italian modeling agent and they signed him up on the spot. We were off to Cannes the next day.

The show provided a driver to take us by limo via the scenic route along the Riviera to the film festival. It was about a hundred and eighty miles, and fabulous. The driver and David exchanged stories, cultures and we listened to music the entire trip.

A few hours later, we arrived in Cannes and took up at the Hotel Sofitel where they had a piano in the bar area. David took immediate command over it. The room was small, romantic, charming, very Frrrrrrench. It was a short walk along the sparkling waterfront of La Croisette to the Palais for screenings, parties and schmoozing. Word got out to the press we were there—I got a shortlist to call—and we hooked up with a publicist who helped connect us to further venues that included a lunch with the festival president, premieres and events at the very private and elite Grand-Hôtel du Cap-Ferrat.

Our mutual friend Alan Oberholzer and his wife Patricia were also there premiering their film, so we met up several times. Even getting caught in the rain was enjoyable.

It was a non-stop, unforgettable whirlwind each time we went to Cannes, especially the year we were married. I had a chance to wear my incredible fully beaded, silver peek-a-boo Bob Mackie gown for one of the premieres on the steps of the Palais where David, in his wedding tux, bent me back in a long kiss in front of hundreds of clicking and flashing press cameras.

There were invitations to every party, people tugging at David for autographs and conversation, the press pushing for interviews. And the best of all was sneaking off, just the two of us, finding quaint out-of-the-way cafes to have our romantic moments. Yes, sigh . . . it was wonderful!

* * *

Another year at Cannes, we attended a press conference, where Martin Scorsese was in attendance and the main focus. David was jonzing to see Marty because it had been years since their last contact. He longed to connect in hopes of re-bonding and working together again. We were among the last to get in and stood in the very back of the enormous white tent. The people up front, on the panel, where Scorsese was, looked like little dolls, we were that far back.

The conference was nearing its close and David's hope of seeing Marty was slipping away. "We'll never get close to him, Blackie. There are just too many people. Look at this circus."

Indeed it was a mad sea of reporters, security guards and literally hundreds of people vying for positions between Scorsese and us.

David lamented again, "We'll never be able to get to him. Let's forget it."

I hated to see him so deflated. It made me all that more determined. We weren't going to give up without trying. I just knew we could do it.

I had to make this happen for my Johnny. "Wanna make a bet? Follow me!"

He looked at my determined expression and smiled weakly, "Okaaaaay."

I grabbed David's hand and led him in tow under partitions and over ropes, detoured around guards, jumped, dodged and dashed in front and back of passersby. We were gaining ground! There was one final roadblock in the form of a beefy security guard. The last hurdle between us and Scorsese was a velvet rope behind beef-cake. I turned to David and said, "Go around me, now!"

I tapped the guard on the opposite shoulder to distract him and said, "I'd like you meet David Carradine!" The diversion worked. David scooted around so when "beefy" turned to where David wasn't anymore, I scooted around the other side and over the rope to get to Scorsese. In one final move, I grabbed David's arm and jerked him from my back to my front. This placed David right next to Scorsese, who was in the middle of an on-camera interview. David stood there waiting for a moment and I knew there was no time because "beefy" was upset and wanted us to step back, so I tapped Scorsese on the shoulder and said, "I believe you know my husband, David Carradine."

Scorsese turned to us and busted open the biggest smile. He grabbed David in a bear hug as the cameras rolled. They hadn't seen each other since *Box Car Bertha*. After their brief chat, we walked out of the tent on clouds. David's feet didn't touch the ground. I turned to "beefy" and smiled. He gave me a wry look as we walked triumphantly away. I would never have done anything like that before I met David. He taught me literally to go beyond the boundaries.

We were walking along the Croisette and passed by the Chopard jewelry window display. I gazed in the window at the "Happy Diamond" designs—diamonds contained in the jewelry that jiggle around as the wearer moves—and pointed out a pair of earrings. It was the pair I wanted to buy at the airport on my way to Luxembourg when I filmed the series

Dracula, but there wasn't enough time or else I'd miss the plane. Elegant gold heart-shaped studs with three small, happy, bouncy, diamonds inside.

David said, "Let's check it out."

Okay, I love to drool over jewelry. Ever since I made my own silver jewelry in high school, I had always wanted to design my own line someday, so to while away time over these Chopard beauties was fine by me.

While the salesman was showing me more of their glittering baubles and treating us to coffee and hors d'oeuvre, David tells the man to remove something from the display case. He was so thrilled about meeting Scorsese again, that to commemorate the accomplishment, he bought me the pair of heart-shaped Happy Diamond Chopard earrings I longed for.

"Here, Blackie. You deserve these. Thank you."

My all-time favorite jewelry, outside the dragon pin he designed for me for Valentine's Day.

* * *

We played a Frank Sinatra CD with the song *I Love Paris* on it as a continual reminder of one of the most unforgettable, romantic trips we took together—Paris.

While working on *Queen of Swords*, we were trying to decide what nice hotel to stay at on our way back from Cannes. David's choice was the George V where he had stayed previously, but the ritzy hotel was now out of our price range. Even if it was affordable, that was part of his history with Gail, and I wanted our own separate place to create memories. That was more than fine with him. Fresh start. One of the men on production highly recommended Hotel Galileo. His word was good enough for us, so reservations were made.

At the airport, we went through our second bomb scare—the first had been in Turkey. This time, people took it seriously and it was a tense hour delay, all because of a false alarm. We chatted in our broken French with the driver who brought us to a bed and breakfast hotel. Quaint, cozy, charming, unique and so close to everything—Arc de Triomphe, Champs Elysées. Our room was very small, but just as charming as the rest of the hotel. It had a section in the back of the room we could close off with a curtain for David to smoke and open the windows, which overlooked the street.

When we closed the door to our mini-suite, we could leave everything behind. Hollywood, the financial battles, demands on David from his family, phone calls . . . it was a peace that we rarely had with each other. It was a calm I never experienced before, but how I always dreamed love would be like. And we had it. Three days of pure bliss. We daydreamed about coming back and taking an apartment there to live and do our artwork, we loved it so much. The apartment never happened, but we did return to Paris and stayed at the same hotel, which was equally as wonderful as our first time.

David could hardly contain himself, he was so anxious to show me the town, with the first stop being Fouquet's for dinner. We decked ourselves out and headed to the five-star restaurant where everything was in its place and perfect. Perfect manners, perfect gestures, perfect decor, service and food. I loved to hear everyone speaking French and gushing over David. The people of Paris treated him with reverence and respect. He was relaxed, happy, and a different "Johnny" emerged. He didn't drink as much espresso or smoke as much. His face had a constant smile and he was consistently sensitive to my feelings. He paid attention to me, remembered things. I didn't have to watch over him. Relief and a bit of heaven. It was like a honeymoon "do-over."

He took me shopping along Champs Elysées, and bought a few pairs of phenomenal shoes, spent hours at the Louvre where he purchased a small Rodin reproduction, and outside bought original artwork from the local artists who were painting and selling their wares on the spot. We were hoping to discover the next Picasso or Monet.

In the next couple days we took in the Arc de Triomphe, the Eiffel

Tower, Notre Dame, Moulin Rouge and many fabulous cafes. It was cold and damp as the rain continued, which made it all that much more romantic, holding hands as we walked through the Tuileries Gardens. David acted as tour guide for each location, relaying its history, what it's like other times of the year and more places he would take me. We stopped at the swanky George V hotel and warmed up with coffee, then headed to "our" hotel to freshen up for a night on the town at Crazy Horse.

That's an experience and a half. An amazing show with topless women precision dancing to fabulous music. Each number was a showstopper. It's strange to see a line up of dancers like that and almost forget they are topless. Their anatomy all looked exactly the same, so it became a kind of eyesight challenge of sorts for me. It's not like one set of breasts looked bigger or a different shape . . . it was kind of . . . odd. David told me that's on purpose, they are all a certain height and shape and all . . . I thought how strange the auditions must be, but then, I guess for them, maybe not. It is sooooo Frrrrrrrench! David was surprised I liked the show. Why not? There was nothing not to like. It was *magnifique!*

"That's my Blackie," he grinned proudly.

It was the most perfect trip in spite of being drenched in the rain with a broken umbrella. Even that turned into a special encounter. We stood at a corner as the umbrella went belly up on us in the wind. David tried to hail a taxi, to no avail. But hey, it was French rain! As we decided to make a run for it, a sophisticated and attractive woman driving a Range Roger type vehicle stopped and lowered the window, and with an unbelieving expression, asked "Are you *David Carradine?*"

David shouted back with a chuckle over the loud street sounds, wind and water splashing around us, "Yeah, a very wet David Carradine."

"Get in!"

We piled our soaked bodies into the warm dry car.

The woman said she couldn't believe her eyes that it was actually him, getting soaked . . . in Paris!

"Oh, I've done some pretty strange things before, but this wasn't planned." We laughed. Turns out this wasn't just an ordinary Parisian, this was Gardner Bellanger, president and director general of Condé Nast France. She invited us out to dinner the next night, and we met her family and visited at her elegant home nearby. It was quite the highlight of our trip to be welcomed by such a gracious hostess under such unusual circumstances. When we got back home we told everyone how she rescued us in the rain.

On each trip to Paris we wandered along Îles Saint Louis and its neighborhood of adorable boutiques, cafes, bakeries, cheese shops, and gourmet shops: its own 17th century quaint world with rustic streets and charming storefronts. One of my favorite stores on the planet is there, Pylones: whimsical, cheery, designer merchandise from kitchenware to toys. I purchased a couple of bike bells and the most adorable green umbrella with rubber frogs on the tips. It was a tribute not only to France, but to our inside joke, " . . . rather see a rain of toads than to hear the sound of baboons on zah road!" Well, I got my rain of toads to carry with me! It still hangs on my guest closet door.

Paris was the most romantic time we ever spent together. For me, it was the most romantic time of my life. David said he wanted to keep Hotel Galileo a secret for us, which made it extra special. It was our "honeymoon hotel."

During our divorce, I found out he took his girlfriend on a trip to Paris and stayed there at "our" hotel. Was he reaching for memories of us there together? Was it a way to still be with me? Wouldn't he want a fresh start with the new person in his life, as he had with me? I couldn't understand why he'd stay in the same place when there were such strong feelings for us there, sharing this little hideaway together. You can't just wipe those away. Those types of shadows always linger. How could he not think of our special time in that hotel together?

* * *

People would say how lucky I was to have these opportunities, and I agree, but nothing is without its price. The work involved in the planning, taking care of David, watching over him pre trip, during trip, after trip—it would have been nice to have someone watching over me for a change. But things were what they were. I'm fortunate to have these very precious moments with David to look back fondly on. They outweigh the angst. I still roll my eyes and chuckle about him spilling the drinks and losing things . . . If I had it to do over again, I'd take along a video camera to remember more.

Chapter Twenty-Eight

THE MELTDOWN MAMBO

I believe the house David and I had in Tarzana—The Rosita House—was haunted. My experiences there were not so much scary, as they were "amusing." Nevertheless, because of all the strife David and I were going through, I turned to our dear friend Patricia to suggest some sort of protection ceremony.

"Oh, I've got a great one!" She instructed me to put a small amount of olive oil in my palm and draw a small cross on every door, window and mirror in the house. As I did that, I was to say an affirmation or prayer to expel *all* the evil from the house and call in divine light. Easy enough. About three days prior to my trip to Toronto for meetings on a project and an audition, I decided to anoint the house, which left me with a sense of peace. And off I zipped to the city that brought so much joy into my life, including David.

May 9, 2001, in Yorkville, Toronto at 2 pm EST

I had purchased a beautiful pair of two-toned blue leather western boots for David as an "I miss you so much" gift and was on my way to meet Mark Breslin (owner of the Yuk Yuk comedy clubs in Canada) for a 2:30 lunch at the Four Seasons' Studio Cafe. I had just talked to David about an hour earlier, and we both said how much we loved each other and I hinted at the surprise I bought for him. He gave an odd response, but I didn't think too much of it, since I thought he was just in one of his funk moods. I thought he was just missing me.

I was hustling down Bay Street, approaching Yorkville, when I got paged. There was a 911 at the end of our pet sitter's number. I felt a shock wave bolt through me, thinking that something had happened to one of our six pets—two dogs and four cats. I had hired Jeanie and Kathy to come in every day to tend our beloved critters because I knew David would either forget to feed or walk them or do something amiss regarding their care, as he'd always done in the past. More than a dozen times, I'd come home to him asleep on the couch with a lit cigarette or with something on the stove burner in mid meltdown.

So instead of worrying or getting angry with him, the gals would visit twice a day and make sure everything was okay. Kathy's voice was a bit shaky. "Uh, I don't know how to put this ... "

My heart was pounding. "Something happened to any of the pets!?"

"Uh, no ... they're fine ... uh ... something is going on here we think you should know about. Uhhhh ... We think David is moving out."

My brain froze. "Whhhhaat?"

"Well, there were all these boxes around, and he was packing stuff, and when we asked him what it was all for, he just said he was making some changes. Uh ... he's packing his clothes and has movers planned. Took a TV."

"I just talked to him about an hour ago! What?!" It was hard for me to catch a breath. "I'll call you guys back. I have to call him." I kept repeating to myself that they were mistaken. It had to be a misunderstanding. This couldn't be true! My fingers were trembling so badly, I had a difficult time punching up the numbers. David answered. I tried to be calm, took a breath and asked "So, what's this I hear about boxes?"

There was a beat. His voice was somber. "Oh, you found out."

My fear turned to anger. I thought, duh, you ass, like the pet sitters wouldn't let me know! Then I felt the fear again and into the cell phone I cried, "What's going on?!"

He continued in a tired voice, "I'm moving out."

There was this awful nauseating, wrenching, feeling that started in the pit of my stomach and radiated over my body in one whoooosh of adrenaline panic: fight-or-flight. I felt like someone had thrown me out of a high-rise and I was falling into a dark, never-ending pit. It was like being in the Twilight Zone. My voice wobbled. "You're what?" I started to crumple to the ground, but dashed into the foyer of a building so I wouldn't be walked over by pedestrians. The echo of my panicked whimpering in the corridor didn't help. "What are you talking about?"

He started to get defensive after hearing me snivel. "See, this is what I was trying to avoid. I knew you'd cry, and I didn't want this."

I started to get angry again. "Of course I'd cry!! You mean you were just going to move and not tell me?! What were you going to do, leave me a note?!"

"I don't know. I thought maybe I'd call you on your way to the airport."

Oh yeah, like that would have been great. At the airport with no one to turn to. Worse yet, if I didn't have time to call anyone and I'd actually be on the plane. I could picture myself having a breakdown and trying to muffle the sounds under a flimsy blanket with everyone on board thinking that I was crazy, or something. How shitty would that have been?! Thank God the pet sitters gave me a heads-up.

He got more defensive, then he took the offensive. "See, it's getting confrontational. This is exactly what I didn't want. I knew if I did this when you were here, you wouldn't let me leave and it would be a big crying scene . . . I have to get out. It's not working."

I tried to use common sense. "But we were going to counseling. I thought it was helping. Don't give up. We're making progress." I pleaded again with another wave of tears. "You can't give up, Johnny. I love you so much! Please don't do this!!!" I honked into a tissue and asked, "So do you want a divorce?"

Then he offered the first of a few thoughtful, contemplative things for me to chew on. "I love you too. I'm not talking about getting a divorce. We just don't get along anymore. I don't want a divorce. I feel like I'm constantly disappointing you. We'll just live in separate places. You won't have to put up with my smoking . . . "

Deep in my shock with tears falling to the ground, I can still remember passersby looking at my pathetic body balled up in a corner of the foyer. My hiccupping cries echoed through the hallway and out the front doors. "I can't believe this is happening. This can't be happening! Please don't leave, Johnny. You're giving up. Please don't give up."

He got pissy. "See, this is exactly what I wanted to avoid!! We'll talk when you get back. I have to go now." He hung up and didn't answer when I tried calling him back a dozen times.

By now, I felt totally integrated with the granite flooring underneath my body. I had melted so tightly into the corner, that I might need a suction machine to pry me out. I repeated a hundred times to myself that this couldn't be happening, as if the mantra would make it untrue. That horrible feeling of knowing it is, yet praying it's a nightmare you can wake up from, then throw yourself around the other person in deep relief when you do wake up. Deep breath. It was just a dream. But it's not. It's real alright.

Remembering my appointment with Mark, I rushed over to the hotel, looking down at my feet so people couldn't see my tear-stained and now puffy face. I headed quickly through the lobby and up the escalator to the restaurant. I looked at his smiling face, which dropped immediately upon seeing me, knowing the answer to his question already.

"What happened? Are you alright?"

I approached him and buried my head on his shoulder, sobbing like Mary Tyler Moore did in her television show. "Noooooooooo! David is moving out. I found out from the pet sitters just now. I talked to him and he had planned to move out entirely without me knowing, while I was up here!!" And I broke down in sobs again.

Mark put his arm around me and hustled me gently into the restaurant, where we got a table that allowed me privacy so I could cry unseen by patrons. I related what happened, updated him about past problems, and even through the trauma, he made me smile and laugh. That is an art, and a true friend. He had been there for me during my Dabney traumas and he was there for me now. Mark ordered me "comfort food" —a grilled cheese sandwich—which I somehow managed to eat part of. For the hour we sat, I was able to pull myself back together a bit. Just enough to get me back to the hotel and put in some other support calls to a couple of close friends.

I tried to get a flight out that night, but it was too late to get to the airport, so I changed it for the first plane out the following morning. I was invited to the Blossom Gala at Holt Renfrew, at which Jane Seymour and her husband, James Keach, were the key honored guests of the evening. I originally had planned to surprise them and thought maybe if I pushed myself to attend, it would help save my sanity for the evening. It would be better than sitting in my hotel room crying my eyes out and not being able to do anything. I didn't know then how right I'd be. In the meantime, I put an SOS call out to my dear friend Marilyn. With her psychic insight, she gave me key things to do and not to do when I returned home, to help pull my power back and ground myself before I walked in the door.

That night, I got dressed up and kept slapping on make-up, crying, smudging it, wiping it off with tissues, and putting on some more, only to start crying again. Finally, after the fourth time, I thought if I rushed out the door, it might keep me from crying again. It worked for the most part, but the pang in my stomach and the feeling of free-falling was still there. There was nothing emotionally to hold on to. I sat in the cab on the way to the gala with my arms around myself for fear I'd fall apart. I got to Holt Renfrew—Toronto's version of Neiman Marcus—and headed upstairs to the event. I wandered around in an aimless daze, seeing how cheerfully everything was decorated and I spotted the cameras flashing off in a corner. Then I saw Jane taking an interview and James off on the side observing. I rushed over to say hello and was greeted by a big surprised smile. He gave me a big hug, and we chatted a bit about how gorgeous

Jane looked. Then he turned to me with a curious look.

"How are you?"

Instead of breaking down on his shoulder sobbing, as I had with Mark, I said, "Oh, fine, except I just found out this afternoon that David was in the middle of moving out without telling me. So . . . I guess I could be doing better. I'm a little . . . in shock." I gave a wimpy smile. He looked at my puffed eyes and put his hand on my shoulder.

His comforting touch made me feel vulnerable again. I took a deep breath, trying to hold in the tears. James said, "C'mon, let's talk." He escorted me over to an area with less commotion and proceeded to spend the next half hour pulling me through my trauma. "Forget David now. You focus on what *you* want. What *you* are going to do for *your*self. You will get through this."

James knew David from way back, well before I did, so he knew what I was dealing with. We talked about alcoholics, dry-drunk syndrome and denial, which helped dispel some of the myths and misinformation I had. Most important, James reminded me to take care of myself first. He treated me with the loving respect of a brother and helped bring me through the experience. His and Marilyn's advice was the magical combo I needed to hold on and to temporarily stop the free-fall. It also not only helped me face the chaos, but ground me for months to come.

May 10, Thursday morning, back in L.A.

The 7 a.m. flight back seemed to take days and I feared what I'd find at the house. Jeanie and Kathy left me a message that the movers were supposed to be there in the morning, but David missed them because he was asleep. When I got to the house about 10 am, it looked like a bomb had exploded. I walked around in each room trying to keep myself together. Then I noticed a spiral notebook had fallen to the floor from the wet bar and papers had fallen out. When I picked them up, I noticed a familiar name. It was a person whom one of David's friends was trying to pass off as having psychic abilities. I didn't like this particular friend of David's because I felt they were trying to usurp my position as David's manager. I didn't like the vibe I got off this other person who wrote David the letter either. I thought they were two sycophants trying to worm their way into our lives. I guess they succeeded. David said he hadn't been in communication with this person for months and had no interest in the psychic thing anymore. He lied.

From the letter, they were not only in constant communication, but I could tell they were giving him "psychic advice" all along for at least a couple of years. Coincidentally, it tied in to when problems between us escalated. I felt the letter undermined me and my relationship with David. There were direct and indirect insinuations of what I had supposedly done in the marriage, and advice to David that his friend was the one to help his career and could be trusted. Like I couldn't?! Like I wasn't honest with David?! I and others proved to David in the past that his "friend" couldn't be trusted.

Did David listen to anyone who was really telling him the truth? Didn't seem like he cared. Then the thunderbolt hit. This "prediction" gave David the dates when he should move out: May 7 to 10! The date on the letter was April 26. The "friend" knew I was leaving town, had all the "inside" information because David would spill the beans. I thought problems we were having were used in this "prediction" as a way to finally separate a vulnerable David from me.

The letter hinted that I was hiding money from him, when it was the opposite. I was outraged by it all, feeling they were succeeding in turning David against me. I couldn't believe he bought into the crap, hook, line and sinker. But, sadly, he did.

I could see Lulu and Thunder asleep outside in the backyard. Then I walked into the bedroom and saw him snoring away in a deep sleep. I couldn't decide if I wanted to throw myself on him and envelope him with pleading love, or attack him with a barrage of hammer punches and screams. I took a third option and stood over him, staring in disbelief, then finally tapped his chest lightly. He woke with a start and stared back at me in silence.

I stated flatly. "You missed the movers. "

He bolted out of his daze. "Oh shit. Oh God."

I didn't say anything as he got up.

"This place is a mess," I said, again flatly, as I left the room.

I took a deep breath and tried to remember all of what Marilyn told me to do. David was trying to get himself together as I stood off to the side and actually began handing him things. "Here you forgot this," and, "You better put this with that or you'll lose track of it."

The movers came and went. Did he know where he was going? No. The only plan was to put it all in storage and stay a while at his longtime pal Peter Jason's until he finished the filming he was going to do with Keith on a cable movie.

The house looked like an empty shell after the last box was removed. He looked around and then went to the hall closet to place a jacket *in* it.

"What are you doing?" I asked.

"Well, I thought I'd leave something here to have handy".

I half laughed "Handy for what? You're moving *out*."

He looked at me like why would I ask a silly thing like that and said, "For when I come to visit . . . have dinner . . . "

My head felt like it was going to explode trying to fathom this logic. "Visit? Dinner?! You want to move. You want out, so go and take *all* your things with you."

With that, I went to the closet and handed him his jacket. He had a disappointed, sad look on his face. No, he didn't expect me to have *this* attitude. "I don't want a divorce," he said quietly. "I still want to stay married. You can still be my manager. Things can still be the same. We just aren't happy *living together*."

The Sicilian in me rose to the occasion and I moved to the front door. "I'm sure you forgot some other things, so I'll gather them up and call you so you can pick them up . . . outside. Bye."

He hesitated and stood there looking at the open door, not knowing quite what to do, then slowly walked out the front door. After it clicked closed and I turned the deadbolt, I headed for the phone and called a locksmith for their first appointment the next day to change the locks.

Then it hit me—he wants to what?! Stay married, manage him, but live apart. Like he's doing me a favor I could still manage him? I let out a wry "Ha!" So in other words, do everything for him so he can now go screw whomever he wishes and have me take care of him and his chaos, which would now be in two locations. Not to mention still be subjected to fighting for my payments, all the deviant behavior and recent physical abuse that would probably only escalate. I donnnnnnnn't think sooooo.

I looked around at the bleakness of the rooms, crumpled to the floor and cried. After I caught my breath, I called Marilyn. "I did it, Marilyn. You were right. I did what you said. I couldn't have done it without you!"

"It's going to be ok, luvy. It will. I know it's hard right now, but it will get better."

My survival instincts told me it had to be this way. There's no way I could have continued on. I wanted out. I knew this was what had to happen in order for me to survive. The relationship was destroying me. I had just wanted our last effort in counseling to have its fair run. That was my last hope of saving the marriage. But David's fear of abandonment wouldn't allow that. He had to be the one to do the abandoning. It's what he did to Donna, Linda, Barbara, Gail . . . and now to me.

Then I wailed, "I'm so angry and it hurts soooooooo baaaaaaaaad!!! Oh God, it hurts soooooo baaaaaad!" Who said cutting the cord would be painless? I felt I was being sucked through a keyhole and then thrown . . . .the free-falling sensation overcame me again.

Then I suddenly realized . . . the ceremony I did before I left for my trip . . . to expel all the evil from the house . . . Gasp! And here David moves out. Oh . . . my . . . God!

That night, the silence of the house, in the darkness . . . it was never this quiet. It was so still I could hear the blood rushing in my ears with every heartbeat. I never felt so alone, so hurt, so angry. I lay there sobbing, wondering, as the haunting lyrics of a song "Wasted Time" by the Eagles played through my mind. I never did think I'd be alone this far down the line in my life. I cried myself into an exhausted sleep, holding on to the feeling that I was being protected by a higher power. Lulu, Smittie, Tai, Talulah and Purjia cuddled close, trying to comfort me.

CHAPTER TWENTY-NINE

THE MESSAGE

May 15, 2001, Tuesday

Psychic John Edward more or less launched our separation, since the celebrity read we did for his television show *Crossing Over With John Edward* was five days after David moved out. It wasn't the same as a bottle of champagne, but my dad and Uncle Sam visited from the "other side."

I waited months for this day to arrive. How it all came about was an "ooooooohoooo" story in itself. It was meant to be. I believe I was guided by my father, who passed on, so I could receive a message. This is what carried me through a very difficult time.

My brother's wife, Maggie, who's as akin to spiritual beliefs as I am, called to tell me about John's show and insisted I try to get an appointment for a reading. "I really think you should try, Marina. You should have a reading with this guy." After trying off and on for a few weeks to contact the number listed on his web, I gave up thinking that I'd get my reading.

About a month later, I was called into my agent's office—Abrams-Rubaloff-Lawrence Agency,—for a voice-over audition. As I was sitting in the lobby looking at my copy, the voice-over dialogue, I noticed a framed picture of John Edward on the side table. Interesting. Now why would they have a picture of him in their lobby? Maybe someone got a reading and was a fan or something? So after my audition, I asked my agent about it and he told me the agency packaged his show. They represented him. *They represented him*! I sped off to Richard Lawrence's office and poked my head in the door. He glanced up and smiled.

"How are you doing? What can I do for you?"

"You can get me a reading with John Edward!"

He popped a "Ha!" He couldn't even get his mother a reading and the wait was at least a year. I remembered they did special celebrity segments on his show and offered, "Well, what about them doing a celebrity reading with me and David?"

His eyes lit up and he immediately got on the phone to contact the executive producers. Within minutes, we were signed up for a segment!!!

* * *

Fast forward about three months later, I didn't call the producers to tell them David and I separated just days earlier for fear of them canceling the segment. So mum was the word. Besides, the producers insisted from day one they didn't want any information about us, as was their policy, and no information goes to John either. That way they keep everything on a top secret level and there's no second-guessing who may have told what.

I waited with deep anticipation for David to show up at our house for the taping, knowing he'd most likely be late, wondering if he'd show up at all. I kept calling and leaving messages to remind him.

The crew set up and I chit-chatted with the producer about moving the sparse furniture around to make room for the crew. I spent the past few days cleaning and re-arranging everything to try and cover up the fact that some things had been removed. It looked lived in, but minimal. The shifting around covered well in the other rooms, but the one where the piano sat was difficult to disguise, so I said I took out some furniture in order for them to have more room for their equipment. John arrived and I got an immediate warm, sympatico vibe from him. We took pictures outside with Lulu and Thunder, but kept the talk minimal since he didn't want any hints about anything. We were busy with setting up the room and getting wired for sound. I did my best "there's nothing wrong at all in my life" smile.

Finally David arrived and my heart raced. We had talked, but hadn't seen each other since he moved out. He didn't really want to do the taping because there wasn't any money in it. I thought it was because he was scared at what information might come through. After all, David believed in this type of thing. We were finally all set and the reading began with John picking up things—messages—for the crew and then he linked up to my dad, his brother Sam and my grandmother on my mother's side. There were many important messages that came through for me in the reading as far as confirmations and there were accurate details only immediate family members knew about.

But the most profound was John telling me that I would be mending a relationship with an older woman and rebuilding my foundation from scratch and getting back to my core beliefs. I didn't realize at the time how long and intense that process would be. It turned out to be my "Dances with Coyotes" experiences that made me start from scratch, dig deeper, look at the realities straight on, face and deal with the pain that came with it all, in order to rebuild, and rebuild in a healthy way. But going through eight years enduring the fire and forging the steel, wondering when it was all going to stop is what brought me back to my core beliefs, faith and trust I had had, and lost during my time with David. I could tell by the way John was talking he seemed to know more than he was letting on in the reading.

I remember thinking, "He knows. I know he knows we separated." There was also the message which I couldn't put together until about a month later. John asked me if I saw the musical Annie Get Your Gun, which I had. He then asked if there was a reference to the song with a joke in it about "can't get a man with a gun"? Which there is. It's one of the main songs, but I didn't know how it applied to me. He said he saw the reference as having to do with the plot or what the song is about. David sat there figiting with his fingernails taking it all in.

Further in the reading John said my dad was bringing up the Annie

Get Your Gun message again. One of the things they edited out of the show was my dad found humor it -- the lyrics. Nothing came to mind for either David or me that fit. I love the musical, maybe he was hinting I'd be doing it on stage? Little did I know David was keeping information from John and me. Even when I asked David later if he knew of anyone named Annie, he denied it.

No one came through for David. No one. We stopped tape after the reading and were to tape the after comments about the messages John relayed, but David bolted from the couch blurting for all to hear "Well, that's been a fucking waste of my morning!" And he zipped out the front door. I started to go after him, but the producer held me back. "No, just let him go. It's okay."

"But the after comments?" I looked at everyone in embarrassment and disappointment.

"Don't worry about it. Just let him go," the producer repeated.

I looked off to John and he nodded like it was okay. I felt awful. After they did my comments, I approached John to talk. He gave me his book *What If God Were The Sun*. I started a sentence, "You know David and I . . .," when he cut in and said, "I know." I started again, "Do you . . . " He finished by shaking his head and saying "No." He knew we broke up and would not be getting back together again. And it was a good thing.

There was a sense of inner peace brought to me by his affirming that it was *a good thing*. Then I had to ask, "Why didn't anyone come through for David?"

He smiled and said, "That's because this reading was really meant for you." I smiled back and related how this whole thing came about and that was what I felt in the beginning.

For the next month, I was consumed with trying to figure out this riddle about the song. Ah ha!! I thought the message applied to the fact we got married on the Western street at Warner Bros! Hmmm . . . It still didn't feel complete—about the joke of the song. Then a close friend at the time told me about having lunch with David and some woman after we separated. Supposedly, David met her before we broke up. That meant he possibly knew this person at the time of our reading with John? And guess what? Her name was . . . Annie! I was told she, or her deceased husband, also had a gun collection.

David finally confessed to knowing her when I confronted him. Liar, liar pants on fire! David lied so much to me in our relationship. I'm surprised he didn't have a tattoo of flames across his ass.

There was another side note to the reading with John. My mother came with me to NY and we stopped by John Edward's production offices so she could view the tape. When John asked about the *Annie Get Your Gun* song, I could see the slightest smile on David's face, which I hadn't been able to see sitting next to him, and him *clenching his jaw*, his "give-away" sign he was holding something back.

In a conversation with executive producer Paul Shavelson, he told me John had arrived at the house and before he talked to anyone there he got vibes and immediately called Shavelson from his cell saying something to the effect that he had just walked into a very messy situation. He did indeed psychically pick up on the fact we had separated, with David moving out, and the vibes were clear it was a bad, troubled time, but he wanted to go through with the taping regardless, for me. And boy, am I glad he did. What a gift that was!

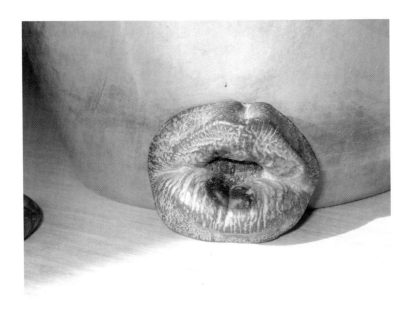

David's lips (one of two different molds) in bronze
I cast in 1992.

The bronze sculpture I did for David for his wedding gift
titled "Ahhhhhh".

Celebrating my birthday at Spago, Beverly Hills, CA, 2000.

David and Jackie
Chan in China
during filming of
David's documen-
tary on China.

The broken fence at the
Mississauga house.

It was more than a
title for the show
segment. It really
was Special Forces
that brought us
together in 1995.

Posing with a puppet made by a fan.

Vail, Colorado.

Golf anyone?
At a charity tournament.

They wanted the shot to be different, so instead of standing in front of the fountain, I suggested to David he jump in. And he did. Singing in the fountain. Hong Kong, China.

My first time in Cannes with David, we met up with friends
Alan Oberholzer, his wife at the time, Patricia Wark.

Romantic dinner at Fouquet's. Paris, France.

At dusk. Hong Kong harbor.

David showing the Abbot of the Shaolin Temple, footage from David's
series – *Kung Fu: The Legend Continues.*

At work in his corner office at our Valley Vista house.

Say "bananas!" In our hotel room on location of *The New Swiss Family Robinson,* we got a visit from a special guest – the orangutan – actor they used in the film. And this was the baby!

One of our many trips to Toronto – David at the piano in Alexander's Bar, Sutton Place Hotel. The same room and piano where he serenaded Quentin Tarantino during our lunch in 1995.

At the Canadian Film Center barbeque hosted by
Norman Jewison during the Toronto Film Festival, 1996.

With famed astrologer-clairvoyant Walter Mercado.

My beloved collie, Lulu.

This was THE pic we used to revamp his image as sexy leading man. It was THE pivotal picture used in my campaign to resurrect his career.

Director's Guild Awards,
1998.

"Come Rain Or Come Shine," our song, is what David was singing to me at our engagement party.

The kiss – our engagement party at Chasen's, Beverly Hills.

This was the moment he first saw me walking down the isle.
Standing next to David is our best man, his brother Robert.

"First dance" – our first dance as husband and wife.

The headstone at his grave.

Part III

Sex, Lies and...

1995-2001

CHAPTER THIRTY

OPEN A NEW WINDOW, OPEN A NEW DOOR

I learned a lot from David. The eye opening experiences we shared motivated me to take a deeper look into myself, and get help. When things inside me started to change, the outside expression of how I felt about myself also changed. Including my expression in the bedroom. Maybe it saved my life. Maybe it will save others.

The dynamics of relationships vary greatly. One person can have great experiences with another, but those experiences may be limited to, say, a working relationship. What works in one relationship in bed might not work in the next, depending on the chemistry and what buttons are successfully pushed or which emotions are triggered. What goes on in private, behind closed doors, can be quite different from what people think happens.

What tweaks a person into certain preferences? What warps one person might twist in another. How did David get *that* dark and damaged? What turned him so on to erotic comic books? Was he sexually abused? That was something he never revealed to me, only alluded to. However, I felt we shared a common experience, which bonds damaged people.

Want to hear details about a celebrity's bedroom playtime? Oh yeah. No matter what anyone's kink is, whatever rocks them on, it is what it is. It's *their* thing. There shouldn't be any shame in it. We're all human beings. David was no different. It bothered me that this subject was fodder for sensationalist journalism when he died, but it was understandable considering David's circumstances and the 2003 court papers that appeared to support those circumstances. The cat was certainly out of the bag. But the focus was on the shock value, not on bringing *value* to the shock or awareness, which can help us understand why people do these certain acts. I received many emails from strangers after the news of David's death, but one in particular hit me:

"I do hope this plight can be brought to the attention of more of the public and perhaps capture some media attention. The toll being paid for the embarrassed silence rippling around this subject is far too high already and probably growing. It is unfortunate that David's death was treated like a media circus instead of focusing perhaps a little more on the painful repercussions these deaths leave behind."

—Sandra Martin Stanchfield

That the underlying motivation or psychological factors of what drives a person to these extremes were barely explored by the press was disturbing. I heard very little, and was disappointed. It would help further understanding of what motivates someone to indulge in acts such as autoerotic asphyxiation if there was more information out in the open.

David didn't care about keeping all that much private. He never liked to lock doors, so it carried over into other areas of life as well. A kind of open door to his life. No matter where he went, from the far obscure corners of the world to the local store, David was recognized. He did not attempt to disguise himself because even if fans sometimes annoyed him, a large part of his ego was relieved he was still in demand. He liked to be wanted. He *needed* that constant attention. You'd think there would be exceptions, but even on our trips to various adult stores, like the Pleasure Chest in Los Angeles or similar stores in Toronto, he made no attempts to hide who he was.

Shortly before his passing he made an in-person visit to an adult store not too far from where he used to live—Suzie's Delights, which oddly enough was only about a mile from our Rosita home—to place quite a substantial order for sex items. Had he wanted to keep this totally private, he would have found a way. But that was David. He was open about the subject of sex. Embarrassed by anything? Yes, but he'd never let you know it. Ever. It's something he told me he learned as a child. Never, ever let anyone know how you really feel. Why? It gives them the upper hand. He did, however, let his guard down for those closest. Was he embarrassed about anything to do with sex? No.

Regardless of what his preferences were, it was the essence of who he was. It's part of what made him fascinating, on and off the screen. Maybe knowing more about this side of the man might add new interest, dimension and perception to watching this intense performer's work.

David often intimidated people, primarily because he was rather unpredictable. As soon as people got to know him, they'd see what a pussycat he could be, and they quickly learned to expect the unexpected with him. Strangers maintained a certain image of him from his past reputation for drinking, and using substances such as LSD and peyote. Others thought he was the parallel to Buddha . . . the all-knowing, centered and at-peace-with-all type of person. They thought he really was like Kwai Chang Caine, meditating and practicing kung fu everyday. They didn't know that the mystical, unspoken attraction he projected was a facade that hid a dark core of dysfunction. His rebellious behavior was a hint at the war that raged inside, which could only be quieted by his drinking, or by love. It was the only way to feel in control of the demons that tempted him to the edge of the outer limits. He had a six-year run with me dealing with all of it sober, but was unable, after our divorce, to maintain that way of life. It proved too much for him without an incentive or motivation.

Certain sexual practices are dangerous and have cost lives. People with similar experiences sent in emails. They too, were searching for answers. Some related how their spouses or friends died trying autoerotic asphyxia or similar sexual acts. They felt people should be more educated about the subject. I agree. The door should be opened to dispel the embarrassment and taboo. If more people were open about their sexual preferences, instead of hiding them in shame, then maybe more people might play it safe, or safer. I'm sure if anyone had asked David, he would have been happy to talk about it at length.

Another email I received from a very concerned person expressed it this way:

"I find it disconcerting that this 'folly' is not exposed publicly for the danger that it is. Just how deadly it is seems to get pushed to the back burner...especially the ways in which it is fatal. My partner survived the 'act', but died lying on the floor afterwards. Apparently there is a nerve near the jugular vein, which can trigger the heart to slow down to as slow as 1/3 of its normal rate. Or to stop altogether. This is, apparently, an attempt to keep the heart from like blowing itself out from too high of pressure (what with the head no longer in the circulation pattern). I found out about this after my partner died."

Maybe the higher spiritual purpose of David's demise was to bring the subject of autoerotic asphyxiation and other sexual variances to the forefront and address the issue in order to dissipate the mystery. He loved teaching people, delving into fine detail and spinning stories. David always liked to be the hero.

Sex was at the top of David's list of favorite topics and a constant to talk about. As he put it, "A man thinks of sex every 20 seconds." And then he'd give this wide toothy grin and chuckle. I'm convinced *he* did.

He told me that practically every choice he made, he had sex in mind—clothes, the house we were to buy, what it would be like to make love in the black lagoon pool, in the dark secret spot in the backyard . . . okay, *anywhere*. He said in a letter that no matter what ailed a relationship, sex was a "great glue" that "washes away all ills" and he craved it with me "with a fire that won't quit . . . "

His sexuality was one of the things I liked about his persona. It was at the center of who he was. I understood that. I embraced it. He took delight in educating me in *The Story of O*—male dominant, female submissive, slave oriented story; Ramba—a comic book character he said I reminded him of; and other sexual "arts," as he referred to them. It was arousing for me to know that my participation turned him on. Afterward, however, I didn't feel good about myself with most of it.

Sometimes David displayed almost a shy, boyish approach regarding sex. He sometimes expressed it in funny cards, like a banana equating an erection. Sometimes he was very romantic, and always gentle. In the bedroom, he never came across as lascivious, gross or crude with his verbal communication or his touch, with the exception of grabbing me in public.

It was all a new adventure and I was not only open to the journey, but also wanted to make him as happy as he made me. However, a nature is a nature. The 20-second philosophy, that a man thinks of sex every 20 seconds, was not what drove me on a daily basis. I was consumed with furthering his career and our future, and the "sexual arts"—in the direction he was pointing—were interesting at first, but it was a rare cup of tea for me at best, something that was indulged in because it was part of our relationship and I wanted to please my man and make it all work. What took place in the bedroom with David was something that I had never participated in before and have not done since.

After a sixteen-hour day I wasn't really in an energetic mood to say the least. The "least" part was a combination of what I felt were betrayals, "hurts," and of course the incest. As time went on, the list of what turned me off got longer. I loved him passionately, but it was difficult for me to be romantic with someone I was starting to resent and dislike much of the time. And the "secret" issue kept gnawing at me.

Since I was taking care of the day-to-day grunt work, David had plenty of time to sleep in, take naps, work on any number of his creative projects— music, writing, drawing, talking to friends, meeting for coffee. He got re-charged while I got de-charged. Come evening, he couldn't understand why I was "in a mood" a good deal of the time.

He appeared passive in our working relationship, with me as the aggressive one, but in the bedroom, it didn't matter. Nothing, it seemed, unsettled David under the sheets.

I recently came across a letter he wrote toward the end of our relationship, complaining about my lack of sexual interest in him. After reading the four-page letter I was in a puddle of guilty tears. How could I have denied him this? What was I thinking? Reality check! David lived in his own world. You could show him a lime and he would still think of it as a chair. And he was not one to take responsibility. Things were rationalized in his favor, and if there was anything he was the cause of, it was denied, set aside to be forgotten or pushed off on the other person.

It wasn't that I didn't want to have intimacy with him. I wanted it as much as my next breath, but I didn't want to do things that repelled or hurt me anymore. It got to a point where even the way he kissed me was off-putting.

Even though we went to marriage counseling, and I sought help on my own, the bedroom was not discussed. Why not? I sit here writing this book and for the first time I realized we never discussed this in counseling. It would be a "duh" factor for me now to talk about, but we didn't. First of all, David didn't think he had a problem, but it had everything to do with the relationship. He thought it was my problem. Well . . . he was right. I didn't want the kinks anymore. The sex issues got compartmentalized to a separate file of their own. I'm still shaking my head why I didn't bring this up.

I finally understood what that "mystery and allure" was in David that partially attracted me to him—the familiarity I couldn't pinpoint. It was a darkness that harbored deviance, the same as in my uncle. Since that was my first sexual encounter, the one with my uncle, it tainted that part of my life in relationships to come.

At first I thought choking was just a different thing to try. Game and fantasy. Fantasies are great. But some are better kept fantasies.

David would again test the boundaries to see how far he could take those fantasies into realities. I didn't realize until later in the relationship with David that they were the core of his preferences and being, to a point where if this wasn't part of our being intimate every time, he was disappointed. The sex games took away from the core of what I vibed on—just him. When I refused to take part in these more extreme sexual activities, David began doing other things in the bedroom as a way of acting out his resentment. If he didn't get what he wanted sexually, or in our working relationship, he was not going to give me what I wanted. Or if he did give me what I wanted, he added something that would give him the pleasure of ruining the whole experience for me by inflicting pain or ignoring me. It burst his bubble when he learned I faked blacking out from the choking. I didn't want to lie when he asked me. After that confession, he said he didn't get turned on from it much because it wasn't real, which contradicted what he wrote me in a letter—that just keeping the fantasy alive was better than not having it at all. All I knew was that I didn't even like the *fantasy* of being choked anymore and that was because I was changing my core being.

Many times, I'd wear seductive lingerie, he'd say he'd be right there to join me, then hours would pass and I'd fall asleep. Countless times I tried seducing David, he'd turn me down or keep me waiting so long that I would just go to bed. Our honeymoon at the elite La Quinta Resort and Club in Palm Springs was terribly disappointing. We had an incredible wedding suite with fireplace and private jacuzzi in the patio and there I waited in bed in my expensive white honeymoon lingerie while David sat in the adjoining room doing a crossword puzzle.

"I'll be right there, honey." Half an hour went by. "Just give me ten more minutes . . . "

Fast forward, I woke up the next morning to find him asleep in the other room. I tried not to make too much of it and focused on the fact we had a lifetime of bliss together. That and insisted we go shopping. Somehow the trinkets just didn't ease the hurt I buried inside.

He told me some time later that he couldn't fathom why he acted like that. He just couldn't imagine not making love to me on our honeymoon.

Yeah, well, a day late and a dollar short. When David said things like that it made me even more sad about everything. What *were* you thinking?

Maybe seeing *Titanic* during our honeymoon stay in the desert should have given me a hint of what was to come? It was at the Rosita house, one late night after I had waited in a beautifully candlelit bubble bath for him until the tub got cold, my fingers turned to prunes and bubbles had long disappeared.

I grabbed the bathroom phone and called him in the office at the other end of the house to ask when he was joining me.

"Ohhh I'll be right there." Then he finally showed up after I gave up and went to bed. "Why didn't you wait for me?" An apology was followed by his trying to seduce me. As if I could deny my feelings and instantly shut out my being upset.

* * *

He had been in his office at the computer working on a nude photograph someone sent him of an Asian woman. He was just trying out a Photoshop application, he said. As if he couldn't practice on a flower or a face? He kept me waiting for our "date" because he was doing *that*? And why would someone send him a picture like that? He gave me a flimsy story and I let the subject drop. So this is what he forfeited a romantic romp with me for? Say what?

But these off times were countered with equally wonderful moments. When he remembered to introduce me to people—he'd often forget— he'd always call me his Bride with the most loving look in his eyes. He said one of his favorite pastimes was to sit in silence and watch me put on my make-up, to write little loving notes to me, create beautiful romantic cards, bring me flowers, buy me presents, even when we couldn't afford it, like a $900 western hat in Telluride. "You're my bride and you deserve this hat!"

I didn't find out until a few years after we divorced that toward the end of the marriage, but while we were still together, he had met with several women at a certain cafe in Studio City. He'd evidently sit in the back in a darkened corner with the femme du jour. No wonder I couldn't get him on the cell when he was supposed to be at the newsstand. I knew something wasn't right when I actually drove to a spot where he was supposed to be but wasn't. While looking at the stand from across the street, I called him on his cell.

"Hey, so are you finished looking at magazines?"

"Oh, just about . . ."

"Good. Which ones did you get?"

"I'll surprise you."

"OK! So where are you? I don't see you."

Silence. "What do you mean you don't see me?"

"Thought I'd surprise you and go out for coffee."

"Uh . . . I just left and was heading out to another."

"Oh. Uhhuh . . . want to meet up?"

"Let's meet up back home."

My body would be trembling. It was fear of being hurt and angry and knowing the truth. And after another hour he'd finally show up with a pile of magazines, including my favorite ones on arts and crafts. He may have bought the magazines, but I didn't buy his story. Again, I just put it in the "doesn't fit" pile and gave him benefit of the doubt. It was easier for me than dealing with the problem. I denied my instincts. To learn years later what he was up to was upsetting.

Chapter Thirty-One

CRY UNCLE!

"Feels good, doesn't it? Does that tickle?" He looked down at me and moved his hand gingerly up my inner thigh, anticipating my reaction. His brown eyes twinkled in a lusty, lascivious way. "You like the gift? How about a thank-you kiss?"

That was one of many unwanted encounters I had with my father's brother, Al. It was difficult to know for sure what I was feeling. After all, I was just seven or eight years old. All I knew was that something was wrong. No one ever educated me to the fact that it was sexual abuse and molestation. These incidents created a kink, damaged the matrix, tainted me for years to come. Only by becoming aware of how much damage they wreaked was I able to start connecting the dots and be proactive in rebuilding myself. And the relationship with David was the defining avenue to my healing

Incest! Say it slowly and it sounds even more lewd. Innncessssssssst! The word provokes a multitude of reactions, quietly muttered in conversation. Fascination, repulsion, nausea, curiosity. A great number of people have experienced it first hand. Most people tend to shy away from the subject, possibly because it's happened to them and they can't confront the reality or the abuser. Maybe they have the inclination or fantasy themselves. Some people are afraid of their own anger, not knowing how to express or channel their emotions. What if they love the perpetrator?

The fact that I chose a partner who had "an incestuous relationship with a family member" slammed the issue at me again. I was already hooked into the partnership with David when he thrust the information upon me.

My being drawn to David had to be for a reason. Was this my chance to finally confront and win my battle, overcome the past abuse by forgiving, releasing the past, and staying with him? This other 'relationship' he had, however, permeated my life with him on an unspoken daily level.

By bringing sexual abuse out into the open, by exposing it, allowing an atmosphere in which more people feel free to talk about it, some of the embarrassment and guilt might be lifted. The more people talk about it, the more people will feel comfortable about getting help: the more that get help, the more that get healthy. The healthier people are with boundaries, the more they hold perpetrators accountable for their actions.

* * *

One Thanksgiving holiday, my family stayed overnight at my uncle's house where he cornered me in a dark hallway, blocking my path. Looking like he was salivating over his prey, he told me if I got scared at night I could always crawl into bed with him.

When I was a kid, the subject of incest and molestation was far more hushed than it is today. My own counseling and research confirmed that the feelings I had as a child were valid. But those feelings were to be pushed back. Ignored. Denied. It didn't help hearing adult role models consistently say, "Oh, don't feel like that." I didn't have the knowledge when I was growing up that my childhood was indeed violated, but I could feel something wasn't right. It wasn't something a kid in those days talked about.

Uncle Al brought me presents and my loving, polite parents would prod me to be courteous, give him a hug or do as he asked and sit on his lap. When they weren't looking or in another room, he'd touch me, inflicting his damaging indecency.

Goodness knows what song and dance uncle dearest gave my parents, because my request for them to make him stop didn't seem to have much impact. My father supposedly talked with him first, but uncle continued his behavior. After my mother confronted him, addressing the issue yet again, is when he then confronted *me*.

"You told your parents on me. You tattled. I didn't think you were a tattle tale." He looked at me with disdain. I could feel my heart pounding, words expelling from my mouth, saying that I didn't like being touched by him.

"You trying to get me into trouble? That's not nice."

The fear made almost a deeper impression than the violation did. Both integrated into the matrix of my being. It should never have come to that. I was "daddy's little girl." Didn't he want to protect me? What stopped him? My uncle should have been banned from being near me at all. Period. Why didn't that happen? He didn't like being shut down by my mother, so he changed his tactics and violated me in other ways with looks, innuendos and invading my personal space by getting too close. I don't remember talking to my parents about it again.

It wasn't until I was older that I devised excuses to leave the house when he came over or I hid in my room. *I took control* and didn't allow myself to be subjected to him. I was happy when my uncle died. Relieved.

Some years ago, I brought up the subject with my mother. She sloughed off the touchy-feely thing. "Oh, that was just the way your uncle was."

She didn't seem to understand his "touchy-feely" wasn't affection. I blasted back, "The way he was? *Yes! A child molester!* Why are you making excuses for him like he did no harm?" Didn't my parents really listen to me as a kid about what he was doing to me? How does it go? You can hear, but are you really listening?

I tried to explain how that affected my choices in men in life, but it's like she wanted the subject to go away. I didn't speak to her for weeks after that, but I finally brought the subject up again and explained again how it tainted me negatively and had everything to do with affecting my choices in life. She finally listened.

My mother apologized, admitting they should have ostracized my uncle from the house. That moment, for her to take responsibility, was a major turning point in my healing. My mother and I bonded closer. My resentments dissipated. She did the best she could at the time with the tools and boundaries she had. My mother has loved me more than herself and to this day she is still proving that. This too was something John Edward said in my reading. I'd be making amends with an older female. Too bad my father had passed away years earlier and couldn't be a part of this healing process. The responsibility, I felt, was mostly his. It was his brother.

In those days things were dealt with differently. David was sixteen years older than me, so when he was a child, it was even more different for him. He told me he was never truly happy as a child. It wasn't so much the things he said, as the things he didn't say, and how he phrased his childhood re-countings that made me suspect something happened to him.

For years, I minimized my childhood events. All those feelings I pushed down, feelings that I thought I had already gotten over—the hurt, the anger and anguish, the feeling my parents didn't believe me, and failed to protect me—started coming to the surface again. I took a few "healing" workshops. In one I took a bataka, a soft foam filled bat, and confronted my dead uncle, bashing his imagined person in a chair, screaming how I hated him, how he damaged me and how he should be castrated. I thought "Yeah, that felt great. Got that out! Cured!" Not!

I thought I had faced my past and it was behind me, yet from one relationship to the next, a pattern began to emerge. It was no coincidence that each "significant other" in my life had light eyes, not brown eyes like my uncle, and most of them had anger and control issues, like my father.

In order to gain perspective and understanding, I started going to counseling again, "conventional" and spiritual, which included a core group of friends, psychics and astrologers. I had done this on occasion in prior years, but I had hit "critical mass" with necessity during my time with David. The healthier I got with my issues, such as self esteem, codependency and sexual abuse, the less I could tolerate the dark side of the man I loved, which included certain activities in the bedroom.

At the same time it made me want to try harder, no matter the cost to me, to help him. My efforts proved futile. I finally got it. I couldn't fix him. A nature is a nature. I couldn't tolerate living with someone who made no effort to deal with the issues or any attempt to heal, so there was no choice but to walk away from the love of my life.

I saw the patterns, the warnings, and the experiences I was supposed to learn from. They all culminated in the one relationship I had with David. That was my PhD. That marriage was my turning point of "getting it."

Not until my marriage to David did I feel the full impact and magnitude of *understanding*. It's taken eight solid years of rebuilding myself strong enough to pull out of incest's tentacled grip. I know how to make healthier conscious choices now. I have the tools and know it's better to be alone than to be in an unhealthy relationship.

After separating from David, I faced my obstacles, the detours, the extreme pain of letting go and starting over again. I had no husband, no children, no job, and no career. To be whole again, to find the core of "me" again . . . finding the matrix, correcting, reprogramming, rebuilding a new, healthier person. Healing was an extremely painful process.

A new life is a double-edged sword.

The steady beam of light that kept me from tanking was my beloved Service and Therapy dog, my collie Lulu. It was Lulu who pulled me through my emotional turmoil and healing process after David. When she knew it was okay to let me go, she passed away, on March 25, the anniversary of my father's death. It was because of Lulu that I was able to let go and finally close the door to David a week prior, on March 16, 2008. She was the reason I had one last conversation with David that night.

The court documents of 2003 that ended up on The Smoking Gun website were meant to be sealed, but by some fluke ended up in our divorce file of public records. The scandalous revelation not only regarding incest, but also deviant sexual preferences, resurfaced upon David's death, since it seemed to support the method by which he died.

My early sexual abuse had everything to do with my being drawn to David. I was finally able to identify that "something familiar" about him, but instead of being repelled, I was drawn in. It was only by becoming aware of how much damage it wreaked that I was able to start connecting the dots and be proactive about rebuilding myself. The relationship with David was the defining avenue to my healing. I'm convinced David was abused himself as well, that it drew him into the preferences that made his world go round, and end. He confided in me once he had an encounter with another man when he was a teen that took place in a movie theatre. He said that was the only time. David had a difficult upbringing on many levels. We were two broken souls.

After our separation, I read *The Courage To Heal*, which had a profound effect on me. I realized no matter how "trivial" or "light" the abuse was, it could have as much of a profound impact as a more physical act. It all depends on the person's sensitivities—their feelings and spirit. It can be something someone says, maybe just once, a look, a gesture, but the impact can be profound and if not dealt with, can snowball. I remember reading chapter after chapter, breaking down and crying for hours. All those years I put up my wall and played down the emotions, mostly because I didn't want to connect with the anger against my parents for their failing me. So the anger emerged in other ways.

David was part of a generation with a different perspective on life. It was a time of indulgence, of experimentation with hallucinogens such as LSD and peyote, which David talked about using. Hallucinogens combined with booze can have psychological effects. The combo can warp a person's perceptions, boundaries and reality, especially someone like David who ventured so often into uncharted territory. From his dysfunctional upbringing, he stretched conventional boundaries and colored outside the lines of acceptance and normalcy. Unfortunately, other people got hurt in the wake of his actions.

Adding celebrity and fame to the mix, being accustomed to perks and getting one's way, stretches the lines even further. Celebrities sometimes come complete with their own bubble and don't think their actions will have consequences. Boundaries, he felt, were inconveniences and impositions—things to defy and go beyond. David certainly defied convention, tradition, and the mundane. He sometimes behaved as if he were above the law, constantly daring, challenging things that some considered risky, including his perspective about "incest." This was looked upon by him as merely an alternative lifestyle, something that should be accepted as it had been in ancient Rome. He saw nothing wrong with it and couldn't understand why more people didn't see things his way. He said "The world wouldn't understand. After all, who determines what is normal? Society?" He'd laugh. The world's viewpoint certainly didn't stop him from making it a reality in his universe.

The involvement with X wasn't just as consenting adults. David knew what he wanted and verbally let X know about it in no uncertain terms when X was a young teenager. David crossed the line and tainted X's life from that moment on. He knew society and the world wouldn't accept his outlook. So he waited. It was more complicated from X's point of view, why and when it all took place in later years. Bottom line, I believe, the reason was to grab any love or affection X could, that X never got from David. Not in a healthy way, that is.

Makes ya wanna cry uncle, doesn't it?

CHAPTER THIRTY-TWO

CAUGHT IN THE ACT

W E would spend considerable time on the set together, and sneak off during breaks so David could grab a quick drink. One evening, we ventured into the hardware department of a local store so that David could do some shopping for the bedroom. Yes, the bedroom. He notified Rita, a sexy, hip Italian assistant director on the show, where to find us if they got to his scene early. After an hour of collecting various and sundry items, which we packed in our cart, Rita appeared around the corner, taking inventory of our . . . er, um, interesting assortment of chains, rope and accessories.

She smiled mischievously. "Building something, are we?"

David laughed. "Caught in the act," he said rather proudly.

Rita nodded, with a blank wide-eyed look, "In the act of what?" And winked as she reported in her walkie, "Rita here, I found Sparky. He'll be traveling momentarily."

Up until that moment, there were only a few people who knew about our living together. Now Rita was in on our secret, within the secret.

That evening, David rigged up the rope, hooks, and chains and built a contraption to tie me up in a rather exotic way. He made sure the rope was soft so it wouldn't burn or bruise and showed me some ingenious knots he had learned over the years. One of which was rather clever—it held tension, but if one end was pulled, the knot released.

His design attached over his chin-up bar installed in the doorway to the den. It was rather exciting in a way, waiting to see what he had in mind. David made the "event" feel very sexy since it was my first time ever doing something like this. It seemed to give him extra pleasure to know he got a "virgin" into this type of participation. He talked in a low, calm, soothing tone as he gave me long kisses and caresses, in between prepping his invention. I wore his favorite choice of ultra revealing lingerie and waited as he began tying me up. Once he had my hands tied in back, he made me wait longer as he worked away on the project. It was part of the "game."

Apprehension crept in. He was making the ties a tad too snug. I wanted them loose enough so I knew I could easily get out of them, but he said it wasn't as fun to make it *that* easy. He enticed me to accept it the way he wanted by more foreplay. As he pulled on the rigging, which tugged on the rope around my neck—with my hands tied in behind me—it got a little *too* tight. He told me that that was part of the experience, then kissed and fondled me to keep the excitement going. He relished every moment.

My anxiety increased, especially since it was at the end of the day and he started to show the affects of the alcohol by getting sleepy. He sat on the floor holding on to the rope, which led to the rigging, viewing his "masterpiece" with a smile. He leaned to the side, which pulled on the rope around my neck, making it a bit difficult to breathe. Then it became very difficult. My face got tingly and numbish, then my vision started to black out, as I could see David start to nod off, and the terrifying fight-or-flight fear factor took over. He was on the verge of passing out, leaning away from me with rope in hand, making it tighter. I started to scream for him to wake up, let the rope go, and untie me. He didn't. He was on the brink now, teetering.

I screamed at the top of my lungs once more, with tears of terror running down my face and neck. "David! DAVID!!! WAKE UP AND LET ME GO!!!!!!! *DAAAAAAVIIIIIID!!!!!*"

He finally snapped out of it. "What's the problem?" And let the rope loose. Needless to say, I was quite shaken. He, however, couldn't understand why I was so upset. It's like I spoiled his fun. Had he blacked out, I believe I could have been hanged to death. Maybe I was hyperventilating and would have only blacked out. Thank goodness we'll never know. Let's just say that to his disappointment it was the last time we tried that one. His funk didn't last long, however, because he had accumulated quite a collection of other toys he was anxious to play with. It was also not the end of his teaching me the fine art of the dark side of his sexuality.

* * *

Like a vampire, he took his appreciation and assessment of my neck a step further. Instead of tenderly caressing it with both hands and merely looking like he was going to sink his fangs into me—well, he did that too—this time he put his hands around my throat and said "I want you to do this to me."

Okay, no problem, but when I did, he laughed and said, "No, like this." And he proceeded to apply light pressure, like he was choking me.

"You want me to literally *choke* you?"

He laughed. "Yeah."

It was something new to me as well and I was all for pleasing him, so I tried, but I wasn't applying myself as he wanted. He wanted it . . . tight... to get him to black out. I was afraid of hurting him. I remember thinking how horrible it would be to have anything go wrong and kill him. Besides, it just wasn't something that pushed my buttons as far as being a turn on, so I lost my excitement. That's when he told me about how it heightens the orgasm. I thought, "Not for me, buddy! That's not what I consider exciting, especially since I'm not a violent person."

He assured me it was safe. That by cutting off the artery in the neck, it causes the blackout and as soon as the person releases the grip, the other person comes to again. Kind of like getting a karate chop on the neck and the person blacks out and falls to the ground. Well, what if he doesn't let go soon enough. Wouldn't that cause brain damage? Geeezzz.

He thought I was cute, but silly, and intent on proceeding. When he tried to choke me again, I got that awful blackout feeling. It scared me so much I started to panic. David wouldn't stop so I had to try and pry his hands away from me as I pleaded. That still didn't stop his pursuit, wanting to try again with repeated reassurances all would be okay. He waited until we were in full swing having intercourse to impose his method again. Unknown to David, I faked passing out and coming to. It was certainly something that cranked his yank—it couldn't have been more of a turn on for him. He came alive with renewed energy at the thought of conducting this type of act and being successful at it with me. He found a new *toy* with which to share his novelty.

I figured there's no harm in pleasing my man as long as I don't get hurt. If faking it like that worked, then, whatever, but I also thought it would only be for those few times. As time passed, I discovered it was his obsession and fascination, and he needed it on a daily basis, which became a problem for me to deal with. Games are great in bed on occasion, but not what I needed or wanted as the constant. I never did get the—excuse the pun—hang of the choking maneuver on him, but I continued to do my best for a while. It took quite a long time for David to finally give up on my efforts. I guess he lost interest because I just couldn't get him to conk out, but not the other way around.

After our first couple of months together he didn't pay as much attention to pleasing or satisfying me. Could be because I refused to be strung up again. He'd come to bed, we'd have great oral sex, but then he'd do the typical rollover and sleep, or in his case, pass out. I kept reassuring myself it's all that he was going through emotionally and with his work schedule, and hopefully soon it would change.

On one of our treks to L.A. during the first few months together, I brought David to one of my favorite hangouts. I was expecting to see the usual crowd and a fun acquaintance, "Tim." I asked the maitre d' if he'd been in. There was an odd look on his face. "Didn't you hear?"

How could I? I was in Toronto. Evidently "Tim" died under suspect circumstances with a woman performing an extreme sex act using a plastic bag over his head. This was shocking. Even though David didn't use a plastic bag, it reinforced my need to put distance between me and one of his preferences. But how could I keep him satisfied, as an incentive to stop drinking, and still enjoy things myself?

To create mystery and intrigue, which David loved, I decided to lead him on an adventure, blindfolded and handcuffed. It was the dead of winter with a fresh thick blanket of snow on the ground. My apartment was already prepped with his favorite fragrance of peaches and I had Chinese paper lanterns dangling from the ceiling of my tiny one-room basement studio. We parked the car in back, hoping the neighbors wouldn't see, since it was broad daylight. Actually David didn't care if anyone saw. He actually liked the idea.

I led him as quickly as I could over the slippery iced walkway, down the steps and into my hideaway. He took a long breath in and let out a long sigh, "Ahhhhhhhh. Peaches. My favorite," and smiled as I sat him down on my futon. He didn't want me to lift up the blindfold until I enjoyed myself and pleasured him with a simple unzipping of his jeans. He knew I couldn't contain myself and it was all we could do to keep quiet so the people upstairs wouldn't hear.

After I lifted the silk scarf off his face, he said with a bold laugh, "I'll have to come here more often!"

* * *

We had many romantic interludes in and out of town. I'd set up "date nights" so we'd have time designated just for us, although we'd often have to change or postpone those plans because of business that would pop up at the last minute. Instead of once a week, they stretched to a couple of weeks or a month in between. But the times we did set aside, David and I would sit and watch a movie at home or go out to dinner and upon our return pretend we were on location and make love. But those very special times became fewer and fewer.

I treasured the times when things were good between us—it was magic. He'd frequently give me lingerie as gifts, year round, any and every occasion, or for no reason other than he wanted to see me in a particular "outfit." Sexy, kinky, classy. A wide variety from leather to rubber to lace to spandex, he covered the bases for selection! Trashy Lingerie was a favorite place of ours along with Fredrick's of Hollywood. Victoria's Secret too. Above all the seductive wardrobe, however, he still liked nude best.

One of the rare times David had to film on location and I couldn't go, I decided to have a special surprise for him when he came back. It was the usual jam-packed scene at LAX with cars and people swarming everywhere. I had to circle around a few times before I could edge my way into the line-up of vehicles waiting to pick up travelers. It was nighttime and brisk, the beginning of winter, perfect to wear my long buttonless black suede coat. I could see David coming through the doors from the baggage area so I quickly got out of the car, holding the coat closed, greeted him with a kiss, and let go of the front of the coat. He was close enough that no one else but him could see that I had "forgotten" to put clothes on. We made it home in record time!

CHAPTER THIRTY-THREE

THE SECRET

Each time X and I discussed the subject of X's relationship with David, I found myself caught up in even more conflict. Part of me pushed back the anger and disgust for anyone who could perpetrate such a thing. The other part of me was very much in love with the man and not about to let go of the union, in spite of knowing and feeling it was against the center of my being, ethics and morals. I still held out hope he would make amends with X, that something would change. That would give me the excuse I needed to justify staying. I also thought that rising above the issue with forgiveness was the answer, so I kept compromising myself by remaining in the relationship. It was like being sucked into the La Brea tar pits. The longer I stayed, the more deeply entrenched I got. I didn't like myself for that, but the alternative, leaving him, was unbearable.

Then there were my feelings toward X to be reconciled. I understood how X felt and wanted to give support, but at the same time I didn't want X around because there was usually some sort of interaction or innuendo between them, even the way David threw a glance. I was blamed as the bad guy, the scapegoat who was accused of keeping X away, which wasn't true. Never once did I say David couldn't see X. I just didn't want to be constantly reminded about their secret by having them around, so I limited my time, not his. He could visit X whenever he wanted, and he did.

He was consistently giving X money before he made sure we even had our own rent money set aside. Since the house was owned by my dear friend Lisa, I was always in a panic about David not coming through and ruining my lifetime friendship with her. I was always looking over my shoulder with David, covering the bases so I wouldn't get dragged into his messes. But I felt he was putting X first before me and our life together, and that didn't sit right. I felt as though he still had a lover he was keeping and supporting. It always turned my stomach when he talked about X because I could never tell if it was true affection or lust he was thinking about. Unless he was on screen, he was an expert at not giving away what he was thinking or feeling.

There was an incident when X was visiting at our Valley Vista house and I walked into the living room unexpectedly. X's jeans were pulled down to the bare essentials. The look on David's face was not embarrassment, but lust.

Like a cliche line out of a movie, I commented, "Am I interrupting something?"

It was awkward to say the least, especially when David's expression didn't change. He remained seated, relaxed and entertained. X, however, was visibly rattled and babbled an excuse. X supposedly wanted to show off how much weight X had dropped. So X had to lower their pants like that? It only added to my feeling that perhaps their particular relationship wasn't over. I thought I was going to throw up and was repelled back into the kitchen to catch my breath.

Funny how denial works. As soon as I calmed my nerves, I chastised myself by assuming the worst. What if I was wrong? Maybe it was as innocent as they explained. I shoved back my feelings. I also knew if I confronted the issue with David, it would start another huge argument or he'd just walk away in silence, as he had before.

But I gave it a try anyway after X left the house. He clenched his jaw as he usually did when he was withholding information or blocked emotions and said I was imagining things. He didn't see anything wrong with the situation. That was it. He gave me the silent treatment again, lighting up a cigarette, retreating into his office space and busying himself with the computer.

Nothing was mentioned by any of us after that, until after our wedding. There were some other issues that surfaced regarding X, which I had to address. X responded with a letter where X poured out the sad, heartfelt and soul wrenching feelings about the relationship with David. I sobbed after reading it, still not knowing what else to do for X, or for me, or how to deal with it emotionally. The letter also propelled me further away from David, especially since I asked him again to go with X to counseling. As I anticipated, he ignored me by walking out of the room without saying a word.

Because of his refusal to help move forward and heal, I lost respect and feelings toward him. I felt he was yet another perpetrator that was getting away with it.

The other part of me was trying to justify that if other people knew and were forgiving of him and could, it appeared, accept what he had done, then why couldn't I? Bottom line, I just couldn't. It went against what I believed in for myself and for others. That feeling pressured me more as time progressed.

After David and I separated, X and I met for coffee in North Hollywood. We talked about X and David yet again and how X longed to have a normal relationship with David, but it was not to be. X recounted the story of how David approached X, and stated what he wanted, and how very different his outlook on social acceptance of such a relationship was. X also wanted to discuss, regardless of the letter, the reasons behind X's participation in the relationship. X had come to terms with things, got counseling and was moving forward in life in a positive way. It was good to hear the words, but in X's voice, pain, anger and resentment still lingered.

I wanted to help in some way, to try and get certain people to understand and support X. I thought X got a raw deal and was regarded as a problem, as if X was the black sheep of the family, instead of David. There were valid reasons why X was the way X was. So instead of being what I thought was tolerated by certain people, X deserved care, love, understanding and support. I always believed that.

As far as I am aware, X did not receive any support emotionally or otherwise. I wanted to be there more for X after the separation, but it was too awkward. It's not like X reached out for me again either, so we drifted apart.

In emails that David and I threw at each other during our divorce, I addressed the issue trying to explain how I felt regarding him and X and "Seeing how you lusted after X still? Your responses every time X made an inappropriate gesture toward you? Please, Johnny. You're not that great of an actor."

His reaction summed it up in two words. The first one started with an "F."

Over the years, I was surprised to find a few people knew or suspected the "secret" and yet it was still kept under wraps. Embarrassment, guilt, the concern of David being a celebrity, his career, protecting the family name, who-would-believe-me paranoia, "I don't want to think of him like that," were some of what people thought might be the reasons or excuses for keeping it quiet. Who knows how people truly justified it, but to my knowledge, David was never held accountable.

Chapter Thirty-Four

PANTY RAID

MANY years ago David wrote a song called "Got No Right To Sing The Blues" in which he sings about wearing his mother's underwear and parading around the room like a queen. He composed many songs with a sense of humor, but they were usually based on his personal experiences. In this song, he says when he was seventeen, he put aside most of that behavior and now he enjoys "being on top than any kind of in-between."

The first time I heard it, it was funny. Then as time passed, I couldn't help but wonder—were these lyrics written to shock the audience or was it based on his world, as most of his songs were?

It had been a while since we moved into the Valley Vista house and I was putting away laundry. In straightening up my lingerie drawer I pulled out a pair of what I thought were a size large women's panty briefs, which had been shoved to the back of the drawer. I primarily wore thongs, and I was always a size small/medium. The panties were black with a touch of lace edging. One problem. They were not mine. Hmmmmmm. How odd.

I brought it to David's attention, who quickly dismissed it as some leftovers of Gail's that got mixed in the move. Uh...no, I don't think so. It had not only been ages since we moved from Mississauga and every stitch of Gail's was gone, but also I didn't have my things near any of her drawers. Mine were in the guest room where the drawers were empty. We had also moved from my condo as well. I knew what lingerie was packed and what wasn't. These were not mine!

"What do you want me to say, Blackie?" This was a long-standing consistent response when he felt backed up against the wall. Moreover, he stood by his theory. I gave the panties the heave-ho, but not my suspicions. Out of curiosity, I snooped into his underwear drawer and found a few pairs of exotic thongs. At first glance, I thought they were women's lacy bikinis, but they weren't. Funny, he never wore those for me. One pair was pretty black stretch lace. Interessssssting. I never asked him about it because I didn't want him to know I was snooping in his dresser. He not only never brought up the lingerie subject again, but also never wore the thongs.

Was it something he wore only for certain people in the past? Maybe he just decided Speedos were more comfortable to wear. Were those panties found in my drawer put there by mistake and they were really *his*? They were a size he could wear. After all, my lingerie drawer was right next to his and he did sometimes open it by mistake. But whom did he wear them for? Or did they belong to someone he was having an affair with? A souvenir? It wasn't just the panties that didn't fit.

My qualms were raised yet again when David took on a new friend, "Simon," who infiltrated our private life. I never had a good feeling about this person, who had become one of David's buddies. There was something off about the way he would look at David, his behavior. It never felt right. Simon was a fan of his so maybe it was because he idolized him?

One day in the kitchen at the Rosita house, Simon was standing next to David at the counter. My mother was there visiting and we were all chatting away. David asked him what he wanted in his coffee. Simon slithered his arm behind David to grab his cup and said softly "Whatever you're having, Dave." He slithered his arm back with cup in hand and looked up at David with a certain smile. It made my skin crawl.

* * *

David didn't like traveling alone so he took a buddy on one of his business trips. David responded to a message I left on his cell phone voice mail, but called me from a hallway instead of his room.

"Why on earth are you in the hallway?"

"I don't want my friend to overhear me. Besides, he's watching TV."

"Why don't you call me from your room?"

"Oh, uh...well, he's in my room."

"No he's not. I just tried *your* room and they said you checked out. They only had his room registered. That's why I called your cell! What the hell is going on?" Busted!

"Oh...yeah I was going to call and tell you...well, I decided to save money. I thought we'd just bunk in the same room."

My skin crawled again. We didn't have to save money like that at that time. Besides, David didn't like to share a room with anyone but me. Once more, I just stuffed my suspicions away.

CHAPTER THIRTY-FIVE

LOVE HURTS I

"JUST because you're my father doesn't mean you're right."

My father reacted by smacking my face with an open heavy hand, leaving more than a hand mark on my cheek. It wasn't the physical pain I minded, it was the emotional bend it made in me.

"What makes you think you're so special? Queen B. You think you're so special?"

I blurted out through a torrent of tears, "I'm *special!* I *am* special!"

My dad's facial expression showed he immediately regretted what he did. Even though he never touched me like that again, irreparable damage was done.

One of those light bulb "ah-ha" epiphanies occurred in the middle of my relationship with David. I finally realized that my entire life I've been trying to prove to everyone, including my father, but most of all to myself, that *I am special*: to show people, to do for people, to prove to myself. I can deal with that. I can change that, I can help with that, I can do for you, I can do without. I can do it all! See? I AM SPECIAL!!!!

I was terrified of my father's angry outbursts until I was in my teens when I felt I could physically defend myself or run away fast enough. He didn't beat me, in fact there was really nothing my dad wouldn't or did not do for me, but there was a fear factor that would freeze me inside because of how angry he got.

I can't remember what set him off, but I have a vivid memory of my father chasing me through our family room in hot pursuit with a steak knife in his hand, swearing he'd kill me. My mother bolted out of the kitchen still holding an open container of oatmeal—today it's almost sitcom funny, thinking of how the oatmeal went flying about as she ran through the room—finally reaching him just as I grabbed my bedroom door and shut it, trembling behind the thin wood. I held it closed as tight as I could until the flimsy flip lock was in place. My mother tried to calm him down, but screaming back and forth ensued.

I was terrified and so stunned he could seemingly hate me that much. Nothing like that ever happened to my brother. Just me. My dad had a difficult time communicating a verbal apology so he wrote me letters instead. Looking back, here's a father who assaulted his daughter with a deadly weapon and nothing was done about it. No counseling... nothing. Swept aside like it didn't happen. It could have ended in tragedy. It took some time, but eventually I put the incident in a "memory bank" and numbed out how I really felt about it. None of this seemed to affect me. Or so I thought then. I adored my father. I never viewed that event with this kind of perspective until some twenty years later when I started to stand up for myself with men again. I didn't realize what impact it had on my spirit.

The first of my three marriages ended in 1983 after eight years of what I felt was an abusive relationship. Within a few days after a major blowup between us, I found an apartment and moved out. I never looked back. My perceptions were so off at the time. I actually had no conception I was seriously underweight—five-seven and a hundred and ten pounds. All those years I thought what this guy needed was to be unconditionally loved . . . and I had that to offer. To prove that was to cater to him one hundred percent. Looking back I could just scream. And have.

The following year, 1984, I took a long hard look at the damage the childhood molestation had inflicted on me, how it had contributed to undermining my self-esteem, confidence and integrity. I got breast implants shortly after leaving my first husband. That had a good psychological effect. For the first time I felt feminine, sexy and in control of using that sexuality. I consciously overcame the fear, guilt and shame instilled in me growing up and started enjoying dating for the first time. I was *thirty-two*. It was also the year my father died and the year my acting career finally got in gear thanks to friends like Walter Hill, Vicki Huff and William Bast. I like to think my dad was helping me with that from the other side.

I ran into an old friend from the '70s, rocker Don Henley of the Eagles. I felt there had always been a strong attraction between us way back when, and even though I felt I was falling in love, I shied away from going to bed with him. I thought it was unrealistic to think he'd be faithful to me, since he had a career about to explode and living the rock'n'roll lifestyle. Besides, psychic George Dareos, who did a reading for both of us, confirmed that it would be better for me to wait. He said he saw us reuniting years later. He also told me that should I get pregnant with Don, to have the baby because I might not be able to have one later.

Years later, sure enough, right after I left my first husband, Don and I did get together. Being a "good girl" I was extra cautious, so I never did get pregnant during that time. For me, it was an exciting, intoxicating, and liberating year and a half affair. Don and I met at a variety of times, places and circumstances. Sometimes he'd walk into my bedroom through an unlocked front door where I'd be there waiting: ready, willing and able. On occasion, he'd have his limo outside waiting, sometimes I'd head out two, three or four in the morning to meet up at a recording studio after they'd finished for the night.

Between 1984 and 1986, I gave hash, coke, opium, and a tad of grass a try as well as a few girl-on-girl experiences at the request of a man I was seeing. I didn't continue any of my experimentations, but I felt bold and liberated for trying them, instead of fearful and guilty. It was a kind of delayed rebel reaction for being such a goody two-shoes all my life. My adventures with Don restored the self-confidence I lost in my first marriage and some self-esteem I never had. I wasn't rejected as I had been in my first marriage. Far from it. It was not only *okay* to be a woman, but I started finally to *enjoy* being one.

I was desired, felt beautiful and independent. I was pursuing my acting career, had an income to support myself, not just from acting, but from a basket decorating business, which was creatively fulfilling. That was just the start of my long journey toward healing the wounded child within and recovering my *self*.

This point in time is when I met my second husband actor, Michael Anderson, Jr. It was at the Hollywood Hills home of actress Kay Lenz. I knew Kay from the days we went to Grant High school together. It was at Kay's birthday party where we all played Pictionary that I struck up a conversation with Michael. He was telling wonderful stories about starring in the western film *The Sons of Katie Elder* with John Wayne as a young actor. I knew as soon as I sat next to him and dropped my fork (I was so drawn to him), I was going to marry him. We had good times together, but it didn't mesh. Bottom line deal breaker for me, he didn't want any more kids. We were great writing partners though, and I still care about him to this day. In fact, we still keep in touch. It was because of my relationship with Michael and his family, my world in Canada opened up.

* * *

Healing is ongoing. The experiences with my uncle started the erosion of my self-esteem and confidence. Being brought up in an atmosphere of fear and guilt about sex, and anger outbursts from my father, did not nurture a healthy outlook on the subject or on how I viewed men, in spite of how I respected and loved my father. I started to realize my choices in relationships needed to improve. Without knowing it, I was always subconsciously trying to "get the lesson" from each. From one to the next, the repeated themes would recur and I'd relive it over and over again, attempting to set it right. I never connected those dots until my relationship with David. Did it surprise me he had angry explosions as my father did?

At first David boasted that he didn't yell as often with me as he had in previous relationships. As time moved on, his rages were more frequent. After he got sober, I was told they could be attributed to "dry drunk syndrome." But what about *before* he got sober? Problem was, when he did get angry it was a volcanic explosion of screaming, breaking things and going off on me in public.

At LAX on our way to Telluride, with my mother in tow, he was angry the airline wouldn't let him carry his guitar on board and had to check it. When I tried to explain an alternative plan and calm him down, he snapped, grabbing and shaking me by my coat collar, as he pulled me up off the ground to my tip toes, screaming nose to nose in my face. This was all in full view of airline staff, my mother and onlookers.

Another time at the Plaza in New York, having a nice lunch, over a small "discussion," he slammed the table so hard the tea cups flipped onto the floor and silverware bounced all over the place. The din of the room ceased as everyone watched him bolt away from the table.

If I was involved in an art project, one of the rare moments I had for myself, he'd get upset about my not reacting how and when he wanted and would rage, thus spoiling my mood and concentration.

In Montreal, the hotel staff will remember a "tabloid moment" when David and I got into an argument and he slammed the door to the adjoining suite so hard it cracked down the center and they had to replace it.

He had more subtle forms of hurting me, instead of embarrassing me, too. He would simply ignore me when we were in public and socializing. Times when I needed to pour my heartfelt feelings out to him, he'd sit there with his quadruple espresso, English Oval cigarettes burning away as he concentrated on his crossword puzzle, totally ignoring what I was saying. I would get upset because he wasn't listening, and he'd retort with his classic line, "What do you want me to say?" and coolly return to his paperwork.

At the end of the relationship, he got physical with me and bruised my wrists. That was the "first strike." The second was kicking a waste paper basket into my leg so hard the "unbreakable" plastic broke off, and bruised my shin for two months. He hovered over me with a satisfied smirk on his face, watching me squirm on the floor in pain and tears.

David knew exactly what button to push to make me feel insecure and off balance. I believed he thrived on keeping the women in his life "disturbed" so that their self-esteem was so far in the toilet, it was hard to see the light, or the reason or be able to climb back up. What he did was sometimes very subtle and kept me in a kind of "gaslight" where I began to doubt myself, instead of realizing this was a calculated plan to keep me in his control. I felt he was a dangerous man, feeding off the energy he got from women. As he told a friend, "I burn women up." The more disturbed I got over something, or the more vulnerable I felt, the more he'd put me down for having those feelings while keeping the degenerating actions going so I'd start to spiral down further.

* * *

David would sometimes catch me totally off guard, especially if I was involved in something where I was focused, like cleaning the house. As many times as he could, if he saw me lean over, he'd seize the opportunity to goose me by running his hand under my crotch and over my butt. It was funny the first half dozen times, even with hurting my head and other body parts when I jerked, but in spite of my continual objections, pleadings and finally anger, he continued. It got to a point where I had to alter my habits and position just in case he snuck up on me to do it again. He thought it was the funniest thing to see me jump. I thought it was sadistic.

* * *

Many of David's actions contributed to my losing respect for him, and caused me to like him less and less as time went on. A few times, it's not a big deal. Time after time, it was like Chinese water torture.

His disregard for what I wanted or needed was subtly saying I wasn't valued. Simple things, like disappearing down the street only to reappear with a cup of hot coffee for himself, when we had both been waiting outside in the bitter cold for a store to open for over an hour. Or talking down to me in front of people, criticizing how I did something, as if I were a child. Or not caring if he woke me or anyone else staying at the house at four or five in the morning by playing the piano or slamming doors. He could sleep late, while I had to get up at the crack of dawn. He didn't care. He didn't think. He didn't want to adjust. It was a major imposition. All that mattered was what he wanted, when he wanted it.

My constant requests for him to stop tweaking my nipples or grabbling my crotch in public were also ignored. He'd usually sneak in a pinch at a social gathering or waiting for our car or . . . come to think of it, he'd just try to grab one whenever. It was difficult not to take it personally and think he didn't have any respect for me. What I should have realized was that *he* didn't feel *he* was worthy, and therefore attempted to make me feel as bad as *he* felt by trying to degrade me. It's a manipulative tactic so that the other person can't "shine," by taking attention away from them.

Even with marriage counselors being adamant with him to stop, he didn't. I believe that spurred him on even more. Authority figures weren't going to tell David Carradine what to do!

CHAPTER THIRTY-SIX

LOVE HURTS II

David always preferred to sing his own music. *Love Hurts* was one of the few songs David would sing that wasn't his own, and he had a kind of a fixation for it. He liked to perform the song and I liked hearing him sing it.

Love can hurt in many ways—it can wound and it can scar and it does take a lot of pain.

"Pain," David said one evening in bed, "is simply a feeling."

When you take the fear out of it and experience the sensation for what it is, it can transform into something else. Even pleasure. This is one area he was a master in. How to manage it for himself, how to inflict it to hurt and how to give someone else pleasure with it.

Many times, rolling with him in the heat of the moment, it was great to get a passionate intense high when some pain could actually be a trigger to even more passion. However, David took it to a new level, as he did with most things. A little pain went a long way with me, and imposing it on another had its limits. David could endure and wanted it to an extreme. He wanted me to bite him. <u>Hard</u>. I could feel my teeth meet on each side as I bit down on his penis. It caused me to literally gag, it was so against my nature. I feared I'd be in the news as the next Lorena Bobbit, but he urged me to continue. In spite of it being a turn-off for me, I continued to try and please him. He loved it.

"Go ahead, you can bite harder. Harder! You're not going to hurt me."

Are you kidding me? The harder I bit, the harder he got. "See, I told you," he said, and the more he wanted. Shouldn't it be the other way around? Yeow! It was like watching some magic trick.

I couldn't understand how he could have that kind of tolerance. He wasn't always like that. I couldn't figure it out. Someone pointed out years later that if he was on meds, he might have had that kind of physical reaction, and only intense pain would get him excited. People indulge in painkillers to heighten their sexual experience and, conversely, doing so also dulls the senses to pain. This in turn supposedly causes the pain threshold to rise so the person can endure more. Even without drugs, it's said that the more pain someone tolerates and turns on to, the more they want each successive time.

We hadn't had any pain meds around for a couple of years—at least not that I was aware of. Besides, I had experienced first hand what he was like on "nummers," it just didn't fit that he was taking any. Nor did it fit with how he behaved. But then, I'm not an expert on this type of subject. Looking back on how he handled the aftermath of his hair transplant and lipo, he was very happy to have the meds on hand. His sexual tolerance points more to his mind set, or self-hypnosis fits the profile better regarding control and indulgence in crossing the line of endurance. Combine that with his attitude toward pain and I think David was someone who was able not only to tolerate the extreme, but thoroughly enjoy it. Besides, he commented many times how fabulous he felt substance free. "The clouds," he said, "have lifted."

* * *

When we first moved into the Valley Vista house, Kansas and I did a complete clean of a medicine box unpacked from Mississauga. There were literally dozens of bottles of prescription pills, mostly with expired dates, which we deemed needed to be tossed. Why would he want expired medicine around? I recognized a few of the brands and types of painkillers such as Vicodin and Darvon. It was quite a colorful collection.

When we told him, proudly, that everything was sorted and thrown out to make room in the small medicine cabinet, his rage was immense. It was like World War III erupted! I could actually see his jugulars bulge. Kwai Chang Caine turning into the Hulk. He slammed objects, and the cats scurried for cover as he ranted on about how long it took him to acquire such a stash. A favorite side trip when he traveled out of the country, ideally in Mexico, was to pick up a supply of difficult to get and inexpensive medications. He didn't forgive me for the longest time for eliminating the "pharmacy." Not until we actually did travel and he had the opportunity to begin replenishing it.

Since he had just recently gone sober, I thought that it scared him to lose his security blanket. Without alcohol and no meds, what was he going to hang on to? Reality?

When David paid a few visits to the dentist, he got a prescription, and he made sure we kept leftovers from the various procedures we went through—my IVFs and knee surgery, his hair transplant. I always took the bare minimum of that sort of thing, so there was always some left. When we both had lipo at the same time, we received plenty for future use. It never occurred to me he'd be taking anything other than for a legit reason. And it wasn't like I'd check by counting the number of pills in each bottle. If David ever took pain meds for "recreational" use, he never mentioned it to me. I trusted he told me everything else, so this wouldn't be something he'd keep from me. Or would it?

* * *

We chose a typical store front in a shopping mall to get David's ear pierced, and I loved buying jewelry for him to wear in his "pirate ear." He wore the tiny gold dragon I designed for him for years, which I now have. He stopped wearing it opting for subtle diamond or ruby hoops. But when it came to other piercings, that was different.

We made belly button piercings an anniversary present to ourselves to celebrate our first year of being together. He already had this piercing, but needed it opened up again, so we headed out to a West Hollywood store recommended by his son, Tom, who had a friend who worked there. The young guy had several facial piercings strategically decorating his face and ears, and a great attitude. He made it an educational as well as a spiritual experience, and coached me through the event like I was having a baby—how to breathe, when to breathe, what to focus on. It was actually an enjoyable experience, except for the two seconds of excruciating pain.

David, the piercing veteran, watched my procedure intently and took it all in stride when it was his turn. He didn't make a sound. The piercing artist didn't need to guide David through anything. In fact, David was giving him tips! It was a little more complicated since his was being repositioned. David looked forward to the moment and Zen'ed out into a space of contemplation by focusing on the piercer and what he was doing. Me, on the other hand . . . well, I couldn't look. I held on to every word the "coach" was gently saying, " . . . and now take a deep breath and . . . " I didn't scream. It was more like a very surprised squeak. Kind of like stepping on a nail.

David was inspired. He was determined to get other parts of my body pierced. Now he wanted me to have my clitoris and labia done. Oh whoopee dooo! It was part of a continuing fantasy that sounded sexy, felt sexy, but the reality of doing it was something I wanted to avoid.

When we were in Toronto, we sussed out a couple of piercing places, but neither made me feel comfortable. I managed to put it off for a while, but now David was like a dog with a bone, he wouldn't leave it alone. He certainly knew his way around the anatomy since he had done his own accoutrement genital piercing, so I trusted he could do it right on me. I hoped.

He got me under his hypnotic spell, as he often did, and after he seduced me in bed I acquiesced to his request to give it a try. He convinced me it would be like the belly button piercing—a split second of pain, but then it would be fine. So he got out a little kit he put together and prepped the needle—which might as well have been a stake the way it looked to me, totally intimidating—with alcohol, a cork, the piercing ring . . . He turned his attention to me to get me in the mood again with considerable foreplay. Then came the moment. It was not just a split second, but seemed like whole minutes of agony held within one silent inhaled gasp. It was so painful I couldn't even let out a sound for a moment. Like that moment in *Godfather III* when the daughter of Al Pacino's character gets shot and he stands there wanting to scream, but nothing comes out.

Then while he tried to pull the needle through the "hollow" in the clitoris area, I couldn't stand it anymore and finally cried out in agony. I probably sounded like Pacino from David's reaction. He withdrew the needle and I bolted out of bed, running for the bathroom, bleeding like a stuck pig. I thought I was maimed for life and would never enjoy sex again. He tried to cover his being rattled about my reaction. "You screamed."

I'm thinking like what in the hell did he expect? A laugh?!

He was more disappointed than he was concerned about any damage that may have been done. What was I thinking? I could have smacked myself, but I decided not to, I was in too much pain. It took about two weeks to recuperate from that debacle and not once did he ask how I was feeling. He was pissed I didn't want to try it again. There was no way I was going to try a labia piercing after that in spite of David heisting a bottle of Zylocaine from a doctor's office. My belly button ring would do just fine!

* * *

It came to a point where I wondered why couldn't he just be excited and happy with me. No games, no fantasies, no "accessories," just me. Wasn't I enough? All he talked about was how much he wanted me, but . . . It reminded me of my first marriage. There always had to be some other "thing" going on in bed, which didn't make me feel . . . special. There was little true intimacy, so it created an emotionally empty experience.

Contrary to what was revealed in the press when David died, he did not tie himself up to meditate during our time together. I never found him in any situation "flying solo," but bondage was certainly a main course on his sexual menu as was another favorite dish—strangulation, whether with ropes, handcuffs, neckties, hands, or scarves. Maybe the passive meditative "exercise" described in the media escalated to where it was with me?

Slowly, as time progressed in the relationship and I started to find my way back to "me," experiencing pain as part of our sexual dance appealed to me less and less. I was experiencing such emotional grief on a daily level, I didn't need it or want it in the bedroom anymore. That's when David started doing things to either hurt or upset me on purpose, in and out of bed.

This other behavior put a damper on our sex life. At least for me it did. He refused to stop when I had reached an orgasm, knowing if he continued, it would become painful. He did it time and time again, which ruined the experience. He'd get a smirk on his face anytime I'd show I was upset by it. It was obvious it didn't ruin the moment for him. On the contrary.

Then, there were the gold piercings he wore, which were great to look at, but at times irritating to my body. One of the jewelry pieces fit at the tip of his penis and part of the chain had broken leaving a jagged, sharp point. At first I couldn't understand why I was bleeding, but quickly discovered what the source of it was. You'd think he'd remove it, but he didn't, even after I told him I didn't want to have sex with him wearing it. That also put a stop to him trying to have intercourse with me with his ruby studded penis ring. It gave new meaning to being given the family jewels. About four millimeters in size, it was embedded in the 18k gold circle which hung from the very tip of his dip stick. Cool to look at, but I insisted it remained a decorative versus "active" accessory.

***

After one IVF procedure, which was intense for me to go through, we made love sooner than I wanted, to please David, and I started to bleed. I panicked, thinking the procedure went awry since he denied having the sharp piercing still attached to him. It was difficult to see because it would lodge itself inside the piercing hole, but upon hands-on inspection, I discovered he still had the same sharp offensive jewelry in place. He lied again, breaking our pact, as well as my trust. Why would he risk hurting me like that? When we went for my follow-up with Dr. Paulson, he was upset as to what happened. The jewelry punctured my cervix and caused bruising. The IVF procedure never took. I had to ask myself, was David trying to sabotage our efforts to have a baby?

* * *

A couple of years after we married, the bedroom wasn't a place I looked forward to anymore, but I held out hope things still might change. He knew what I wanted, but refused to please me. He only participated the way he wanted. The experience consistently left me feeling incomplete and hollow. I wanted more than just oral sex. I guess he felt if he couldn't get what he wanted in his world of fantasies anymore, in or out of bed, then why should he give me what I really wanted?

The thought of going topless, exposing myself as we drove down Sunset Boulevard, was fun at first flush of our relationship, but once was enough. I didn't want a repeat. He did. Then there was his constant talk of walking me nude with collar and leash down the isle of Levant. It was part of his fascination with the *Story of O* book. Fine in fantasy, but he was serious in one day making it a reality. As I was getting counseling for my problems with David, my self-esteem started to come back and these fantasies didn't have much appeal anymore. I got tired of the submissive scenario, much to his disappointment. I longed to feel as I had in the beginning of our relationship, like he loved every inch of me. No matter where he touched me or what he said was loving and gentle and I melted. Now, his words were still loving, but his actions were not. There were too many contradictions, too many things to try and figure out.

Early fall 1996, and we had just moved into the house on Valley Vista in Sherman Oaks. The carpet had been removed and David was in the process of trying to refurbish the hardwood flooring. Wearing a pair of Bermuda shorts, he had purchased a mass of supplies and was diligently working away with chemicals to remove adhesives from the parquet he installed. It was a noble attempt, but it never looked quite right. The side molding never got installed. Many of the projects he would undertake remained unfinished because he'd give up and there wasn't enough money to get them professionally fixed.

I approached David as he sat on the floor working away. His hair was mussy and he seemed to be having fun. There was something on his leg that looked somewhere between a bruise and a burn. I called his attention to the mysterious red-blue-yellow-and-purple marking but he dismissed it as being an allergy to the chemicals he was working with. The mysterious markings were further up his shorts, upper thigh to be exact, and it didn't make sense that he would have been exposed to any chemicals. Not that high up.

Second-guessing myself, I thought maybe he got careless as he sometimes did and splashed the chemicals or rubbed his hand there. His shorts didn't appear to be stained either, but I accepted the explanation. When I touched the marks, and asked if it was bothering him he said, "No." I couldn't understand his peculiar expression, but tossed it off anyway. There was also a mark or two on his wrist area and upper arm.

It was a couple months later I noticed similar marks on his other upper thigh, arm and chest area. Before commenting, I asked if he had worked on the flooring while I was out, but he said he had been busy writing. These marks looked worse and more like burn blisters. They also didn't hurt him when I examined hands-on. He chuckled this time.

"It tickles?"

"No."

"Then why did you laugh?"

"I don't know."

"They don't hurt and they don't tickle . . . what the hell are they?" He never answered me. Just shrugged. I'm thinking they might be herpes, but they didn't look like that either. Peculiar. I noticed this one more time, but only very, very small marks on his forearms. Could they be . . . rope marks? Nah. I dismissed that quickly. I had adamant trust David wouldn't cheat on me. But something wasn't right. There was a neighbor who retrieved Thunder once. I could tell David was hiding interest in her. There was another woman who was in contact with David. I long suspected she wanted to get him back. It was all very hinkey, but I maintained my belief he was true to me. So what were these things?

I came across a letter from David years later where he wrote: "This marriage has become something like the most sexually exclusive relationship I've ever had." So what exactly did that mean? He was faithful *after* we were *married*? And what did "something like" mean? I always had suspicions about the before, but held fast that he was completely faithful once we were married.

Fast forward to one September morning in 2002, about 4:30. I bolted awake with the solution to what the mysterious marks were . . . Gasp! Ah! I can't believe it, they were . . . hickies!!! Why didn't I realize that before? It just didn't connect. They looked different from the garden variety, and besides I was in such denial before. My pillow took a beating as I pummeled it in frustration. I felt so blonde! No wonder he laughed.

* * *

David loved it when I lavished myself in perfume. He'd inhale deeply and say "There's nothing like a woman smelling like a French whore house!" He appreciated "the smell of perfume on women period, especially if they were naked," he'd joke. Sometimes, he'd come home with samples he liked from the store for me to try out when we made love. A couple of his favorites were Sublime and Angel. I wore Angel for the six years we were together. Now I can't stand even one whiff of the scent. He thought it smelled like mangos and peaches. Peach fragrance reminded him of the trees on Ben Avenue where he spent part of his childhood. David indulged in all the senses when it came to our intimate moments. Nothing was off limits for him. He was totally uninhibited. He explored every orifice he could and wanted me to do the same. He wanted me to do anything and everything to him. Literally.

CHAPTER THIRTY-SEVEN

WHAT'S WITH *THAT?*

An animal marks its territory in a new space, but a person? After we moved to the Rosita house, our beautiful new home in Tarzana, David's dog Thunder yielded to his natural instincts and began marking his new territory by peeing inside the house on furniture, on the rugs, the lamps . . . He'd be fine for a while, then I'd hear the sound of water puddling on the carpet and run screaming into the room, "Noooooo!" Thunder would look up with his soulful brown eyes and cower, knowing he did wrong. Did David clean up after his dog? No.

Shortly after this most loved canine began his habit, I walked into our kitchen to get a drink. Something smelled funky. My male cat, Tai—whom I suspected didn't like David because he had a habit of peeing over his boots or whatever else David had in the closet on the floor, and occasionally on our bed—jumped down from the counter. Gazing down into the pristine stainless steel basin, I saw a pool of yellow colored liquid reflecting part of my image. Leaning down and putting my olfactory sense to use, I deduced that it was . . . urine. Great. My cat was using the sink as his litter box!

I knew moving might be upsetting for any of the pets, but never thought this would be the way Tai would express it. I vented my disapproval at him and he scampered out of the kitchen. Could it be the male marking instinct again? Could he be taking his cue from Thunder? He was still using our baskets of magazines as an alternate kitty litter box, wasn't that enough?

The next day, after an exhausting twelve hours in the home office, I sludged my way into the kitchen to find *David* taking a leak in the kitchen sink! It was *him*, not my cat. Dumbfounded and disgusted, I watched in amazement, until he turned around, passing me with a smile like nothing had happened.

"You just peed in the sink!"

"Yeah" He said with a slight chuckle like it was a "duh" factor.

"What the hell are you pissing in the kitchen sink for? It's called a toilet, Johnny!"

"No it's called a sink." He loved to really get me going that way.

"That's disgusting, one. Two, not sanitary and three, it's got to stop."

"I'm saving water."

"Excuse me?"

"Instead of using the toilet every time, I'm saving water by using the sink. Lighten up, Blackie. It's only urine."

The logic of this was beyond my comprehension and my limit of tolerance. "This is where we do the dishes! Where we prepare food! *It's the kitchen not the bathroom!*"

Before I could continue, he walked out of the room with a smug look on his face. This is a guy who would also eat food picked up off the floor and shovel dog dung with his bare hands if there was an accident in the house. He didn't care.

Regardless of my countless complaints, pleadings and anger vents about his golden showers, he continued to do it with or without the sink full of dishes, and on occasion the bathroom sinks for the year we lived there, until he moved out.

Between him, Thunder and Tai, it was here a piss, there a piss, everywhere a piss piss. Why couldn't he just walk outside and water the backyard lawn with his donation? Oh, he did that too.

What could I do? The next time I caught him at it, I had a fleeting fantasy of some reptile like Alien crawling up from the garbage disposal connecting with a firm snap on his genital wand, but his urine sent it shrinking back into the sewer system.

Let's just say the household budget for disinfectants skyrocketed. Unless I assured friends who knew of his habit—yes, I couldn't help but vent to a few—that the dishwasher was used, they preferred plastic glasses straight out of the box and opted to go out for lunch.

If he had been the outdoorsy type then following an urge to take a whiz outside would be one thing, but that wasn't David. He simply liked to relieve himself in a variety of places when and where he felt it suited him, such as an awards event in Las Vegas that Jaki Baskow of Baskow & Associates booked for him. In a recent conversation, we laughed over the memory of David whizzing behind the backstage area in a corner.

When David was a guest on Sharon Osbourne's show, she recalled a moment when he climbed over a wall at Wimbledon and "took a pee on it."

It's hard to top Wimbledon, but there *was* the day David was a guest on the *The Mommies* talk show, hosted by Marilyn Kentz and Caryl Kristensen, to promo his book and projects. Even though David was in a grumpy mood and didn't want to do the show to begin with, all went well. We walked out to my car, which wasn't far from the production building, when he decided he needed to use the bathroom before we headed out on the road. Instead of going back into the studio, he went around to the side of the car and to my exasperation, rained on the garbage bin instead. "No one's going to see me."

Years later, after our separation, I bumped into one of the hosts of the show who related to me part of the staff wanted to meet David before he left. She stood in the doorway with them as they watched David in that rare performance. We both burst out laughing. Needless to say they didn't rush out to the car. I guess they were afraid to shake his hand.

* * *

Sometimes David could be very naïve. Most often he didn't do things in a pre-meditated way. If he did plan, he often wouldn't think the whole thing through. He'd often speak before he thought about information he was giving out, and his actions also often gave away the truth he was trying to hide.

After we separated, it was sometimes difficult to reach David on the phone. He said he was getting a new cell phone and number and would let me know. A few weeks passed and he never brought up the subject again. One evening my phone rang and a strange number appeared on the caller ID. When I answered it, there was no one on the other end. I called it back and the outgoing message was David's voice.

About half an hour later he called from his regular cell phone number. I asked if he ever got the other cell phone he was talking about and he said he changed his mind and didn't get it.

"Well that's odd cause your number appeared on caller ID a half hour ago."

"How can that be, I'm calling now."

"Yes, you are calling now from *your other cell phone*."

There was a long beat of silence.

He gave a heavy sigh, "Okay, you found out."

"You lied to me. You out and out lied to my face!"

Then in a higher almost childlike whine he retorts, "Well I only lied for a minute!"

CHAPTER THIRTY-EIGHT

SHRINK-RAP

FINDING a good therapist can be difficult. It was for us. We consulted with several. It was a ping-pong game of who approved of the next choice, trying to find the right fit. David went along with me practically dragging him, each time saying he wasn't the one who needed the counseling because he wasn't the one with the problem. He was right. I had the problem and it was him. Most of the time he'd sit there in utter boredom, looking at the walls, down in his lap, the floor or out the window, anywhere but to the situation at hand.

I thought a female shrink would be more receptive so we started there. The office with its own private entrance was in the back of her chic monotone decorated home in the hills, surrounded by beautiful shade trees and hummingbirds. Tranquil beauty. The pulled together, naturally grey-haired, sixty-something woman was very understanding of my plight on the first session. She understood the bare minimum I wanted was to feel safe and leaving the doors unlocked and not setting the alarm was not being supportive for someone with post-traumatic stress disorder, let alone good safety. She agreed that since David was a celebrity, he was more of a target.

"You have me to protect you," David would boast. Yeah Kung Fu man, like that's going to do us any good if you leave the door unlocked and we're sleeping and someone has a gun. Is that common sense? I thought he was fricking delusional. He didn't see it that way.

She also agreed with the counselor I had for my PTSD, that it would be beneficial to me if David stopped calling me paranoid, and criticizing my safety concerns.

In our next session with her, since David defied all her suggestions, I was in full rant mode. He engaged her in philosophy and other topics and our $175 worth of fifty minutes was soon up. He did most of the talking and I could tell she was enamored. She was also single. The only suggestion for the day was that he "try harder."

Following week, the same issues were brought up and more, but this time she did a one-eighty on me and said I was being too demanding and so what if he left the doors unlocked. I was now being *unreasonable!* David wanted to go back the following week. No way! I'd rather spend $175 on extra toilet paper the way the crap was being handed out.

Our agent at the time recommended his marriage counselor who was great. The shrink nailed David, and me, on each issue, but when it got to the part where he suggested David not touch me inappropriately in public and the subject of a baby, I crumbled into buckets of tears. David sat there casually, sans shoes in a semi cross-legged pose staring at the wall on the opposite side of the room. Like he was in another world.

The therapist told him he was being insensitive. "Look at your wife, David . . . She's in pain. Does that matter to you?" Silence. "Do you care how she feels? Did you hear what she was saying?"

"I care."

"You're not showing it. Your actions aren't saying that."

The therapist felt badly for me. After David walked out of the room, the therapist said that it was not possible to help the two of us because David clearly didn't want to participate or make any adjustments. It was like talking to a wall. David refused to go back for another session.

One last try, with yet another male counselor, David spun the truth around a problem, which sent me over the edge again. I was on the verge of divulging "the secret," since David was accusing me of not wanting X around and making me out to be a cold bitch. I tried to dance around the issue without giving them up. It was almost as if he was egging me on, daring me to say it—to tell the therapist about the incest. It was all I could do not to blurt it out. "Do you want me to tell him?!" But I didn't because I was honoring his secret. I wish I hadn't because maybe revealing it could have helped us and saved the marriage. Maybe it would have helped me, but I put David as first priority again.

When we got home all hell broke loose. "Do you want me to divorce you, Johnny? Because I will. You want to throw it all away? How can we get help if you're not being truthful? How can you tell those lies?!"

He got in his car and left, and he was gone for hours. When he returned, he came back with flowers and my favorite magazines. He tried to make some adjustments, as I did, but it only lasted for a couple of weeks. That Valentine's Day in a card he said he'd marry me again and wanted to know if I'd do the same. It tore at my heart. I was stuck for an answer. I was burned out and hanging on by a thread. Had there been money to hire people to help, things might have been different in many ways. But there wasn't. With the personal issues, nothing really changed.

I made another appointment, and I vowed to myself everything was going to be brought out into the open this time. I couldn't take stuffing it away anymore. Being accused as the bad guy with David withholding and twisting around the truth made me boil. Like the victim being blamed for a perpetrator's actions. The next session never happened, however, because he moved out.

David had great pride. He also shifted his interests if he felt he'd be better served by another. A close friend of his related a story about an elderly woman who lavished gifts on David because he reminded her of her deceased son. She promised him a new expensive car, but when she didn't come through with it, he cut off all ties with the woman. She was very distraught by his cold disconnection. I was told he was upset he didn't get his car and had nothing else to gain from her. Maybe the situation reminded him of his stepmother, Sonia. As a child, David adored her and thought she adored him as well, until he overheard a phone conversation in which she related to her friend that David wasn't that special to her. It hit him hard and had a profound effect on him. Based on his younger years, David had great fear of abandonment. Now, he'd rather be the one to walk away, to avoid the pain of yet another person abandoning him again.

Donna, his first wife, I was told, was the one who worked tirelessly choreographing David's audition for a show, which was key to him landing a lead role in *Royal Hunt of the Sun*. As soon as it opened on Broadway, he walked away from her, leaving Donna to raise their daughter Calista for the next twelve years.

During his relationship with Barbara he strayed to actress Season Hubley. From Linda, his second wife, he strayed to Gail. From Gail he strayed to me.

Was it because he feared being abandoned and took action first, or did he use up the usefulness each relationship offered him in order to further his quest for something he thought could fill a never-ending void? Or maybe deep inside he felt he didn't deserve to be loved and hit his self-destruct button? None of the above?

What attracted David to each one of us? Many people have commented on the physical common denominators of most of David's wives. With the exception of Gail, we all had dark hair and similar builds and features. From what I've observed and know about each of us, and I have met them all, it's more than skin deep.

* * *

From a letter David wrote to me, he tried harder with me than he did with any of the previous women to make the relationship work and to "conform and compromise" to a lifestyle other than what he was used to—which was doing what he wanted, when he wanted, how he wanted, with whomever he wanted. He had no healthy boundaries, nor did he, as I found out much much later, want to have any.

Whenever he told me he was doing the best he could, I believed him, but it was always a temporary effort. The few things I ever asked of him were not held to. He let me know that smoking in another room, locking the doors or setting the alarm, for example, was a major compromise for him. He wanted to be free. He didn't want the responsibilities he felt people placed on him. It was okay for others to dance around him, to cater to his needs day and night, but he only contributed when he felt like it.

* * *

It's said that the inside of a person's home reflects what is going on inside that person's being. The house could be neat as a pin and not more than ten minutes after David got home, you'd never believe it had been cleaned. Clothes strewn, cigarette ashes, shoes tossed in the middle of the room, shopping bags on a chair, something on the stove burning over . . . What does it mean when one person has to constantly clean up the other's disorganized, dirty mess?

It was suggested that I put all his things in a pile and let him deal with it. Good idea. Tried it. The pile would get bigger and bigger until finally David would blow up.

"Have you seen my shirt with the crane on it? And the belt with the turquoise buckle?"

"Yeah. They're in the pile."

"It's all wrinkled," he raged.

"Well, you should have hung it up," I'd calmly responded.

He'd stomp out of the room. It remained a mystery why our problems escalated when we moved to the Rosita house. It seemed nothing went right there. Anyway, the "pile-up" exercise was one that worked to an extent, but I was still spending considerable time picking his messes up to put in the pile!

My own theory is that men like David, and women too, tend to feed off the energy of others. If that energy is removed, they feel deprived or abandoned, which can cause fear and anger. They are actually angry at themselves for not being able to step up to the plate and do things for themselves. And maybe because the desirable qualities they see in others, they think they can't achieve for themselves. This can cause resentment and jealousy. This anger, fear, jealousy and/or resentment builds to a boiling point where they will either deflect that negative energy onto someone else or onto themselves. The bedroom seemed to be one of the arenas where this drama was expressed.

At least, that's what I've experienced.

CHAPTER THIRTY-NINE

SHRINKED

WHY would a person get a charge out of something like autoerotic asphyxiation? If they are the aggressor in the act, does it mean that they are symbolically killing someone they love? That they feel deep down that they don't deserve that love? Is it hate, for themselves or for the other person? And what if they are the one being asphyxiated? What does that mean?

Apart from the inherent danger autoerotic asphyxiation presents, why is it considered a disorder? Why is it more than merely a dangerous, perverse preference?

It's said that the attraction is the heightened sexual arousal it gives to participants, but with David, it seemed more complicated. Nothing was simple about the man.

I had pushed aside these questions and more for years, but in the media storm that followed David's death and the revelation of the condition in which he was found, the whole issue all flew up and hit the fan again. Even though I started to write the book years ago, the current events regarding David dictated addressing this part of my life with him. I realized that these questions deserved answers, and I felt impelled to pursue explanations. I also knew I needed help in putting some of the pieces of the puzzle together. I wanted clarification and understanding of some of the issues that had troubled me for so long. It was one thing to draw conclusions based on my personal experience, but I felt it was also essential to hear a professional perspective.

In selecting a psychologist or qualified professional to interview for this book, I reviewed a list of names that were either recommended, or that I knew about from having seen them in the media.

The one I zeroed in on was Dr. Drew Pinsky, an expert on addictive behavior and host of the VH1 television network's successful *Celebrity Rehab with Dr. Drew* and *Sex Rehab with Dr. Drew* programs. Dr. Drew, as he likes to be known, is a graduate of the University of Southern California's Keck School of Medicine, where he is now an assistant clinical professor of psychiatry. He is board-certified in internal and addiction medicine, as well as a *New York Times* bestselling author.

Within two days of placing a call to Dr. Drew's publicist, Valerie Allen, I was on the phone with him in an intense conversation.

It was an encounter I had looked forward to for a long time, and though I had envisioned myself inquiring with the objectivity and skill of Barbara Walters, I instead found myself often tongue-tied, caught up in the emotions that the discussion dredged up.

Dr. Drew spoke with quick-paced, high energy, and keen insight. His responses to my questions were immediate and to the point and he projected a friendly feeling, as if we had spoken many times before. There was an instant comfort zone with him. This was fortunate, because while he certainly ended up confirming many things I had suspected, much of what he said forced me to confront behaviors in David and myself that I now realize I didn't see (so much so that I have felt obliged to edit out almost every "wow" and "geez" that escaped me in reaction to the revelations and confirmations, because they were so frequent).

Conversation with Dr. Drew:

[*After relating my experiences with David and concerns from women who e-mailed me with the same and similar issues, I asked my first question.*]

MARINA: What causes people to do this: strangulation and autoerotic asphyxiation?

DR. DREW: Please keep in mind Marina, these are casual speculations of an armchair quarterback. I do not and did not know David. Everything I will be saying is built from pure speculation based on what you are telling me and frequent clinical patterns that I have observed. That being said there are two common themes. One is, if a child has been physically abused in childhood, they will tend to be aroused by physically abusive kinds of scenarios. There are various theories about why this is. I like to think of it as the arousal of the system being sort of burned out by terrorization in childhood. And to get arousal back again you have to go to very extreme lengths.

The other issue is that experiences of terror in childhood are converted to arousal and attraction in adulthood. We don't know why this is, but it's why people who are sexually abused become prostitutes or strippers. They compulsively repeat the traumas over and over again. Some people theorize it's like bonding to the trauma. Almost like a love connection to the trauma itself and thus therein lies the arousal too.

MARINA: The complication is that I was sexually molested by my uncle, my father's brother when I was young. It wasn't a rape. It was a very touchy, hands-on lascivious kind of a thing, but nevertheless it carried through relationships as to what attracted me to certain people. Coincidentally, I get into the relationship with David and I start connecting the dots. There was incest between David and X as an adult . . .

DR. DREW: We might speculate that perhaps David had been sexually abused at a certain age for him not to perceive those boundaries normally. And that history is remarkably common among celebrities. And of course remarkably common in the population at large.

MARINA: That was my kind of kindergarten perception. In talking with someone like you, it grounds the truth in there more.

DR. DREW: It makes it likely. Now there's another piece to this puzzle, which is that addiction is a peculiar illness.

MARINA: Because he was an alcoholic.

DR. DREW: It has people doing things they wouldn't do in their normal state. So when people are using, they may have poor boundaries, they may have predilections in this direction, but when they are in their addiction, they can go to really egregious lengths.

Let's say he had sexual abuse "lite"—a turn of phrase meaning there was unwanted touching and not overt sexual abuse of some type—in childhood but then becomes a severe addict. That's a situation where people can behave in all kinds of crazy ways. Regarding the asphyxiation, one of the more common things we see these days—and this may or may not apply to him [David]—are opiate addicts. When they come off opiates, the arousal system is sort of blunted or burned out. So it's very common for people with a history of opiate addiction to go to asphyxiation as a way to feel sexual satisfaction. A lot of my opiate-addicted patients die that way when they are in the first year or two of their sobriety.

[All during his explanation, I had been getting "ah-ha" epiphanies. But when he said this, my mouth dropped open, and I silently gasped.]

MARINA: It's interesting you bring that up because . . . David had an arsenal of painkillers.

DR. DREW: There you go. Those are opiates. Perhaps he was an opiate addict.

MARINA: But that's something I thought he never continued on. I dumped all those painkillers. And he threw a shit fit. He was totally clean and sober for at least two years [that is, not drinking or taking pain pills], but he wanted to make sure those painkillers were on hand. I could never tell if he was taking anything, but . . .

DR. DREW: Let me repeat what I said. You've got to listen carefully. My opiate addicts particularly in the first one or two years of their sobriety, get into this asphyxiation stuff, and some of them get into it for life. They can never feel sexual satisfaction after what the opiates do to their brain. That's one thing. So he may fit that profile. And secondly, if he had opiates on hand, he was using them. Period. That's the way addicts are. And that too would predispose him to the behaviors we are discussing here.

MARINA: The strangulation and asphyxiation started at least a year before I was with him . . . He had a pain level that was not to be believed

. . . It took me aback . . . I couldn't understand how he . . .

DR. DREW: Well, he was using. Painkillers.

MARINA: That's an eye-opener.

DR. DREW: I didn't know him, I don't know for sure. An opiate addict who has opiates around simply can't not use. I've never seen that happen.

[*At this point, I was feeling that this couldn't be right. David couldn't have been an opiate addict. But everything Dr. Drew was talking about fit. David made sure there were painkillers on hand. Why else would he want them other than to use them? My brain was wrapping around the information as we forged on into the next question, hoping the answer would give me an excuse to deny David had been what everything was pointing to.*]

MARINA: Wow . . . and there would be no other symptoms or personality behavior to . . .

DR. DREW: Well, there can be. People can spend years and years on opiates before the house of cards begins to fall. It's a broad spectrum of people who seek that [*asphyxiation, strangulation*]. I don't think you can say it's only this one source or kind of person that does that. It is a common pattern in my opiate addicted patients. Some people have physical abuse in childhood and they find it highly arousing as part of their S&M practices. For other people, it could be some genetic biological issue where they don't feel arousal and they are looking for ways to intensify arousal and they come upon this. It's a relatively small population. The most common thread amongst the group is trauma. The way to think of it is, you don't feel arousal normally; you need to intensify it, and you aren't particularly interested in intimacy when you are being sexual. So things that divert from intimacy are sought after.

[*I was thinking that from what Gail said to the press, and from what I experienced, it appeared that David's satiation requirements were escalating. Years after we separated, and from how he died, it appears that it never stopped escalating.*]

MARINA: Ah ha! Whoa! Combined with years and years of abuse, and I guess, to get more and more and more, it just kept escalating . . . I guess.

DR. DREW: It's hard to put it all together with great accuracy. It may be that he was into some stages of early kind of a sobriety. Was he going to meetings twice a day?

MARINA: [Laugh] No, no, no. He did it on his own, cold turkey.

DR. DREW: He was using.

MARINA: Once a year to get his birthday cake, . . . [*I related to him the incident at the Malibu AA meeting*]. And he only went to a few meetings during the six years together.

DR. DREW: There just really isn't, and I don't want to say never, but there isn't such a thing as stopping opiates on your own. It doesn't exist in nature. I've just never seen it. And I've treated 10,000 addicts. Call me crazy, but he must have been doing something. Was he smoking pot? Was he doing something?

MARINA: We didn't have that [*pot*] around [*then I remembered*] . . . it was around at some point, but I was definitely aware if he was doing that because I'm very keen to that sort of thing—the behavior and symptoms—maybe two to three times in the six years. Outside of that, no, I definitely believe he was not using grass. [*But I was thinking, how would I know what he was or wasn't doing when I wasn't around?*] There were a few plastic surgeries, [*we each had them*] here and there, and we'd always have leftovers from me 'cause I barely used that stuff, so it's not like I went to count the pills, but . . .

DR. DREW: Who knows? It's all very suspicious.

MARINA: Wow. Because it dulls the senses and therefore they have to have more of the . . . whether it's the pain or the heightened . . . [*I was thinking of his wanting me to bite him full force on his penis.*]

DR. DREW: It changes their system so that they can't feel sexual satisfaction whether they are using or whether they're off. In both situations, they don't feel sexual satisfaction very well.

MARINA: Now, turning that around, he liked to inflict pain on me, which I wasn't really into. It seemed to give him perverse satisfaction to know that it hurt me.

DR. DREW: That goes back to the physical abuse scenario. So you surmise that he was hurt or witnessed people being hurt or something as a child. Again, terror becomes attraction. Terror becomes arousing. It's not that he's experiencing terror when he's doing this to you, but the wiring is set up by the terror in childhood. Terrorizing circumstances in people, which would normally be a source of aversion, suddenly become attractive, arousing . . . attraction is the main ingredient.

Experiences that cause terror in childhood become repeated magically in adulthood and they are repeated because the people and places that remind that individual of those terrors are somehow converted into attraction. So they are attracted to people and places that are reminiscent of the sources of terror in childhood. Not in any kind of conscious way, but some sort of deep subconscious drive, people theorize that this is "traumatic bonding," that you literally bond to traumatic experiences and perpetrators. That bond becomes recapitulated later as an attraction to someone whom you want to bond with, someone very much like the perpetrator.

MARINA: So my being afraid of my uncle, would that create possibly the attraction to David?

DR. DREW: Right. You like somebody and you're freaked out by them or can't understand or it doesn't make sense to you or it's perverse and yet still it's attractive on a certain level.

MARINA: When I started getting counseling and became more, say, healed within myself, I started to be repelled by that and hence the problems in the marriage

DR. DREW: Right.

MARINA: Inappropriate touching the same thing? Because he would grope me in public.

DR. DREW: Right, but that used to be the thing you were attracted to. By the way it's more that, as much as anything, you're attracted to the type of person who will oblige you by repeating the traumas. You know what I mean? You may not have ever seen them do those things, but somehow intuitively you know it's that person, it's that kind of person. And of course they will oblige you most of the time, by doing the things that person did from childhood.

MARINA: Whoa.

DR. DREW: It's a dance. It takes two.

MARINA: Yeah . . . Symbolically, for him to strangle someone he loves, is it maybe literally killing what he loves, like he doesn't believe he deserves something? His self worth . . .

DR. DREW: I'm sure somebody has made those kinds of . . . now this is pure speculation okay? But in my head when I think about the kinds of connections that men make, men have some level of wanting to . . . you know the French call orgasm, "la petite mort," the little death, and I think men on some level have a desire to sort of have a woman succumb through orgasm. And this just becomes a more explicit, highly arousing, and very aggressive manifestation of that.

MARINA: Well, he was into . . . you're probably familiar with it, the book, the *Story of "O"*?

DR. DREW: Yes.

MARINA: He was totally fascinated with that book.

DR. DREW: Here's the deal. He grew up in an age of culture where people were "Hey man, whatever you're into, just go do it. Explore. It's your thing man."

MARINA: Right.

DR. DREW: But "your thing" has meaning. We now know that. "And it may not be healthy what you're into man." And so in this case you both are re-enacting all these traumas over and over again and it diminishes intimacy when you do that. As much as anything else, it's dangerous and unhealthy, as you have discovered. And here you go, you know?

MARINA: Yes, totally. And I was having a big problem with all of that. In a way, was there maybe a little bit of a death wish of his?

DR. DREW: You're trying to find rationality in an irrational drive. Making these kinds of explicit interpretations, I think, becomes by its very nature, inaccurate. However, I will tell you that addicts are sort of aroused by death. They sort of . . . they have a unique relationship with death, addicts do. And I've just noticed that. Not all of them, but opiate addicts particularly. It's sort of, something they don't mind flirting with. They kind of get aroused by it.

MARINA: There was something about that with him, too.

DR. DREW: I treat so many trauma survivor addicts, but I don't know if that's the trauma or the addiction or both. It's a common thing I see in addicts.

[*I was thinking of the first line in David's song "Cosmic Joke," where he says, "I'm not afraid to die," but he was "afraid to live a lie." There was usually more to David's lyrics than you thought, which prompted the next question as I flashed on the lyrics to his other song "Got No Right To Sing The Blues."*]

MARINA: What about men wearing women's lingerie? I suspected he was into that, too.

DR. DREW: That could be a lot of different things. That's a hard thing to put in a particular drawer the way I can so many other things. It's a little more fluid phenomenon. In other words, that's a child searching for a sexual identity at a certain period of development when they are traumatized. It's a little more complicated in my experience.

MARINA: Okay. What on earth would make him piss in the sink? Is that just a guy thing or what?

[*I burst out laughing and could hear a smile in Dr. Drew's voice.*]

DR. DREW: That's a guy thing. I don't know what they get from it. It's easier?

MARINA: David came up with all sorts of excuses: save on water, it's convenient.

DR. DREW: I can't speak for that behavior, but men by nature are kind of lazy and reaching down to pick up a toilet seat can be a tall order for men . . . [*we're having a good chuckle*] . . . and, oh, by the way, we're used to splashing . . . a little more right there . . . [*we laughed some more.*] I wouldn't make too much of that.

MARINA: What is the basic definition of a narcissist? I tend to think David was one.

DR. DREW: Most trauma survivors have narcissistic traits, what are called "cluster B personality traits." Borderline, Sociopath, Narcissist. In a personality disorder there are cluster B personality disorders. Pretty much all trauma survivors have some sort of cluster B phenomena. A lot of them do these days. Fundamentally it's a deep empty core surrounded by a false self, a pseudo-self that the person has to sort of use the world to keep puffed up, to keep buttressed up.

MARINA: Wow, that was pretty much David.

DR. DREW: The liability of having that personality style aside from being very hard to feel good about yourself, to really feel good about yourself, is that it's hard to have relationships, it's hard to be intimate, and the big liability is, you have potentially a lot of envy and you have difficulty with empathy. You can't really appreciate other people's feelings very well. Envy and empathic failure are pretty unpleasant things to be around. So that's a big liability of narcissism.

Other than that, the only person who suffers is the narcissist. They never feel filled up, they never feel good enough, they never feel whole until the next arousing, whatever makes them feel good.

MARINA: That's a part of what was so sad about David. No matter how wonderfully things were going in life or between the two of us—and it was great for most of the time—there was a core of sadness about him. Morose I would say.

DR. DREW: Again, these things are never all . . .

MARINA: One thing or the other.

DR. DREW: Yes. For instance, let's just go back to his addiction. An addict who is white knuckling, trying not to use is always miserable, depressed and anxious. By the same token an addict who is trying not to use, but using and telling everyone they're not using is always depressed, miserable and anxious and an addict who is using with impunity is always miserable and anxious. So there are a lot of things going on here pretty clearly.

MARINA: Yes. It's a complicated thing.

DR. DREW: Yes. That's why it takes so long time to treat and sort out.

MARINA: How do you go about breaking the pattern of being attracted to a perpetrator, that type of perpetrator, whatever that person's trauma is?

DR. DREW: Have some trauma treatment of your own. When the trauma is metabolized or processed in some way, it loses its power. By the same token, in therapy when you learn to have a healthy bond, healthy intimacy with a therapist, you start seeking and are sought by healthier people. One of the basic phenomena of therapy is that you just learn to be close to a healthy person. And that teaches you to do that. You can process trauma through various techniques like EMDR [*Eye Movement Desensitization and Reprocessing*]. Some people might look at this, whose behavior never breaks, as a sexual love addiction, so there's the twelve-step approach as well. There are multiple modalities out there. Usually this kind of thing we approach with a program called S.L.A.A.—Sex and Love Addicts Anonymous—and a therapist with a lot of experience treating this type of thing.

MARINA: Thank you so much.

DR. DREW: Great topic. I commend you for having the courage to step up and do it and do it thoroughly and do it properly. I think that's a very good thing.

* * *

We ran out of time, but I could feel the puzzle pieces click-kachinking into place. The interview had given me a greater sense of completion. I now possessed a certain solidity of focus, an improved confidence. It wasn't so much that I had guessed accurately what was wrong with me or

David, our relationship, or the road to my healing, but that I had received confirmation that by my following my gut feelings, I was on the right track, that this was the right thing for me, the right path for my healing.

Nevertheless, the information Dr. Drew had given me spun me around and took a couple of days to digest. Was I in denial about David being an opiate addict? I still am in a way. At the time, the thought never crossed my mind. I didn't have a clue what the symptoms are, so there was no way I could have been aware.

The nonsense now all made sense.

Why else would he go into a tirade about throwing the medicines out? Why else would he make sure he stocked back up? How else could he tolerate the pain levels he did? His behavior fit. I still wanted to cling to my initial opinion, to believe that it was mind over matter, that it was his inner strength that got him sober. He had had that ability, I was sure of it. Maybe it was both? Emotionally I tried to grab for every straw.

How David died meshes with the way opiate addicts need to up the ante. Hell, David pushed the envelope with anything he could. As awful as it is to think this, I believe David's high pain threshold and his thirst for more escalated into more of that alternate sexual experience.

Even if he wasn't actively using, previous addictive use, evidently would still alter sexual satisfaction and would never be the same or "normal" again. And that makes sense. But somehow my ego is still getting in the way. Even though he stayed sober from alcohol, there's a good chance that he was secretly addicted to painkillers the whole time. It is plausible, but no one will ever know for sure.

Emotionally it's very difficult to think of David as an opiate addict. Why? Maybe because I feel guilty that I missed all the signs. Maybe I could have done something. He never voiced any concern about being an addict. Of course, he also never considered himself an alcoholic either. But why couldn't he have been one? He was pretty much everything else! See, I'm arguing with myself! My head is spinning from all the information. I have to take a deep breath and think it through again later.

I feel sooooo "shrinked!"

PART IV

DANCES

May 2001 – Present

CHAPTER FORTY

DANCES

May 10, 2001 to 2010

Looking back, at times I felt the marriage was like doing six years of hard labor. David once called me "his savior," but all traces of that gratitude seemed to disappear into the abyss of a game called money. The least he could have done was hold to his legal and moral obligations—what he promised me and my mother. Once we separated, however, I was strung along with empty promises and every minor issue became a major exhausting battle.

I never stopped loving him. The "Blackie" part of me allowed tears to well up in my eyes when I thought of how much he must have loved me to try and stay the Johnny I fell in love with. The Johnny who was moral, ethical and loving. But the "David" part of him wasn't one I liked. Maybe the resentments of his childhood took over and wouldn't allow the *Johnny* in him to continue.

So being "in love" faded, but even now the love remains for the Johnny who disappeared. I've always seen the potential in people and felt I could help bring out his best, but I wasn't paying attention to his *true* nature. A wall of reality smashed me head-on as the harsh truth of what our relationship was and wasn't set in. I should have paid attention, seen all the signs, and listened to my inner voice.

Deep down, I believe David felt undeserving and hit the destruct button. The self-confidence he built up for himself during our six years together ebbed when things didn't happen as fast as he wanted, so he drifted back to his old beliefs and patterns. He allowed the riffraff back in—the sycophants, the dishonest leaches who kow-towed and deceived him. It was a sorrowful thing to happen to our marriage. One of the biggest disappointments of my life. His demons are what led to his demise.

These negativities claimed more and more territory. My efforts to work with him on that failed. He wasn't willing to open the door and shed light on it. Instead, in 2003, a blazing beacon in the form of a court document illuminated the problems and brought him into the light of day.

He got stuck again in a self-made tar pit of booze. Maybe to punish himself. Maybe he couldn't pull himself out again. Perhaps he didn't want to because he realized too late what a mistake he made by walking away from—as he said to many—the best thing that ever happened to him. Could that be what drove him further back into the abyss of alcohol and whatever other dysfunctional habits he might have been indulging in?

The next several years for me, as a single person again, were an unending series of struggles, battles, delays, fighting for my rights, keeping my head above water, rebuilding my life, and doing it alone, defending myself on a battlefield of deception and angst.

The emotional turmoil of dealing with attorneys, the court, the foreclosure on the house, realtors, being stalked and threatened, a frozen housing market, loans, financial problems, health issues for myself and family, and moving three times nearly pushed me into a breakdown. Seeing the door close on being able to have children and not finding a love in my life capped the list of woes and threw me into depression. I had to confront the past, deal with the present, and prepare for future demons that would haunt my daily life. I knew I deserved better than the crumbs I got in the relationship with David. The anger was particularly difficult to endure and overcome.

At the time, I didn't take full inventory of what David removed from the house when he moved out. I couldn't deal with it. But as I rearranged things in preparation to move back to my condo in Valencia, I noticed more and more missing things that were "ours" and not "his." He took the most expensive gifts from our wedding—a Picasso that Jay Bernstein gave us, a collectable movie poster from a dear friend of mine, a Michael Bowen painting that he promised to give me because I loved it so much . . . it was quite a list.

Regardless, I couldn't deal with any of it and didn't even bother to argue it as part of our divorce agreement. I wanted it to be a smooth and loving transition, as much as it could be for us.

But doubts kept creeping in each day. Was it the right thing? Was I expecting too much? I was not happy with who he became or who I was anymore, yet I wasn't happy without the love between us either. I often wondered if I would have been happier staying in my misery with David. And each time I came up with the same answer. No. Even though I missed the mutual exchange of love—that feeling of being so into and such a part of each other you could crawl inside each other's soul.

Freedom can be excruciating, especially in the beginning when seeking truth and healing. It can be a lonely road to a healthier being. I opted to be miserable for a while in my newfound freedom and finally found a measure of happiness.

The core problem, that one little pea under the mattress, that itty bitty detail called incest, ballooned into the size of Godzilla. It couldn't be ignored, let go, swept under the rug or accepted anymore. The sexual deviance didn't help matters either. I fought so hard to accept all of it. Even though he was the one to leave, I had already hit the border and was ready to cross the line out of the marriage.

In that last counseling session, I wanted to openly talk about the incest. The fact the session never happened was actually my answer. It was only a short time before I would say "that's it." David knew it. He wanted to be the "abandoner," as he was in his other relationships, rather than be abandoned by me. I so desperately wanted that last chance with the counselor, but it was apparent to me he didn't want to get healthy.

That was one of the reasons I went to Toronto that May. To get away and think about what I was going to do. I created a few meetings as an excuse to have a few days to myself in a town where I had close supportive friends who I knew would help me sort things out. He beat me to the punch by packing up first.

So on May 10, 2001, off David went to stay at the guesthouse of a friend, stashing everything else in storage, until he could figure out a game plan for himself. He didn't have me or anyone to keep him organized, so over the next few months he floundered on his own, moving a couple of times and finally landing at a rental in Hollywood.

A few months earlier, I had a healing with Rosalyn. She told me, referring to my energy field, "If you look this way again the next time I see you, I'm going to tell you to get a divorce." This, from not only my healer and teacher, but the minister at our wedding. The day after our reading with John Edward, I went to see Rosalyn for that "check up." I could hardly wait to see her and hear what she had to say about David leaving. I showed her that horrid so-called prediction and she stood there a moment to read it.

Her eyebrows arched and she shook her head. "This isn't about you. It's about them. We know what the truth is here." I agreed. If he was going to allow himself to be influenced that way, then it was time to stop trying.

Six years of battles were eating up all my energy. My health was compromised. I let go of more tears lying on her table as she worked on me. Her radiant energy reached deep into my chakras and I could feel my strength start to come back. The panic started to subside.

She looked at me as she scanned my body and said softly, "Get a divorce. The sooner the better." Stay married and still manage his career? Why? For who's benefit? This was certainly no way to live my life anymore. I knew at that point I had no choice. Either I get sick or get out of the marriage and survive. Change was upon me.

* * *

To save money, I hired a paralegal to file the divorce. I called Keith to let him know what was happening so he could be there for David. I didn't want David to be alone when he got served. I guess I was afraid David was going to start drinking or. . .I didn't know what or how he would deal with it, but I knew he'd be okay with Keith there. He sounded distressed by the call, but grateful.

They would be leaving for Australia on another movie for *Showtime*. David would be served with the divorce papers at the airport since it was the only time and place I could pin him down. I even called the process server later to check that David was alright. I was told he took it in stride, as if he was expecting it.

Even during his filming, we were in communication over various matters and the contact was still very loving. I simply didn't like him much anymore. That dislike intensified greatly over the next few years during the divorce battle, but it never killed the love. During this trip to Australia, David lost his wedding ring. He said he made initial efforts to find it, but I found myself calling the hotel and the airline to see if it turned up. Then I thought...why in the hell was I doing that?! I couldn't help but feel that, symbolically, losing the ring pretty much said it all. There was no going back. It was over.

It took me years to finally release my wedding ring. When I was strapped for money, I turned it and some other jewelry in for cash when the market for gold went up. That decision still bothers me, but it's called survival. I cherished wearing it so much. I loved everything about it—how we decided on the special Celtic weave design, special ordered it from a little store we visited on location when we filmed together in Galway, Ireland, how it felt when he placed it on my finger when we got married. The ring represented my entire world. It was everything to me. I never took it off. But I had to let go of it. The engagement ring, which I decided to sell as well, sits in a jewelry shop in Studio City.

Just days after serving David with the divorce papers, I flew to Montreal, Canada, to guest in a segment of the series *Largo Winch*, directed by David Wu and cast by producer friends Phil Bedard, David Patterson and Larry Lalonde, whom I had worked with on prior shows. I had chunky dialogue, which wasn't compatible with my being an emotional basket case. I couldn't stop crying at the airport, on the plane, at the hotel, in my dressing room . . . and no matter how many hours I spent on the dialogue, it wasn't sticking. I almost had a panic attack just before filming because I couldn't retain the lines, but as soon as I hit the set and we got our blocking, by some miracle, the words came to me and I flew through it without missing one. Working with my friends again felt like being home and helped ease the pain. I confided to a sweet soul in wardrobe what I was going through and she gave me the beautiful pantsuit I wore in the show as a gift. It was from Paris, France. How appropriate. How could I possibly say no?

Back in L.A., there were still projects left in the works for David and it was up to me to follow through with them. It was also a constant struggle to get my commissions. One excuse after another was given why I hadn't received my money, and each time I'd find that he had received his. It was a constant dance, a do-si-do and allemande left around his obligations.

David had already filmed a day in Switzerland on one of those projects, *Crisis in Havana*, with one more week to be filmed in the Caribbean. Time ran out in the contract for the production company to film by a certain date, so the balance of the money was released to pay David. However, it was understood that if they resumed production, the money would be credited to him finishing the shoot, if they accommodated his schedule.

A short time later, after the deadline, the company informed us they had put the project back into production. The company rescheduled for David at least twice, but he wanted more money as compensation for his inconvenience. Ultimately, he refused to finish the film altogether and told me he opted to do an autograph convention another person had arranged for him.

One of the producers told me they not only had to recast, but re-shooting cost them considerable extra money, not to mention the chunk they lost in paying David.

During the first few months after our separation, David denied seeing anyone and maintained that he was still in love with me, trying to see if I'd change my mind and maybe call off the divorce. It was like pulling teeth to get his cooperation in paying the money owed to me. His actions betrayed his words. I made it clear there was no chance of reconciling. Besides, I didn't believe he wasn't seeing anyone. I suspected it even before we separated, and found I was right.

There were brief moments of humor at the time. I asked David to help me with some heavy physical labor in order to get the house ready for a showing, to sell. He and a friend came over to move a couch from one room. They were like Laurel and Hardy, trying to figure out how to maneuver the sofa. I suggested tipping it on its side to avoid damaging the doorframe. Instead, he poked a 2-inch hole in the middle of the door and carved up the doorframe. How did they get the couch out of the room? Only after they retracted and moved it the way I initially suggested. Who had to repair and paint the door? Me. The sofa? I sold it.

* * *

In one of my phone conversations with David, he wanted my opinion on putting in a trip to Austin, Texas on his credit card in order to try and hook up with Tarantino again. It was going to be expensive and it was all a risk whether he was going to be able to contact him or not. I felt strongly the trip was going to be beneficial, so I encouraged him to go ahead with it. He called me with good news from the film festival. He indeed did meet up with Tarantino, which led to them making plans to get together when back in L.A. David still sought my guidance and I couldn't stop myself from helping him. Isn't that what loving people do for each other, even if they are divorcing?

Problem was I still hadn't learned my lesson. No matter what I did to help him, he took it for granted and I was still catching him in evasions about the money issue. So why was I still helping him? What would it take before I stopped?

During that summer, he courted me as much as I'd allow. It was almost like we started over again. He even acknowledged my going out of my way for him. We met often for coffee or a movie. We even made a few public appearances where I joked by introducing him as my soon-to-be-ex-husband. He remained silent, clenching his jaw.

His cell phone would go off often, and with certain calls he'd get an exasperated look on his face. As the weeks wore on, his reaction to the calls were sometimes more agitated. He'd comment on occasion that it was a friend calling, but still not take the call. Observing this behavior, I couldn't help but wonder if that's what he did during our marriage, when I tried to reach him while he was out for hours "getting magazines."

If something didn't feel right with what David told me, I'd repeat the same questions over a period of time, a method I learned from attorneys when I had to give depositions. This would result in different responses, because he often didn't remember what he told me previously. The truth would eventually hold, or a fib would slip or I'd find out from other sources if David was lying or not.

At the end of our many rendezvous, we'd depart with a kiss. I tried to keep it to his cheek or just a light touch to the lips. Sometimes I couldn't resist and had to feel his lips on mine again. We'd often look at each other, not saying a word, and turn to our cars. Unhappiness was obvious in each other's eyes. We had a soul connection, an understanding that didn't need words. We missed each other deeply.

It had been months since we slept together and I missed his romantic ways of holding me, a tender smile and kiss, spooning at night and falling asleep with him wrapped around me. I wanted it to be something it couldn't be anymore, and wasn't for the longest time while we were together. Something we had that disappeared into the past, leaving me feeling empty. I missed knowing my love was there with me, but I didn't miss the list of things that spoiled the relationship. It was also a practical relief to be out of his cigarette smoke.

Unless there was something for him to pick up at the house I didn't want him there. Many times, I could hear the distinctive sound of his Maserati drive by at various hours of the day or night, probably checking to see if I was home or had visitors spending the night.

September 11, 2001

It was early morning and I was on my way to Valencia to prepare for my move when someone called to tell me a terrorist had crashed a plane into the World Trade Center in New York. It didn't compute in my head that this could possibly be happening in our US of A. Turning onto the freeway ramp I called David, out of habit. He was still my friend and the one I called first with major news. He sounded half asleep and hadn't heard the news. All I could blurt out was, "Turn on the TV! We've been attacked in New York! Terrorists!" He non-coherently mumbled he'd check it out and we'd talk later.

On television, I watched the twin towers disintegrate before my eyes, as if they were a mirror image of my marriage crumbling in ruin and disintegrating into ashes of its own. It was difficult to think of anything else, feel anything else except the grief, loss, hurt, anger and trauma of my country, as well as of my private life.

* * *

I didn't want to be living in the Rosita house with all the animals there and people milling in and out during realtor showings. It was too difficult to shuffle my schedule around and I was afraid they'd leave the door or gate open and one of the critters would get out, a death sentence given the coyotes and speeding cars down the street. So in order to sell the house, I was forced to move back to my condo, which I'd owned since the '80s.

I was not only in trauma with my pending divorce, but was also fighting similar battles with the homeowners' association (HOA) when I moved back to Santa Clarita. A band of homeowners, including myself, wanted proper accounting and justification for major HOA expenditures of funds. This coincided with my court battles with David. I and others in my group experienced a series of weird events and attacks on our safety and privacy. We were causing too many waves for certain people to deal with. My confrontations with one particular person who I thought was eerily similar to David—ended up in court where, for fear of my safety from him, I tried to get a restraining order issued. This, along with needing money for surgery, was the additional catalyst for finally deciding to move out of the "Stepford community."

I lost about eight pounds from all of the stress, having to pay the bills and upkeep on the Rosita house while waiting for reimbursements and for the house to sell. I had no doubt David was courting other women, freely spending money and ignoring his promise to take care of me and his debt to my mother. Explanations weren't forthcoming and my patience was stretched thread thin.

David blatantly told me his monetary obligation was to the new girlfriend he moved in with, and not to me. Since the house was in jeopardy due to lack of mortgage payments, I decided enough was enough and filed the lawsuit against him.

David had many very valuable guitars, memorabilia and other material possessions he could have sold or auctioned, but he wouldn't part with any of it to ease the monetary situation. I felt he'd rather *I* sell my possessions, have *me* panic and my mother sick from worry than be honorable and pay up. When I said I had no choice but to sell my engagement ring, he said he'd sell two of his guitars if I promised *not* to sell the ring. He never did sell the guitars and I couldn't get a decent price on the ring. It wouldn't have been enough for half of one month's mortgage.

During this period of time, in all the chaos, I struggled to get work. If there was any energy left over, I had ever so brief, fleeting moments of fun, mostly with Lulu participating. She was my pure joy and refuge.

Any time I thought something grueling had ended, another torment would take its place. The emotional traumas kept right on coming and I barely had a chance to recover from one, before the next started. It got to a point where I thought my severe post-traumatic stress syndrome and sleep deprivation would send me over the edge.

I kept remembering what John Edward told me in our reading—that I'd be rebuilding my foundation. I held that in my mind as a kind of mantra to reassure myself this was all for a reason, that it was going to be good for me. It never occurred to me it would prove to be such a struggle! Waking up in the middle of the night, crying in panics, shaking in the morning from unknown fear of what the day would bring. It truly tested my limits and challenged me to remember my core beliefs. I never thought someone who loved me would do what he did to me or my mother. He said I was the best thing that ever happened to him. And this is how he showed his thanks?

Spiritual counselors helped get me back to a place of remembering how powerful I and other women are who have been through this type of experience and worse. They helped me put those pieces of the puzzle together, to reconstruct my life. Visualizing and grounding exercises helped carry me through day to day, along with the companionship of Lulu of course.

It was shaky at times through the years, but finally, like forged steel through the fire, I'm stronger than ever. I have been blessed with several incredibly supportive friends who have listened to me rant and vent and sob. My family has also been there, but they heard only a fraction of what I've poured out to my tight circle of friends.

It was a slow recovery process out of codependency, reclaiming memories, myself, and my world. Any time I traveled to places we had shared, I would do various ceremonies to take back my power. Instead of feeling melancholy about being there without him, I celebrated my freedom. My final journey to release the past was my trip to Toronto in 2003, venturing back to the house in Mississauga.

As part of my healing, the year before we separated, I vented about daily pressures by writing notes and stories, which turned into this book.

Yes, I've tangoed, tap-danced and swirled my way around the dance floor of life these past nine years. It was just as John Edward told me. I would rebuild my foundation and return to my core beliefs. Not only that, I found I'm a damned good dancer!!

CHAPTER FORTY-ONE

DANCES WITH COYOTES

Fall 2001–*Johnny Went To Soldier*

Just as I was typing the title, I goofed and typed Johnny went to SOULdier. To me, things like this are little hints of meanings more profound that lie beneath the surface. Just after I had my hearing in court in which the judge agreed with my intent and interpretation of my divorce agreement with David, I stopped on my way home at a little out of the way store called Cie Marie that had a select variety of home furnishings and gifts. While puttering around and choosing a knob hanging, I heard over the music system a woman singing what sounded to be a very old Irish war song: "Johnny Went to Soldier." David was part Irish, our wedding rings were Celtic . . . It was about her love going to war and her feeling he probably wasn't going to return.

Well, I had just been to court with my Johnny. We were in battle and I took this as my confirmation he was never going to return to my life as my partner. We would not get back together. I went to the counter to pay for my trinket, and in a bowl by the register were these little wooden sachets carved in the shapes of apples. They were exactly the same as the ones I had on my desk in Mississauga all during the time we were there. I made sure I packed them for our trip to L.A., so they were in my office here as well. They had the exact same scent of apple and cinnamon. A rush of emotion overcame me and the tears started to flood. Like the feeling you get when you've eaten too much horseradish, your nose hurts because the rush comes on too quickly. I bowed my head, turned away and walked around a bit more. The song still played on. The signs were there.

I saw the real David. Not the public façade most people saw. One of his friends told me "David is like a piece of film. He projects what people want to see." I looked through to the core and experienced who he really was. No one is all bad or all good. We are all complex mysteries and blatant patterns of both.

It's *understanding* and deciding for yourself what you want to live with and what you don't. I made my decision when I filed for divorce. It was one of the most painful decisions of my life. When you still love someone so deeply, but you know for your own well being you cannot continue, that there is no other choice to make, then it's agony. There's a naturalness to death—if it's from disease or old age. I find divorce very unnatural. It's where love and hate can meet at that fine line. I could understand why some people take drastic measures to stop the pain by stopping its source. There was a time I saw red. Ironically, the joke among friends was not *Kill Bill*, but Kill David.

Even sleep didn't ease the nightmares I woke up sobbing from, only to fall asleep from exhaustion again, leaving me totally debilitated through the coming day.

It is also difficult feeling you got a raw deal from someone, leaving you behind while he continues to benefit from your hard efforts. Living what looks like the highlife while the other who made the sacrifices is struggling. Lesson? Life is not fair.

The divorce settlement proceedings in court were almost unbearable. I felt I got a law degree. I never sued either of my two previous husbands for alimony, or any other payments. This time I was standing up for myself. It was far more complicated.

I was hit with one problem after another. It was a struggle emotionally, mentally and spiritually, getting through each challenge, since each has its own unique "freak-out factor." I'm into the metaphysics to the max and

I've tried countless modus-operandi to help overcome the stress and still have a sense of humor.

David and I had what I thought was a very basic agreement, which was reviewed by one of his financial advisors and an attorney, both of whom, he told me, approved it. However, after he entered a new relationship, things changed. He hired a different attorney who argued points in the contract to the court. He wanted to pay me the least amount of money possible

The first attorney I hired used what seemed to be a generic form to write the agreement. Up to that point, the lawyers I spoke to wanted thousands for a retainer fee, which I didn't have. I was backed up against the wall and tried to make due. I had to have some agreement between us to protect me. I found myself having to rewrite the agreement, with the attorney supposedly looking it over and adding legal jargon. I wasn't comfortable with it by any means, but I had no alternative at that time. The lawyer wasn't much of a help.

David kept balking about signing our divorce agreement. I practically had to bribe him with the beautiful blue leather western boots I bought in Toronto. He finally did. I don't know if he ever wore the boots, but I could tell by his reaction he loved them. It was a heart rendering moment for both of us, symbolized by the boots as another step closer to the end of the marriage.

Another sad moment. I learned later the contract had considerable problems with the structure and was deficient in protecting me. So I demanded my $500 back, which I eventually got, and found another lawyer. But the basic damage was done. The document was clear to me, and it was clear to David, but he argued it in court and, I thought, made it sound more confusing than it was. What do they say? "It ain't worth the paper it's written on?" Just because you have a contract doesn't mean you are "safe."

For a one-year period of time, the last year of my management contract, I was to receive fifteen percent or a base fee of $3,000 per month, which ever was greater. Sounds like a good deal, but that was it. No long term spousal support, no money from his residuals, no part of his pension and only six months of health insurance. I was also to pay for all my own bills as usual. David was to pay the house mortgage for a short period of time to allow it to sell. During that one year, it appeared commissions due me were sometimes spread over longer time frames so I'd get less money in the long-run.

For example, let's say David got one job on a film that involved one week of work and that was the only job he would get paid for in that calendar month, then I was to get $7,000 in commissions. The next month, if he didn't work, I would receive only the minimum base fee of $3,000. So, for those two months I would get a total of $10,000. However, if he made arrangements with the production company to split the amount he was to receive into two monthly payments, then I'd get $3,500 in commissions for each of the two months. That totaled only $7,000 for me, which is $3,000 less in commissions than the first, straightforward, way. Was it being creative and clever with the money, or did it just happen that way with certain projects? Based on previous history, I believed it was "creative."

There was cash for his per diem payments, which added up quickly on location. It could also be arranged that what went on record in the contract was one figure, but payments were made in cash on location to keep it off the books and off the contract.

* * *

The battles over our settlement got out of hand. I never should have had to battle him to try and save the house, which involved my mother. Why was he doing this?!

Perhaps David wasn't the core of why it was happening. Maybe other influences were dictating to David how things were presented in court and he was complying. I knew David's modus operandi and this wasn't it. Or was it? I was told Gail endured similar battles, and had to fight for her half of the residuals from the series, which she supposedly never got, even with an initial judgment in her favor. David often let others wage his battles for him, to avoid confrontation and remain the "innocent good-guy." That left him with time and energy to do what he wanted.

If other influences turned David against me, it could result in less money being paid out to me. That would leave more money available for him and others to grab. Hence the battle for the green. If I hadn't witnessed the divorce with David and Gail, seen how he handled it, I wouldn't have known better.

We were in court I thought, for an accounting and contract issue, not a personal one, yet I felt my character was attacked in an attempt to make me appear as a gold-digger and as someone who hurt his career instead of helping it. The accounting for David's income was very confusing. To investigate David's earnings, a forensic accounting would have cost $5,000 to $10,000. For the amount of money we were asking, it wasn't worth it. As someone in the CPA business pointed out, what is generated in someone's computer can be altered. The numbers presented can be anything they want people to see. Even bank statements aren't going to give an accurate accounting because cash can be taken from a deposit and only the net amount will show in the statement as the total amount placed in the account. Unless the actual receipts or paystubs or other primary documentation are reviewed to see how much and when they came in— a forensic accounting—then you are going by what is presented by "the opposition."

I spent weeks delving into it myself and came up with different numbers from David's accountings, yet mine weren't submitted to the court. It supposedly wasn't enough of a difference to matter. I didn't agree. The process was foreign and intimidating to me, as well as extremely frustrating. David let the house payments go, but paid on spousal support. As David put it, "I can get a full write-off for spousal support, not mortgage. You worry too much. It'll work out in the end." It not only didn't work out in the end, but most reimbursements I received were deducted from my spousal support, which they shouldn't have been.

Each diversion, each argument, each aggravation kept building in me, yet I still made attempts to keep things as easy between us as possible.

By the time we got to court and payments were being received, the house was going into foreclosure with high penalty fees incurred.

My trust factor was sub zero with David and my instincts told me he was holding out on revealing income. I suspected he either placed funds into a hidden account, as he did when he battled Gail, or maybe put off signing on to other projects until after the year limit, in order to evade paying my percentage. Having a corporation, I was told, makes it easier to shuffle the peanuts around in the shell game.

David stated in a document presented to court the number of bank accounts he had, but I discovered yet another active credit union account that he omitted. Documentation was presented to the judge, who asked David point blank if there were any other accounts. He responded innocently that there weren't. The judge then displayed the paper and asked about the one mentioned in our complaint.

David sat there speechless for a long moment and replied that was one he "forgot" about. He wasn't reprimanded, let alone penalized, in any way. That's when I learned the word "disingenuous." I strongly believed that was the account into which he placed cash income from conventions and whatever else he wanted to hide from me. No one requested bank statements to see what activity there was either. That was it. There was nothing else I could do.

Autograph conventions were a considerable source of income for David, but a document presented to us stated he didn't attend any during that year. Even though I had proof David attended several throughout that time, which could certainly generate considerable cash for him, a percentage of which I was entitled to, I was told there was no way to prove the amounts since it was . . . cash. It was another lost cause and another bone of contention.

* * *

January 2002, I finally closed that door to the personal side of our relationship. I was tired of trying to smooth feathers in hopes he would cooperate and end the court proceedings by paying up.

I was only asking for the one year left in our management contract and it was as if he was doing anything and everything either to pay me the least amount or to get out of paying me altogether.

When it came to the house, the payment I was finally awarded by the court was too late and too little to save it from foreclosure. A short sale was accomplished after five more months, but my mother's lifetime impeccable credit rating got trashed, along with the $32,000 I put in as the down payment. It was a gray day saying goodbye to the Rosita house, and at the same time a relief. We were not happy there.

CHAPTER FORTY-TWO

THE LIMBO
How Low Can You Go?

September 8, 2003

R*EFLECTING about the past. Eight years ago to the day I took that flight up to Toronto, moved in and began my life with him. And here I am in the final throes of the divorce court battle.*

I thought it wasn't just a coincidence that I was able to get a phone consult with Rosalyn today. . . of all days. Just hearing her voice helped ease the pain. Friends think of me as a "toughie" in that sense, especially my mother. Able to weather it through any circumstance, but it's been one rough ride.

Rosalyn said I was doing much better. I was healing. I knew from talking to many of my female friends that they too were going through long periods of emotional extremes and facing the most difficult situations. We were no longer taking the abuse. We were fighting back. I believe that by forging through all this, we emerge the strong goddesses that we have always been. We just got . . . sidetracked

I never felt as married or as close to any man in my life as I did to Johnny. So . . . eight years ago we began our dance, our romance, our rocky road, and our wild ride

* * *

The first years after we separated were agony. After having to sell my condo, undergoing surgery, living with my mother for six months and breaking up with my boyfriend, I moved into a two-room apartment in Studio City. Last time I lived in an apartment was 1988. No complaints, I liked all the apartments I ever lived in, it was just. . . I felt totally derailed, losing ground instead of maintaining and progressing with the success of what I built with and for David. Looking at the bright side, it was a great location, and I could walk to everything, and it had an area out back for Lulu to romp and pee. The sounds of children at play echoing from the school just down the street were like music. The daily walks through the neighborhood with Lulu brought me a temporary peace.

It was a harsh contrast to my previous lifestyle with David, however—the glitzy parties, dining out at expensive restaurants daily, having money not only to cover my basic needs but also to splurge without worry, and being debt free. Even though my credit card bills were building up rapidly, I had a roof over my head, clothes to wear and food to eat. I was grateful for what I had, made the best of the circumstances and was relatively happy.

I went from 2200 square feet to 550, but I got creative with the limited space and made do. The bedroom became my walk-in closet, filing cabinet/storage and cat room—there was nowhere else to put the kitty litter because the bathroom was dinky. My futon couch converted into a bed, with the living room serving double duty as my office as well. No room for a coffee table, so I ate off a typewriter table next to the futon. In one corner next to my closet washer/dryer was my art table and desk, so I could get back to my painting and crafts. For atmosphere there was a small gas log fireplace, and a wonderful view out the back patio onto a lush ravine full of trees. At night I could hear wild animals like skunk, raccoons and coyotes socializing outside, and wafts of jasmine would drift inside from nearby bushes.

Since I was on the second floor, I had privacy, serenity and a little sanity too, which was a relief after all those crazy-making years living with David. Except for the absolute essentials, everything I accumulated in my life was held in two storage units miles away from easy access. For the next four years, I lived in limbo. I questioned everything in my life. I often wondered if I had done the right thing in divorcing David, but always came back to the same answer. Yes.

One scene from the TV show *Frasier* hit home. Sometimes when I had doubts or was tempted to even think of getting back together with David, I remembered when Niles, who had just separated from his wife, was living the life of a stereotypical bachelor, in an apartment, wearing Hawaiian shirts and having pot-luck dinner with neighbors. He starts to pick up the phone to get back together with his wife, but hangs up. Frasier commends him. To go back to her and all of the tyranny and unhappiness would be a mistake. Referring to Niles' new apartment and lifestyle, Frasier says, "This is but a small price to pay for your freedom." Niles agrees. It rang true for me too. And I still love wearing my collection of Hawaiian shirts!

* * *

The stress level reached critical mass with the declaration David submitted to the court in what appeared to be an attempt to discredit me with the court.

The distortions came in a document I received Feb 20, the anniversary of our wedding. I found it hard to believe David ever thought in this calculating way. It wasn't how his mind worked. Was this coincidence or a planned maneuver to try and get me not only to hate David, but to ruin my memories of our wedding? It didn't work. Nothing could take away the glorious wedding memories we had.

Such a document, which appeared to degrade and discredit not only my professional life, but my integrity as a person, had to come, I thought, from a vicious, bitter being. I didn't think David could ever be either. His document didn't mention I had anything to do with his career revamp over the six years we were together, but implied that he never earned as low an income as he had since he signed on with me. His document did not say how difficult it was to get him work because of his previous bad reputation. It ripped me apart. With all the money issues he seemed to be getting away with, I was not going to stand by and let him denigrate my integrity, or my accomplishments, so I filed my response. I would never have done anything as daring as that before my relationship with David. I had changed. He taught me.

I wrote the truth about the sexual deviance, incest and other issues. I revealed his demons, which were the major underlying factors in the demise of our marriage

I had less than twenty-four hours to get my response in to the court. I was up until the early morning hours writing it and first thing that morning, Feb 21, I was on location with Lulu, doing the First Miss Dog Beauty Pageant. I had to keep running between the stage and the production office to make sure the fax went through—they had a fax glitch—and so my attorney was able to get the papers typed, signed by me, faxed back and messengered to the court in time.

Overcoming the obstacles and getting this response in to the court minutes before the deadline seemed to be another affirmation that it was meant to happen. I've often wondered if David actually wrote the document himself. If he did, was it to hurt me as much as he was hurting? Did he resent the fact I wanted no part of him? Whether he read his own papers before he signed them or not, his signature was on the dotted line.

The second Lulu and I got home from the dog show filming and walked in the door, it all hit me. The adrenaline had kept me going. The emotions I held back and didn't have time to let out now flooded over me. I was overcome with incredible waves of anger, loneliness, fear, panic and anxiety. Tears and more tears flowed uncontrollably down my face . . . a feeling of almost unbearable pain from all over my body . . . wrenching emotion . . . an absolute soul-screaming mix of agony and anger, the depths of which surprised me.

I sat on the floor, looking up to the heavens and asking, "When is this going to stop hurting? Please take away the pain! Why is he doing this to me?"

Echoes of my voice from the past, screaming at my father, "*I am special!*" The little child in me fearing David couldn't possibly think I'm special if he was treating me this way! *He can't possibly love me anymore.* I thought he was trying to punish me for being strong and taking a stand.

With this tidal wave of emotion, I understood how a person can get to a limit of what can be endured. Intellectually, I got why people drank and took drugs to numb out. Was this the limit David had reached -- why he drank?

I had now reached my own personal limit—the line between me and the brink—and could contemplate in fleeting flashes of fantasy going beyond it. The pain doesn't stop and the person that perpetrates the circumstances causing the pain continues. My depression got me to a place at one point where I looked at the kitchen carving knives and wonder how much it would really hurt. It wouldn't be nearly as agonizing as what I was feeling at that moment.

Then I'd look at Lulu and the thought would instantly pass . . . she grounded me . . . she made me smile, laugh and feel loved. She was the reason I wanted to go on, and why life was worth living.

Lulu gave me one soft nuzzle on my hand with her long perfect snoot to grab my attention. I looked into her brown worried eyes as she whined and barked, as if saying, "Mommy, are you okay? What's wrong? Please don't cry. I'm here for you. Aw, c'mon, cheer up!" Licking the tears off my face, she brought everything back into perspective. We sat there for what seemed like hours. My arms wrapped around her tight and my head nuzzled into the crook of her neck. She made little grunty and licking sounds whenever she was being hugged like that. Then a satisfied relaxed sigh. Knowing I was ok, she ran to the door and barked, as if she were saying, "Okay, now that you snapped out of it, I gotta pee!"

It's not the situation, it's how you handle it. David wasn't worth wasting my energy on anymore. My motto in dealing with "crazy-makers" got plastered up by my desk: "There's no sense in trying to make sense out of nonsense."

This event pushed me further into my core beliefs. I had never known such negativity and hurt as I did with David. It tested my faith to the max about Karma. The kind of "evil" I felt does not let go without divine action. The "let go and let God," re-trusting, getting my faith back, was a difficult road back to "home," but Lulu guided me there.

Instead of turning to drugs, drinking or smoking, I had her, the cats I adored, and I turned to my friends and spiritual counselors. I hadn't attended church with groups of people since I was a child, when my Catholic maternal grandmother would take me. Occasionally as an adult, I'd stop by a church in Beverly Hills I had gone to since the '70s. This time, as I did in the past, when it was empty, I sat in a pew under the magnificent multicolored images in stained glass. Holding my eyes shut tight, I sniveled out a prayer in the silence that wrapped me in a blanket of comfort. All was quiet and calm. I felt an invisible "someone," a higher force, beside me, holding me. I wasn't alone.

On a more practical level, watching Classic Arts Showcase and HGTV (The Home and Garden channel), helped too. I'd tune in for hours on end, and into the wee hours of the morning. Then, emotionally exhausted, I'd go back to bed again, only to have nightmares. The dark clouds lifted occasionally, but I still had a long way to go in the storm. I did end up with quite a few great decorating ideas and craft projects, though.

* * *

That next court appearance, I refused to look at David or give him one ounce of energy. Even when he opened the doors to the courtroom for me, I glanced beyond him as if he were a stranger. With all that vitriol in his document against me, why would he look at me longingly and open the door for me?

The judge asked if I wanted to retract my declaration, to which I responded, "No." It was difficult to tell if the judge's expression was in disapproval of my document or for what she might have wondered regarding David. Approval was granted to have certain pages sealed, which was fine with me.

David wanted me to pay his costs to get the record sealed because I refused to withdraw my declaration with the court. I felt that would have been like making an apology. This was the only way I could show him that I would not back down for anyone in defending myself, regardless of how much I cared about the other person. I would not go quietly anymore!

* * *

I wanted to make sure my declaration would actually get sealed, so I decided to observe the proceedings. I also thought it would be interesting to learn what they do in a session like that, not to mention make an interesting entry for my book.

I didn't want his attorney to know I was there, so I decided to disguise myself. I felt as if I was in the middle of my own episode of I Love Lucy. Decked out in one of my blonde wigs, black-framed glasses and a demure suit, I got to the court early and nervously waited in the hallway. Just before court time, David's attorney appeared with a very tall, stocky man, both wearing sunglasses. That registered as odd for some reason. The tall man looked like a bodyguard-detective, not an attorney. Why would David hire him for the sealing of the records?

I followed them in and kept my head down. When they were looking around for a seat, I quickly turned and nodded to a man seated in the back row, as if I knew him, and sat next to him. David's attorney and "associate" went up front to check in and I kept busy, with my head down, pretending to be looking at documents. They finally sat up front to the side. If they turned to their right and looked back slightly, they could see me, so I made sure I hid behind two people in the seats directly in front of me.

It was hide and seek through the procedure. When they were called up, I ducked down to the floor, pretending I dropped something, until they were standing with their backs to the "audience," and would occasionally pop back up to watch the judge, the same one who handled our divorce.

All went well. They were granted certain pages to be sealed, but until his attorney could pull those separate pages and re-present to the court, the declaration remained unsealed. This seemed to upset his attorney. I remained on the floor "searching" until the attorney and her escort walked by me and out the courtroom. I waited a few more cases, just to make sure they were gone, dodged out of the courtroom and drove to my attorney's to deliver a thank you and update on what had happened.

At my lawyer's office, the staff giggled at my blonde disguise, but my attorney was perturbed and scolded me for attending the court proceedings. I couldn't understand. It was open to the public. Why not? David's attorney was supposedly being stalked and the man with her was a bodyguard, that's why.

I handed her a beautiful bouquet of flowers as a thank you for handling the situation so that I wouldn't be in jeopardy of paying David's attorney fees.

Her mood changed. She graciously accepted the gift and said brightly, "I saw you on TV last week!"

"Oh?"

"Something where you had on different dresses and went to a premiere."

I was pleased she caught the show. "Oh, the E! Fashion Emergency show!"

She looked at me carefully, "You look better now than you did then. My husband thinks the same."

I laughed sardonically, "It must be the lack of stress."

"I'm serious" she said, "You look much younger. There's a difference."

When people ask me about getting plastic surgery and they happen to be in an unhappy marriage, I tell them to get a divorce. It's better than a surgical facelift.

* * *

About two weeks later, I got a call from The Smoking Gun.com, asking if what was stated in my court document was true. *What?!* My declaration, which was supposed to get sealed, wound up in our public file. Now The Smoking Gun had it and the document was blasted worldwide on the internet and in other media, causing a tornado of its own. This felt like someone "upstairs" was showing me that David was not going to be able to hide anymore. His attorney wrote a blazing letter to the court, but there wasn't anything anyone could do to stop the media frenzy at that point. Word was out and there was no retrieving it.

October 29, 2003, Court session

David kept looking at me, trying to get my attention, from the minute I entered the corridor to the court. He looked misty eyed, romantic, sentimental, almost the same look that he gave me when I walked down the aisle. We stared at each other for a solid fifteen seconds or more, until I felt I was going to burst out laughing. I made an exaggerated face at him like "cheeeeese!" With a glint to his eyes and a subtle smile, he bowed his head like in the *King and I* in acknowledgement.

In the court session, he sat in front of me off to the left so I could see his profile well. He looked gaunt, sad, upset, unhappy and worried. It was the first time he didn't look well. And for the first time, I felt no attraction to him. I felt repulsion to a man I now saw as twisted, demonized, and stuck. I saw him as a sad, lost soul. A shell of the man I fell in love with. A small amount of compassion softened my edges, and eventually turned into forgiveness.

Celebrity Justice wanted to cover our divorce. So at the courthouse reporter Chrissy, and Hugh the cameraman took us outside at the end of our session. I was looking off, over the shoulder of the reporter, across the courtyard to where David was in my line of vision. He kept staring at me with a soulful, longing look, watching my every move during my on-camera interview.

When it was his turn, he gave them a sound bite saying he wished I would get on with my life. As if fighting him in court for my rights and my money wasn't moving on with my life?

Somewhere in the middle of the years in court, my attorney received a rather nasty message on her private voicemail and appeared to be disturbed by it. I asked if it was a threat of some kind. She hesitated, looked as if she wanted to tell me, but responded simply that the call was disturbing. Could it have been something the mystery caller said about me? Could it have been a threat? Maybe it was partly because of all the delays and the time consumed with "tactics" on David's part, costing my attorneys more time?

2004

When the dust settled, after almost two and a half years of delays, excuses, dancing around the money and the issues, my attorney bill would have been over $70,000. I'd be surprised if David's attorney bills were any less.

Instead of participating in the supposed millions David profited by after his career re-launch, I saw a low to mid double-digit figure from the divorce, that included the money owed for months of due mortgage. After paying my attorney, the remainder was barely enough to see me through one year.

Six years together and two and half years in legal combat. That was my "reward." The amount of money he spent in battling me, he could have just paid me, and saved himself thousands of dollars in attorney fees. I believe if he was truly happy, he never would have fought against me like he did.

When people learn I was married to David, they often have the misconception I walked away a wealthy divorcee. As they see me getting into my eight-year old car, I chuckle, "Yes, I am wealthy. The experience was priceless."

Chapter Forty-Three

WATER BALLET

The Flying Goddess
All women are Goddesses.
We were born that way.
We just have to remember our inner power . . .
Which gives us our wings to fly!

—Marina Anderson

I was thrust into celebrity-hood for the six years with David and when it was over, it was as if I sank into a hole and disappeared. The attention I got as "Mrs. Carradine" was easy to get used to. It was more than being "Mrs. Somebody." People knew how much I was helping David. They could see and experience the difference, the change he had made for the better. The charge I got from being on David's arm, proud of him, proud of us, and having our picture taken on the red carpet, was indeed an addictive "high." Now all the attention was quickly slipping away. I literally suffered withdrawal from a lack of social life. The press, parties, invite lists, which had contributed to my feeling important, dwindled.

Until people got to know me as a person in my own right, their interest was mostly an avenue to get to, and use, David. That's one of the drawbacks to being a spouse to a famous person. To be suddenly axed from "friends'" party lists and industry premieres was difficult to deal with.

There was a large event held at a Beverly Hills hotel every year on

Oscar night David and I attended for years. We got to know one of the hosts and their spouse as friends. I had to twist David's arm to attend the event initially, but he found it enjoyable so we brought in other celebrities to the venue. The host told me they were very appreciative of my talking David into participating. We even got together at their home a few times over the years.

When Oscar time came around again after we divorced, I didn't get the usual invitation in the mail, but heard that David was attending. I called the host to inquire if possibly the invitation got lost in the mail. I don't remember the exact words, because my brain froze from being so stunned by the insult. First they tried to palm the issue off on someone else and a committee working with the event. When I questioned the excuse, they changed their response to the effect that I was now only an ex-wife of David Carradine and basically a nobody. There was no invitation for me. Is that what I was now? A . . . "nobody"? I'm not special anymore? His words whacked my ego.

Not one to hold grudges, when I heard a few years later this person was seriously ill, I called to give my support. They seemed very appreciative, telling me I was missed and hoped to see me soon. Next year, no invitation. I still have not received one. So it goes in Hollywood. It is all an illusion.

This was just one of many slaps that made me all the more determined to create something for myself again, instead of being in the shadow of someone else's light. Especially a light I helped to shine again. I began a campaign to pursue my writing projects—which included children's books, one of which is *The Adventures of Lulu The Collie*—TV shows, film, teaching, acting, and performing again.

The daily chores of dealing with the divorce, moving a few times, having major surgery to remove a suspicious mass, which turned out to be benign, my mother having cancer surgery and surviving (she is now ninety), and taking care of my furry companions occupied pretty much all my time. It was a daily struggle to keep above the bills and my debt was building. At times I felt I was treading water. A water ballet of sorts.

Looking graceful to all those watching me swim patterns in the water, but feeling I couldn't hold my breath anymore and at any time I could drown. I'd come up to the surface gasping for air, trying to look in control with a smile. There were only a few close confidantes who knew what I was going through.

Managing other clients proved to be less than a satisfying experience. At one point I had five psychics, a few actors and a couple of musicians on my roster. The nature of the beast of being a manager, most of them needed considerable attention and babysitting that I did not want to give anymore. One client who was starting out and whom I had nurtured for at least a year called me the day after Lulu died, ranting about my taking time off from work and that their career was more important than my grieving. I dropped that one like a hot potato. There weren't enough hours in the day to get things done. Besides, David had burned me out. So I dissolved all the working relationships.

Barely anything in my life seemed to click or bring me any kind of creative expression or satisfaction. The things that did, didn't bring in enough money.

There were other questions to be answered. Big someone-is-under-the-bed-and-going-to-grab-your-feet scary questions that kept me awake many nights. What now? How am I going to support myself? Did my years away from acting to manage David hurt me long term? Had I been out of the game too long? I was older now and even though I looked ten years younger than my real age, it didn't seem to matter. Somehow an industry internet website got my real birth year and posted it on the site coincidentally in the beginning of my court battle with David. They refused to remove it. I felt someone did it on purpose. It seemed like I lost more opportunities and auditions because of it. Casting and producers would get enthused about me, but then punch up that website, see my age and not call me in for a role I was totally right for. In spite of my picture posted on the page or what was sent to them, they probably couldn't believe that was what I really looked like.

Given the bridges David burned, it seemed more difficult for me to get an agent and, without a strong one with clout, almost impossible to get auditions for anything decent. Being the ex-Mrs. David Carradine didn't seem to hold weight, and changing my name didn't help much with the acting jobs either. My daily exercise routine consisted of bouncing violently back and forth between relief and blind terror. I was working at trying to get work sixteen hours a day. When situations got too much for me to deal with, I'd take Lulu for a walk or blast Latin music in my apartment or in my car to try and energize me out of a mood.

Every once in a blue moon something cool would happen, like doing a webisode with a couple of friends—Brent Roske, producer, and Kate Clarke. I was the co-lead opposite Kate in *Sophie Chase,* a lightning quick shoot that was submitted on a lark to the Academy of Television Arts and Sciences for Emmy consideration. And it got nominated! The first in the history of the Academy for the category of Outstanding Achievement in Video Content for Non-traditional Delivery Platforms. Or in short, New Media.

When the divorce proceedings came to a close, instead of pursuing one last legal possibility, I put my energy into developing a jewelry design taken from my business logo, The Flying Goddess. It was divine guidance taking my logo, a half nude winged female, flipping it over and making it complete. In the process, it formed a heart. All of one minute, the design was there. I drew a backside to it so when the charm was flipped over, you could see the "hiney." The lyric-affirmation and a white feather accompanied all the pieces. The Flying Goddess caught on. Many celebrities have one, including Fran Drescher, Maya Angelou, Shirley MacLaine, (who sold them on her website), Rachelle Begley Carson, Jillie Mack, who is married to Tom Selleck, and Jan Rooney, who is married to Mickey. It was great to focus on something creative and positive for a change.

* * *

Everywhere I went, Lulu grabbed instant attention. She was so intelligent it was spooky. I could teach her a trick in five minutes. She knew over thirty silent hand commands. Even Bob Weatherwax, her godfather, was impressed. So I decided to take it a step further and get her out in the limelight. That brought both of us great joy. She was such a social butterfly and a healing being. I got her certified as a Therapy Dog and we made the rounds at convalescent hospitals until our schedule got so busy we couldn't do it anymore. Lulu instinctively knew how and when to approach people in the facilities. It was incredibly rewarding, but no money was involved and I needed to pay the bills. Television shows and film productions started calling to use her and we had a blast. The jobs also paid well. She was a favorite on *Desperate Housewives* (they called her the Wisteria Lane collie) and Nicolette Sheridan was a gem, making sure Lulu had everything she needed, including steak for lunch. When we walked the picket lines in support of the writers' strike in front of Universal Studios, Marc Cherry, creator and executive producer of the show, met Lulu for the first time. He said to the press as he posed with her, "Now that's the real bitch of the show!"

Lulu got so popular, *she* was getting invites to red carpet events and fund-raisers. A jeweler gave her a diamond "L" necklace to wear, which glittered when she walked the red carpet in her Swarovsky-encrusted silver leash.

After Lulu passed away, *Desperate Housewives* production asked me back to do a foot-double "acting" gig on *There's Always A Woman* segment, where the feet of the guest star have to express an orgasm as the character Carlos gives her a back massage. The entire cast and crew watched my scene and I got it in one take, to huge laughs and applause. The director, Matthew Diamond, insisted I put it on my resume. From then on, I was known as the "orgasmic feet" on the show. Funny stuff. Okay, it wasn't my face, I didn't have lines, and it wasn't a guest star role, but I had a hoot of a time and now have infamous feet!

I filled in my days with more "bits" on television, a couple of nice roles on shows that haven't aired yet, film and reality shows, to bring income and put myself on tape for audition requests for guest star and series roles in Canada. To make my insurance again, I even took to doing stand-in and background work, which opened up a door to a different world. I worked with director's and producer's wives and other relatives, out-of-work Emmy-nominated actors, other people from various professions in survival mode.

A lot of people think it's a "cush" job, but can be a butt-busting gig. A lot of extreme hours, sometimes extreme weather conditions, sometimes being treated with respect and sometimes being treated horribly. But there were a lot of fun "shoots" as well. Sometimes a group of us would bond and turn the day into a party. If the ADs knew we had acting resumes, we'd be given "bits" and put up front with the main actors. If I got picked, I'd try to turn *away* from the camera so I wouldn't be recognized as background, in case someone I knew might watch the show. Then there were times they placed me in main scenes, doing actual acting work, but with no lines, and even given close-ups, but no pay bump. For the most part, I stopped caring about having to do "bg" work (background work). Anything to take care of basic necessities and get health insurance again.

I also went back to doing freelance writing—everything from enhancing actor bios to scripts, publicity and make-up work for indie films, photo shoots and weddings. Something I always loved doing, and was good at, plus it paid well. Then I ventured into agenting, repping children at an agency, but it didn't pay enough for the hours put in to revamp the entire department. I segued into teaching again and coached a kid's class in the morning and adults in the afternoon on Saturdays, which was a blast. It also paid well. The same people who headed up the classes brought me in to overhaul their school, but that lasted a short time and I was let go due to the economy—they couldn't afford to keep me on staff. Oh well. My jewelry line was doing well and I coached privately on the side along with career consulting. Putting it all together, along with pushing my acting career, selling my artwork, other miscellaneous jobs, seven days a week, twelve to sixteen hour days got me out of debt, and when the market went down, I borrowed from my family to buy back into a condo.

I'd hear stories about David drinking, and they kept getting more frequent. That told me he wasn't happy, regardless of the money and his newfound success. I felt something was missing for him. It was amazing— I'd be in conversations with strangers and somehow the subject of David would come up and time after time, I was told he was seen here and there and "didn't look happy" or "looked miserable" or "something wasn't right" or . . . he looked like he was drinking. I tended to believe these "candid" observations, versus the friends we had in common, for whom I thought David would put on his best "happy face." I knew all too well how that worked. We'd have a raging argument one minute and be out for dinner the next and to close friends all was hunky-dory. The last thing he'd want anyone to know, especially the press, is that he wasn't happy. Never let them see you vent.

In 2004, a call came in from Eileen Bradley at E! Entertainment Channel asking if I would like to be interviewed for a special they were doing on ex-wives. She remembered me from my earlier days with David and thought I'd be a good guest for them. They heard about my managing David's career and were impressed. Naturally, I was thrilled. They covered my jewelry line and couldn't have been more supportive. Over the years, E! has called me in to participate in other pilots and shows. The special, E! *Hollywood Wives Tales* aired for a long time and brought me the long awaited validation I never got in my relationship with David.

That December, I got a call from a close family friend who attended David's Christmas party. The friend told me he didn't seem himself and hinted David might have been drinking. David made an announcement he was going to marry Annie (who he had been living with), in the next few days, but didn't appear as happy as one would think. After the announcement, my friend said that David disappeared and wasn't seen for the rest of the time they were there at the party. He couldn't be found to say goodbye either. Quite a contrast with how he announced and celebrated our engagement. I wasn't as upset by the news of his impending marriage as I thought I'd be, which was good, but it still stung. I couldn't help but wonder what he was really feeling.

Throughout this time, hearing how financially well off David was, while I was struggling to make ends meet, sometimes put me in a tail spin. Unjust? I thought so. Then I'd look at the bigger picture. The spiritual overview. We each had our journey. I was learning the lesson in mine.

CHAPTER FORTY-FOUR

TORONTO TANGO

September 9, 2003, The Final Voyage

ANOTHER Toronto Film Festival was under way. Because of my mother's illness and to change my pattern, I decided to fly up the day *after* September 8, which would have marked eight years ago to the day I flew up to Toronto to start my relationship with David. I was always happiest living in Toronto. I needed to "reclaim my city," make it my own again by creating new memories there without David. Part of my therapy was visiting where we used to live in order to achieve a final release. Weepy on the plane and already exhausted, I had to catch myself. Hey, the trip hasn't even begun yet! It was only 9:30 a.m. But just the thought of how I felt eight years and one day ago, flying into David's arms to start our life together, got the tears flowing. I was distracted from my melancholy by the in-flight movie, *Bruce Almighty*. It gave me the laugh endorphins I needed to get through the flight.

Going through the all too familiar routine of customs I got to talking to a woman, Dawn Hudson, executive director of IFP West, now Film Independent, which I had coincidentally just joined. We shared a cab and chitchat into town and exchanged cards. I quickly unpacked in my HoJo hotel room—Mark Breslin's nick name for the Howard Johnson's—which was great for the price and perfectly located a half block from Whole Foods and two blocks from Yorkville! The money I saved on a hotel I spent shopping for little trinkets with my credit card to celebrate being back. Ooooohhhh, we like that! Pulling out my wardrobe I noticed I had *so* over packed.

At about 7:00 p.m I made a dash for Yorkville to check out the scene and indulged in my favorite Movenpic ice cream cone, Carmelita and Tiramisu. It was a double-scoop celebration. God I missed Toronto. It was hard to believe it was a year since I'd been there. Tooling around the village with cone in hand, I spotted director Atom Egoyan. I was so tempted to approach him but he scooted around the corner. This was the moment the synchronicity started once again. It was eight years ago that I set up the lunch entertainment David provided for Tarantino and Egoyan on piano at the Sutton Place. After putting in some phone calls on my cell and grabbing my gourmet smorgasbord dinner from Whole Foods— sesame salmon, string bean salad, tofu—I settled in my room to get some zzzzzzs. Wednesday was going to be busy!

September 10, Day 2

I crammed in two doctor appointments, banking, phone calls, picked up my festival tickets for the closing gala screening and party, and connected with friends for plans for tonight and the rest of the week. All by 2 p.m. In L.A., it would have taken all day to accomplish because of having to drive everywhere. Toronto is such a convenient city. It's easy to meet friends for coffee on the fly and then head to a meeting or work. Things are much more available and . . . convenient. It's more conducive for connecting than is L.A., which is sooooooooo spread out.

Here, I grabbed my day pass for the subway and zoomed everywhere, and when I felt like it, grabbed a quick cab. So nice not to have to deal with a car and parking, plus I got great exercise walking! Tonight was schmoozing with agent-friend Ralph Zimmerman, who owns Great North Agency. We met at my favorite hangout, Bistro 990, to hook up with other friends of his and headed off to a film reception. From there it was a screening premiere of festival film *Intermission,* produced by his friend in Ireland, and then off to a bash at the Roots store on Bloor St. Roots did all the fabulous leather crew jackets for David's show. By that time, about 1:00 a.m., we both pooped out and called it a night.

September 11, 2003, Day 3

I was looking forward to connecting with certain people. Jonathan Hackett, who was one of the producers of David's show, and Terry Ingram who also worked production and then directed. Peter Mohan, who was a writer-producer on a fun show I did in the early '90s called *Sweating Bullets,* filmed in Puerto Vallarta. All three were now on *Mutant X* and I targeted them all on a one-day visit. The timing on that was . . . synchronistic. It felt like old home week reminiscing a bit about David and the show, a tale told or two . . . bittersweet nostalgia. Terry showed me pics of the kids and Linda, his wife, who also worked on the *Kung Fu* show. Then I bumped into Kristine who had *also* worked on *KFTLC.* It was quite a reunion! We exchanged more stories about behind the scenes of the show. Eight years and everyone looked the same. Time warp. The hour went by quickly. It was sad to leave. I wanted to be a part of it all again.

I sat outside in the warm sun waiting for the cab. Looking at the blue sky, I compared every thought and feeling to the past. Memories of what it was like at the studio out in Mississauga at 565 Orwell Street—which was later used to film *La Femme Nikita.* My first show on the series was show #13, which has always been a lucky number for me. Shit, I just missed being on a soundstage!! It was starting to hurt too much and in the nick of time, the cab arrived. I knew this was just an emotional warm-up to what I had in mind to do before my Toronto trip was over. Every time I thought of it, I'd get pangs in my stomach and clammy hands. Gasp. It was time to go "lollipop" shopping—buying an inexpensive trinket to ease my angst.

I had on my call list to get together with Mary Gail, whom I had met last year via my friend Dee. I didn't have a number for Dee. Every time I thought of calling, I'd get caught up with something else, like shopppppping! Mary Gail had tried to connect me with her sister who's a producer off and on during this last year. I made attempts to connect but she was always out of town. I wanted to check out one of my favorite stores in Yorkville—ICE, where I bought David the silver tri-band ring with Latin inscriptions—but decided to venture through the lobby of the Four Seasons instead as I had last year where I chatted with Gabriel Byrne and Stephen Baldwin. I figured, I can make some calls, drink my Starbucks frappe . . . relax the toes. I moseyed up to a couch where a woman moved over to give me space, and I settled in doing my thing.

About ten minutes later, I coincidentally get up at the same time as the woman and I see she moves up to greet a familiar face. It was my friend Dee! Synchronicity. We squealed hello and she tells me they are on their way to the restaurant inside to meet Mary Gail and . . . her sister, Suzanne, the producer! We all gathered at a table and yakked away and I find Suzanne is producing a movie starring my ex-step-sister-in-law—did you all follow that? —Laurie Holden, daughter to Adrianne Anderson, my ex mother-in-law. Yeah, it's a small world. When things like that happen, I know I'm on track. It was a great visit. We exchanged numbers and I was off to get changed for dinner with another friend.

September 12, 2003, Day 4

I was on a roll catching up with friends and events in town and decided it would be a perfect day to trek out to Mississauga and revisit the house I had shared with David. I'm on the subway and had already transferred to the westbound toward Kipling when I had this niggling thought there was something else I had to do that day. I pulled out my date book and realized I was supposed to meet my agent, Kevin Hicks for coffee. Shit! I panicked and glanced at my pager. 2:30 p.m. Whew! Had just enough time to backtrack to Yorkville, and would venture to Mississauga tomorrow. A ping shot through my stomach. Maybe I won't be able to get out there.

Maybe something will keep me from it. We'll see. I have to reclaim my city!

I was just on time to meet Kevin. It was a special visit in that we talked about everything else but the business. We originally met when we worked on a segment of *Top Cops* together. He was the "top cop." Years later he thought of giving agenting a try. I could definitely relate. It lifted my spirits in spite of the fact that there were no auditions this trip. Things were slow again. Sigh. What we could both relate to and griped about is the irresponsibility of some actors and having to baby-sit them and scold them for things like, "why didn't you check your messages in four days?!" Actor Responsibility 101—*check your frickin' messages!*

Later, I met up with my friend Mark Breslin. I have a permanent spot reserved on his shoulder to cry on, I've used it that much. He took me film gala hopping and kept me laughing as usual, through the evening.

September 13, 2003 Day 5

This is it. This was the main reason for the trip. This is *the* moment. I almost forgot to bring my camera and as planned as this was, I completely forgot to check to see how much film was in it. Turned out it was just enough. There was such angst wondering about how I'd react to seeing the old house and how I'd feel, but I just had this compelling feeling to visit it one more time. I knew it played an important part in my healing.

I subwayed it out to the Kipling station, which was the last stop on the westbound. There was that niggling feeling again to call Marilyn. I know she said she'd be out of town until the next day, but some feeling compelled me to call to see if maybe she came in earlier. I flipped out my phone and called. Sure enough, she answered! "Just got in, luvy!" Timing. Synchronistic. We made arrangements to meet after my visit down memory lane.

I flagged a cab and climbed inside with my rolling cart—these are popular in Toronto; they are like colorful bags on wheels for groceries and things—filled with my purse, water and sundry items. My cabbie was Francisco, which I found a curious coincidence because I had an aunt by the name of Francesca. Anyway, I explained my purpose and said he might have to wait in the car for me while I took pictures. So with Francisco at the wheel and me giving directions in the back, we were there in no time.

All the while I thought I remembered the number of the address and I had it wrong! Thank goodness I remembered to bring an old phone book because it not only t had he correct address, but also detailed directions. Another whew! As we rode along the freeway, familiar sights came into view. The more memories that came back, the more I started to tear up and get clammy and shaky with anticipation. I could tell we were getting closer since everything now was looking all too familiar. Before I knew it, we were at the entry gate to Sherwood Forest. A hit of adrenaline pumped through me. We navigated around the streets until we finally got to Prince John. Ohmigod.

We both scouted the street for the house address and I didn't recognize any of the houses as our house. My head spun. Wabbawabba. Huh? Oh, we were looking on the wrong side! Back around we cruised, slowly. Wait! There's the address, but . . . where is the *house*? Ohmigod—it was gone! This was the address all right. I recognized one of the beautiful pine trees on the front corner of the lot. But gone was the circular driveway where we embraced. Gone were the apple trees. Gone was the other magnificent pine tree. In its place was an impressive stone house with one central driveway to the main door that looked to be where our original door might have been. It was a shock. I stared and stared and suddenly remembered I should take my pictures, dragging my cart with me, Francisco waiting in front as I clicked away. As I wandered to the right side, I looked down the side of the house, where the garage was, and spotted a man literally puttering around on the grass. He had a miniature putting green!

"Excuse me! Excuse me! Hellooooo!" I called out.

An attractive man with golf club in hand met me as I walked toward him in an effort to get a better look at the house again.

"I used to live here."

I told him who I was and he gave me a broad smile. "It's a little different than what I remember!" I joked.

Ray and I chatted away about the house and stories neighbors had told him. He pointed out a section of broken fence and said his neighbor next door told him and his wife that David had kicked it in during one of his drunken rages.

"Would you like to see?" he asked in a light accent.

"Oh yes, it sounds like that was something David would have done," I laughed. "I'd love to take a picture."

And that I did. We joked that a little brass plaque should be placed above the broken wood slat, "Kicked by David Carradine." Hey, so far I wasn't crying! I asked to see the yard and he gave me a mini-tour. It was now fenced in so they don't see the red fox that used to romp through the yard and there was a meditation area off to the side with a statue of Mother Mary. It was like I had arranged and decorated the yard, it was soooo me.

I told Ray about the prediction that was given to me about the river. He appeared to be very interested in the history and explained how the old house had extended out to here and there. I was trying to take it all in and remember this new vision, all the while remembering how it used to look—the side entry to the office David used, the kitchen with the mouse that would climb the curtains with Purjia the cat watching in amusement.

"Does the basement still have the sauna and fireplace? We enjoyed it so much." On a day like today, with the air crisp, overcast with just a hint of mist, I'd have scented candles and bubbles prepped for David's arrival home and thick cozy terry robes to wrap ourselves in.

"Oh, no, it's been entirely rebuilt" he replied. "We redid the entire thing. Rebuilt the entire foundation from scratch."

It was a jolt that the house that I felt was my home had been torn down, but to hear our wonderful basement "playland" had been wiped out hit deeper. But when I heard this, my mouth dropped open as I stared at the man for a silent moment, flashing back on the words of John Edward echoing in my head. I would be rebuilding my foundation *from scratch!* It was a surreal moment and an affirmation. Another confirmation that my trip had special purpose and that I was on the right road in my life. A new beginning for me and . . . for the house.

A flood of memories now overwhelmed me. Wonderful memories. And I still wasn't crying! I was smiling. It was so nice to see that there was a beautiful new house with what appeared to be good people enjoying the property.

"I like to think this property is blessed," Ray said.

"Oh, yes. I was very happy here. I believe it is blessed and you will be very happy here."

I took a deep breath, a few more pictures and we exchanged phone numbers before saying goodbye. As I climbed into the cab, my nose hurt from the tears finally coming on. I took a last long look as we pulled away and headed slowly down the street for the quaint small shopping village we used to go to at the edge of the estate entrance. All the ghosts rushed in on me. Francisco and I parted and as soon as I turned to face the restaurant we used to inhabit, the tears rolled down. Grabbing a tissue, I entered what previously was the Friar & Firkin, but now transformed into the Rosewood Bistro.

Lighter in decor, it was pleasing to be in. I stared at the bar we'd sit at for hours. The bar David would hit first thing in the morning when it opened. The bar he'd be at for last call at night. The bar we'd meet at after work. *The* bar. The haven for David to run to.

Yes, this was where David broke down, saying "I can't do this again. I just can't start all over again!"

I was jarred out of my daydream by the manager asking me if I wanted to be seated. "No, just remembering".

He looked at me with an odd smile. I walked out to gaze at the little village that now had a Starbucks, a French cafe and other additions. I looked back at the bar again and sighed heavily.

I had an outdoor lunch from the little Apricot Cafe and ate my yummy chicken crepes on the bench facing the same fountain in front of the bistro. It felt okay now. Yes, I felt . . . ok. Finishing off with a Starbucks and pastry from the cafe, I walked around the village and found Rouges, the little romantic restaurant where we'd sneak in the back way to avoid gawkers. We'd sit at a small cozy table in the very back by the door and talk about the future. I had never been romanced like that before. I never fell so hard before. Every moment I felt alive. Everything was wondrous to me. I had never been happier.

I called Marilyn and grabbed a cab after one last pic of the entry to the Sherwood Forest development. It was a speed-visit, but it was great to see the smiling face that I missed in the past few years.

It was time to go and she drove me to the subway station so I could get back and change for the festival closing screening and gala party. We had some good laughs in the car along the way and it was sad to say goodbye again. It was a full day already, but I felt relieved, lighter and energized, as if a chapter had closed. As I made my way downstairs into the station, there was a man on guitar singing "That Old Feeling." His voice had a haunting quality that was emphasized by the echo through the tunnel as it got faint in the distance, faded away and finally abruptly drowned out by the noise of the subway car, as I boarded back to town. It couldn't have been a better song for this movie soundtrack, as I started to recall my drive up to the Prince John house. "I got that ooooooooold feeeeeelllllllinnnnng . . . ." I sat motionless for the entire ride back, staring out the window of the rail car remembering . . . remembering . . . remembering.

Now, as I write this, I'm looking out the lobby window of the hotel, waiting for my cab ride to the airport. I just finished a conversation with dear friends Larry and Carol Lalonde. It was very disappointing not being able to see them, but his production schedule was chaos plus. The sky is grey today. How appropriate. Beautiful and sunny my whole stay and grey the day I leave. There's the typical fall chill in the air too. I remember days like this when I'd be busy with errands for David, and go from Mississauga to the studio, and the happiness of feeling fulfilled carried me lightly through the weeks.

CHAPTER FORTY-FIVE

THE TWIST

They say dreams are the messages of the soul's yearnings, working out our waking problems, subconscious fears, hopes . . . or they can be prophetic.

I had a dream since childhood, and it kept recurring every so often during the marriage and divorce. I'd be running down the street, but couldn't run fast enough, so I'd grab hold of the ground and pull myself forward to gain speed. Other times I'm grabbing onto poles or cars and pushing myself forward and running faster. Sometimes I'd sense I was running away from something, but I always seemed to know where I was going.

There was a recurring dream I had a few times when I was with David After we separated, it happened more often. I'd be jumping up in the air and kicking up my heels to the side . . . higher and higher in each jump, clicking my heels together and kicking my legs out further and higher. It was my affirmation of happiness. I literally started to get my "kick" back.

I hadn't talked to or seen David for about a year, since we had our last court session. I was in the throes of a seven-month relationship with my boyfriend Jimmy Swan. We fell hard for each other, but he still wanted to sow some more oats. He was fifteen years younger than me, and as painful as it was I understood. Especially since he is a very hot-looking musician and women are drawn to him like magnets. Tall, slender, head full of thick brown curly locks, shocking blue eyes that could laser your heart, and one of the most gifted singer-composer music talents I've ever encountered.

First of all, I wasn't happy or in the best state of mind with the problems in the relationship. Compounding everything, I found out David was up for a Golden Globe for Kill Bill, Volume 2. I didn't feel bad because of the nomination, but because I wasn't going to be with him for the event. That was yet another part of what we dreamed about together and I worked so hard for.

So in a moment of frustration, I accidentally called Jimmy, "Johnny!" I thought the only way to find out what I was really feeling was to call David. What if it opened up the wounds again? I would be taking a major risk.

A few days before the Golden Globes, at 5:30 a.m., I bolted awake, unable to go back to sleep. That was a drag because I had a major meeting for a reality show about Hollywood ex-wives and I wanted to be at my best. I thought, there was a reason I wasn't able to go back to sleep. I wanted to give David a chance to acknowledge how I helped him achieve this moment—getting a Golden Globe nomination. Maybe he was afraid to call me, afraid of being rejected. If I didn't make the effort, I would never know. This would be his opportunity to finally give me some credit or words of . . . *something*, for helping him. Okay . . . that does it! I'm calling David.

It was always his pattern to stay up all night and go to bed around six or seven in the morning. My hand trembled as I punched in the numbers to his cell phone. What if this messes with my emotions and my interview? My heart pounded. I have to do this. He answered. Gasp! I couldn't tell if it was a drunken slur or sleep . . . maybe both . . . It's almost impossible to tell with him.

"Helloooo."

With clammy palms clenching the phone, "Hi Johnny, it's Blackie".

"Who?"

"Blackie," I said slower and louder.

Yet again, but stronger, with a slur, "Who did you say?"

"It's Blackie!"

There was a long pause. "Ah. Okay."

Silence. "So how are you?" I asked cheerily.

"I'm good," he said slowly.

"Did I wake you up?"

"Well . . . yeah, what do you think?"

"Well, you were always up at this time." I'm also thinking that no phone ring would or could wake that man. He's slept through alarms, calls, screams . . . pounding on doors . . . Nope. I didn't buy that.

Another long pause . . . "Yeah . . . well . . . " Silence.

I didn't know what else to say. All this time we hadn't seen each other or spoken and I was at a loss!

"So how are you?" I asked again and hit myself for asking the same question.

"I'm doing good."

"So . . . do you think you're missing taking a certain someone to a certain award ceremony coming up?" I smacked my forehead. I couldn't believe I blurted it out that way. Well, if there was any doubt about him thinking about me or including me, here was his chance. I held my breath.

"Uh, no," he answered gently. Then his voice got emotional. "Look, uh, I just can't deal with this right now. I'm going to have to hang up. Goodbye."

And with that, he hung up before I got a chance to say the same. It was okay. The tone of his voice said it all. He didn't want to be reminded or face the fact that I helped get him to that point. I was okay! I didn't feel the twisting in my stomach. My heart was down to a calm rhythm. The world was at peace. I didn't miss him. I didn't feel anything but relief. I went back to bed and slept like a baby.

Chapter Forty-Six

MERENGE

January 4, 2006

Had errands to run today and thought of wearing a vest. Went into my closet and came across a leather vest my David had given me, which I never wore because it was so big. Even after it was taken in I still didn't wear it. But today, I decided to put it on. I even wore a jacket I hadn't worn in five years, one that was given to me when we did a public appearance together. I had second thoughts about wearing it because it had his vibe, then I thought, nope, I'm going to enjoy the vest and jacket! There was a change in plans I made previously, so I did my errands as they came up, spur-of-the-moment, which included hitting the vitamin store to get things I forgot last time.

Well, I was in there, grabbed my vitamins, turned around, and . . . there he was! David! It had been almost two years since we had seen each other in court. I stood for a few seconds in disbelief and finally blurted out, "Well, hey there!"

He was wearing glasses in order to read the label. On auto-pilot, reacting before he realized who I was he responded, "Well, hello." He looked over the top of his spectacles and realized it was me and beamed, "Well, what do you know?"

"Weird, huh?"

"Well, not really. We both used to shop here together."

We hugged and stared for a long beat, then he kissed me on the lips. It was nice, but caught me totally off guard. My nerves were rattled and I tried to remain cool and collected, calling him Johnny when we talked. People milling about in the aisles were looking and trying to catch bits of our conversation. While he took a phone call, I took a good look at what he had in his cart, thinking he found some new herbs or good remedies. There was tea for pregnancy, which was for Kansas, who was expecting, and bottles with strange names to them. Pointing to one, I asked, "This is a strange one. What is this good for?"

He chuckled and cleared his throat to make it sound funny, and in a deep animated voice said, "For the libido."

I looked at him like he's got to be kidding. "You don't need that."

He cleared his throat again and gave a small shrug and laugh, "Yeah well . . . "

That's when I caught a glimpse of his left hand. "Let me see your hand." I pulled it to my face and stared at his ring finger, gasping, "You found the ring?! Wait, it's . . . " And I rotated his hand around to get a better view, like it was going to change. "This is . . . Did you...Wait, you lost your ring."

"Yeah, I did." He laughed nervously.

"But this . . . "

"It's Celtic."

"I can see that and I can see it's the same ring."

"It's not the *same* ring."

"It's exactly the same except . . . "

He cut me off, finishing with, "The weave is closer. Ours had more space in the weave."

I was wide-eyed. I tried to read his expression. "How could you . . . " I was stuttering, "Why would you . . . What . . . Celtic or not there's a lot of patterns to choose from. This is *ours*." My expression soured, which made him laugh. "I wouldn't want anything even similar. There's no way I would want anything close to the rings we had. Nothing could compare with what we had."

I looked at him straight on. That caught him off guard. He gave me a look like he realized our marriage still mattered to me. He kept staring at me with an odd smile, finally admitting it was "ordered" for him. Really? So what did that mean exactly? I didn't ask. Whether it was ordered or chosen for him, why would he want to wear it? Did his wife know about this? How could he look at it every time and not think of me and *our marriage*?

"That's just too weird."

He chuckled, shrugged. We realized we had been holding hands the whole time and I let his hand go, repeating, "That is just way too weird."

We chit chatted, catching up about the family, and had a few laughs. He looked at me with a gentle, loving smile, "In case you wanted to know, you look the same." I wasn't about to ask. He read my mind. Caught me off guard again. He asked how I was doing.

"Doing okay and my jewelry is selling well."

The Flying Goddess jewelry I was wearing made a big hit with him and we discussed what the process was to design and make it. The only show business we talked about was the movie I was trying to get a crack at that he did, the updated version of *Richard III*. Lori Petty got the role I wanted. He said he did his role in a "strange way," which I complimented, saying, "Johnny, you've always made interesting choices in your work. That's one reason why you're so good." He looked at me with that Gary Cooper shy reaction of his, as if he really appreciated my saying this. Grateful is probably more the word. Yes, he was grateful.

We talked as we stood in line for checkout, with more people getting an earful of our conversation. It didn't matter. I felt I might never have another chance to tell him things I'd wanted to for a long time. So I did. I said all the loving things I wanted and needed to.

"The love will always be there, Johnny." That hit a chord with him. He looked a bit hurt, and to avoid my gaze glanced down as if he had to re-focus. There was that jaw clench too. For a second I thought he was about to tear up. I sure started to. It was just then I remembered what he told me in 1994—he always loved the women he fell in love with.

By this time, it was his turn to pay the cashier and we said our goodbyes. I glanced at him walking out the door and into the parking lot. A solemn calm overcame me as I went through the motions of paying the cashier and headed out the door. When I looked up, there was David waiting for me. He could have driven off by that time, but he was still outside milling around. Evidently he was looking for my little Miata, which I no longer had.

He showed me the new cream-colored Jag convertible he was driving. "What happened to your Maserati?" He told me about its demise, but beamed that he now had a Ferrari! The Jag was his wife's car. I couldn't help but feel a little tweak about it all, but it quickly dissipated when I invited him to say hi to Lulu, who was patiently waiting for me. He leaped at the invitation. When we walked up to my four-year old SUV, David looked at the car curiously, as if he was wondering how I got the money to buy it. He commented it looked new and asked why I got a different car.

"Lulu needed some tail room. The Miata was way too small for her."

I opened the hatch so Lulu could say hello. Usually she would be hyper-happy and bouncing around—it was over five years since she'd seen David—but she took one look at him, lowered her head and tail and remained unusually calm. She was so in tune with everything. I thought her behavior might be from remembering the time David slugged her in the chest for jumping up on a painting a fan had sent him. Not long after that, we separated. But Lulu was ultra gentle, sweet and loving to David, giving tentative slow licks and nudges with her long snoot. Being made of pure love, she couldn't help it.

David was in ecstasy as he kept fawning over her with his hands. I told him about Lulu being a Ralph Lauren model for the Kids Polo Fall collection, the television dog show and more. He got a real kick out of how she was a working pup in the biz and couldn't believe how gorgeous she grew up to be. Well, hell, her dad was Lassie VIII for goodness' sake!

I finally had the chance to thank David for helping me choose her, and told him that I'd always be grateful to him for that. Suddenly, he said he had to get going and gave me a tight hug. He felt light, like he could be blown over in a strong wind.

As the embrace started to relax, he took his time kissing me sweetly on the lips again. It was an awkward moment as we looked into each other's eyes. I searched deep in his for answers—was he happy? It was like looking into an empty room. When I got into the car, Lulu was her perky happy self, wagging her tail and barking hello. Interesting. I looked over to David. His demeanor had changed back to serious as he faced the road and we both drove off in our chariots.

CHAPTER FORTY-SEVEN

MASHED POTATO

October 6, 2006

I ran into David at his son, Tom's showing at an art gallery in Beverly Hills. Actually, I planned it. I heard about the showing and I wanted to see Tom again to make sure he was "okay" with me after David and I had divorced. My friend Winslow had ventured into town, his first time in Los Angeles, and I thought he'd get a kick out of a celebrity party, so I brought him along. Besides, I was glad I didn't have to go alone.

The space was jammed with friends and relatives, including Barbara Hershey with her love, Naveen Andrews one of the stars of the television show *Lost*, David's brothers Bruce and Keith, who warmly greeted me, with wife Hayley. Calista and granddaughter Mariah rounded out the clan.

I was nervous about the family's reaction to my being there. Tom gave me a wonderful hello hug as I handed him his birthday present. He seemed genuinely happy to see me. Whew! What a relief. I was very fond of him and his wife, Teddie, who was there as well. Turns out they divorced too, but remained friends.

I waited in nervous anticipation of seeing David. The last contact I had with him was April 5 when my beloved calico "sweetie-cat," Smittie, passed away in my arms. She was twenty-one years old. David supposedly adored her, so I thought he'd want to know. From his first words on the phone, I could tell he wasn't in a good mood. The only thing he had to say was a dry, "Well, shit happens." That was it. I shook my head and chided myself for calling him.

From the corner of my eye, I could see him enter the doorway and lock in on me standing toward the back. He made his way through the crowd, heading directly for me. The raucous background suddenly got so quiet it was like someone flipped the volume switch to off. We looked at each other, smiled and moved into an embrace, with David giving me a big bear hug and slap on the back.

"You don't miss a beat, do you?"David laughed.

"Well, you otta know I don't!"

He laughed again and moved on. There was a palpable relief you could feel from onlookers that there wasn't going to be an ugly encounter and everything went back to its high noise level.

When David hugged me, however, he got a bit off balance and seemed very light. Similar to how he felt when we ran into each other at the vitamin store in January that year. There was no substance to him anymore. He looked gaunt, pale and empty. There was no light behind the eyes. His speech was slow and slurry. It saddened me to see him like that.

A bit later I went up to him at the bar to chat.

Curious, I asked, "You know it's Free's birthday, don't you?" Tom's birth name is Free. David looked like he was trying to log it in.

"Mine was yesterday...remember?"

Then he chuckled and said, "Well, you know with so many wives and all these kids around, it gets confusing."

One of the gallery people told me he purchased at least one of the paintings, so I guess he made up for his forgetfulness. I had a casual chit-chat with Calista here and there as we milled about the gallery. She looked good, as if she had been working out. She told me it was too difficult to remain friends with an ex-wife and have a relationship with the current one. From thirty years of experience, with all of the exes, that's what worked for her. We both got a good laugh out of it.

When my friend and I left, David was sitting outside with Calista and Mariah. He behaved as if he were clearly in another dimension. I gave him a hug, feeling his face against mine. It was soft, like I remembered. Then took his face in my hands—trying to lock eyes, but his gaze drifted slightly in his altered state—and planted a big kiss on his lips. He kissed back and gave a big sigh. Almost an "Ahhhhh," as he refocused and smiled back.

"Bye, Johnny." Our eyes finally locked as I turned away. That was the last time we ever touched or looked at each other. How fitting it was with a kiss—*the* goodbye kiss.

December 1, 2006

Walked in to a book store in Studio City and saw David's *Kill Bill Diary* in the window display. Couldn't resist going inside and taking a look. I fanned the pages, stopping at a random point to catch a paragraph or two, where he talks about connecting with Tarantino. You could have steamed a pot of veggies with what was coming out of my ears when I read the segment. Well, almost. He didn't mention me and didn't even get the year right. David had a vivid memory of not only the meeting, but the initial psychic, my friend Michael Bodine, who told us in 1995 of the destiny driven prediction. But he didn't mention the second clairvoyant, Maurice Amdur, who in 1997 predicted the same thing, standing in our Rosita house kitchen, announcing in his bold proper British accent, "David, you are going to make it big again and with Tarantino. I can see it as clearly as I can see you here." Why David omitted him was beyond me.

Me? That could have been a combination of things, his doing, or the influence of others, but ultimately, I felt, an attempt to obliterate me from getting credit for anything. A repeat of how and what happened during our divorce.

I bought the book, but couldn't bring myself to read it until after I finished writing my own. I was sure it would be too emotional for me. I was right, because I took a sneak peak four years later, in 2010, and felt that old anger and hurt resurfacing. One thing that caught my eye was a paragraph about his sculpture of a bust of one of his ex-wives, who he referred to as a "bitch." The sculpture he was referring to was of Gail. Because I knew a good deal of what they went through in their marriage and divorce, it prompted me to call her. I heard how she had to fight him for her residuals from the series. In our conversation, she said she never got the payments because of legal complications. How could that be? She got a judgment, didn't she? Her story was involved and it was difficult to follow her explanation, but it appeared I wasn't the only one who ended up with barely anything from giving David almost everything.

* * *

February 8, 2007

Longtime friend of mine, actor-composer Patrick Dollaghan recommended me to Robert Madrid, a producer-actor—you have to be a hyphenate in this biz nowadays—who was looking to hire voice-over talent for a film he was doing, *Treasure Raiders*. He needed someone to loop the English speaking voice for the lead Russian actress. After talking on the phone, he decided my voice was an ideal match and booked me for the ADR job—automated dialogue replacement. I'd be subbing in dialogue for the *entire film* and David was one of the male leads! Madrid didn't associate me with being David's ex because I was using my Coco d'Este name and Patrick didn't let on. I didn't dare tell him about it for fear of losing the gig—sometimes people don't want exes working on the same projects. Only after we broke for lunch did I let on. Evidently it didn't matter. Madrid thought it was a gas about the coincidence and they were very pleased with what I was doing. It was very strange acting in a scene with David again, especially with him not there! If he only knew!

CHAPTER FORTY-EIGHT

PASO DOBLE

Mᴀʀᴄʜ 25, 2008 was the darkest day in my life. It overshadowed my grief about losing the marriage, the financial problems and the battles. Anything and everything paled in comparison . . . the light and most precious being in my life passed away on the anniversary of my father's death. My most beloved collie, Lulu. The air keeping my world alive was gone. Everything since has been a shadow of reality.

One week before, I was desperate to get Lulu more medical help, but I didn't have the funds. I had maxed out financially and left no stone unturned in my efforts to help her. My dear friend, Dabney Coleman, who adored Lulu, paid for her MRI, and Actors and Others For Animals also contributed to medical costs as a thank you for the many fund-raisers Lulu helped them with.

She was dying, but I was in denial. I swallowed my pride and decided to call David for help. I fought back my feelings that if he had done what I felt was the right thing by me, I wouldn't have had to make this call. I would have had enough funds of my own. Oh well. As the song goes, "love has no pride." Because David was so happy to see me when we last met at the gallery, and so happy to see Lulu at the vitamin store, where he clearly showed his affection for both of us, I thought he'd be willing to help. He loved her, didn't he? Just one or two vet visits would, I thought, help her more.

I held my breath and nervously punched up his cell number.

"Hi Johnny, it's Blackie."

Silence.

"Are you in shock or is it that you can't hear me? It's Blackie."

He sounded sour saying he didn't think he'd ever hear from me again. I gave him an update on Lulu's condition. Going to over twenty vets and the tests to find out what her problem was. It was a nightmare with each misdiagnosing, prescribing unnecessary and expensive drugs and treatments. Losing precious quality time, dragging her to all those places she came to dread. Complications from giving her raw dog food, as many recommended for the "natural enzymes" to help her. She got bacteria . . . the details were too gruesome to describe. She suffered needlessly. It took a receptionist to ask me if the vet suggested getting a stool sample, which they didn't, and by getting that simple test, we found out how to deal with the secondary complication. It was eight months of hell for her and me.

He grunted in sympathy when I told him it was a tumor in the spinal canal in her neck. Too dangerous to operate or radiate. I thanked him again for helping me choose her and said that she was the light in my life ever since that moment. When I got to the bottom line of asking him to help out, he responded by saying he couldn't do it. He told me that after "the stuff" I did, and put them through, there was no way. "If she found out I gave you or your dog money she would just fucking flip." He said he was surprised I would even call him after the "shit" I put them through.

What?! I put *them* through?

When I questioned what it was I supposedly did, he retorted I should know. I reminded him calmly how I helped him, his career—that if it wasn't for me he wouldn't be alive, to which he said he was going to hang up the phone, and not to call him again. Click.

It didn't make sense. He had every chance to say these things to me in person when he saw me the last two times, but didn't. Quite the opposite. His attitude now contradicted how he behaved then, with kisses and loving looks. So what happened in the past two years? I reminded myself of my motto: There's no sense in making sense out of nonsense.

The perpetrator trying to make me out to be the bad guy. He sounded like a miserable person and had lashed out at me, so I'd hurt and be as miserable as he was . . . he knew Lulu meant the most in the world to me. Even though he didn't say *he* personally didn't want to give me the money, and put it down to the fear of the wife finding out, had he wanted to, he could have helped me out on the side, as he did in the past with other people behind my back. He could do anything he wanted and he had the money and means to do it. But he didn't. Was he afraid of retaliation if someone found out? Or was this the one way he knew he could hurt me the deepest, by not helping Lulu?

I kept thinking Karma . . . remember Karma. Let go and let God.

With the click of that receiver, I felt every ounce of affection I had left for him dissipate instantly. The umbilical connection and bond to him—I didn't feel it anymore. He turned his back on my girl. And with that, I turned my back on his life and everything to do with him.

I still keep her website up, www.luluthecollie.com as a memorial to my girl.

July 8, 2008

I was invited by my good friend Kate to the *No Bad Days* movie premiere and got to talking to the wife of one of the film's actors. Her husband had worked with David previously and she commented that meeting me was a reminder she had to give David a bottle of some alcoholic drink from the Philippines he loved so much. In between details of my past with David and how I came up with the design for my jewelry, she related in so many words how David put LSD in an eye-drop bottle and supposedly the housekeeper, thinking they were actually eye drops, got messed up on it.

From this story, it sounded like David had returned to his previous recreational indulgence so typical of the days he filmed the original *Kung Fu* series. I truly hoped this woman I talked to was mistaken, but I doubted it.

Chapter Forty-Nine

D-DAY II

"Born December 8, 1936, Hollywood, California
Split June 3, 2009, Thailand"

"Hᴵ there! Um . . . yeah, well, you sort, uh, got me. Uh, and leave a message if you absolutely have to, but you know, the truth is, you're better off just calling me back because I *rarely* check my messages." That was David's outgoing message on his cell phone.

The last conversation I had with David a week before Lulu passed away closed the door on him. Without emotional ado, upon hanging up the phone, I released him. I felt no anger, no pain, no . . . nothing for him anymore until I got that call June 4, 2009. All the emotions and more flooded back in.

I thought David's death would be the completion of my journey and ending for my book, but it wasn't. The lessons continued. I may have snatched the pebble out of the master's hand, but there were still many challenges ahead.

Like my life with David, the series of events that followed as a result of his death was like a tornado, leaving friends and family devastated in its wake. What pulled David and me apart never kept us apart in spirit or soul. The "forces that be" kept us bonded.

There were still things I wanted to say, to amend, to get answers to

. . . that last chance was gone. Even though it was a fantasy, it was the one thing I still daydreamed about regarding David, that maybe one day things would change and we'd have another chance together. His death was final and I couldn't even hold on to the fantasy anymore.

It was non-stop with the calls and the press wanting interviews. Some people think that would be exciting. It angered and scared me. I understood why they wanted a story, but I had enough of the negative. There were statements to the press that my declarations in the 2003 court documents, which had resurfaced again in the media, were false. I felt as though I was being painted as a liar and was therefore obligated to defend myself once more. The interview requests were an opportunity to counter the bad by remembering the good things about David.

Inside Edition and *Access Hollywood* provided me the opportunity to spin something positive about David. To talk about his talents. Take the focus off exploitation and sensationalism. To put more loving things about him out there. In spite of all the vitriol between us during the divorce, great love remained. In 1994, as we sat in the Inter Continental bar, with my arms around his waist, he told me that I reminded him of all the women he ever fell in love with, and that he always remained in love with every woman he fell in love with.

Prior to any interview I gave, the members of the media knew ahead of time I was not going to out the incest victim, nor detail anything else regarding the sexual deviances. They asked anyway. It was their job. I trusted these two particular shows because they had helped us in the past. *Inside Edition* was the first to help with David's career revamp in 1995 and *Access Hollywood* did wonderful coverage on our wedding. They stepped up to the plate in his death as well, with excellent interviews showing the good things to remember.

Other publications made me reel with anger, writing articles that made it appear as if I said a particular thing, when I didn't. They didn't even print retractions as my attorney requested. The lesson, little grasshopper? Never do an interview with print media without recording it yourself!

A couple of the tabloids were literally pounding on my door and calling every fifteen minutes. I was so upset by this I went out and got a steel security door installed. So much for a gated community and unlisted information. I have since moved as well.

I tried to set aside any emotion. I put on my investigator's hat to do my own research into David's death. Something did not feel right about it. The day he died, I put in calls to two clairvoyants to get a handle on what happened. Michael Bodine, told me he felt David was disoriented and pissed off. It was difficult for David to accept he couldn't "connect" to his body anymore. He supposedly couldn't understand how it happened to him—the fact that he'd actually died. Bodine told me he had warned David years earlier to be careful. David supposedly said he knew what he was doing and had things under control.

The other call was to clairvoyant Sloan Bella, a gifted, sassy blonde, who said what she was getting from David was he couldn't understand why he ended up in a closet when he had been in his bed. She agreed he was disoriented about what had happened. I barely had time to catch my breath when I got a call from astrologer and intuitive friend, Clarisa Bernhardt in Canada. She had just heard the news and was immediately overcome by powerful impressions that this was not an accident, but foul play. I was stunned. That prompted me to call Weiss Kelly, who gave me more details. I asked her to explain what she saw in his chart and to put it all in writing for the book. This is her letter:

Marina has been a client of mine for over 30 years. Charts can be a wonderful source of insight and timing. Making the right choice at the right time supports the right outcome. (I am sure all of us have looked back and said I should have done that then!) A Lucky time is actually an opportune time. All opportunities are temporary. I do not make decisions for my clients. We all create our own experiences.

I recall her telling me about her meeting with David Carradine—there definitely was an astrological attraction. Marina is a Libra. David's birth moon is in the sign of Libra. That in itself is one of the cosmic geometric connections.

Astrology is a language of symbols (planets, signs have meanings and correspondences to certain interests, and subjects). Libra relates to marriage, and partnerships. Libras seem to have more marriages than any other sign. So is the case with Marina and David. I did see the strong potential of a legal marriage taking place as it happened in 1998. They wanted me to give them a marriage date, and I did, but I cautioned Marina that she would be the giver and most likely contribute more to the marriage [than] he.

It was Marina that put his professional life back together and did all the leg work. The film Kill Bill launched and gave him a second chance at fame. What were the warnings that indicated it would not last? A planet named Pluto. It brings a complete transformation to whatever area it transits, and those changes are irreversible. Pluto entered his sun-sign in 1995. It was midway into his sun sign in 2004 when Kill Bill was released. By 2008 it made its exit, which meant it brought a completion.

David is a Sagittarius, they love their freedom and space. It's an excessive sign that wants to do it all and they can. The sign relates to cultures, religions, philosophy (Kung Fu, his earlier successes). The dilemma of his moon in Libra kept him marriage bound for a while.

I have to admire Marina with her trying so hard to hold it together. Why? Because her natal Saturn in Libra (commitments, perhaps Karma) conjoins with her natal sun and David's moon in Libra. She really was trying. I so admire her for that.

I received a call on June 4, 2009 from her, so distraught that I could hardly understand her. She said that she heard David died by suicide. Could I look at his chart for that day? I said that I did not believe David hung himself as rumored. I told Marina that there are two qualities there at the time—sex and money. The moon that day was in Virgo (work) opposite his natal moon in Pisces (films, drugs, certain deceptions). In addition, the sun in the sign of Gemini (information) was also opposing his natal sun in Sagittarius. Gemini is a dual sign. Perhaps he was not alone. This was not a favorable month for him. Maybe he never should have gone to Thailand to do the film.

Was he a victim? Could be. We may never know. There was certain vagueness there in the chart. Oppositions and squares showed in his chart on that day.

I can't help think as I look at the autographed glossy he sent me that hangs on my office wall. It reads, "Weiss, when destiny calls, answer."

He answered. I have had many conversations with Marina about the book these last several years. Presently, Saturn is transiting her sun in Libra. Saturn is related to the past, challenges and commitments. Marina is reviewing her past. Now destiny has called her and she is answering.

What did happen?

I believed the reason David passed away as he did was to open the door wider to help people with what he couldn't do on this earth-plane. I believe he, yet again, handed over the baton to me with a mission, and from the other side is helping me to help others.

The sexual subject matter is something that shouldn't be shoved into the shadows in embarrassment or shame, but should move into the open, into the light, so that more people can learn from it. There are reasons why people participate in these acts. Getting to the core problem and finding a healthy way of dealing with life and its issues is key. If people know how dangerous this and other acts are, then maybe they will either get help or take further precautions.

I wasn't about to let David's death remain stigmatized. I did what I could at the time to try and divert attention from the negative and into the positive. In so doing, I was caught in another tornado he created, a world where I was acting on autopilot through my own grief and trauma. A few days after I did interviews—I did not accept any money for them—I wanted to see how Bobby and his family were doing. I had talked to them a couple of days before and things were fine between us. Now, Bobby's wife, Edie, hung the phone up on me. No explanation why.

I assumed it was because I gave the interviews, but to this day I have no answer as to why they won't talk to me anymore. It was extremely upsetting. I adored them all, especially the kids. Not having children of my own, they were "my special loves." To have that taken from me remains incredibly painful.

I thought Keith might reject me as well so I never called him. I was hurting so badly. I regret that I didn't reach out to him, but I couldn't subject myself to one more possible slam or major rebuff from David's clan. I didn't lose just David that day. I lost the whole family. Only recently, I found the phone number for Bruce, David's older brother, and he took my call. It was brief, but at least he talked to me and gave me his email address. He was the one brother I had a few in-depth conversations with in the past about David. He's kept the door open to me, so far.

June 10, 2009

I was told by other spiritual counselors and friends that they believed David has not only apologized to me, but opened the door for this book. In looking back at the sequence of events, how and why certain things have come to the surface, it's like it was one big plan for his karmic release.

The signs are all around, if you look for them. If you're open to them. Tinkerbell is a symbol to me that my dad is sending me a message. The day David passed away I went to see Rosalyn to help me with my shock and grief. Coming out of her building, there was a new Tinkerbell wind chime hanging outside one of the apartments. Okay! I felt my dad was letting me know he was looking out for me.

June 10, 2:00pm

I went to a local hardware warehouse to order a security door and the car parked next to me had a Tinkerbell decal in the back window. Okay . . . interesting, an affirmation that getting the security door was the thing to do. The man whom I ordered my security door from—his name was *David*. Okaaaaaayyyy. Feeling on the verge of the Outer Limits, I stopped to get gas and as I'm thinking to myself I still can't believe David is gone, I looked up to see a black car parked in front with a license plate that read: RYL DEAD...His nickname for me was Blackie. It was a black car. At that point I believed David was laughing in response to my consistently saying to myself I can't believe he's gone. And there, as if it were his response, the license plate read: RYL DEAD.

Just like his sardonic humor. How profound is that? I could almost hear David in the etheric realm, "Thought you'd get a chuckle out of it, Blackie."

That prompted me to recall the lyrics of Cosmic Joke, that crowd pleaser, "laughing song" favorite. I could hear David's deep base vocal as he starts the song by singing he wasn't afraid to die, but afraid to live a lie. Can't say I was chuckling about it, but it did bring a slight smile to think he was communicating with me.

June 11, 2009

Today marks one week since David died. I wasn't invited to the funeral, which will be held in the next couple of days. That was very hurtful. I decided to have my own closure with him and go to Dan Tana's restaurant. My friend Kate, her mate Joe and my cousin Nunzio helped me do a little release and "goodbye" ceremony as a tribute to David.

In my mind I replayed his announcing our engagement there— standing up, saying, "My name is David Carradine and I have an announcement to make. I'm going to marry this woman! We just got engaged. Her name is Marina and she's going to become my bride . . . . " I could hear his booming voice echoing through time like it was all a dream.

So there we were tonight, sitting outside on the benches, having a cappuccino with "vitamins"—alcohol. The weather was perfect, people were talking and laughing. Ryan Phillippe was waiting for his car. We had our own sidewalk party going, mingling with people. A man stepped outside for a smoke and Kate and I chatted away with him for a while. Turned out to be Steve Kroft of *60 Minutes!*

One of the regulars at the restaurant—we'd seen one another there many times but never knew each other's names—came up to me and said, "Here, I want you to have this." He handed me a beautiful long-stemmed red rose. Not the dark burgundy red, but a beautiful brilliant, almost incandescent red. I was so surprised. "How did you know?"

"Know what?" he said, looking blank. I saw he really *didn't* know what I was referring to.

"My ex-husband passed away a week ago, David Carradine, and we were doing kind of a small send-off."

He had no idea I was married to David. The man expressed his sympathy and said he liked to buy roses from the guys outside to help them out. He felt he wanted to hand me the one he bought. His wife was inside the restaurant, but he felt motivated to give it to me.

I was overcome with the symbolism. "Thank you so much. Out of all these years I've seen you here, I've never gotten your name. What is it?"

He extended his hand, "David."

My mouth went slack. If that isn't a message from my David, offering his love, I don't know what is. In that instant, the sting from not being invited to the services disappeared. I didn't need to go. *This* was direct communication from my David to *me*. The red token was placed in a beautiful blue vase on my counter for a week. I even took pictures of it. Thank you, Johnny.

I emailed Bobby about this experience. He emailed back, thanking me for sending the story and that he thought David was now having fun. That was the last I heard from Bobby.

June 12, 2009

When I got home, I brought out an entry I made in a journal, sometime in September 2003. I remembered speaking to Patricia about it at the time, the friend who called me June 4 to give me the news:

The dream I had last week was a profound confirmation.

I dreamed David had died. I was attending a memorial service elegantly done all in white. My thinking was "Oh, my God, he's really dead." The feeling was a sense of relief. I didn't have to deal with the hurt anymore. He couldn't hurt me anymore. Then the finality of it all hit me. I found myself talking to some people and pleading with them—crying profusely for them to understand and listen to X. This person needed people to listen and understand. I woke up with a feeling of detachment from David. From then on, it's been better . . . lighter, a bit more each day.

We had two white limos for our wedding. Then:

Saturday, June 13, 2009

I flipped on the television as I made dinner. The news anchor announced, "Coming up, coverage on a final goodbye to actor David Carradine. Stay tuned."

The news coverage showed various attendees, including Tom Selleck and Jane Seymour, then cut to a new *white* hearse parked outside the chapel and slowly moved down the drive. I gasped. It was white like my dream in 2003. I picked up the phone to talk to Patricia. I hyperventilated as I related what I just saw on TV. She too, gasped in amazement.

David and I discussed this only once, but he thought of himself as a phoenix rising from the ashes, as he wrote in another one of his songs. That, he said, would be the way he wanted it. To be cremated. It didn't make sense to me why David wasn't, unless maybe he never expressed it to anyone. Or maybe he changed his mind? But that song, he told me, was definitely an expression of how he thought of himself. David's inner self. His personal life, professional life . . . his soul rising from the ashes . . . to be free. I heard his daughter Kansas named her daughter Phoenix. Perfect.

June 22, 2009 Monday, 5:15pm

It was almost closing time and I had only minutes to get to the post office in Tarzana and get my overdue mailings out. The line, when I got there, was short, but slow. I was so relieved to get in, and to get this assignment off my hands, that I didn't mind the wait.

"Next!"

I stepped up, plopped my mailings on to the counter. I couldn't help but become aware of a rather energetic person next to me talking to the other postal worker about her packages. I glanced over at a woman with long black hair and black sunglasses trimmed with a tad of glitz on the edge. I thought hey, I have a pair similar to those. There was something familiar about *her* too. Back to my mailings, and I glanced again, but this time she took off her sunglasses and I could see she looked like . . . nah! . . . there was something different about her. But I had to ask. I thought I'd regret it if I didn't say something.

"Excuse me, Annie?"

She looked at me.

"I'm . . ."

She knew.

I chuckled and said something to the effect of how weird it was for the two of us to run into each other. "Go figure." She had a slight smile and acknowledged that, yes indeed, it does happen. Again I laughed awkwardly and said "Yep. Well, I guess it does!" and turned back to the postal worker to grab a form to fill out.

But I couldn't resist asking her a few questions, which she politely and sparingly answered.

I had to know about Thunder. She took a beat and told me he passed away from old age a couple of months before. Wow, the timing of that. Just a couple of months before David. He *loved* that dog.

I fiddled with the form, then I felt compelled to tell her one last thing. I just wanted her to know that no matter what happened in court or with David, I had nothing to do with the 2003 papers getting out. I looked her straight in the eye and said I wanted her to know, coming directly from me, that what I said in the document was the truth.

She looked at me intently and her expression softened a bit. It was an awkward moment, so I turned back to finish my transaction. As I left, I turned and waved, with a smile. "Bye, Annie." She turned quickly and smiled back a polite goodbye.

Adrenaline caught up with me quickly. Only one week after David dies and we run into each other. What's with that? I was shaking by the time I stepped outside only to see a beautiful new burgundy car parked in the shaded corner slot. David's favorite car color like the Maserati he loved so much. It had a Montecito advertisement in the plate area so it had to be the new car media reports stated David just got. I was in such a daze, I didn't even notice what kind of car. It didn't matter.

I called Bobby to tell him of my pleasant encounter, but mistakenly called Edie's cell instead. She answered, but as soon as she heard my voice, hung up on me. I called back and she hung up again. No chance to find out why she was so upset or to defend myself. As I wrote in my email to Bobby that night, people have a right to know why and what they are accused of. There was no response.

Some months later while having dinner at Tana's, I ran into Martha Plimpton, Keith's oldest daughter. It was a bit tense, but she got up and greeted me in the aisle with a big hug. It meant the world to me. We chatted briefly before she left. Maybe not all the family hates me.

Then it was time, I felt, to visit David's gravesite. Having no idea where it was, I called the main funeral office at the Burbank location. A younger woman answered the phone and asked me to identify myself, since they don't give that information to just anyone. Her tone went from friendly to cool after I told her who I was. She put me on hold for a few minutes and said I'd have to get permission from the family before they could tell me where David's plot was. I was not on "the list." This upset me for weeks. I was not going to be denied the right to visit David's site.

A blazing hot day, I had an audition over at Warner Bros. Casting director, John Frank Levey was good enough to call me in to audition for another show after I kind of bungled a prior one. Before that I hadn't read for him in over 20 years—not since that time David read with me for his show. It all sort of caught up with me—the nerves. As I mentioned before, I blew that original audition with David too. This time, however, the audition went well. I stopped by the gift shop for a blended latte to celebrate before heading out again. Since I was in the neighborhood to the cemetery, and memories of reading with David were fresh from my current audition I just had, I decided to give it a shot. Determined, I drove up to the gate and asked the woman in the booth to give me directions to David's gravesite. She looked into a computer and on a map, then turned to me, "We don't have anyone here with that name."

"Try John Arthur Carradine."

Sure enough, she gets out a map and marks the directions for me. My hands were shaking so badly I could hardly grab the paper from her hand. Up the long driveway to the top trying to block out the creeps coming upon me. For the next hour, sweating in the sun, I searched high and wide for the number on the map. An older gentleman even tried to help me in my quest. Tip toe-ing over the plots and apologizing for any disturbance to them, I was so upset I wasn't finding it.

"Yeah, Johnny, I'll bet you're finding this funny!" I grumbled to myself.

As the sun started to go down and it got cooler, I noticed a few cotton-tailed rabbits scrurrying about over the grounds. More and more popped out of the bushes and stopped to look at me. Sweet. But I still hadn't found where David was. I drove back out to the entrance, but the guard wasn't there.

A woman was exiting the funeral building and I pulled alongside her, explaining my plight. She took my map and said, "Follow me."

With that, she led me directly to where David rested. Finally. There was no stone set yet and he was placed in a single plot between a "stranger" and a small tree. There was no room for anyone to join him. He was . . . alone amongst strangers. Not such a funny parallel, but David could be in a room full of people he knew and still feel alone. Now he really was. It's not how … or where I'd picture his final resting place. Emotions caught up with me. I couldn't believe I was looking at this. I said a prayer and left. It took me a while sitting in my car to get through a few tissues before I could drive, it bothered me so much.

Chapter Fifty

ICE DANCING

Many people have asked me what happened to David. I've asked myself the same thing over and over. A detective might ask—Was it planned by someone who held a grudge? Was there an insurance policy? Was he worth more dead than alive? What about the secret societies? Was it robbery, or simply an indulgence gone wrong? Who had motive? And so on, down a list of things to investigate.

Theories abound. And they all had their fifteen minutes worth in the press and the other media. But David passed away in a foreign country—Bangkok, Thailand—so there were many roadblocks to getting immediate or accurate answers.

An anonymous email to me contained the awful death picture of what was supposed to be David. I tucked my emotions in a corner and scrutinized the fuzzy image for anything that would tell me it was him for sure. Nothing. Maybe I just refused to accept that it was among the last images taken of him. Maybe it was the dark hair that didn't seem right. Was it something he was wearing for the film? Was it a wig? I didn't know.

I thought when the autopsy results and the reports of what was on the surveillance tape came in, the case would be solved. But when Michael Jackson and Farrah Fawcett died, the media blitz took over and David's case was not only put on the back media burner, it almost completely disappeared. By January 2010, seven months since David's death, the only new information I could get that was different from repetitive reports off the Internet was an article published in the November issue of *Maxim* magazine. After reading Mark Ebner's investigation, which he conducted himself in Thailand, I was amazed at how it coincided with what the clairvoyants told me.

Bangkok, it appears, was definitely a place David would have enjoyed. It's evidently a city where people can get any kind of sex they want and at any time. And for someone like David, for whom sex was a major part of his being, it would be, I think, a paradise. In the full-page picture of a shirtless David that accompanied the article, I couldn't help but notice he was still wearing the Celtic wedding band that was a double for the one we had and talked about in the vitamin store.

Ebner's article recounts viewing morgue pictures. One supposedly provided proof that the picture on the internet, showing what was purported to be David with dark hair, was a fake. However, another picture supposedly showed a deep laceration on his neck, filled with blood, and blood covering the right side of his head, which had matted in his hair. A thick ring on his middle finger was noted on his *left* hand in the article. The autopsy picture I viewed online showed the thick ring, which looks like it's in the shape of a devilish face, on the middle finger of his *right* hand. Looking at a picture, it would have been on the viewer's left side, but on David's right hand. Or, as we say in the biz, looking at the picture, it would be "camera right." His *left ring finger* showed what looks like his wedding band, and that Celtic ring. He wore it until the very end.

With blood in his hair, could this mean he might have accidentally hit his head so hard that he passed out? If he did, there was nothing in any article or report to the public that I was aware of, mentioning that type of injury. If that was the case, then how could he have died from lack of oxygen, as was reported?

If David was engaged in autoerotic asphyxiation, by himself, then how did his neck get deep ligature marks filled with blood? This certainly wasn't something he would self-inflict. More like be inflicted upon him. Sadomasochistic or even dominatrix inflicted? From my personal experience with David, knowing his high level of pain tolerance, that was plausible. But the object of this sexual game was not to inflict pain or induce pain for pleasure. Or was it? If opiates were in play during the years after we separated, then maybe things escalated even further.

The aim of autoerotic or sexual asphyxiation is to heighten sexual gratification by cutting off oxygen, and that doesn't take a lot of pressure to accomplish. The markings on David's neck I viewed in an online autopsy picture, looked like blood from strangulation marks that went way beyond the call of the game

The initial conversation with Ebner sparked my Libran urge to seek justice, and I felt compelled to launch my own mini-investigation into what happened to David. I started my preparation by talking to Dr. Steven Pitt, a nationally known forensic psychiatrist who has been involved in several notable cases, including the Kobe Bryant sexual assault trial, the Columbine High School tragedy, and the JonBenet Ramsey investigation.

I asked Dr. Pitt first to clarify for me what a forensic psychiatrist does.

He was precise: "It's the interface between psychiatry and the law, applying psychiatric principals to legal concepts in a variety of contexts."

In a forensic psychiatric investigation such as those Dr. Pitt undertakes, the investigator must delve deeply into the background of the subject. And, like the ripples that emerge when you drop a rock into a lake, the investigation inevitably extends far out from its center. What the investigator does is perform a retrospective analysis of behaviors, a psychiatric autopsy. He or she gathers information on the person's family, job, state of mind, all to get a solid picture of the person in the days, hours, and minutes leading up to the incident at issue.

Dr. Pitt emphasizes that "You have to go by what the physical evidence shows [and] not speculate on what you think happened. In a case such as this, one looks for the use of a ligature, and, if [this is] found, you look for signs of a self-rescue mechanism, for example, the presence of a slip knot or knife nearby. Also was there any evidence of sexual paraphernalia in the room, like vibrators, dildos, or fetish items? Were there any props such as photographs, pornographic films, or mirrors? You look for signs of cross-dressing and self-mutilation. An investigation also secures collateral information from friends or intimate associates who have knowledge of the decedent's behavior. When assessing whether or not you are dealing with a suicide, you look for the presence of a suicide note. Equally important is evidence that points away from a suicide, such as whether the subject was reported to be in an upbeat mood, spoke about future plans, or had no reported emotional or psychiatric problems."

"What do you think happened to David?" I asked him.

"What I suspect happened was that this was an attempt to achieve increased sexual arousal through a form of asphyxiation—autoerotic asphyxiation that went bad."

He had reached no conclusion as to whether it was done solo or with others, but he did feel it was not suicide. He felt confident David had been into this sexual practice for a long period of time.

"Because seldom, if ever, does the behavior happen in a vacuum," he elaborated. Based on what Dr. Pitt knew, had seen, and had read about, he felt it was too intricate and too sophisticated for this to have been a first-time foray into that type of behavior. Evidently it takes time and practice to get to a point where the act is fine-tuned to the participant's preferences, and, in David's case, that scenario fit.

"When it comes to sex, it starts with a fantasy, followed by experimentation, practice, and then refinement of behaviors that give the subject or subjects the most pleasure." So it is a long process. A person takes the time to figure out what it is they like or don't like, what works, what doesn't, and what is most gratifying.

With this initial guidance, I began my journey.

* * *

Khunying Pornthip Rojanasunan, Forensic Pathologist, M.D., Director General of the Central Institute of Forensic Science (CIFS), Ministry of Justice, Thailand stated, "If you hang yourself by the neck, you don't need so much pressure to kill yourself. Those who get highly sexually aroused tend to forget this fact."

So how did David get what looks like blood-filled marks? I tried to reach Pornthip directly, and was given her cell number, but it kept disconnecting. From what was supposed to be her personal e-mail, I was informed she did not perform the autopsy and couldn't answer my questions. I was referred to the hospital where the autopsy was actually performed, but given no name to contact. Great. I was getting frustrated with the language barrier, time difference and the expense to call there. I wracked my brain trying to think of anyone I knew that spoke Thai. When I emailed Pornthip back, asking for a statement for my book, there was no return response.

Producer David Winters theorized in *Maxim* and in other articles regarding David's death about the possibility of lady-boys—a male-to-female transgender person or effeminate gay male in Thailand—drugging people and robbing them. This coincides with the messages the clairvoyants gave me months prior to the article. My inner voice was telling me a piece of the puzzle fit, but wasn't complete.

I called Ebner. From what I had read online, there was a lot of conflicting information, but Ebner's article rang a bell of truth for me. And for me, the fingers were pointing to foul play and cover-up. Ebner confirmed the information in his article. He expressed, in so many words, that the type of marks on David's neck didn't look accidental.

Maybe there was something embarrassing on the surveillance tape and someone didn't want the public to know, so the evidence was quashed? Who reviewed those tapes? What about the conspiracy theories?

David was fascinated with the Freemasons, a secret society, and had a few books on the subject. There was a jovial guy who worked at a place where we used to get our pictures duplicated who was a member of the

Freemasons. The two of them would gab away about it, but nothing beyond an occasional conversation. David also talked about both Bruce Lee and son Brandon dying under mysterious circumstances. He heard the rumored theories, and wondered if something beyond what was presented in the press had occurred. So he was into the talk, but unless after we separated he got deeper into them, I pushed the secret and not so secret society theories aside, to the far end of the spectrum.

If there's a cover up, the question is why? The most logical answer is that to have such a major international star as David die in a hotel, accidental or not, is bad publicity and bad for business. For any hotel, let alone one that caters to tourists. Especially if there was foul play involved.

* * *

After doing intense research on the Internet, I made a list of key places and people in Bangkok to call. What came of that slowly solidified the clues, omissions and theories.

Emotionally, it was extremely difficult to handle. In order to detach myself enough to be able to remain objective and talk to people without tearing up, I had to put myself into an emotional state of anger at David again. Just enough to keep the journalistic side of me keen on grabbing the information without getting "soft." Sometimes, when I was exhausted, I could park the emotions in neutral for a while, but it didn't last long. I found myself yelling at my cats for no reason or reaching for the chocolate bars too often. Too much emotion built up and not vented. I can't eat when I'm tense and upset. Over the time writing the book, I lost eight pounds. Two of which was during this research.

Before and after each conversation, I had to take short breaks and either walk around, call friends or my mother, drink water, or have a crying jag to release the emotions triggered by the information being given to me.

There's no way I believe it was suicide. And David was not one to "fly solo," so the autoerotic didn't fit. Neither did the statements Gail made to the press about David tying himself up to relax or meditate. That never happened with us, although it could have been something he had done before me, and then his preferences could have later escalated. Sexual gratification, however, was not something he enjoyed doing alone. He'd rather remain "horny" or put his energy into some other activity, like his computer art, or pound at the piano, than indulge himself by himself. He even wrote me a letter on the subject expressing it all when we were having problems. Granted, that was nine years ago, and who's to say he didn't change preferences? His past pattern suggested to me, however, there was someone else in the room with him.

A spur of the moment stop at Susie's Delights in Tarzana, on my way to Whole Foods, proved of little help. The shop and its owner were in the media regarding the paraphernalia he purchased there before he died. The 60-ish blonde shop owner wouldn't talk about David or the large order he supposedly placed before he left for Thailand, as reported in the news. She said in her European accent she wanted him to rest in peace and what he purchased wasn't important anymore. She liked David very much and had come to know him over the time he frequented the store. The owners of the coin shop next door said David frequented their place as well and socially schmoozed at their house. A place to sell and pawn items, the shop has an eclectic assortment of inventory from knives to fossils to vintage coins that evidently attracted David to it many times and he spent considerable time perusing the merchandise. The owners spoke fondly of David as well.

February 18, 2010

My next call was the result of at least twenty-something frustrating chats at all hours of the day and evening because of the time difference, with people in Bangkok speaking English as broken as a mosaic tile project you have to assemble with no directions. Colorful, but difficult to piece together. I finally hit pay dirt with someone at a key facility who actually said they could look up David's autopsy file. With the file they said was in front of them, which included the autopsy pictures, I was told that David was found completely naked with his *hands on his knees,* half sitting on his knees in the closet. Translation to mean, kneeling? Cause of death was from lack of oxygen caused by compression of the artery. The toxicology report, they said, showed alcohol in his system, but not to an extreme. To a "happy" or partially tipsy level, not totally drunk. There were no drugs found—no amphetamines, cocaine, morphine, diazepam . . . and no sign of struggle or defensive wounds.

From the police report and after the autopsy and toxicology reports, the conclusion was death due to *asphyxia,* and an *accident* from autoerotic *or* sexual asphyxia. Even though it's been emphasized in the media as "autoerotic," by one's self, there is still a possibility of another person being present, since asphyxia could be self-inflicted or inflicted by another.

Reading further in the thick dialect and broken English: a medium-sized yellow rope or cord made probably of silk was found around his neck and hands. The rope or cord was bound around his neck, with one end of the cord, and continued in a double-loop to hang over the closet rod, where clothes are hung. Then the end of the cord tied up around both wrists.

They then said, still reading from the report, that the *hands were found a little over his head,* which contradicted what they initially told me when they were looking at the autopsy pictures. So, was one picture taken as they actually found him and the hands had dropped when the cord was released? When I asked again, the answer changed. Translation misunderstanding? One online article actually stated he was found "curled up," which would explain the hands on his knees.

The person went on to say the hands acted as the mechanism that he could use to release the pressure of the neck by pulling up or down, causing the oxygen deprivation. Evidently, this time the brain had continued the loss of oxygen over his body limitation, and he died.

This was the first I heard of a *yellow* cord being associated with David's case. This same person went on to say it was a type of luxury rope, the kind used for curtains, soft, *so it wouldn't mark the body*, but they added it was not from the hotel, that David—I'm thinking "whoever"—must have brought it. Other reports had stated the cord, with no color specified, was from the hotel. Yet other articles had mentioned only the black shoelace/cord, which supposedly tied around everything, hands, neck, genitals.

I asked if there were red marks and if they went around his neck. They confirmed the red marks did run *around the neck*, but were explained to be from his body weight coming down on the rope when he died. If his weight was forward, how could he get such red marks on the back of his neck? The person insisted it was from his body weight. When I asked if the closet bar was strong enough to hold David's weight, the person assured me it was strong enough. How would they know? Were they at the hotel to test it, like Mark Ebner was? Ebner questioned this in his article: if the closet rod in David's room was anything like the closet rod in Ebner's room, it wasn't strong enough.

The person said the bar had only to be strong enough to cut off the oxygen, not hold all of his weight. Being in a kneeling position, it wouldn't have to hold his weight, just enough to give him control to cut off the oxygen.

It still doesn't explain the deep red marks around his neck. Wouldn't that require considerable force? If it was considerable force, then would the closet bar hold? The person answered by repeating what they previously said.

How could he tie his own hands? They didn't know. They suggested he tied his genitals first, then neck, then the hands.

David was quite dexterous and I believe he could tie his hands together. He showed me he was adept at a variety of knots, including one that would tie tight, but a tug on one of the cords, and it would release. A safety mechanism. There was no mention of David having any safety mechanism. I don't believe he would do such a thing without a type of knot that would give him a release.

This person also stated that there was no women's wear of any kind in the room, just a men's black g-string. Whether they meant thong or an actual g-string wasn't clear. They were sure the underwear was for a man because it had the opening in front. Based on my personal knowledge, unless David was naked, he wore Speedos. Of course there were those thongs I discovered in his drawer, which he never wore for me.

Any sex toys or other paraphernalia, like porn or . . . ? They assured me no there was nothing unusual in the room. He was by himself and it was accidental.

What about any DNA testing? No. Nothing abnormal was seen on his body. It was clean. So they didn't test for blood, urine, semen, saliva, nor skin or other traces under the fingernails. Nothing? Nope, no such tests.

I wanted to scream.

I concluded this first conversation by giving them the link to the online autopsy picture, about which I had other questions. This person was to get back to me as soon as possible with further answers once they received the picture.

Friday, February 19, 2010

My call to Dr. Michael Baden, a medical doctor and forensic pathologist in New York, was short, but telling.

He was hired by the family, not the state or any other public entity, to do an independent examination—a second autopsy—to find the cause of David's death. Legally, he could not tell me anything except to confirm his official statement to the press: "The cause of death was asphyxiation, an inability to breathe." In other words, a lack of oxygen.

Who or what caused the asphyxiation and inability to breathe is a question not answered. Was it caused by another person? My impression was that the police in Thailand were to correlate their findings with

Baden's and pull it all together to come up with a determination if it was accidental or not. A determination of asphyxiation doesn't necessarily mean it was autoerotic, just that it was some type of asphyxiation.

The comparison would be akin to figuring out how a bullet killed someone. You know the bullet did the damage, but how the bullet got there would be the question. Baden said in so many words that pathologists' findings aren't always agreed upon by other parties. Was that a hint?

When I asked about the position of David's hands, Baden said something to the effect that in the pictures, it was reported, David had his hands above his head. I don't know what source or time frame the pictures he was talking about were from, though.

Any other information, I'd have to get from the family or next of kin.

Saturday, Feb 20, 2010 – Anniversary day of our wedding.

The weather today was exactly like it was the day I married David. It had rained the day before and on our wedding day, the sky was blue, the sun was out with rain clouds here and there, threatening, cold temperature, but clear and glorious for our sunset celebration. Never thought I'd be spending this or any anniversary of our wedding typing up notes from conversations with contacts in Thailand about his death. It's all so very unreal and disturbing.

I kept looking at the clock. This time we were in the limo . . . This time we were at the studio . . . walking up the aisle . . . having our first dance as husband and wife . . . riding away in our white stretch limos and back to the house for our Italian dinner. Which I just realized is what I made for myself tonight. Shaking my head in dismay, looking out the window at the now black sky . . . I continued to type away at my computer.

Tracking down David Winters in Thailand was very distressing, yet confirming. A longtime friend of David's, Winters spoke in a gentle, elegant British-accented voice, which helped to ease the uncomfortable conversation. He was passionate and adamant about what he stated in the

Maxim article and in an article by Antonio Pineda, *Endgame, The David Carradine Affair* for Magick Papers & Nightlife Thailand. The belief is that David was not alone and that it was either murder or an accident. Winters explained it would take at least one to two people to move a man David's size into a closet like the one he was found in. Lady-boys, who are prevalent in Bangkok, could very well have been able to do that. The women there are very small and not heavy, so they wouldn't physically be able to handle someone such as David, according to Winters.

A theory is that whatever happened to cut off his oxygen, which appears to be via strangulation by a cord, whoever was with him, moved David to the closet and tried to make it look like suicide. A sex act gone wrong by either design or accident.

Winters confirmed the information about the morgue pictures, not only about the blood in David's hair, also described in *Maxim*, but there was supposedly blood in the room, according to an informant of his. I asked Winters to let me know if he could get me any other pictures or further evidence from his connections about the blood in the room, but I never heard back from him. As part of the alleged cover-up, supposedly the entire floor that David's room, 352, was on at the Swissotel Nai Lert Park, has been renovated and the rooms re-numbered so the room David had doesn't exist anymore.

An important point of "trivia," Winters pointed out, was that there was never any mention of David having a watch. He was right. I know David never traveled without wearing one of his watches, all of which were expensive. His favorite, which he wore constantly, was a Patek Phillippe worth thousands. I never knew David to be without a watch. Even if he took a swim. In fact, in the picture for *Maxim* magazine, he's seen wearing a watch that looks like the one we got at the *Ahead with Horses* fundraiser hosted by William Shatner. The amount of money David had with him was brought up again. He was supposed to have about $10,000—$15,000 for upfront money, as well as per diem in cash. This was consistent with David's previous pattern, to get large sums of money in cash on location and to bring it back "under the radar." During our years together, he only did it a couple of times, which made me a nervous wreck for fear of being a target, so he stopped. I can't help but think that had he not done this, he might still be alive. Winters was told that as David went up to his room, he smiled and he waved to the people in the lobby. Definitely not the action of someone depressed on his way up to his room to kill himself.

Surveillance tapes? The Thai police are supposed to be in possession of the tapes, but won't release them for viewing. According to Winters, the authorities have supposedly stated that there was nothing suspicious on them. He sounded exasperated about the situation, that there were so many matters washed under the table, like so many things in Thailand "when it comes to rich people" and killing. If there's nothing to hide, then why don't they show the tapes? He indicated informants thought the tapes have probably been tampered with anyway.

One of the key players at a major newspaper evidently told Winters that all the usual sources for information in various departments around town had nothing on David's death. This was evidently very unusual. Winters agreed it was like everyone was being hushed up. Money, it's said, rules the city. With that in mind, could the whole situation about David really be a major cover-up?

Monday, February 22, 2010

I hadn't heard back from the source regarding the autopsy file, so I called the person back. I wanted them to look at the picture I found and comment on not only the red laceration marks, but also an oval red blotch on his left forearm. I also wanted to get the measurements of the width of the yellow cord as well as an explanation of the blood seen in David's hair. That person has yet to respond again, even after promising me today they would have an answer by the evening.

I also still had not had a response back from Col. Somprasong Yenthuam, superintendent of the Thai Lumpini police, regarding the list of questions I emailed at his request. It's been five days. I was even given a cell number for the man—or for Yenthuam, it was difficult to understand which it was—whom I spoke to at the Lumpini police station. He said Yenthuam was standing beside him—I could hear a man in the background spouting off in Thai—and requested I send my questions in an email, which I did along with a few follow-ups requesting a response. Nothing. I called the cell number today, and the man who answered, who could speak English in a thick Thai dialect, said I had the wrong number. I repeated the number back and he said it was wrong. Looking at my call log, I had dialed correctly. Hmmmmm. I called the Lumpini police station and they gave me the same phone number I had just dialed. Trying the number again . . . no one would answer.

Tuesday, February 23

No email or calls from the Thai police and still no one answers the cell phone. What makes me think they're not going to respond? Just as I'm about to wrap up writing my final chapter, I got a correspondence from my source with the autopsy file, who answered my remaining questions.

The red oval mark measuring about three centimeters on David's left forearm evidently was from a small and recent bruise before his death. I thought it might be a defense wound. In the online picture, it looks *far bigger* than only three centimeters. So their information didn't coincide with the picture.

They stated there was no blood at the crime and the blood that was seen in other photos, they explained, was supposed to be from the autopsy. Blood evidently can drain from the head and body. If they didn't clean the body well, then there might have been what was seen in other pictures. They didn't mention, however, in our previous conversation that any blood showed in *their* pictures. Why was this not mentioned? If autopsy pictures viewed by others showed blood, why didn't this person comment on it? There wasn't any blood on the rope either. The red mark

I viewed around his neck was from an abrasion caused by the rope, but it wasn't the type of wound that openly bled. This type of wound gets darker in color. It wasn't a "slide" type of abrasion, but from pressure.

The black shoelace that was wrapped around his genitals was attached to the yellow rope that went around his wrist and neck. A picture of *the* yellow rope was sent to me as well. It's actually gold in color and the ends are neatly taped off like a fabric store would do to prevent the ends from fraying. The size/diameter seemed to match the markings seen around David's neck in the picture too.

Thursday, February 25

Today marks my father's birthday and the day I'm wrapping up the investigation and the book. My efforts to get a few more questions answered from Dr. Baden went by the wayside. No one called me back. I turned to the Los Angeles County Coroner's office where the Chief Medical Examiner explained this was not an area where they could comment because the case was not in their jurisdiction. Undaunted, I called back in verbal disguise as a writer doing research for a novel. After a five call shuffle to various departments, one of their doctors did answer some general questions.

Is it possible for blood to passively drain from a victim's head into their hair, if they died of asphyxiation? They confirmed it was possible, because of the procedure to check for a broken hyoid bone, which could bruise muscles in the neck and the back of the tongue area. The exact description of the procedure they gave me was too gruesome to write about. As it was, after the interview, I had to take a break and get on the treadmill to relieve the stress and try and shake the images I had in my imagination.

The doctor said if someone died of autoerotic asphyxiation, there usually aren't any marks on the neck. Pressure abrasions are not usually found in those types of cases, but are usually part of strangulation by another party. Even if the victim falls forward, marks, if any, would usually be on the front, not the back of the neck. If there were such marks, it could point to foul play. They said a decision is dictated by the circumstances in which the body is found. Participants in autoerotic asphyxiation "avoid leaving any marks," since the purpose is to give pleasure, not hurt.

Comments regarding the color of the pressure abrasion were in agreement with the other informant, as was the progression of any bruising colors. However, the color and size, observed in the autopsy picture I viewed, on David's left arm looked very large, much larger than what the other informant reported to me.

Donna Hennen, who I met several years ago, is another excellent astrologer with a keen ability to hone in on the nitty gritty in a chart. She gave me brief, precise additional information regarding that third day in June. I was up until three in the morning writing and was half asleep when she called. I could hear her voice echoing from the answering machine in the other room. In yet another direct confirmation to what Weiss told me, the astrological aspects for David were this:

The transiting Saturn, which was in Virgo on June 3rd, was in opposition to his natal Saturn in Pisces. That natal Pisces, that Saturn, was in conjunction and very, very close to the transiting Uranus—the planet of unusual, unexpected and unforeseen. This was in opposition to Saturn—the planet of limitations, restrictions and losses on that day, so it showed a quick and unexpected loss— things that are taken away. It has to do with a very significant aspect of Saturn in his chart on that day, June 3rd, and what was there when he was born.

Seeking yet more knowledge from those with the ability to tap into information from the other realm, I called my cousin, Averi Torres, Malibu's Psychic to the Stars. I have no idea, really, why I didn't call her months ago, but as they say, everything in its own time. Before I wrapped up this book, I had to see if there was any other information I could get to confirm my feelings of what really happened.

Averi came through with the most detailed reading yet, which gave me goose-bumps. I was sitting in Alan Weissman's living room, waiting for him to get an email from the photography retoucher on my picture for the jacket of this book. Being in the hills, reception was cutting in and out, but I could hear what she said about David loud and clear.

Averi's first impressions: although David had personal problems and was not happy about a certain relationship he was in, emotionally he was at "a good place" with other things in his life. He was not suicidal, but he did like to numb out with substances, because it was an escape.

Averi thought there was more than one "young boy" (between sixteen to eighteen years old). Rather short with dark suntanned complexions. They might have been lady-boys, but she didn't see their appearance as being dressed in women's clothes, although they were effeminate, with one of them having lipstick and eyeliner. They were not street urchin types, but their attire was clean and they were *very* well put together. They were definitely in the sex trade and used drugs. In fact, she got the vibe that at least one of them was high at the time and had drugs for David. Her feeling was that David had his own as well, and might have been using two drugs or substances at the time. She believes these two "boys" knew who David was and targeted him with the intent to rob, taking him for everything he had. Averi thinks this was premeditated and David was set up.

The chilling impression that came through was that it was no accident he died.

What does all this mean? A "www?" Wrong place, wrong time, doing the wrong thing?

CHAPTER FIFTY-ONE

THE WALTZ

"I'm lookin' for a place ..."

— David Carradine

Davɪᴅ had a fear of growing old and being forgotten. No one can convince me he was a happy man either. His return to drinking showed me this.

He didn't understand why directors like Scorsese never worked with him again. Especially after he got sober. He was being such a "good boy" and was hurt when he was not rewarded by those from whom he wanted it most. A bit like being ignored by a father figure again. People he looked up to and revered, but felt hurt by. The one major director that did give David "the love" was Tarantino. But even after *Kill Bill*, top roles with top directors he wanted to work with didn't come his way. Why? Were the roles just not right for him? Was the word out he was drinking again? It was a definite bone of contention during the years we were together, and from what I later heard and read in interviews with David, he was starting to show a fringe of bitterness. The alcohol usage made its own statement regardless.

He always seemed to live on the edge and found solace in his work, whether it was writing, acting, his music, art ... or sex. Even though he got into funks, and was theatrical about it, I don't believe for a second he would take his own life. As he put it once, that's quite "an irreversible thing."

The findings I was able to gather to add to the mix still leave questions. Based on the information at hand and from my own investigation, I believe David was murdered. It was that one autopsy picture I viewed that turned the corner for me. Unless another expert can explain it away, to get marks like those around his throat points to considerable force.

I went to a fabric store and found cord/rope the size and material as was described to me. Hiding off to one side in an aisle, I wrapped it around my various body parts including my neck, to see how much force it would take to make marks such as I saw. That convinced me what I saw in the picture of David could not be caused by body weight from hanging in a closet. Nothing that would come from an autoerotic act. And since that type of act—to achieve its goal does not require much force, those marks are beyond the border of enjoyment.

We may never know the definitive answer. On this earth, David was an enigma, and he will remain so. The mystery surrounding him will continue, as it did with Marilyn Monroe, and JFK, for example . . . and he will not be forgotten for his many accomplishments.

The week of David's birthday—December 8, 2009—I got a call from a newspaper publication asking me if I had any comments about the gravestone that had been placed at his cemetery site. Since I didn't know about it, I was glad they called. The reporter didn't know what the inscription was from—a book, lyrics—or what it meant. When he read it off to me, I knew immediately it was from one of David's songs. Wishful, reflective, with a touch of that wry, David humor. A song called *Paint*. The lyrics express his search for the perfect place to be, wondering if there was such a place. Then again, maybe it is just . . . paint?

A few days later I went back to visit his grave to see the completed resting place for the barefoot wanderer. The man I so adored and at times so disliked. This time at the gate, they had no name in the computer at all for him. I just drove up the hill before they could say anything else. The bunny rabbits were out again to greet me as I made my way to David's gravesite. Again, the tears were dripping down my face before I reached it.

He was, as we all are, a mere human being, full of complexities and imperfections. David wasn't religious by any set standards, but had what he called a cosmic awareness, and I thought mystically inclined. He commented to me once he thought death was more of a condition, like the stars and planets in conjuction. How prophetic. Astrology was something he was interested in, but he didn't spend time getting chart updates or consults, as I did. He also told me he thought of God as a cosmic force. It's obviously expressed in that "laughing song," *Cosmic Joke*.

I remember we were at a dinner party once and the subject of reincarnation came up. David said he believed in everything. That in an Einsteinian universe, what you imagine, exists. He laughed, saying he wondered if he'd ever get it right and thought he'd have to stay until everyone else goes, because that was his "deal."

I reached the gravesite. There in front of me was the bronze headstone with both his names emblazoned across it. A heart-shaped stone. White sage and plants remained as love tokens from previous visitors. Very appropriate using the lyrics, and the loving, written tribute was fitting. One picture is worth a thousand emotions. I had my little talk with David as the tears obscured my vision. I felt him beside me as a gentle breeze caught my hair and blew it into my face, just as it had as the harpist played *When Blackie Lets Her Hair Down,* for our first dance together as husband and wife. As I looked up, the rabbits were staring back. It was very quiet except for the sound of my feet carefully retracing my steps over the grass and back onto the sidewalk to my car. Looking over my shoulder to where he rests, I could hear in the stillness him singing "the laughing song."

Maybe he *is* laughing now. Maybe this is just one great big cosmic joke, as he said. Maybe it is a poke in the ribs from the guy in the sky. I can hear his deep bellowing, knee-slapping laugh now.

"Don'cha get it?!"

Yes, Johnny. I get it.

As the song plays in my mind, there is more of his belly laughter and then his satisfied . . . sigh . . . into silence, as I drive quietly away, back down the hill and out the gates.

The Legend continues.

PART V

THE GOOD, THE BAD, and...HE DID *WHAT?!*

D AVID always made an indelible impression. I thought it would be enjoyable to include some stories from a few friends and working comrades. I asked them to write about the story or incident that immediately came to mind when they thought of David. These encounters and memories made us laugh fondly.

He was unpredictable, entertaining even in the most awkward predicaments, as well as caring, humorous . . . and, well . . . unforgettable.

Mark Archer
Director/Co-Producer, "American Reel"
"American Reel" Memoirs
27 January, 2010

Meeting David Carradine

The first time I ever met David Carradine was in the Summer of 1997. I had just come off a publicity wave from my first feature film, *"In the Company of Men,"* which had won the Filmmaker's Trophy at the 1997 Sundance Film Festival and subsequently vaulted several of us into instant careers. While the coals were hot, I was anxious to secure my next project. Working to put together a deal to shoot this script called *"American Reel,"* however, was a process that I would never forget.

The producers of the film, Darrell Griffin and Jordan Rush, had a laundry list of names for the lead role in the film, which was the story of an aging country-western singer named James Lee Springer. We would get together a few times a week at Darrell's home in Sherman Oaks and strategize on stars. David Carradine was always on our short list, but he was not the top pick if it came to a vote among the three of us.

Every time I would bring his name up with someone in conversation, the reaction was nearly universal, "David Carradine? You mean *Grasshopper*? Is he still alive?"

Even to a then 23-year-old filmmaker, Carradine's checkered past and reputation for being "slightly difficult" was no secret. The odd thing is, the thing that Carradine held over my head throughout the production—his vast experience and the obvious age difference between us (he was old enough to be my *grandfather*)—was probably the one thing that brought us together in the first place. I guess I was young enough and dumb enough to not be intimidated by the man, which I think irritated him more than he would have admitted.

I asked if I could meet Carradine in person, since he had come highly recommended by Ally Sheedy, who was supposed to play opposite Carradine in the film. I had had a long conversation with Ally about the film a few weeks prior, and about Carradine in particular. Of course, after making the hard-sell for Carradine herself, Ally dropped out after we signed Carradine. We replaced her with Mariel Hemingway. I guess the fact that she dropped off after we signed him up should have been a sign, but in the end we all survived it.

We met Carradine one afternoon at the Bistro Gardens Restaurant in Studio City. We all sat and talked about the project, and talked in particular about the music aspect of the film. It was a typical Hollywood "meeting." At this point, we hadn't officially offered the role to him, so he was still on his best behavior. Carradine wanted desperately to write the music for the film, which worked to our advantage. In a way, he wanted us more than we wanted him at that point.

Somehow or another we got onto the subject of church hymns, and I looked at him and said, "James Lee Springer could probably sing *Amazing Grace* to the tune of *House of the Rising Sun*. (Carradine's character's name in the film was *James Lee Springer.*) The challenge sat on the table like a cocked and loaded pistol...nobody moved. Carradine thought about it for a few seconds, and said, "No, that wouldn't work...no...wait . . . " At that, he got up, strolled across the restaurant to the piano and sat down. He plinked a few test chords, then belted out the first verse of *Amazing Grace* to the tune of *House of the Rising Sun*. We all sat stunned.

"You're James Lee Springer!" I yelled. His eyes lit up and he looked at me and said nonchalantly, "Yeah, I know!" And that was the first time I ever met David Carradine.

The Stabilizing Force

During that same meeting at the Bistro Gardens Restaurant, we all met Marina Anderson (later Carradine) for the first time. It was only a few months later, during the early production of the film, that we realized what a huge effect she had on him.

Working with Carradine was a challenge. That's about the nicest way you can say it. He was at least an hour late to set *every day* of filming. I can't count how many times he drove my hair/make-up artist to tears. And, he had his own ideas on a great many things—like how the director should do his job, for example. Had it not been for Marina being there on several key dates, the film likely would not have been finished.

On the 6th day of filming *American Reel*, which was a Saturday, we were shooting the large concert scenes for the end of the film. We had rented an auditorium for the day, heavily publicized it, and packed it with over 1000 unpaid extras from around the area. People were driving in from 2 and 3 hours away, just to be an extra in a David Carradine film. Carradine had somehow gotten the idea that we were spending extra time that day filming for a potential music video for the title track, *American Reel*, which he had written and performed. That was news to me.

Someone had promised him that we would cut a music video for his song. When I was talking through the shot blocking with him in the morning, I explained the angles I was getting and which portions of the song we were going to use in this scene. This was 1997, and HD didn't really exist yet, so we were still rolling 35mm film. I only had 60 thousand feet of film for the entire production (which isn't much), so a large, expensive concert scene with lots of long takes and opportunities for things to go wrong was just a killer on my film budget. I didn't have the film or the time to spare. Extra shots and setups were not in the budget. Carradine listened to my explanation of the day's shooting plan, then walked away and started mumbling something. He turned around and said, "What about the music video?" "What music video?" I asked. "We're supposed to be shooting coverage for my music video!" he retorted, then stormed off the stage to his dressing room. I stood there for a moment, then looked at my 1st AD, Guy Camara. He sort of smiled and said, "We're shooting a music video today?" "Where's Darrell?" I asked. We went looking for Darrell Griffin, the producer.

What transpired over the next 3 hours was nothing short of a temper tantrum. By the time Guy and I had found Darrell, Carradine had locked himself in his dressing room and refused to come out until we agreed to shoot extra footage for a music video.

Darrell went in and tried to reason with him, but to no avail. I went in and took a turn, but nothing changed. He had dug his heels in and refused to even allow hair/make-up to work on him until he got what he wanted. We were all at a loss.

We had over 1000 people now, sitting in the auditorium, waiting to be in a movie. We had a whole film crew sitting, waiting, for the production day to start. It was a nightmare. The only thing that got him out of that dressing room was Marina showing up and talking some sense into him. After she talked to him for a few minutes, then came out and talked to us, she went back in and shut the door. About 10 minutes later, Carradine came out and walked down to hair/make-up. Nothing more was said about it.

There were several other occasions where we all had wished that Marina had stuck around. During the last week of filming, Carradine announced to the entire crew that I was "f-ing up the film" and didn't know what I was doing, then stormed off the set and went to his RV. That outburst stemmed from his misunderstanding of my scene blocking, but it nearly shut the film down again. In the world of low-budget independent films, you can't afford to take a day off to stroke someone's ego. You have to deal with it and finish your shoot day or you're done. Had Marina been there, I'm certain that incident would have been avoided.

The work experience with Carradine was not all bad. In the end, we finished the film and we were pleased with it overall, though when I think of how much time we spent waiting on the man just to show up to work, it sickens me. There was a lot of arrogance there, but deep down I think he was just a lonely man.

I never saw him get so softspoken and almost come to tears like when he would talk about Marina. In fact, one of the tracks in the film that he wrote was called *And Then She Smiles*, which he revealed to me was all about her. I remember being in a conversation with him at one point, just the two of us, and I brought up the song. We were discussing the scenes that would go together in the film to make the montage for that track. He got very quiet, looked at me and said, "You know, I wrote that song for Marina."

I remember looking back at him and saying, "I think Marina anchors you back to earth, doesn't she?" He just sort of smiled in his usual, nonchalant way and said, "Yeah . . . she's good for me."

People have asked me many times over the years if I had that film to do over again, would I still work with Carradine? In the years immediately following that project, the answer was usually "No!" It's hard to feel amicable to a man who literally challenged you at every turn, cussed you out in front of your cast & crew, and eventually wrote a 3 page letter to the producers and executive producers to explain all the reasons why my name should be removed as the director of the film. When you got done working with someone like David Carradine, you felt all at once like you had been grafted into Hollywood history while at the same time ground up and spit out the other end like hamburger. You felt like you had earned something, just for *surviving it*. David Carradine, though, was, and still is, a *legend* in Hollywood, and I feel honored to have had the chance to work with him when I did.

Phil Bedard
Writer/Producer

The Nose Story

It was the first day back after the *Kung Fu* Christmas hiatus. I'd arrived early that day and decided to grab a few quiet moments on the darkened studio set. I was an on-set producer that first season of *Kung Fu* and the set was usually a chaotic, noisy place; to find it dark and quiet was unusual so I grabbed the opportunity to sit there and enjoy the peace and quiet. After a few moments I heard David enter the studio area with a couple of other people. As I sat in the darkness and the small group headed past me towards the rear of the studio, I figured they couldn't see me. But David did. He stopped in his tracks, called my name, and made a beeline my way. I was a little taken aback because we never really had any kind of a relationship, but here he is, approaching me like I'm the best friend he ever had. He smiled that shit-eating grin of his (which could be both amusing and terrifying), walked right up to me, took my face in his hands, opened his mouth and pulled my nose into it in what I assumed to be some sort of friendly gesture of greeting. I forget what he said after that. But I'd learned by then that you never knew what you were going to get with David—only that it would likely be unforgettable. . .

1st Meeting

. . . Like the first time I met David. We were in the early stages of prepro-duction on *Kung Fu: The Legend Continues* in a bungalow on Warner Bros Ranch lot (where they shot much of the first series). David wanted to come in and meet the writer-producer group (executive producer Michael Sloan, supervising producer Maurice Hurley, my fellow coproducer Larry Lalonde and me) and put on a little demonstration: his way of immersing us into the world of Kung Fu. He showed up mid morning saying he'd spent the last 48 hours in a recording studio, working on a series theme song. We sat on a couch in Maury Hurley's office as David demonstrated some Kung Fu stick fighting moves using a heavy four-foot-long metal bar which he swung repeatedly over our heads. I recall there being some concern about his balance after he'd gone 48 hours without sleep, but we emerged from that part of the meeting with our skulls intact.

That part of the demonstration over, David wanted us to hear some music he thought would be good for the series. There was no cassette player in the office so David herded us out of the building into the parking lot where his driver had parked his white convertible Cadillac Eldorado (complete with cassette deck and license plate that read "I KungFu"). Michael Sloan and I climbed into the back seat, David and his driver sat in the front and Larry and Maury stood beside the top-down car . . . and we listened to the music. It was David playing flute and singing what was known as a saga sell—a series theme song with lyrics that explain the series (c.f. "Gilligan's Island"). It would never fly because of Canadian content regulations and I knew that would cause some tension, so I kept my gaze firmly affixed to the floor of the car, and noticed that it was littered with Kibbles and Bits . . . no doubt from David's beloved dog, "Sasquatch" . . . and a couple of empty vodka bottles, Stoli, I believe. And it was there that I realized we had been very lucky not to be brained during the stick-fighting display.

Memories—Sort Of

Years later, I was producing a series called *Largo* based on a very popular series of European graphic novels about a young man who inherits a massive fortune when his estranged father is murdered. We were looking for someone to play the father—an actor who would only be in the first scene in the pilot (his murder) but whose presence would play throughout the series. For that you needed someone unforgettable. I suggested David and the networks loved the idea. David came up to

Montreal with Marina. He was fantastic on camera of course (so good we brought him back to play his character's double), but he was also in great shape. The three of us had a great time, David regaling Marina and me with stories about the business. And that got him onto talking about *The Legend Continues*. He said he'd love to reshoot the series . . . because he remembered very little of it.

And that statement was David in a nutshell: funny, down to earth, smart and a straight shooter.

Mark Breslin
Owner, Yuk Yuks

New Year's Eve, 1995, Marina and David are in Toronto and I took them to a hip loft party. David is already roaring piss drunk. We walk in, there's a couple of trestle tables set up with a beautiful midnight banquet, and David drunkenly crashes through them, wiping out all of the food onto the floor. Everybody runs over, angry as fuck, and then sees David sprawled on the floor covered in food.

"Hey, it's David Carradine," somebody yells.

Everyone forgets about the food and lines up for autographs . . .

Lisa Knox Burns

How David Made it Real

When Marina called and asked to rent my mother's house on Valley Vista in Sherman Oaks, I was happy because Marina is a friend from childhood and I knew she loved the house. This was not long after the 1994 Northridge earthquake that devastated parts of Sherman Oaks, and the house had been replastered, repainted, and (as a consequence of mistakes made by the company who rebuilt the masonry fireplace) reroofed. During the renovation, I decided that it would be best to paint the original 1950s maple stained wood cabinets, in the partially updated kitchen, white.

And then Marina showed the house to David. To my surprise he objected to the freshly painted kitchen cabinets. He wanted them to look like what they were: wood. As a decorator, I argued that white made the kitchen look sunny and bright. But David didn't care about that. He was concerned that the wood BE what it was: wood. We had to strip the paint off the cabinets. Truth in decorating was part of David's ethos.

Later, without telling us, he pulled up the wall-to-wall carpeting we installed in the living room, exposing the original narrow plank wood floors that had not been refurbished. He did this so that his Steinway grand piano could better resonate. Music trumped comfort. It was more important that the décor complement the music—it didn't matter to him how it looked. Beauty was in the eye of David the beholder; and David really didn't care what other people thought.

I remember the time when David presented us with what appeared to be a generous offer of paying for wiring throughout the house for a security system. Later I found out that he needed that kind of protection because one of his ex-wives was stalking him. David was good at looking out for himself.

If you were wondering about the closets—and I don't mean to be insensitive—but they were too small to hang upside down in. This house has since been razed to build a McMansion; another fatality of a quaint mid-century home by an ostentatious one. Definitely not the Tao of David.

Looking back on that period in the "gay '90s," I regret that I never really got to know David, except for his actions on the Valley Vista house. I hope the reader does not find my impressions too harsh, but I mostly remember him as tall and arrogant. Only in reflection do I realize that he was more of a "searcher." As Joni Mitchell wrote, "chicken-scratching for our immortality." Rather than being satisfied resting on his acting chops, my senses are that David was searching for what we now fashionably call "authenticity."

Rita Colucci

There was a time where David was being called to set and every AD was out looking for him. I saw a cool bar a couple of blocks away from the set so I set out to investigate. It was my first experience with his infamous "wandering" reputation. I venture into the bar with all my gear. The place is packed and I have a hard time getting through all the folks. I go up to the bartender to ask if he's seen David over the live music playing. There onstage on the grand piano is David. He's playing a beautiful blues number. I radio back to set so they understand he's taking more than five here. After his song the place fills with applause and I approach.

He says, "Hey, Coluch, have a drink with me."

It's my first union show and unsure what to do I radio back to the 1st AD and bravely estimate "10 mins."

I order a shot and he has a drink, and starts to tell me a story about his father. A long time ago when David was a boy, his dad was upset with him and threw out all his comic books. He hated that his father did that because he had an amazing collection of them.

"I'm sorry to hear that. Sometimes dads do shitty things. What did you do?" I asked.

He couldn't recall and added, "They'd probably be worth a lot today and still be fun to read." I agreed wholeheartedly. We shot our drinks back and made our way back to set.

Zale Dalen
DGC, Director

He was a remarkable man, and an amazing artistic talent. He could take a big lump of plasticine and turn it into a perfect likeness that looked like it had come from the hands of Rodin. He could take a smashed Martin guitar and patiently repair it to playable condition, and then play it. He could sing the blues. He could compose songs of his own. He could do a passable piano lounge act. He could tap dance. He also wrote books. Actually wrote them himself, and they were not only readable, they were fascinating.

Most of all he could act. He could act far better than most people will ever know. Take a look at *Bound for Glory*, the Woody Guthrie story, if you want to see David outside of his Kwai Chang Caine persona. The guy had chops.

One episode of *Kung Fu: The Legend Continues* stays with me. It was really Chris Potter's show, and Chris was putting his heart into it, doing a great job.

David only had one line—to walk through a surrealistic nightclub where his beloved wife, deceased, was sitting at a table, pause and say: "I can't talk now. I have to save our son."

David, who at that time was drinking heavily, walked into the scene, paused, delivered the line, and a single tear rolled down his cheek on cue. When I called "cut" the crew applauded. A rare event on any jaded television series set.

On his way off the set, David turned to Chris and said, "Top that, kid."

A bit later, sitting on the curb outside the nightclub where we were filming, I said to him: "David, you're a prick."

"No, I'm not," he replied. "I'm mischievous."

And he was. This, after all, was the guy in the fringed buckskin jacket who rode his horse to the take-out window of the Dairy Queen.

I don't mean to take anything away from Chris Potter by telling this story. Like I said, Chris was doing a great job and is a talent in his own right. He really aced that episode ("The Bardo" for all you *KF:TLC* fans.) But David was a star, and everybody knew it. He lit up the screen, as he did in his big come back movie, *Kill Bill*. He had his demons. But what I loved about him was that he was human all the way. He gave me insights. He talked to me, and he didn't get mad when I talked back. I'll miss him.

I should add that I expected David to be dead within months of the cancellation of his series. Booze was obviously killing him. It's a tribute to Marina that he had a few more good years, and a comeback career.

Story 2

I was directing an episode of *Kung Fu: The Legend Continues* and the producers were not happy that their star, David, was forcing his daughter, Calista, on them as a character in the show. They didn't like her acting, described it as "way over the top," and asked me to work with her to get a more realistic performance. So I did, and it was a pleasure, because I like Calista and she's actually a good actor. We worked on her character, the street person, and how that character should be feeling in the scene and in relating to Caine. Then we shot her big scene. I thought that Calista took the notes I'd given her to heart, and really turned in a great performance, adding depth and feeling to a character that had been all one note.

Of course when you make artistic decisions, you aren't really one hundred percent sure you are doing the right thing.

David had his own opinion: "You turned her lights out."

David was furious with me. I felt sick, literally. My confidence was shaken. A man I greatly respected was telling me that I had ruined his daughter's performance. The worst part was the pain in his voice when he told me how he felt. The rest of the day was a dark blur of depression. I was working on autopilot, going through the motions, with that "you'll never work again" feeling.

Toward the end of the day, the AD told me there was a phone call for me. David wanted to talk to me. I was dreading taking the call. But David was calling to apologize. He had seen the rushes, and he realized that Calista's performance was much better than he had thought. To say I was relieved would be a great understatement. I don't know how many stars I've worked with who would have had the humanity to make that phone call, admit or even recognize a mistake, and apologize. Certainly not many. And this was one of the things about David that I really loved. He was every inch a star, but I could still talk to him like a real person, and he would come back at me like a real person. He had a sense of humor. He could be charming and play the star. But he could also be real.

Ellen Dubin
Actress/Producer

I first met David Carradine at a Studio City, California chiropractor's office. I was lying in a tiny examination room hooked up to all these electrodes to relieve neck and back tension. I had seen that David and his wife Marina were in the waiting room, but I got called in first to have my treatment. So I am lying in this small cupboard of a room with my eyes closed and in wanders David C. in a hospital gown and socks. Before I had time to talk, he bent over, gave me this huge deep kiss on the lips and walked out with this absolutely mischevious look on his face. I said *Oo, what the hell!* but I couldn't move, because I was hooked up with all these pads and wires, to run after him. I was also afraid to watch him leave for fear he may not have had any underwear on under that gown. You never know with a guy like David!

I never told his wife. Hell, she knows now! Hilarious!

Emrie Brooke Foster
Artist

I was brand new in Jay's (Bernstein) life and very young at the time. I had no idea who David was or what his work was when we all met for dinner. Jay always wanted everyone to feel good and respected, so when we all were waiting for our table, Jay told David that I was staring at him because he was such a movie star and that I am not used to or have never seen a movie star before. First of all I was staring at him because I was dying to have a cigarette and he (David) was smoking and I was trying to quit. The whole thing was very funny.

David got so uncomfortable and walked outside to finish his cigarette and I followed and asked for one as well. He gave me one and walked right back inside. The moral of the story is that he was a very down to earth natural man who did not want any fuss over him.

Sidney Furie
Director

I had always been a huge admirer of David, even before working with him. It seemed to me that some actors act the part and are known as very good actors, but others like David inhabit the character and there's no acting at all going on, they are the characters and when you see it in front of you on the set it is scary!

I had that experience with David. It was frighteningly real! He *was* Woody Guthrie in *Bound for Glory* and maybe every other character he ever did. Think of his work in *Kung Fu*. Amazing!

Julie Harding
Personal Assistant to David Carradine

One snowy day I arrived at the house and David was not filming. He came into the office and said that he was waiting for his driver to pick him up as we were going to pick up the Maserati, which was in a garage somewhere near the Don Valley Parkway (the other side of Toronto). I did not think anything of this statement, as I thought his driver was going to drive David there and David would drive the car back to the house.

When his driver arrived, David said, "We should all go for lunch before picking up the car."

To which I said, "Me, I have got work to do."

David said, "That can wait, I will buy you lunch before [y]ou drive the car back."

I was shocked as I am a nervous winter driver, it was snowing, I do not drive on the freeways and *me* drive David's beloved Maserati.

So I turned to David and said, "David, I don't do freeways."

He laughed and said, "Is that why I got you so cheap?"

After explaining that I could not possibly drive his car in this weather, David and his driver picked the car up.

Story 2

I had taken a couple of telephone calls from a man in New York, I can't remember his name, I think he wanted to do some work with David. David was not returning his calls. One day I asked David if he had returned his call and he said no, that the guy was getting on his nerves. Then he asked me if I would do him a favor and call him back and in my best English accent tell him to "F--- Off," only if I was not offended by telling him that. I said of course.

I called, he had a strong New York accent and I told him that I had a message from David. He said he would be offended by the message if it had not come from a lady who made those two words sound so nice, and that David should not get his English Butler! to do his dirty work. I explained that I was not David's butler, I was his personal assistant and that it was my job to return calls for David as he was a busy man. So he asked me to give David a message to, "Get his balls out of his cowboy boots and call him." I don't know if David ever called him back, but it gave him a good laugh.

Donna Eubank Hennen
Astrologer

Who didn't grow up watching *Kung Fu* with David Carradine? But David always seemed a little too far out there for me. Fast forward to 1996. Craig Campobasso, my dear friend, and brilliant casting director, hosted one of his amazing dinner parties and invited me. Lo and behold, there in the flesh was David Carradine. He seemed pleasant, articulate, funny. We engaged in simple conversation, but when his wife Marina joined us I was in awe. I thought to myself if this amazing woman is in David Carradine's life, if he is lucky enough to have someone like this care so much for him, then I should really rethink Mr. Carradine. All I can say is she walked in grace.

Larry Lalonde
Writer/Producer

Musings on David: #1

I met David on the Warner Bros. lot a few months before *TLC* was to go to camera in Toronto, where I lived. Michael Sloan, Maurice Hurley, Phil Bedard and I waited for the big moment in our offices. I was excited and nervous. The star of *Kung Fu*—a show that had meant a great deal to me as a kid—was about to walk in. My career in TV was just getting started and David, for sure, would be the biggest star I'd ever met. I remember Michael walking in and saying, "He's here," with a certain amused tone. This did nothing to calm my nerves. We'd heard, of course, that David could be a bit wild.

David walked . . . *careened* in, wielding some kind of long metal tube; going on about how cool it was that this thing was much heavier at one end than the other. It seemed to mean a lot to him. He started waving it over his head and struggling to maintain his balance. If I wasn't certain before, I was now. Kwai Chang Caine was shit-faced. Needless to say, when a drunk is waving a metal object in your face you become somewhat wary. David provided many other moments like this in the months that followed that sealed my relationship with him; avoid at all costs.

He finally sat down and I could breathe again. He never made eye contact. I've heard since that he was quite shy, but at the time I assumed he was too drunk to focus. Michael handled the moment very well, saying all the ego-soothing things he could think of, I suppose. But then David said he'd been up all night writing the new theme song! . . . It took a second or two for the air to come back into the room.

We walked out to David's convertible. There was a butt-ugly dog bigger than a pony in the back seat. The car interior was inches deep in kibble. David poured himself into the driver seat and played us a cassette demo tape of the new theme song. I've blocked out most of it, but essentially it was David, middle-of-the-night blasted, barely holding a tune as he sang, "There was a man . . . a very lonely man . . . " or some similar cloying garbage. He had accompanied himself, fucked-up-guy flute, as I recall. I looked at Hurley and he must have seen my panic. I was pretty green, then. Maury just smiled. I guess he'd seen this sort of appalling behavior many times in the business in L.A., but for me it was a shock. I just wanted to go home.

Musings on David: #2

Three months of creative prep in L.A. came to an end in June of '92. I'm not sure I can convince anyone that there are situations where it is a godsend to leave California for Toronto, but this was one. I'd had a terrible three months. The stress of writing hour drama (which I'd never done before) and the added pressure of doing it for Warner Bros. had taken a toll, but it was the dread of working with David for twenty-two episodes that had made me a bit crazy. When I arrived in L.A., I was a fit 185 lbs. When I left, I was a demoralized 225 lbs. You don't gain 40 lbs in three months unless a) you eat *only* bone marrow, or b) David Carradine is the star of the show.

When the lead actor of a series is poison, that poison trickles down. I know David never intentionally set out to make *TLC* a miserable experience, but it became one for me because of him. David was usually late to the set, often by more than three hours. You'd have to ask Warner Bros. how much that cost them. If the crew call was, say, 8a.m., you could bet that David and Gail and that swamp monster they called a dog would stroll in at 11a.m. as if nothing had happened . . . and that he'd be drunk. The curious thing was that as long as David was AWOL, there was light in the office. But as soon as word reached us, "He's he-eeere," that changed. It was as if you could feel the building shudder.

Despite this, when circumstances were such that I could not avoid David, as in the few instances when he wanted to discuss the script, he wasn't all that bad. He called Phil and me down to his trailer one time, but not to rant. Turned out he felt a speech I'd written for him had too many words. He was right, but the thing was he'd only looked at the lines moments earlier. I doubt he ever studied his lines the night before, probably because he knew he couldn't possibly remember them.

It got to the point where David was so out of it that the ADs started writing his lines on strips of paper and taping them up off-screen. This is why that in most of the later episodes of the first season what looks like Caine searching for heartfelt inspiration is actually David searching for the paper strips and his lines.

I'd have to say the most impressive thing about David—if impressive is the right word—was that somehow the talent never went away. He could be miles away in a sea of booze and on "Action," none of that mattered. He'd summon Caine from somewhere, somehow, and be brilliant, paper strips and all. For this he was forgiven every folly. I'm not sure he should have been. Things might have turned out differently.

Musings on David: #3

In the summer of 1998, Phil Bedard and I were shooting *Top of the Food Chain (a.k.a. Invasion!)*, a sci-fi comedy feature we'd written and were producing in Toronto. Marina and David came to the set. Six years removed from TLC, and having heard how Marina had somehow managed to get David off the booze, I looked forward to seeing him. It was like meeting a complete stranger. He looked healthy. He made attempts at eye contact. He smiled. He was interested in what was going on around him. But mostly I noticed how shy he was. I wonder if his drinking was in some way a coping mechanism for that shyness. At any rate, he was *present*. I'll never forget the one and only time I met the real David Carradine.

Musings on David: #4

TLC and David's fans will want to save a special thank you for Michael Sloan. With David the way he was for most of the run, only someone with Michael's Zen-like producer skills could have held *TLC* together and produced a show that the audience grew emotionally attached to. I have a feeling the experience took its toll on Michael, but I never heard one complaint from him. I will never forgive Michael for those goddamned 8 a.m. breakfast/story meetings, mind you. Most days I managed to hold off puking up my eggs and coffee until after the meeting. Most days.

Musings on David: #5

I had a friend who married a traveling pasta salesman. There's nothing wrong with selling pasta for a living, but one can reasonably question its long-term earning potential and one might wonder just a little about investing one's heart in a man who, after careful consideration of life's possibilities, chose to focus on macaroni. I attended my friend's wedding with roiling mixed emotions. I did my best to convince myself that if she was happy then I was happy for her, but the attempt was unsuccessful. What I really wanted to do was rush the altar and drag her away, toss her into a getaway car and ask her a very simple question . . .

Years later, when Marina told me she'd agreed to marry David, the same unspoken simple question popped into my head, but her happiness restrained me. Today, as regards both [nuptials], I realize I may have saved my friends considerable suffering if I'd had the courage to ask that simple question . . . "Are you fucking nuts?"

Oh, well. We all have to learn our lessons the hard way.

Musings on David: #6

Gail wasn't the only one living with an alcoholic. We all were. There is no way to predict what a drinker will do or say; no way to know each day how their drinking will affect things. So you're always on edge. Television, with its tight budgets and meatball surgery mentality relies entirely on careful planning to get the job done. With alcoholics you can't plan, you can't schedule. What happens next is always a coin toss. For this reason you live in chaos and try to find ways to cope.

Towards the end of the first season I had an epiphany. I would grow a playoff beard. You see them a lot in pro sports. Men's pro sports, of course. I have no idea what professional female athletes grow during the playoffs and I don't want to know, but for men the beard is a response to added stress and a way to signal defiance in the face of that stress (that sounds good enough to me). Sounds silly, but it works. It was my signal that I'd had enough; that in the wake of this Carradine-inspired nuthouse I was going to . . . make facial hair! Yeah. That's showin' them.

John McIntyre

Toronto, 2010

As David's driver for three of the four seasons of *KF:TLC* in Toronto I got to know him, in some ways, as well as anyone could. Being David's driver entailed quite a bit more than the average film-driving gig. I didn't simply pick him up in the morning and drive him home at the end of the day. He needed his driver to actually come into his house, find him, wake him up and get him going. I had a key to the front door, but I can't remember that door ever being locked. We were never on time in the morning and we rarely went straight home at the end of the day. In the beginning I felt stuck between the production company and a very high-maintenance actor with seemingly few redeeming qualities.

But somehow after a few weeks he endeared himself to me and over the course of those three seasons we became very close. Though he sometimes had trouble remembering what happened yesterday, his mind was a fascinating fountainhead. He could speak with great insight on subjects as diverse as French wines, music, Shakespeare, Ferraris and film history. Equally fascinating were his personal stories from his childhood, details of the ups and downs of his career and his encounters with luminaries like Bob Dylan and Paul McCartney. He was intensely loyal to those close to him and I was, and still am, reluctant to tell compromising stories about him. When pressed, however, there's one or two that I sometimes recount.

David loved his dogs and often brought them to the studio. His English springer spaniel, Champ, was very intelligent and often displayed a quiet wisdom not unlike that of his master on a good day. One evening at wrap David became enraged about something-or-other and stormed upstairs to confront the line producer. Champ and I followed. As a heated exchange began in the line producer's office I stayed in the outer office, but Champ slipped in and quietly sat down in a corner.

The line producer paused in her attack, pointed at Champ and loudly declared, "And I've told you before—dogs are not allowed in the office!" A strange silence ensued as Champ rose, and with bowed head, slowly padded across the floor to leave. But when he reached the doorway he paused and nonchalantly lifted his leg, leaving his short comment on the doorframe before making his way back down the stairs.

I'm not sure how the meeting ended because I quickly exited on Champ's heels and gave him a treat when we got downstairs. When David joined us he did the same, as we laughed ourselves to the point of tears.

Another evening after work David said he didn't want to make our usual stop at the local bistro but instead wanted to go straight home. He planned to take his then-current wife, Gail, out himself. We were in the middle of a January blizzard so, as I dropped him off, I pointed out that it was still snowing and many of the roads had not yet been plowed. He said it didn't matter—he was going to take the four-wheel-drive Jeep. I suggested this might be a bad idea but secretly thought that, once inside his nice warm house, he would be unlikely to venture out again.

How wrong I was. When I got to the house the following morning I noticed that the Jeep had been moved. I also noticed that half the front bumper had been pulled forward 90 degrees, producing a wreckage of cracked plastic and Styrofoam backing. It was clear from the tire tracks in the snow that when returning home last night, David had taken the alternate driveway to the house—a trail that meandered through an apple orchard. It appeared that David had slid off the trail, gotten hung up on an apple tree and reversed his way out, ripping the bumper forward. I went into the house, started the process of getting him to the studio and, for simplicity, decided to avoid the whole topic until later.

David was never much of a morning person. As we left the house his hair was disheveled, his shirt was buttoned up wrong and he stepped through the deep snow wearing only slippers with no socks. Just as we were about to get into the car, David suddenly raised his finger as if remembering the previous night. I followed him over to the Jeep where he examined the damage. He bent over and thoughtfully broke off a piece of the mangled bumper's Styrofoam backing. Standing back up, shifting his gaze from the Styrofoam to me, he said in a gravelly, deadpan voice: "That's not the Jeep we won World War II with."

Wherever you are now, David, we miss you and hope you have found peace.

George Mendeluk
Director

TAKE OUT TURKEY

It was a bleak, bitterly cold afternoon when Victoria my wife and my 8-year-old son Alexander drove up to David's rented house on Prince John Boulevard, a four thousand square foot rambling structure in Mississauga, with an orchard in the back. I had moved back to Toronto, Ontario where I grew up, alternatively directing David Carradine and Christopher Plummer who were starring in two different series at the time. Carradine and Plummer, two legends in their own right, presented a challenge to directors; they ate them up and spit them out. But if you knew your stuff, and were prepared, they were a thrill and a joy to direct, especially if you had a sense of humor and finished your day before five p.m.

My family and I arrived early, around one or two in the afternoon, and somewhat apprehensive as to what to expect, especially with Alexander being eight years old. But being on the road is a lonely existence and a home cooked meal on Thanksgiving is something you don't pass up. I recall that we brought flowers and wine and that Gail, David's wife at the time, greeted us warmly and ushered us in. In the background, David was singing the blues. Immediately we were introduced to "Dr. Feel Good," a short, rather hyper and recently widowed doctor who David somehow discovered. It was Dr Feel Good who was prescribing the vitamin B shots that David was getting on set.

After the introductions, I noticed that there were none of the usual show business crowd invited—no actors, nor directors; in fact I was the only one. We relaxed. It was going to be a normal Thanksgiving, I thought, or as normal as could be expected with David. Pounding on the keys, Gail joined him in a duet. David was dressed casually, but had on a pair of brown, worn, two-toned shoes. They were tap shoes actually. David loved music, and musicals. He could wax and wane on the subject.

It was something we had in common—a love of music. David greeted us graciously, but you could tell he had been drinking more than usual. Usually, it didn't show. But as always he kept it together. He was a pro at that. But Gail was clearly plastered and continued going strong. They were singing traditional blues, and would slip into an occasional Broadway tune. But it was getting dark. I thought perhaps other guests were going to arrive. But Gail said no. We offered to help in the kitchen? Gail waived off the offer. Victoria and I exchanged looks.

Soon it was after six, and still there were no familiar cooking aromas. "Don't worry," Gail offered, "I will make sure you will get more shows to direct. David feels comfortable with you." I thanked her, but suggested that perhaps we should go. (We didn't mention the obvious). Our excuse was that Alexander had to be up for school the next day. And it was true. (How an eight year old wasn't bored by this time still amazes me!) Suddenly, it appeared to dawn on her. David was still entertaining at the piano, the guests had arrived, but there was no turkey in the oven! Gail started to dash around, but she wasn't upset. It was kind of funny to her.

The bird must have arrived well past eight, from a restaurant. Who marshaled it on Thanksgiving, I'll never know. There might have been some pizza too—I can't remember—but we dug in unceremoniously and the bird was quickly gone. David continued to grin, play and sing as if nothing was the matter. Did he know it was Thanksgiving? Did it matter? When we drove away, his repertoire had changed: no more traditional blues, or Broadway tunes. David switched to playing his own material, which he enjoyed best; his voice a sort of Tom Waits wail and growl. I don't even know if he even touched the bird.

THE CROSSING

It was a gorgeous summer day, a cloudless sky, a flawless blue ocean. I was about to cross the border from the United States to Canada, en route to Vancouver, when I saw the long line of cars ahead. I knew that it was going to be a long wait. I opened the passenger window and looked out. Something metaphorical about a crossing, I remember thinking, whether it's a border, an ocean—whatever.

How I ended up calling David, I can't remember. I hadn't spoken to him in months. There was no reason to call. Maybe it was about a part in a movie I had written, *Hollywood Wolf*; perhaps it was about a role in a movie I was going to direct in Vancouver, or it could have just been an impulse, an intuition.

At any rate, I had about an hour to kill, and I suddenly had the inexplicable urge to speak to David. It was a long and memorable call. He was very open, and personal. David was often loquacious, it wasn't that. But he would speak knowledgeably on a great variety of subjects without revealing much about himself. This conversation was different: we covered the business, the scars, the joys, the moments on set working together. As the sun began to set, and the line of cars got shorter, we began to share more of our personal selves—more than at any time in our seventeen-year-old friendship. He shared with me personal insights about his marriages—he especially mentioned Marina—personal sexual things that took me aback. I know that I must have brought up *Hollywood Wolf*, a true period love story that takes place during the golden age of Hollywood. How David loved to speak about that era, about his father, and about acting! And directors. We spoke about Tarantino. I complimented him on *Kill Bill.* Then I mentioned that an actress had auditioned for Quentin and that he told her after looking at her resume that he liked my work. I found that odd. "No George. I am sure he knows your work. He used to work in a video store. He knows [e]very picture ever made and who directed it! He also watched *Kung Fu.*"

I must have asked him to read my script again. I wanted him to play the part of a father, a poignant character who was dying because of years of working in the gold mines. Somehow I must have mentioned how badly I wanted to direct this movie. I must have said, "if it's the last thing I ever direct." I know that I shared that I had some issues with my heart.

And then he said something I will never forget. He blurted it out. It was so emotional, so unlike him. David said: "George, you must look after yourself. The film business needs you!" I thought he was being very kind. It was very unlike David. I am under no illusion that I am invaluable to the film industry, that somehow there will be a void when I'm gone. But it touched me. It was a compliment in the sense that we are all part of a fraternity. Suddenly, I reached the border. The guard ordered me off the phone. Literally the sun had set as we said our last good bye. I realize now that I was about to cross the border, and David was about to cross to the other side.

THE INITIATION

It was 7 in the morning when I was summoned by David to his trailer. I was apprehensive when I was offered the opportunity to direct David in the new *Kung Fu* series. I had heard of all the horror stories about his drinking, but I hoped for the best. I have always loved a challenge. However, when I opened the door, I realized that all my apprehensions were true: there on the table sat an opened vodka bottle with a grinning David Carradine behind it. Maybe a leering David Carradine is a more apt description. He was friendly enough, but he wanted to establish his turf.

"You know that I am the executive producer as well as the star," he smiled. He was mischievous. "I know now," I said. "Good." Then he offered me a drink. "It's too early for me, David. Besides I don't drink when I work," I replied. "Well I do. Got a problem with that?" "Not if you know your lines and hit your marks," I said. What had I gotten myself into, I thought! David laughed. "Well, I do and I will." And he was right. In the three years that I ended up directing the show he rarely, if ever missed a line, and never his mark. It was remarkable. Sure, his reflexes were slow, and the fight scenes needed to be doubled, because he was drinking, but he was a total professional. It was amazing. Other actors with fewer lines came on the series and blew lines left and right, but not David. I respected him for that. And we became good friends.

Sometime later, perhaps it was on the first show that I directed, David and I were on set, and he hauled off and hit me on the chin. To him it was probably a playful tap. But I can still feel how it felt being hit today. It was like a bag of cement hitting me. At first I didn't know what to say or do—the man assaulted me! But I realized later that it was like an initiation, a sign of endearment. He might have been constantly plastered, and he needed stunt doubles to pick up the pace of his fight sequences but he was a physically strong man. That part wasn't fake.

The other thing I remember about his drinking was how he tried to make up for the abuse with daily vitamin B shots administered on set; how he used to take Chinese medicine—one was a bizarre concoction of fetid snake that had been buried in the ground etc.—in order to give him strength and help his liver. It was bizarre, but whatever it was, or he took, the man had stamina.

ACTING

David's true passion was acting: it was as simple as that. He loved the technique, the process, the history of the craft, and the true greats of the stage and cinema. And unlike some legends, he also liked directors. He respected you as a director if you knew your craft and, in turn, respected actors. It was a throwback to the old days of Hollywood when directors like John Ford, Michael Curtiz and John Huston were in their heyday—although arguably I don't know how many of the old greats truly loved actors!

I can't remember the occasion, but David gave me a gift which I cherish to this day. I have always been a fan of Stanislavsky and Sandy Meisner, but David gave me a book by Richard Boleslavsky entitled: *Acting: The First Six Lessons*. Inside the front cover he inscribed the following:

> George, my love; read this and you will understand the rest of us:
> (The actors) Read it and reap.
> David

Recently, I had the pleasure of directing Robert Carradine. He said that David raised him, and that he was like a second father to him. I showed Robert the book. When he returned it I found this inscription:

George, thank you for your care and kindness
Bobby Carradine

That is the way I would like to remember David. He was a consummate actor, who lived and loved his craft. He was unique, he was kind and generous. And I miss him.

Jalal Merhi
Producer/Director

David and I kept in touch, it was rough thru his divorce with Gail, then he introduced me to Marina, who helped him clean up and get away from the drinking thing. We did the movie *G.O.D.* in Victoria Island and he was there for two weeks, it was a charm to work with him, he was amazing, knew his and others lines, always on time.

We stayed in touch and talked about other work, connected him to other producers, then he went on to do *Kill Bill*. After *Kill Bill*, he needed some paperwork from my production company concerning his taxes, we stayed in touch having a coffee here and there. He was driving his vintage Maserati then when I got him a gig meeting fans in Kazakhstan and in Toronto on a project called *Blizhiny Boy* in Dec 2005.

He came to the set of the film blasted, he hugged me so tight, I felt he could have crushed me. He was very affectionate.

In one scene at a fancy friend's house, as soon as we walked in, David saw a piano. And went directly to it, then started playing, it was amazing. However, he kept going and going while the crew was waiting, and the owner of the house being hospitable and bringing him one drink after another. With all of that, David was patient with the newcomer actor, and he knew his lines.

The next time we met, it was in L.A. I invited him for lunch, he arrived in his black vintage Ferrari, and he had been drinking. We had our lunch and a long frank discussion about his alcohol use, his answer was "I'm bored," no good roles, nothing challenging. We spoke on the phone a few times after that. That was the last time we met.

Jan Rooney

I first met David on the set of *Tom Horn*. Mickey and I had just gotten married in 1978 when my manager Tim Lane from Atlantic Records took me on the set with my guitar in hand and had me meet David Carradine, who was resting in his trailer at the time.

David and I sang up a storm. Donovan was big in those days, so we had a lot of fun singing folk songs. David gave me one of his records and politely asked me if I would record one of the songs he'd written called "You And Me." I was quite honored he would ask, but I feel bad because I never actually got around to doing it.

I was happy to hear David absolutely adored Mickey and spoke so highly of him. The fondness carried on since they reunited on David's series *Kung Fu: The Legend Continues* in Canada, where my son Chris joined Mickey on a couple of segments as well.

In 1997, Jay Bernstein was throwing one of his parties at his home in Beverly Hills. He had been Farrah Fawcett's manager at one time. That is where Mickey and I first met Marina, along with James Coburn and his wife, on a lovely summer's day, as I recall. Marina and I have been good friends ever since.

My best recollection of David is that he was soft-spoken, kind of shy and a very sweet man. He was laden with problems, but he always tried to hide his feelings in public. Mickey and I both sensed a deep sadness in his face. We were brokenhearted at the news of his disturbing death and will miss David for the good and kind traits he possessed. Mickey and I shall always remember him and the magnitude of his enormous talent.

Daniel L. Unger

Time with Jack

While growing up in Los Angeles in the 70s and 80s, running into celebrities and movie stars was almost a regular occurrence. You might bump into one at a restaurant in Hollywood, or maybe at a local sporting event . . . but for me it was a little different as a kid in the small town of Lomita in the South Bay, because my father was Stan Unger, one of David's oldest and dearest friends for over forty years. As a youth I recall a couple of visits to Malibu to see David and Barbara Hershey, we would eat dinner together and watch the waves roll up to their front deck. Later on in my teens, my time with David, whom my father always called "Jack," was spent up at his ranch. We would take pictures of my Dad's classic cars with David in them, so that we could sell them as part of his "private collection." Stan would pay David a couple hundred per car and we would make a lot more at auction! It was similar to the kind of wheeling and dealing they did some forty years earlier, as a "semi-grifting sales duo" in San Francisco, which is well documented in David's autobiography in the chapter entitled "Beatnik."

Having David as your Dad's good friend was sometimes arduous, occasionally dangerous, but absolutely and positively never boring! David's stories resonate in my memory banks like I heard them yesterday. It was the first time I could get the facts from a different perspective other then my Dad's, who was known to alter the truth from time to time . . . just to improve the quality and shock value of a good story! David's memories of amazing episodes of his life, like walking around South Africa with Tina Turner in the turbulent 1970s, was told almost poetically by Stan over the years. Although I don't quite have the baritone and overall storytelling skills of my father, I will continue to tell those tales to anyone interested enough to listen.

When David got sober, with the help of Marina especially, I met a new "Jack" who relished and spoke proudly of his time as a Beatnik, occasionally calling my dad to help him remember certain situations and stories for his autobiography. Thankfully for David, my Dad was one of his only living friends who wasn't a drinker at all, so he counted on Stan's unusually vivid memory! Most of that chapter in his book was written by Stan, you can tell because he includes his own name over 10 times! It was my Dad's "fifteen minutes of fame he never got, but instead lived vicariously with Jack throughout the years! Stan Unger passed away in January of 2002 at the age of 68 . . . even though he was a Jew turned Atheist later in life, I'm sure he got some kind of reprieve to hang out in Heaven on occasion, just to keep people entertained with his longer than average, mostly true stories, of growing up as a good friend of a Carradine. If Heaven does exist, I hope those two guys somehow made it and are concocting their next way to make a buck!

Publisher's note: The accounts in Part V have been minimally edited to retain the authors' original text.

Acknowledgements

Special dedication to my family:

My parents, Mariana and Joseph Benjamin

Mom, you've always been there for me. I couldn't have done it without you.

Brother Dan and wife Maggie; Grandparents: Charles and Mary Dottore, Lillian Benjamin, Sam Benjamin, Smittie, Dalton, Cinelli, Tai, Talulah, Purjia

Everyone at Transit Publishing, *merci!* Pierre Turgeon, for listening to your inner voice and helping to complete my mission; Francois, Gratia, Dwayne, Tami, and Christine; and Clare McKeon, my editor, for "getting it" and helping to give my voice clarity.

To my cherished friends—who saw me through thick and thin, listened tirelessly to my venting, employed me, supported me, nurtured, inspired and made me laugh when I didn't think it was possible . . . to those who contributed to my life past and present, and to this book . . . including:

Adrianne and Michael Anderson, Michael Anderson, Jr., Maurice Amdur, Joe Anderson, Mark Archer, Mario Azzopardi, Tony Barr, William Bast, Phil and Mary Bedard, Larry Beckerman, Ed and Rachelle (Carson) Begley, Sloan Bella, Steven Berg, Clarisa Bernhardt, James Best, Mae Bodine, Michael Bodine, Richard Borchiver, Deirdre Bowen, Mark Breslin, Rosalyn Bruyere, Lisa Knox Burns, Craig Campobasso, Jamie and Sean Carmody, Sandra and Will Carradine, Jon Cassar, Cast, crew and production of *Desperate Housewives*, Cast and crew of *Without A Trace*, Central Casting, Kate Clarke, Dabney Coleman, Rita Colucci, Jon Comerford, Miria Cook, Roger and Julie Corman, Spice Williams-Crosby, Leslie Cyril, Zale Dalen, Don Dalesandro, Jesse Daly, Dan D'Or, Jennifer DeChiara, Ed Delvecchio, Peter Deyell, Patrick Dollaghan, Ellen Dubin, Bob Ellison, Ray and Wyn Evans, Nunzio Fazio, Tom and Christine Fishwick, Sharon and Susan Forrest, Emrie Brooke Foster, Judy Friend, Sidney Furie, Mark Ganzel, Jennifer Gold, Jan Glaser, Joshua Graubart, Julie Harding, Mark Harris, Donna Hennen, Sean Hennigan, Deborah and Jeff Herman, Walter Hill, Dr. Antoinette Hubenette, Vicki Huff, Neville Johnson, Marv Josephson, Edward Kalpakian, Weiss Kelly, Aron Kincaid, P.K. Knelman, Michael Tobin Lambert, Michael Lamont, Larry and Carol Lalonde, Joey's List, Karina Lemke, Brian Levy, Leanna Levy, Jeff McGaver, John McIntyre, Marilyn Mazzotta, George Mendeluk, Jalal Merhi, Michael Misita, James Moore, Tony Morrone, Caron Nightingale, Richard Ohanesian, Lisa Parasyn, James Parriott, Doug Patterson and Talent Group Toronto, Robert Perault, Dr. Drew Pinsky, Dr. Steven Pitt, Stephanie Raphael, Jan Rooney, Susan Rothschild, Leslie Rugg, Ralph Senensky, Michael Sloan, Rodney Smolla, Dr. Bronte Stone, Jimmy Swan, Lily Therese, Averi Torres, Dan Unger, Stan Unger, Stephen Viens, Brooks Wachtel, Patricia Wark, Ken Weintrub, Alan Weissman, Ruby Pollock Werdesheim, Kerry Zirin

And a very special thanks to my school teachers, who inspired and encouraged me:

Dixie Elementary: Bonnie Anderson–Principal, Gladys Clark, Mrs. Delicate, Barbara Fawcet, Roger Fetcher, Mrs. Gaylord, Donald Gelb–Vice Principal, Mrs.Kent, Francis Larago, Mrs. Peterson

Millikan Jr. High: Mrs. Jewel, Ms. Gray, Ms. Harmon, Judy Hunter

Grant High School: Mr. Alboher, Mr. LaFontaine, Rodna Shutz, Ms. Ulrich

L.A. Valley College: Margo Chandley, John Larson, Patrick Riley

BIOGRAPHY

MARINA ANDERSON is an established actress, with starring and supporting roles in many television shows and feature films, including appearances on the *King Fu* series, *Ghost Whisperer*, and *Desperate Housewives*. She is much in demand as a voice-over artist. Currently she has two television series in development, including the kid's ecology show *World of Green*. She designs The Flying Goddess jewelry and wrote the children's book *The Adventures of Lulu the Collie*, about her real-life beloved collie, who was a daughter of Lassie VIII. She divides her time between Toronto and Los Angeles, and shares her home with many, many furry creatures.